EDITH WHARTON AND HENRY JAMES
The Story of Their Friendship

Edith Wharton
&
Henry James

THE STORY OF THEIR FRIENDSHIP

by

Millicent Bell

George Braziller
New York

Library of Congress Catalog Card Number: 65-10196

First Printing, February 1965
Second Printing, September 1965

Printed in the United States of America

To my parents, Mae and Mac

Preface

THIS BOOK is a biography neither of Henry James nor of Edith Wharton but rather of a friendship that flourished between them for only a portion of each of their long lives. James had had a many-chaptered earlier history and his literary achievement was nearly complete when he began to know Mrs. Wharton in his sixties. She herself was then a mature woman, though a beginning writer. She would produce over twenty books under his eye, but she would outlast her older friend by twenty-one years and go on to complete a second half of her shelf of forty volumes after he was dead. But the period of their association was not only James's final one, it was his ripest time, when he had reached, as few writers do, an old age of assured mastery and confident vision. Though often ailing and shaken by personal losses, his sense of what life, for him, was all about only deepened; his interest in it only intensified, his wisdom grew more profound, and his personal tenderness for others seemed to increase along with an Olympian insight and objectivity. For Edith Wharton, the period of this friendship saw her greatest artistic growth which culminated in the three remarkable works she wrote close together—*Ethan Frome*, *The Reef*, and *The Custom of the Country*—novels that now seem the summit of her work. These years also witnessed a personal metamorphosis no less striking, during which the member of New York society transformed herself into the untrammelled professional author and emigrée and during which her marriage foundered into divorce and her emotional needs became fully clear to her. James's ultimate, richest moment met her climactic one in one of the unique attachments of literary history.

Henry James was already famous when they met; Edith Wharton was soon to be. The friendship between two such picturesque and distinguished persons could hardly go unnoticed and continues to be mentioned whenever she, at least, is discussed. Nevertheless, the full and circumstantial account of their relations has not been told at all. No one has till now described the drama of their mutual discovery of one another and of their developing intimacy, the history of their reciprocal affection and criticism, the occasions and circumstances that brought them together from year to year, and the private events and concerns of each in which the other found himself involved as close friendship can involve one. This, considering the prominence and interest of the pair, is certainly curious.

In her autobiography, *A Backward Glance*, which was published in 1934, three years before she died, Edith Wharton devotes some evocative pages to the figure of her great friend. She also emphasizes the importance of his presence in her life, beginning a chapter completely devoted to him with the remark, "I cannot think of myself apart from the influence of the two or three greatest friendships of my life, and any account of my own growth must be that of their stimulating and enlightening influence." Elsewhere in the book she identifies the lawyer Walter Berry, with whom she was in love for many years, as "the one friend in the life of each of us who seems not a separate person, however dear and beloved, but an expansion, an interpretation of one's self, the very meaning of one's soul." James's is her other greatest friendship, and while he must always have remained a distinct and separate person to her—the fondest affection would hardly have presumed to regard Henry James as "an interpretation of one's self"—he was unquestionably the human being who most aroused the reverence of her proud spirit, and the friend of whom she was most proud.

Yet the chapter on James in *A Backward Glance* is curiously disappointing, for it is no more than a collection of diverting anecdotes which illustrate the charm, the wit, the eccentricities of the man, anecdotes which many other friends might have duplicated. It contains no history; it holds a polite door shut between the reader and any view of James's and Mrs. Wharton's

8

Preface

shared private life. This, of course, is the characteristic evasiveness of the whole work. It has often been observed that Edith Wharton's account of her own life is full of blanks barely covered by a few vague explanations, and it is now generally understood that for several years preceding her divorce in 1913 (which she does not explicitly mention) her personal life contained features she preferred to conceal from outsiders. Yet these features formed a large part of the view of her open to a few close friends, and it is precisely because of them that her account of her friendship with Henry James is no account at all. We have not been given any true view of James as the witness and counsellor who stood at her side during a long period of emotional turmoil because that undiscussable turmoil was for them a constant subject of communication, a shared concern.

Mrs. Wharton's reticence about her personal life was scrupulously respected by those few who were in her confidence, and no published reminiscence by any of her friends goes further than her own admissions. Henry James wrote no history of his own life beyond the fragmentary autobiography that stops short long before his later years, but it might have been hoped that Percy Lubbock's *Portrait of Edith Wharton*, published in 1947, would set her in a more circumstantial context, for he was her close friend as well as James's. Yet this graceful sketch is as tantalizingly vague as Mrs. Wharton's own autobiography. There is no question that she and James both would have wanted it that way. James had an almost morbid fear of posterity's prying interest in his affairs and those of his friends, and he burnt many of his papers before his death, quite probably most of Edith Wharton's letters to him, for the packet he had saved which was returned to her at his death contained only the letters she had written him from the French fronts during 1914 and 1915. But what about James's half of their correspondence? When Lubbock published a two-volume edition of James's own letters in 1920, he included no less than twenty-seven letters to Mrs. Wharton, yet these added little biographic information. They were riddled with ellipses, and whether or not there had been many—or any—other letters to her besides them was not disclosed. Edith Wharton's own collection

9

of correspondence was, after her death in 1937, disappointingly withheld from scrutiny; not until 1968 will certain closed archives in the Yale University Library, where they have been deposited, be opened.

Yet, as readers of this book will discover, the story of the friendship of Henry James and Edith Wharton can, in fact, be told now, along with the necessary explanations about her shadowed private history. (It is my own guess that the closed Yale collection will contain fewer revelations than most scholars have supposed, and its existence has, perhaps, needlessly deterred investigators from looking elsewhere.) For the particular story I have wanted to tell here, the facts proved actually available and plentiful.

Among the mass of unpublished James letters housed in the Houghton Library at Harvard University, I found, to begin with, the precious James half of the Wharton-James correspondence. Though the letters themselves are not there in manuscript form, the library possesses faithful transcript copies assembled by Percy Lubbock during the course of his work on the 1920 "Letters." We have Mr. Lubbock to thank for the fact that these copies, as well as copies of hundreds of other James letters to other correspondents were preserved and eventually given to Harvard even though he selected only a few for publication. The typescript series of seventy-four letters of Henry James to Edith Wharton, fifty-seven of which have never been printed in whole or in part, forms one of the foundations of new material which has made this book possible. The Lubbock volumes had excluded, I was also aware, hundreds of other James letters to other friends, and many of the letters to them in the printed collection were mere fragments which might be significant only if the complete originals were examined. A rich source of further facts and insights was thus to be found not only in typescript copies collected by Lubbock, but in the collections at Harvard of manuscripts of James's letters to others. In particular, there were the letters to the members of what Edith Wharton called their "inner group"—the friends of both herself and James who met frequently and corresponded still more often, such as Howard Sturgis, Gaillard Lapsley, Walter Berry, and Lubbock himself. Then there were the letters James wrote to such mutual friends as Charles Eliot Norton and his family, which proved almost as valuable, and even the letters James wrote to his own friends and to members of his family in whom he was likely to confide information and reflection about Edith Wharton, only a small fraction of which have yet been published. The results, as the reader will find, proved richly illuminating. Not only did these letters of James's help one to see Edith Wharton as she had not before been visible, they exhibited James in new dimensions. James as Mrs. Wharton's friend and critic, James as satiric humorist and as tragic moralist, inspired in both moods by the spectacle of another life, and, not least, James the creator of literary variations on a theme within the epistolary form—all stood freshly revealed.

In addition, it proved possible, after all, to examine Edith Wharton's letters to a number of friends during the same period. At Harvard and also in a number of other libraries and collections I found her letters to the Norton family and to other friends of James's, and her letters to the members of that inner circle already mentioned, notably to A. John Hugh-Smith, as well as letters to her editors at Charles Scribner's Sons, particularly William Crary Brownell, who became a lifelong friend. Other individuals had acted as links between the two, and themselves provided points of insight into the nature of James's and Mrs. Wharton's attachment—for instance, the eccentric literary Englishwoman, Vernon Lee, whom each knew at a different period, and another common friend, the French novelist Paul Bourget. James's letters provided fascinating comment on both, it turned out, and their own letters were also available for comparison.

Gradually, as details from these and other sources, chiefly manuscript, accumulated, the design of friendship between these two became clear, and it was ready to be told. Only one question remained—*should* it be? Was it possible that even now, over a hundred years after her birth, there might be some valid objection to "exposing" some of Mrs. Wharton's affairs in the course of my narration? It will be obvious, I think, that only a former age and not our own would regard her troubled experiences as discreditable, in the first place. For the present day's reader they are, in fact, a source of new understanding and sympathy for the gifted woman whom we have tended till now to regard as coolly as she seems to regard us in her books and portraits. As for James, the portrait of him already set forth in print by other biographers has now, as I have said, a new and glowing detail.

Although the chief "sources" of this book have been unpublished manuscript letters, I have been prompted in my interest in the lives of James and Edith Wharton by other writers. Seventeen years ago, in a now-famous essay on Edith Wharton, Edmund Wilson asked a number of questions about her private life and suggested that full understanding of her as an artist and person depended on their being answered. The pertinence of his questions has become obvious to many readers of her works, and I hope some of them have finally been answered here.

My use of unpublished sources has been very full, and I am grateful to those who have made such use possible by granting me the necessary permissions and assisting me in my research. I should like to set down here my particular gratitude to the Trustees of the James estate and the officers of the Harvard University Library and to Prof. William A. Jackson, Librarian of the Houghton Library, and Miss Carolyn E. Jakeman of the Houghton staff for courteous assistance. I am also grateful to the various other holders of manuscript materials (particularly Edith Wharton's) consulted by me: to the Amherst College and Yale University Libraries and to the firm of Charles Scribner's Sons which permitted me to examine its files; and I remember with special appreciation the courteous help at these places of Miss Rena Durkin, at Amherst, of Prof. Donald C. Gallup, at Yale, and of various members of the Scribner firm, particularly Mr. David Randall, then of the Scribner Rare Book Department. For th[e] use of unpublished Wharton letters themselves I wish to tha[nk] the administrators of Mrs. Wharton's estate, in particular M[rs.] Elisina Royall Tyler, legatee of the estate, who granted me ac[cess] to them at the start of my inquiry. Various other individuals [have,] in one way or another furthered my knowledge of Henry Jam[es] and Edith Wharton. Caresse Crosby has shown me her collection of Walter Berry's papers and books as well as given me the benefit

Preface

of her own recollections of Walter Berry and Edith Wharton;
and I have had the help, in slighter ways, of a number of others
who had known one or another of the characters of my story
and were, at the least, able to suggest the evanescent qualities of
personality which fade from written records. To all of these,
whether named or not, as their wishes dictate, I feel grateful.
I also want to thank the editors of *American Quarterly* for permission to reprint in the appendix of this book, the material on
Edith Wharton and the house of Scribner. For efficient mechanical
help in the preparation of the manuscript, and the benefit of an
alert editorial intelligence behind the machine, my thanks to my
typist, Miss Lowell Eayrs.

M. B.

Contents

PART ONE

The Personal Relation

I

Foreshadowings and Beginnings

As EVERYONE KNOWS, they were friends. For a dozen years they
were often together, at his house or hers, or, most typically, on
the move touring and making visits, whether in France or England or even western Massachusetts. In the dimming light of that
recent past, the early years of this century, we can still call them
into view in a sort of double portrait, almost as though they were
a married couple or acknowledged lovers. We see them as so
many witnesses did, for their meetings were frequently witnessed
and sometimes later recorded: his figure rotund and slow-mov-
ing, top-hatted and silk-waistcoated, and on his arm his taut, elegant, "dearest Edith." The memory of others also helps us to hear
them as they pass: the extraordinary, slow, masculine voice mur-
muring its periods from the wide, ironic mouth while the rolling
brown eyes search out objects for study and mirth, and the sharp,
feminine laugh keeping pace as she accompanies him with her
own quick glance and crisp remarks. Henry James and Edith
Wharton—they were, the observers agree, a pair!

But besides this lantern-slide glimpse, what remains? What
kind of a friendship was it, after all? What did these two do or
fail to do for each other as writers and as human beings? How
did they judge each other in the many moods of their long asso-

ciation? Does their joint history have, as James might say, a "story in it"?

We must dispose summarily of the persistent impression that theirs was simply the literary alliance of younger and elder writer, pupil and master. Intellectual interaction was inevitable between them; they were the sort for whom the play of mind against mind was an essential element of any friendship. But discipleship or even the sense of shared problems possessed by literary companions-in-arms may have been less important than other ingredients. Undoubtedly writing, as well as mutual friends, accounted for their initial acquaintance. He was the great author of many works long admired by her, when, at nearly forty, she had just begun to do some work of her own; she was one of the younger writers he had begun to hear about, to hear (to his annoyance as much as to his curiosity) described as writing in imitation of him. But their literary connection hardly accounts by itself for the relationship that developed from about 1903 until James's death in 1916.

"I had never doubted that Henry James was great, though how great I could not guess till I came to know the man as well as I did his books," Edith Wharton wrote late in life. She revered and delighted in the man even more than in the writer, making a distinction difficult for a later generation which has retained the broad shelf of his books, but lost the person. To him, too, she appeared at first as only another writer, but soon emerged from her background of wealth and privilege to stir his imagination as the kind of American woman who might have figured in one of his own fictions. He was interested in her books, but he was fascinated by her personality.

Yet, as far as one can tell, he was never her "admirer" in the old-fashioned sense of the word; she was never "in love" with him. Love, indeed, is the most fugitive of biographical quarries in the lives of these two aloof spirits, and no biographer can be altogether sure he has not missed the silent, protectively-colored creature among the reeds. Henry James's seemingly celibate affections for younger and older women are still a matter of surmise; his dearest feminine friends seem to have remained just that. Undoubtedly Edith Wharton, married for years to a man she did not love, found a "respectable" woman's fulfillment in the loyalty of bachelor friends like James. Undoubtedly, too, there came a point when this must have failed to suffice, and she discovered in herself an unambiguous passion for one particular bachelor friend who was not Henry James. Yet he was deeply involved in her griefs and hopes. He knew all about the tragedy of her marriage and probably about her feelings for this other friend (who happened to be a good friend of his as well); indeed, he knew nearly everything about her private affairs during these years. For so dedicated and determined a watcher of life, there was a sense of passionate participation in his interest.

It is this feeling of urgency that gives so remarkable a quality to James's vision of Edith Wharton. As our narrative of their friendship proceeds, the reader may find himself—as do readers of James's novel, *The Ambassadors*—aware of two dramas, one taking place in the lighted center of the story, like the affair of Chad and Mme. Vionnet which Strether has come to Europe to investigate, the other enacted in the mind of Strether himself. In the end, Strether's feeling that he has not lived, as have the pair he studies, appears as a paradox. So intense has been his participation in these other lives that it is he, not they, who has really lived. Perhaps it is even he who has most truly loved.

The relationship of Henry James and Edith Wharton was of that rarest kind between a man and a woman. It contained humor, ordinarily the enemy of infatuation, if not of love; it was the achievement of detached intellectual enjoyment and a sympathy qualified by irony. Each cast the keenest, and most appreciating, eye upon the other. Strangely, too, each had a kind of imaginative anticipation of the other. In a general way, her type had long figured in his experience and writing; and his own image was not only foreshadowed in certain of her earlier friends, but resembled the sort of man she would come to depict repeatedly in her books.

"She was herself a novel of his, no doubt in his earlier manner," Percy Lubbock once quipped. James might well have considered her fate a promising *donnée*—his word for the sand grain of reality about which a fiction writer builds his fable—but he never wrote about it. He was nearly done, of course, with his long series of novels when he came to know Edith Wharton; he had all the projects he could manage in those last years. He might simply have known too many facts about her to leave any room for fiction; he was too close to this story. We know he preferred to have just a hint, no more than the oyster's grain, to start with, and would long to stop a dinner companion who was elaborating a suggestive anecdote before it was buried in details. Yet Mrs. Wharton's career drew his studious observation, stirring the novelist's impulse to comprehend a perfect subject.

Women fascinated Henry James as they have rarely fascinated more amorous men; few writers in the history of literature have drawn so many remarkable female portraits. And here was a living lady to sit for a portrait like that of Isabel Archer or Milly Theale or Maggie Verver, or their blighted sisters Madame Merle, Kate Croy, or Charlotte Stant, or even that wilful innocent who first made him famous, Daisy Miller. But James did not write her story, except to friends. It is in his private communications that his portrait of Edith Wharton is to be found.

Yet she might easily have suggested another study such as he had made before of an American woman gifted with position, wealth, and intelligence, with the blessed conditions of free choice, and possessed by the very American energy and hunger to freely be, seeking that freedom abroad, and then somehow, in a very Jamesian way, making some blind, imprisoning, fatal mistake in the process. Freedom, that most American of themes, was after all the great theme of his fiction.

In *The Portrait of a Lady* James had most perfectly expressed his ponderings on this subject long before he knew Edith Wharton. He had endowed his Isabel Archer with all the most favorable conditions and had set his heroine afloat on the broadest sea of opportunity in Europe—very much in the tender spirit of his Ralph Touchett, who transfers to her a legacy of sixty thousand pounds, explaining, "I should like to see her going before the breeze!" Isabel Archer does, one remembers, fly bravely over the waves, and finally, freely, choose her anchorage in Gilbert Osmond, of all choices the most fatal and limiting. Necessity, the novelist seems to be saying, has worn its most insidious disguise precisely where freedom has been greatest; the money and opportunity, which were to give Isabel happiness and cause her germ of self to blossom in some splendid and perfect way, generate only evil in the plot against her of Osmond and Madame Merle. Necessity then overtakes her, after all, though it does not end the story or her search. Suffering and guilt, indeed, may yet give her another access to life, the freedom not of Eden but of knowledge.

Here, in the master-work of his middle years, is James's central myth, the myth of innocence and experience, and its central representation, the trial of an American woman. For its setting and conditions the story makes use of his favorite device, the international theme by means of which the innocent American spirit is taken across a literal and symbolic gulf of ocean and immersed in the European medium, which is at once richer and more corrupt. The myth was capable of many variations, and in suggesting its relation to Edith Wharton's experience we do not mean that she enacted the history of Isabel Archer—or indeed of any of James's female protagonists. But it would appear that she seemed to him to have the qualities of his type of the American woman, and that he saw in her experience of self-development, enacted on European soil, a poignant lesson not unlike that administered to his wonderful Isabel.

Henry James did not, of course, invent this mythic design out of thin air. He was accustomed to the sight of his young countrywomen, so many of them delightfully pretty, superbly dressed, thronging to Europe by the hundreds with their disarmingly innocent effrontery that so baffled the Europeans. Among them there were some—like his cousin Minnie Temple, or Clover Hooper who became the wife of his friend Henry Adams—who possessed a quality of intellectual and moral courage of the very purest sort. Yet always he would sense in this type, in its very innocence and attachment to life, a *hubris*, an infatuated drive towards self-fulfillment which could prove tragic. He would recognize variations of this drive at its brightest or brashest in many

American women he knew; numerous examples contributed to the fashioning of an Isabel.

In Edith Wharton's case he must have noted some of the familiar ingredients: the energy and intrepidity and yearning for self-expression, the gifts of mind and body, the material advantages—and the egotism and capacity for tragic error. He did not think of her as a "dove" like his Milly Theale, but came to see her as a "golden eagle" whose high and dauntless flight stirred his wonder and fear. In his books he had certainly foreseen something of what he admired in her, and something of what filled him with terror, also. Like Isabel Archer, she had all the conditions of freedom—wealth, looks, mental and emotional energy of the highest order—and the added bonus of talent as well. Yet could it not be that despite her superior intelligence, her cultural sophistication so quickly gained, she remained as ignorant as poor Daisy Miller of the limits of freedom?

Lady writers, of course, were a special breed. James had met them before, and discovered the peculiar modifications of relationship with a woman who was a professional competitor, when she was not a clinging apprentice. Seldom, if ever, did he get to know a woman writer who was his creative equal in so proud a sense that no question of rivalry was possible, as was the case with Turgenev or William Dean Howells or Robert Louis Stevenson among his masculine friends, writers for whom his personal affection was mingled with an admiring joy in the other's intellectual character. George Eliot, whose fiction always stirred his spirit and even challenged his conceptions of the art, and about whom he wrote his first signed critical article in 1866, might have been such a friend if he had had the opportunity of doing more than merely make her acquaintance. He met her in 1869, and again in 1878, and each time was as impressed by her personal quality as he had been by her books. Describing her appearance after the first meeting in a letter to his father, he wrote, now in this vast ugliness resides a most powerful beauty which, in a very few minutes steals forth and charms the mind, so that you end as I ended, in falling in love with her. Yes behold me literally in love with this great horse-faced blue-stocking. I don't know in what the charm lies, but it is a thoroughly potent, and admirable physiognomy: —a delightful expression, a voice soft and rich as that of a counseling angel—a mingled sagacity and sweetness—a broad hint of a great underlying world of reserve, knowledge, pride and power—a great feminine dignity and character in these massively plain features—a hundred conflicting shades of consciousness and simpleness— shyness and frankness—graciousness and remote indifference— these are some of the more definite elements of her personality . . . Altogether, she has a larger circumference than any woman I have ever seen.

George Eliot was a unique human encounter; it was manifestly impossible for a literary giant like Henry James to "fall in love" with most women writers after this fashion. Perhaps he came closest in this regard in his enjoyment of Edith Wharton's genius; she was not a George Eliot, but she was the most ponderable and productive female talent among his friends.

He kept running into women who wrote, both Americans and English; and some became his friends, some he disliked. Often he responded to their appeals for literary advice; often he regretted doing so. There was Lucy Clifford, for example, widow of the celebrated English mathematician, W. K. Clifford. James was very fond of Mrs. Clifford, author of the now forgotten *Love Letters of a Worldly Woman* and *Aunt Ann*, and in sending her to an American friend with a letter of introduction, he wrote, in 1912: "Hold out your hand to her for my sweet sake—almost as if I were in love with her & you wished to be sublime." He conscientiously tried to do the office of a literary counselor, too, and advised her at least once.

He had tried long before to do the same for his successful English contemporary, Mrs. Humphry Ward, also a social acquaintance, if not so dear a friend. In both cases, he drew back, in the end, from the task of refashioning a talent really incommen-

surable with his own, apologizing in almost identical words—
though the occasions were nearly thirty years apart—with the
observation that his only way of criticizing, after all, was to re-
imagine the subject of the work before him, to imagine himself
writing another book of his own, "thereby often differing from
the author and his or her way." He said exactly the same thing in
1902 in reference to Edith Wharton's first volumes: "If a work
of imagination, of fiction, interests me at all . . . I always want to
write it over in my own way, handle the subject from my own
sense of it."

Sometimes the literary ambitions of women friends made for a
certain awkwardness, for they expected aid and flattery—gallantry, in a word—and not his really ruthless offer to cast aside
their weak designs and tell them what he would have done. In the
end, if he liked them, he tended to ignore their literary side as
much as he could manage without administering overt snubs. The
American novelist Constance Fenimore Woolson understood this
perfectly when she wrote to him, "You do not want to know the
little literary women. Only the great ones—like George Eliot. I
am barring myself out here, because I do not come in as a literary
woman at all, but as a sort of—of admiring aunt." It now appears
that he was as intimate with Miss Woolson as he was ever to be
with any woman, and we can appreciate what an exceptional
effort he made in her case when he included an essay on her very
minor talent in his *Partial Portraits*. Leon Edel is right in concluding, in his recent biography of James, that this "admiring aunt"
must have held his affections by other means than her modest
contribution to literature, so obviously does he strive to do her a
favor in his essay. In the case of Edith Wharton, there was far
more valid reason for him to pay her work the compliment of his
public attention; she was a literary colleague quite worthy of his
notice. Yet he hesitated a long time and spoke only once about
her in print.

He did not entirely trust the mixture of femininity and literary
ambition. He had had some lamentable experiences. There was
the case of Vernon Lee, whose real name was Violet Paget,
whom he met in Florence in 1884. This remarkable English-

woman of twenty-seven was already the author of some distinguished volumes on the Italian Renaissance and eighteenth century, and she had just undertaken to apply her powers to the art of fiction. James was impressed by her brilliant conversation and called her "the most intelligent woman in Florence" (where she lived nearly all of her life). But he was not at all charmed by the novel she was writing, and he was embarrassed when she dedicated it to him. It seems, nevertheless, that she thought him encouraging: "Henry James takes the most paternal interest in me as a novelist, says that *Miss Brown* is a good title, and that he will do all in his power to push it," she wrote her mother. "He says that his plan in life has been never to lose an opportunity of seeing anything of any kind; he urges me to do the same." When the novel came out, he offered her some blunt wisdom: the book was too violent, exaggerated, and reeked of the personal reference. "Cool first—write afterwards," he told her, and she apparently accepted his critique gracefully.

He continued to see and qualifiedly admire Vernon Lee until, without warning, in 1892 she wickedly satirized him in her story, "Lady Tal." The story tells of an American novelist and his interlude in Venice with an English lady-writer who resembled the author in all but physical appearance. The hero undertakes to read the manuscript of the lady's novel, while privately committing himself to a study of its author for a novel of his own. The following passage suggests the quality of Vernon Lee's cruel and shrewd appraisal of Henry James in the person of the novelist:

This passion for investigating into the feelings and motives of his neighbours was at once the joy, the pride, and the bane and humiliation of Marion's placid life . . . Indeed if Jervase Marion, ever since his earliest manhood, had given way to a tendency to withdraw from all personal concerns, from all emotion or action, it was mainly because he conceived that this shrinkingness of nature (which foolish persons called egoism) was the necessary complement to his power of intellectual analysis . . . To be brought into contact with people more closely than was necessary or advantageous for their intellectual comprehension; to think about them, feel about them, mistress, wife, son, or daughter, the bare thought of such a thing jarred upon Marion's nerves. So, the better to study, the better to be solitary, he had expatriated himself, leaving brothers, sisters (now his mother was dead), friends of childhood, all those things which invade a man's consciousness without any psychological profit; he had condemned himself to live in a world of acquaintances, of indifference; and, for sole diversion, he permitted himself, every now and then, to come abroad to places where he had not even acquaintances, where he could look at faces which had no associations for him, and speculate upon the character of total strangers.

There was enough truth mixed with malice—or enough malice mixed with truth—in this portrait to have made James wild. He was in London, in January, 1893, when he heard about the story and he wrote in high alarm to William James who was then in Florence at his brother's suggestion, visiting Vernon Lee among others. Her act, he cried, was "a particularly impudent and blackguarding sort of thing to do to a friend and one who has treated her with such particular consideration as I have . . . don't caress her . . . she is as dangerous and uncanny as she is intelligent—which is saying a great deal. . . . she's a tiger-cat! . . . I should be glad if (though I am quite conscious of the loss of good talk entailed on you by it—she is far away the most able mind in Florence) you could oblige yourself not to respond to her any further than civility requires."

That, pretty much, was the end of one personal relationship which must have increased his caution about befriending petticoated fellow-professionals. He thought about the subject enough to conceive of a story based on the thesis that the friendship of man and woman could not be easily combined with joint pursuit of the literary goal. He made a notebook entry in November of the following year:

Isn't there perhaps the subject of a little—a very little—tale (*de moeurs littéraires*) in the idea of a man of letters, a poet, a novelist, finding out, after years, or a considerable period, of a very happy, unsuspecting, and more or less affectionate intercourse with a "lady-writer," a newspaper woman, as it were, that he has been systematically *débiné*, "slated" by her in certain critical journals to which she contributes? . . . The point of the thing is whether there be not a little supposable theme or drama in the relation, the situation of the two people after the thing comes to light—the pretension on the part of the reviewer of having one attitude to the writer as a writer, and a totally distinct one as a member of society, a friend, a human being. They may be—the reviewer may be—unconsciously, disappointedly, *régulièrement*, in love with the victim.

That, of course, was the most dangerous possibility in these relationships; the writing lady, like any other kind, might fall in love with one. Perhaps she was more liable to, since she could fancy herself infatuated with the man's books. This was probably the deception Constance Fenimore Woolson practiced upon herself. She liked to tell James of her "gratitude" that was not for him personally, but for his books: "You may be what you please, as long as you write as you do," she wrote him, and she called his writings, "my true country, my real home," adding, "nothing else ever is fully try as I may to think so."

James may not have understood her full feelings; quite probably, even she hardly understood them, for most of their friendship. But if Leon Edel is right in his analysis, she did at last understand her personal, not merely literary, need of James sometime near the end that she brought about by casting herself out of her window in Venice one day in January, 1894. Subsequently he spoke of her as "a close and valued friend of mine—a friend of many years with whom I was extremely intimate and to whom I was greatly attached (Miss Fenimore Woolson, the American novelist, a singularly charming and distinguished woman)", and she unquestionably deserved his most tender memories, for she was a person of self-effacing devotion, hardly a Vernon Lee. Yet it must have seemed to James that his involvement had surely proved pregnant of disaster.

Neither the grotesque (as with Vernon Lee), nor the tragic (as with Constance Fenimore Woolson), was to mark his friendship with Edith Wharton. Their long comradeship would have its tensions but remain unthreatened by the disasters he might have dreaded after these experiences. It seems probable that she found him not merely older but more guarded than he had been a decade earlier. Of Miss Woolson's pathetic story Edith Wharton may have known very little, but she was safe from the hazard of the solitary person and she did not run the risk of exclusive dependence upon James. Nor did she deceive herself that his books alone attached her to him. She herself concluded that it was the man himself—his sparkling company, his personal warmth—who was the greater revelation to those who were privileged to be his friends.

Vernon Lee became one of Edith Wharton's intellectual initiators, almost a model of the literary woman, when they met a year or so after the episode of "Lady Tal." If James, whom Mrs. Wharton did not get to know well for another decade, ever gave her his "tiger-cat" view of Vernon Lee, it does not seem to have affected the mutual esteem of these two ladies of letters, which lasted into the old age of both. Still, she may have known enough about the old disaster to absorb its warning. She never dedicated a book to Henry James, for example, though she did dedicate volumes to other, lesser mentors, such as Edward L. Burlingame, her first editor, and Paul Bourget. Nor did she ever put James directly into a book, though his general type was one her imagination fastened to, first and last.

As Edith Wharton's type had long interested him, so Henry James had been anticipated to a degree by other men she had known. Among the dull throng of relatives and acquaintances in the New York of her youth, when she was Edith Newbold Jones, there were several masculine figures who stood aloof from the vulgar preoccupations of their milieu and gave her a special sympathy and guidance. These men, who were generally her seniors, offered her the romance of intellectual initiation which other intimacies could not provide. She had just been married, in fact, when she met the first of these initiators, a descendant of two colonial governors by the name of Egerton Winthrop, of whom she later wrote, "books are alive enough to an imagination which

knows how to animate them; but living companions are more living still, as I was to discover when I passed for the first time from
the somewhat cramping companionship of the kindly set I had
grown up in and the cool solitude of my studies into the warm
glow of a cultivated intelligence."

Winthrop directed her to books she had not known the existence of—the new French novelists and historians and critics and
the early pronouncements of Darwinism which were still thought-
igniting in the 1880's; above all, he disclosed to her the delights of
conversation about ideas, an experience she had hardly known
before. But like other such men she came to know, he was no
more than a genteel dilettante who collected rare books and
eighteenth-century art and planned perfect small dinner parties.
"Never, I believe," she declared long afterwards, "have an intelligence so distinguished and a character so admirable been combined with interests for the most part so trivial."

There were a few other such early friends—men of sensibility
as well as wealth and family—but always there was some subtle
disablement of spirit, if not actual physical handicap, which kept
them from employing their real gifts. There was Robert Minturn, for instance, whose "exquisite culture" was the compensation for his chronic ill-health. "One by one he had given up the
activities and enjoyments of a young man's life; but he never
allowed these renunciations to dull his appreciation of what remained—the love of art and letters, the love of nature, and above
all, exquisitely vigilant and tender, the love of his friends." Too
handicapped to be that tough person, a literary artist, he was a
connoisseur of language, "an accomplished linguist widely read in
certain lines, a sensitive lover of words, indefatigable in the quest
of their uses and meanings, handling them as a gardener does his
flowers, or a collector his precious jewels or porcelain, and deploring above all their barbarous misuse by our countrymen."

Unlike Henry James, the Winthrops and the Minturns were
either not gifted enough, or not courageous enough, or perhaps
simply not robust enough to find an active role for their abilities.
And yet, in their detached and ironic attitude towards the human

scene as well as in their sensitivity and cultural sophistication, they did in their way resemble him.

They were also, like James, frequently bachelors. Winthrop had been widowed early and thereafter remained unattached. Somehow, the vow not to serve the vulgar gods of caste and class seemed to prohibit matrimony, with all its commitments to social ritual. Any man may have complicated personal reasons for preferring bachelorhood, but these aesthetes and detached observers would have shared some of the novelist's cogent reasons, given in his "The Lesson of the Master." In that story an older writer warns a younger against the "idols of the marketplace," among which are included "placing one's children and dressing one's wife." For the lover of the beautiful and the perfect, "marriage interferes," the master counsels. James added an ironic conclusion to his story; the older writer, having persuaded the young man to break an engagement, then turns about and himself gets married. Whether marriage in his case would "interfere" is left for the reader to imagine.

James himself never risked the possibility. "I am too good a bachelor to spoil," he told a friend. Moreover, he saw a social purpose in the bachelor role. Once, complaining about the frequent urgings towards marriage he received, he wrote another friend: "What strikes me most in the *affaire* is the want of application on the part of society of the useful, beneficent, and civilizing part played in it by the occasional unmarried man of a certain age. He keeps up the tone of humanity—he stands for a thousand agreeable and delightful things." Certainly it was true that in the complicated social design in which the man of sensitive intelligence found himself caught, marriage was an added impediment to the free functioning of taste and judgment. Edith Wharton, seeking mental companions among the men of her social world, found, almost inevitably, that they tended to be bachelors.

The type of bachelor-dilettante-observer figures in some of Mrs. Wharton's early short stories and her later fiction, but is most perfectly realized in Lawrence Selden, the chief male character of her novel published in 1905, *The House of Mirth*. Selden lives alone in the midst of New York's frivolities, part of Society and yet apart from it, too. He collects "fine" books and cultivates the finer perceptions. He refuses to enter the round of getting and spending—and marrying—which preoccupies the other young men of his class. What he discloses to the heroine, Lily Bart, is the existence of a "republic of the spirit" which she may learn to inhabit if she will. It was to this same "republic of the spirit" that first Winthrop, then others, invited Mrs. Wharton during the difficult years in which she groped for self-realization.

In her analysis, their shortcomings as well as their virtues are exposed, for Selden's enervated spirit can offer comment and advice, but not action, not love. As Lily Bart spirals downward from society's upper levels to its lower, finally to death by an overdose of sleeping-drugs, he can only stand by in musing reflection. His failure to save her from her doom is made clear by the author of *The House of Mirth*. As he kneels futilely at her bedside at the last, he sees that "all the conditions of life had conspired to keep them apart; since his very detachment from the external influences which had swayed her had increased his spiritual fastidiousness, and made it more difficult for him to live and love uncritically."

As an exact model for Selden, Edith Wharton had her friend Walter Berry, whom she met in New York in 1884. Only three years older than herself, Berry was a young man of her time and place and class, and, like her, the odd exception to the frivolous norm. Though born in Paris, he was the grandson of Stephen van Rensselaer, the New York general and politician who was known as the "last of the patroons," and, again like her, related to some of the oldest New York families. His education had begun at a Paris school, but had continued at St. Mark's and at Harvard. When Edith Wharton met him he was completing a law course in Washington, D.C. at Columbian College.

Her comment on their first meeting is significant:

"We had seen a great deal of each other for a few weeks, and the encounter had given me a fleeting hint of what the communion of kindred intelligences might be." The communion of kindred intelligences—how, indeed, she hungered for it! But the next year she was married to Edward Robbins Wharton, who had been judged "the handsomest man in his Harvard class"—a dashing young Bostonian very much in love with her. Berry had passed his bar examinations and begun the practice of law in Washington, and they did not meet again for another five years, when he dropped in to see the Whartons at Newport.

Though seriously devoted to his law career, Berry was a connoisseur of the arts who, in Edith Wharton's description, was "born with an exceptionally sensitive literary instinct." He was, however, burdened by "a critical sense so far outweighing his creative gift that he had early renounced the idea of writing," and he remained an intellectual dandy, a sort of gourmet of aesthetic comestibles, for the rest of his life. After he became a permanent European resident—like his friends Henry James and Edith Wharton—he was a familiar figure in certain circles of Paris society. He was an intimate not only of duchesses, but of Marcel Proust to whom, at the onset of their friendship, he gave a book from the library of the Guermantes, stamped with their coat-of-arms. Proust dedicated to him his *Pastiches et Mélanges,* and in writing the dedication, which praised Berry for his devotion to France, he confessed a difficulty over the phrasing of his compliment: "You must choose the art wherein it seems to you most creditable to have displayed an 'unrivalled ability.' Is it eloquence? Is it style? You have so many gifts that one is confronted with the difficulty of making a choice." With due allowance for Proust's characteristic tendency to effusion, Berry's versatility is clear. What is significant is that his abilities were never more than personal ornaments. He was content to be the witness of the endeavors of others. In the case of Edith Wharton, he was witness and advisor, her most treasured, until his death in 1927. It was to Berry that she submitted the first of her books, and for many years those that followed, and he read them in manuscript chapter by chapter, with what effect we shall never exactly know.

Though Edith Wharton herself cannot be compared with her frivolous heroine who is destroyed by the society of which she is a product, Berry, as early in the relationship as 1905, may well have seemed a Selden to her. Eventually, he may have been guilty

34

of a kind of defection which she probably attributed to his "detachment" and "spiritual fastidiousness." She herself never spoke of him save with love and thankfulness, but "none of her friends," says Percy Lubbock, "thought she was the better for the surrender of her fine free spirit to the control of a man of strong intelligence and ability—but also of a dry and narrow and supercilious temper." It was generally observed that he was never as exclusively devoted to her as she was to him; whatever the reasons, he did not choose to marry her as she had undoubtedly hoped, after her divorce in 1913. He remained her friend, her counselor—and a bachelor.

Henry James, of course, was the greatest citizen of the "republic of the spirit" Edith Wharton would ever know, and the most distinguished and profound of those elegant and ironic observers, both members and exiles from the "polite" world, who became her friends. But his greatness does not obliterate in him a quality he shared with these others. He, too, this eminent bachelor friend, was to be an intellectual initiator and guide, far more important by the power of his example than even her closer intimate, Berry. While there is little possibility that she was ever let down by him herself, she may have sensed his capacity for withdrawal and ultimate rejection, for being, in a word, a Selden.

Confirmation of such a possibility may be found in his own fiction. Life and art are curiously mingled here, for James, with a certain degree of self-portraiture, also places a Selden character centrally in his novels and stories. In *The Portrait of a Lady*, there are two men of opposite virtue who possess some of the characteristics we have been identifying. On the one hand, there is Isabel's intelligent and kindly cousin, Ralph Touchett, whose love for her is nullified by his invalidism—all he can give her is money; and on the other hand, there is the soulless dilettante Gilbert Osmond, who marries her for that money and who is incapable of either loving or appreciating her, for all that he is as expert a connoisseur of things and persons as Ralph. Both men serve in different ways to suggest the shortcomings of the detached aesthete.

James returned to this personality many times in the course of his writing, so repeatedly, in fact, that his concern with its meaning seems obsessive, particularly personal. Again and again, such male characters in his fiction are coupled with an eager and loving feminine spirit which they subtly or harshly disappoint by an inner coldness. The most famous and terrible of his fables on this theme is the long story, "The Beast in the Jungle."

At the same time, James was most unlike this haunting demi-hero of his own and Edith Wharton's fiction in being a productive man of letters, a type unrepresented among Edith Wharton's early associations. James could remember Emerson calling upon his parents one day and Thackeray another, not to speak of a constant procession of lesser figures from the world of art and literature during his small-boyhood, but Edith Wharton probably did not meet a real writer until she was a married woman. Unlike the elder Jameses, her parents, "though they held literature in great esteem, stood in nervous dread of those who produced it." As their daughter remembered:

> Washington Irving, Fitz-Greene Halleck and William Dana were the only representatives of the disquieting art who were deemed uncontaminated by it; though Longfellow, they admitted, if a popular poet, was nevertheless a gentleman. As for Herman Melville, a cousin of the Van Rensselaers, and qualified by birth to figure in the best society, he was doubtless excluded from it by his deplorable Bohemianism, for I never heard his name mentioned, or saw one of his books. Banished probably for the same reason were Poe, that drunken and demoralized Baltimorean, and the brilliant wastrel Fitz James O'Brien, who was still further debased by "writing for the newspapers." But worse still perhaps in my parents' eyes was the case of such unhappy persons as Joseph Drake, author of "The Culprit Fay," balanced between "fame and infamy" as not quite of the best society, and writing not quite the best poetry. I cannot hope to render the tone in which my mother pronounced the names of such unfortunates, or, on the other hand, that of Mrs. Beecher Stowe, who was so "common" yet so successful. On the whole, my mother doubtless thought, it would be simpler if people one might be exposed to meeting would refrain from meddling with literature.

Young Edith was not "exposed to meeting" writers up to the time of her marriage and, indeed, for several years later. The first professional writer she got to know was, significantly, a foreigner, Paul Bourget, who came into her drawing-room almost by accident, after she had been married for eight years. In 1893, Gordon Bennett, who had read Bourget's novel *Cosmopolis*, just then published, and admired its accomplished definition of various international scenes, conceived the notion of commissioning the novelist to do a series on American society for the New York *Herald*. It was Bourget's first visit to this country, and he came bearing letters of introduction which would open to his view, he hoped, the varied aspects of the social landscape; one of these was from old Franco-American acquaintances, the Ridgeways, who directed him to their cousins, Mr. and Mrs. Wharton, then spending the summer season at Newport. He came to Newport promptly—"the American Deauville" was to be an important part of the picture he intended to draw—and called at the Whartons', expecting to find a typical society couple who would furnish illustration for his survey.

Edith Wharton, on her part, prepared to receive the famous French author with mingled terror and joy. She had read many of his stories and novels, subtle dissections of the passions which seemed overly intellectual or else shockingly decadent to most of his Anglo-Saxon readers, few of whom, however, were to be found in Newport. She did not know anyone, she thought, who could possibly interest him; nevertheless, she asked some guests to meet him at dinner, little realizing that the more mondaine they were, the more they would serve Bourget's purpose. "At least," she thought, looking out of her windows which faced the open ocean at the eastern promontory of Newport's rocky shore, "at least he will be able to enjoy our incomparable view!"

Bourget, who was extremely near-sighted anyway, showed little interest in the Atlantic breakers, but peered at Mrs. Wharton, her husband, and her guests with a sociologist's curiosity. One imagines that he had a difficult time "placing" his hostess—this "smartly-gowned," perfectly-mannered socialite, with her only faintly suppressed bookishness and intelligence that seemed to make a paradox of her setting. He was surprised, but also charmed. On her part, she was dazzled by this first representative of the literary life. Bourget was a particularly flamboyant specimen of his kind. He had lived nearly all his life in the atmosphere of intellectual conversation which surrounds the Parisian *littérateur*, and he was himself an accomplished talker whose remarks ranged from the philosophical to the anecdotal with untiring grace and energy. Even Henry James, himself a master of this art, later declared to Edith Wharton that Bourget was "easily the first" of the talkers he had known. One can imagine the effect upon her of this meeting, for Bourget represented at once all the worlds she longed to enter—the profession of letters, the traditional culture of Europe, the free intercourse of sophisticated minds. Eventually Bourget helped her to take possession of all three of those worlds.

It is significant that she was not swept off her feet by his powerful influence. She had already decided before meeting him that she did not really like his fiction. There was too much explanation and too little left to the reader's perceptions, too little conveyed by the power of direct presentation; she disliked the excessively analytic quality that pervaded all Bourget's stories. It was a judgment that did not alter despite the development of their friendship and the increasing strength of their intellectual bonds. When Bourget died, many years later, she confessed in an essay of "souvenirs" addressed to the French public that it was "painful" but true that she had never developed a taste for his fiction. It was an admission made particularly awkward by the fact that Bourget had always generously praised her own work. Early in her career he had helped her gain overseas recognition by writing a warm preface to the French translation of *The House of Mirth* (a translation done at Bourget's suggestion, by Charles du Bos). It is possible that she owed a little more than she admitted to his technique as a writer. Nevertheless, direct comment either by him on her work or by her on his quite early became impossible.

We often spoke of the art of the novel [she wrote] for both of us cared passionately for the technique of our craft; and soon I realized that Bourget's ideas were entirely opposed to mine. As soon as he began a novel, Bourget mounted the pulpit; every character had to be a pawn in a clever game contrived beforehand, and from which the disconcerting unexpected events in life were totally banished. Having discovered that our theories never could be reconciled, we wisely decided not to talk any further about our respective work; but, in return, we permitted each other to relate the themes of our future books.

The irony and the sadness of human destiny we both envisioned in the same manner. Every incident supplied us—him as well as myself—with a new theme, and we passed hours in recounting them to each other. Bourget always chided me because in my books I did not explain people enough; I answered him that he underestimated the intelligence of his readers in supposing that it was necessary to analyze in advance the motive of every act, almost of every word, instead of letting these be revealed by the speech and action of the characters.

When they met that day in Newport in 1893, she had just been reading his recent *Essais de Psychologie Contemporaine*, a study of modern French writers based on Taine's formula, "la littérature est un psychologie vivante." She admired it much more than she did Bourget's fiction, but when she met the man himself, she was moved to regret. "Why was it necessary that the qualities which made the conversationalist so bewitching—the gaiety, the irony, the light and vivid manner in which he recounted an anecdote or imitated a conversation—why need all that made his conversation so brilliant and so flavorsome have to disappear every time the novelist took up his pen?" Eventually she concluded that it was the vivid person himself, his wit, intelligence and human charm, his tolerance and humor, his devoted friendship, that held them together, and not interest in each other's books.

Aside from Bourget, Edith Wharton made no significant friendship with a fellow-artist until she met James. When her first volume of short stories was published, in 1899, she could still declare that Bourget was the only novelist she knew, and that she had just two friends who at all shared her interests, without being writers themselves, Walter Berry and Egerton Winthrop. "But one was a busy lawyer who did not live in New York, and who, as his practice grew, had less and less leisure; while the other, a man many years older than myself, and of very worldly tastes, could not understand my longing to break away from the world of fashion and be with my own spiritual kin." Even as her opportunities widened, even after she knew James, her circle did not include any other important fellow-craftsmen. Men of talent, men of perhaps one novel, like Howard Sturgis or Percy Lubbock, became in time her closest friends, but where were her real confrères, aside from James and Bourget? Nor did the pattern of her friendships enlarge to include her peers when she finally made a life for herself abroad.

How different from Henry James, who made friendships with great writers in three countries! There is pathos in Edith Wharton's complaint, in her autobiography, that William Dean Howells was an "irreducible recluse, and though I was in a way accredited to him by my friendship with his two old friends, Charles Norton and Henry James, I seldom met him. I always regretted this for I had a great admiration for 'A Modern Instance' and 'Silas Lapham,' and should have liked to talk with their author about the art in which he stood so nearly among the first; and he himself, whenever we met, was full of quiet friendliness. But I suppose my timidity and his social aloofness kept us apart; for though I felt that he was amicably disposed he remained inaccessible." Of course Howells was twenty-five years her senior and he was only seven years older than James, with whom a long friendship, personal and intellectual, dated from their youth. Still, one cannot help wondering why her timidity was so great. Perhaps she never really overcame the "nervous dread" of the producers of literature which her parents had implanted in her—not even after she had long become one of the producers herself.

Her Doucet dress, a beaded tea-rose pink, was all she could offer to his notice, Edith Wharton felt when she was introduced to Henry James in 1887 or 1888. She was twenty-five, a socialite nobody with a well-hidden appetite for letters, while he was forty-five and the famous author of *Daisy Miller* and *The Portrait of a Lady*, who had just published *The Bostonians* and *The Princess Casamassima* in a single year. The occasion was sufficiently auspicious—a dinner party in the Paris home of Edward Darley Boit. Boit was a water-colorist from Boston whom James had met in 1873 when the artist and his wife Louisa (a vivacious woman who loved horseback riding and dragged James to picnics) formed a part of the American art-colony in Rome. They had long resolved upon permanent residence abroad and may have suggested to young Mrs. Wharton the kind of life that might be taken up there. But nothing came of her meeting with James that evening. Tongue-tied in the actual presence of a writer she had read with reverent admiration for years, she wistfully hoped that her new dress would catch his eye. But in vain; he never noticed her or even remembered the occasion when she mentioned it long afterwards.

The situation was exactly repeated a year or two later, this time in Venice, upon the occasion of an invitation from another ex-Bostonian, Daniel S. Curtis and his English wife Ariana, who lived in a Renaissance palazzo on the Grand Canal. Here was another significant glimpse for Edith Wharton of the world which Henry James inhabited, for the Curtises had been settled in "The Barbaro" ever since 1885, and, like *cinquecento* patrons, had entertained the novelist for long visits. The Curtises were part of that Venetian milieu which included James's (and Robert Browning's) old friend, Mrs. Arthur Bronson, also once of Boston, whose more modest *casa* was his other favorite resort in Venice. The Barbaro, with its Tiepolo ceilings, its marble floors, its portraits of the Doges, was shortly to reappear as Milly Theale's Palazzo Leporelli in *The Wings of the Dove*.

In this second setting of Americans in Europe Edith Wharton felt the same dumb awe as before. As she remembered years later: "Once more I thought: How can I make myself pretty enough for him to notice me? Well—this time I had a new hat, *a beautiful new hat!* I was almost sure it was becoming, and I felt that if he would only tell me so I might at last pluck up courage to blurt out my admiration for 'Daisy Miller' and 'The Portrait of a Lady.' But he noticed neither the hat nor its wearer—and the second of our meetings fell as flat as the first."

Both the Curtises and Boits were old Boston acquaintances of Mrs. Wharton's husband, but this could hardly have mitigated, one imagines, her sense of insufficiency. However his friends might value Edward ("Teddy") Wharton, his claims upon their interest were never in the remotest degree intellectual. And the young wife he had married in 1885 had done nothing much since she had written sentimental poetry in her teens to justify any secret pretensions to the literary life. The Whartons must have seemed to James typical examples of those numerous well-to-do Americans he was always encountering, who wandered annually across Europe, called on countrymen resident abroad, and returned to Boston, New York, and Philadelphia, their provincialism quite unaltered. It would be ten years, in fact, before he began to distinguish Mrs. Wharton among the numerous friends of friends he was always hearing about and running into. When he did, the cause was not her feminine hat or costume, but the reviews, probably, of her first book, a collection of clever stories called *The Greater Inclination* to which the critics drew his attention by tagging it an imitation of his own work. The year was 1899.

At that moment, the contrast between Henry James and Edith Wharton could hardly have been more complete. At fifty-six, he had been settled in England for over twenty years, and had just moved into "Lamb House," in the quiet Sussex town of Rye, which was to be henceforth his home. His life had already an established pattern. Though an essentially solitary spirit whose innermost vibrations were communicated only in his art, he had a wide acquaintance on both sides of the Atlantic. His correspondence was voluminous, not only with members of his family and early friends still in America, but with English and Continental friends. Doors in many places opened eagerly to him whenever he was willing to leave his writing desk, but this he did less often than in earlier years. He had already come to that completeness of self-knowledge in which his aims and needs were entirely clear; nothing, indeed, that would subsequently happen to him, no human encounter, however stirring, would alter his view of why and how he wanted to live.

He was, of course, already famous. To many perceptive readers of English letters, and to his fellow-craftsmen especially, he was acknowledged to be a master of the art of fiction who had altered the possibilities of the short story and novel. After the success of *Daisy Miller* in 1878, he produced a succession of novels, and became, as he wrote of Alphonse Daudet, "not an occasional or desultory poet but a soldier in the great army of constant producers." The number of his readers did, indeed, shrink distressingly during the eighties when *The Bostonians* and *The Princess Casamassima*, ambitious attempts to venture into new subjects, were popular failures, though the critics and his fellow-writers sensed their extraordinary quality. His resolution to persevere in the novel almost wavered during the next few years, and he tried, with appalling ill-success, to win a new following by writing plays. But soon he was producing long works of fiction again, resolute amidst his discouragements—among them *The Spoils of Poynton, What Maisie Knew, The Awkward Age*, which represented new assaults upon the problems of his craft, new efforts to formulate his personal vision. His work was less saleable now, but he had reached the condition of inner calm which prepared for his final artistic triumphs. Just ahead of him lay the great triple range of his "major phase"—*The Ambassadors, The Wings of the Dove*, and *The Golden Bowl*. Despite personal illness—he was always something of a hypochondriac, but also a real sufferer from constant minor indispositions—he was assiduous and happy in the practice of his art as few writers have been.

Edith Wharton, in 1899, was hardly in her earliest youth. At thirty-seven, a serious writer might be expected to have gone beyond the preliminary of a first book of stories. But she was, as a matter of fact, at the very opposite end of the cycle from James; her career as a professional writer was making its tentative first steps. She was still so much of an amateur that most of her acquaintances in the tight world of New York Society in which she had always lived did not think of her as a writer at all. She was a "society matron," properly equipped with a house in New York and a cottage in Newport, and a big, handsome, sports-loving husband who took the same pride in her little literary success (for her book, surprisingly, was a success) as he would have in triumphs wrought upon the embroidery-frame. Few of the members of her social set were aware how deep her desire to be a writer was. In all the long procession of wealthy New York-ers from whom she descended—Schermerhorns, Pendletons, Stevenses, Ledyards, Rhinelanders, and Joneses—there had not been a single artist, not even a single person with marked interest in the arts. Yet it was remembered by some of her contemporaries that little "Pussy" Jones was often surprised bending her head over scraps of paper, "always scribbling" or reading—first all the books in her father's unused "gentleman's library," then classics in English and German put into her hands by her governess and the bluestocking daughter of the rector of Calvary Church.

It is often asserted that her family tried to suppress her childish urge to write. As a matter of fact, they took a certain natural pride in her talents, as long as they were those of a precocious child. Though her mother was a person of circumscribed interests, a Rhinelander who was known as the "best-dressed woman in New York," she gave a packet of her daughter's verses to a Newport printer, paying for its publication, when Edith was sixteen. The following year, 1879, her verse was displayed for the first time in the public press. Having read the pathetic report of a child suicide in the New York *World*, the young poet had sent the editor a doggerel ballad based on the story, girlishly signed "Eadgyth," and he promptly printed it.

Her family was not, apparently, alarmed by the event, for it was her brother who then showed some of her poems to Allen Thorndike Rice, the future editor of the *North American Review*, who enclosed them with a letter to his distinguished relative, Henry Wadsworth Longfellow, and Longfellow benevolently passed them on to William Dean Howells. The great editor, to the Joneses' amazement, then actually printed them in the *Atlantic Monthly*. Nevertheless, it is probable that she was not expected to persevere in this youthful hobby. The fact that she "came out" at seventeen, a year earlier than most of the débutantes of the day, suggests that her parents wanted to hasten the putting away of childish things. During the next few years she led the life she had been bred to, went to balls and the opera and found her place in her hereditary sphere in New York, shifted to the diversions of Newport in the summer and one autumn went with her parents to Europe. At twenty-three she was married irreproachably—to a friend of her elder brother and member of a wealthy Boston family. The young couple moved immediately into a cottage on the grounds of her mother's Newport estate.

Her life continued to be perfectly predictable in outward form for several years. From June to February, the Whartons were at Newport, where they soon had a more imposing home of their own at the end of the famous Cliff Walk; from February to May, they travelled in Europe; after three or four years their calendar included a stay in a town-house in Manhattan for the early part of the winter. Hedged in by her inherited associations and ceremonies as she was, Edith Wharton's life still contained glimpses of a freer world. Though the scribbling had stopped, her youthful habit of reading continued and good books accumulated around her as meaningless bric-a-brac accumulated around the other ladies of her circle.

When Paul Bourget called upon her in Newport he was astonished to discover library shelves stacked with literature. Even the furnishings suggested something; there were odd pieces of eighteenth-century furniture which the Whartons had collected while travelling to Italy, following a bent imparted by Vernon Lee's and Bourget's own books. Travel, instead of being the empty excursionism of most rich Americans, had itself become another way of entering the forbidden realm of culture. Art, history, the cross-references of differing traditions, all these were available to the serious explorer who left behind her the frivolities of watering places and Paris shops.

The taste for travel became a ruling passion in Edith Wharton's life. She could never understand, in later years, when she ranged like an eager huntress through the entire length and breadth of France, how Bourget was content to take the same route from Paris to the Riviera every year, when innumerable possibilities of delight for the mind and eye lay in the parts of his own land which he invariably by-passed. Travel was to become a most important part of her relation with Henry James.

In a way, she was repeating something of his own history. The James family, of course, was a very different starting-point from the home-circle of Edith Newbold Jones. William James once said wittily of his brother that he was a "native of the James family," an environment so peculiar and important for both of them that it had more to do with the shaping of their lives and characters than any externals of milieu and geography. Certainly no household could have been more unlike that of the conventional Joneses than the family of the elder Henry James, the distinguished and eccentric Swedenborgian who once explained his own nature by saying: "My intelligence is the necessary digestive apparatus for my life." In the place of Edith Jones's two dull elder brothers, mostly away at school when she was growing up, the younger Henry had the companionship at home and at various schools they attended, of a veritable genius of an elder brother; in addition he experienced the constant stimulus of a sister and younger brothers whose sparkle of personality was an unceasing challenge to his own developing nature.

But, the family is only a small hedged area beyond which lies the world that meets one upon the first outward step, and it is certainly true that James and Edith Wharton shared the same early scene. It was that "Old New York" whose focus lay between Washington Square, where he had been born in 1843, and Twenty-Third Street, a mile further uptown, where she was born nearly twenty years later. Boundaries social as well as geographic defined this polite nineteenth-century Manhattan, and gave it a "family-party smallness" as James described it, in which everyone was connected with everyone else by family recognitions and habits of association inherited for several generations. The Jameses inhabited this "small dusky homogeneous New

York World of the mid-century" until Henry was twelve; his history of his childhood, *A Small Boy and Others*, is full of sights and sounds and family names that would come to be Edith Wharton's own earliest associations. She, too, reminisces of this vanished society in her autobiography, and she remarks of James: "He belonged irrevocably to the old America out of which I also came."

However far each would go from their beginning, Henry James and Edith Wharton both cherished a wistful affection for this world that by the early years of the new century already began to change irretrievably; it was a bond between them. *Washington Square* is his special bitter-sweet memorial to his youth; the square which is his story's background is almost an actor in the drama and deserves its place in the title; Edith Wharton's own memorial was to be a novel written many years later, *The Age of Innocence*, which is, as its title declares, the full portrait of a vanished time. It is interesting to reflect that both James and Mrs. Wharton were at once critical and nostalgic about this world they left far behind. It was small and provincial; it could never have contained either of them; nevertheless it was better than what came after it. A sweet, clear flavor of American vintage lingered on the palate and nothing Europe had to offer ever quite matched it.

The sea-girt backyard of this New York was Newport, and both Edith Wharton and Henry James had the experience of a youth in which the picturesque, unfailing natural scene, with its opportunities for rambles on cliff and beach and the tonic of sun-drenched air and water, were oddly mixed with visions of familiar full-skirted belles of the ballroom at archery or tennis, polished victorias or barouches bearing their elegant passengers behind high-stepping horses along Bellevue Avenue, and parties, whether indoor or out, rivalling in flutter of finery and general pomp the social entertainments of the city.

In 1858, the James family returned from three years in Europe to settle for a couple of years in Newport. Henry was seventeen at the time, and much later he looked back upon this Newport of his youth:

47

American society—so far as that free mixture was to have arrived at cohesion—had for half a century taken its whole relation with the place seriously (which was by intention very gayly); it long remained, for its happiness, quite at one with this most favored resort of its comparative innocence. In the attesting presence of all the constant elements, of natural conditions that have, after all, persisted more than changed, a hundred far-away passages of the extinct life and joy, and of the comparative innocence, came back to me with an inevitable grace. A glamour as of the flushed ends of beautiful old summers, making a quite rich medium, a red sunset haze, as it were, for the processional throng of charioteers and riders, fortunate folk, fortunate above all in their untouched good faith, adjourning from the pleasures of the day to those of the evening—this benignity in particular overspread the picture, hanging it there as the Newport aspect that most lived again. Those good people all could make discoveries within the frame itself—beginning of course to push it out, in all directions, so as sufficiently to enlarge it, as they fondly fancied, even for the experience of a sophisticated world. They danced and they drove and they rode, they dined and wined and dressed and flirted and yachted and polo'd and Casino'd, responding to the subtlest inventions of their age; on the old lawns and verandas I saw them gather; on the old shining sands I saw them gallop, past the low headlands I saw their white sails verily flash, and through the dusky old shrubberies came the light and the sound of their feasts.

This was Edith Wharton's Newport, too, the Newport of the seventies, which she so tenderly described in *The Age of Innocence*. She herself recalled Arcadian summers of her girlhood when the Jones house, "Pencraig," was full of the gaiety of young people and her brothers brought friends to play tennis on the lawn in tail-coats and whale-boned dresses, or led forth fishing and boating parties from the floating boat-landing on its margin. To the romantic mind of young Edith Jones, these handsome, beautifully-appareled creatures were the Gods and Goddesses of those classical legends she had just discovered in her adventurous reading. She did not yet suspect how little her brothers' friends could answer the longings of her hidden self.

48

In James's Newport bouquet there was a special fragrance—vanished by 1906, when he revisited the place—contributed by the winter population that lingered on after the splendid summer,

> when the strange sight might be seen of a considerable company of Americans, not gathered at a mere rest-cure, who confessed brazenly to not being in business. Do I grossly exaggerate in saying that this company, candidly, quite excitedly self-conscious, as all companies not commercial, in America, may be pleasantly noted as being, formed, for the time of its persistence, an almost unprecedented small body—unprecedented in American conditions; a collection of the detached, and yet of the resigned and contented, of the socially orthodox: a handful of mild, oh delightfully mild, cosmopolites, united by three common circumstances, that of their having for the most part more or less lived in Europe, that of their sacrificing openly to the ivory idol whose name is leisure, and that, not least, of a formed critical habit. These things had been felt as making them excrescences on the American surface, where nobody ever criticized, especially after the grand tour, and where the great black ebony god of business was the only one recognized.

Edith Wharton recalled that in the little society in which she had been born, business was similarly unworshipped: "for the most part my father's contemporaries, and those of my brothers also, were men of leisure—a term now almost as obsolete as the state it describes." Yet the uses to which her father and her brothers put their leisure were relatively primitive; literature, art, music, even the theatre played only the most minor part.

James's cosmopolites, with their experience not merely of European travel but of European residence and their "formed critical habit," included an element more highly civilized than any it was Edith Wharton's fortune to encounter either in New York or Newport when she was a girl. It was in this rather precious winter Newport that he discovered his first artist friends; in the studio of William Morris Hunt, for example, he found the younger painter John La Farge, who was the first to offer him a light along his true path. La Farge introduced him to the works of Balzac and other modern French authors, and to Browning, then the awakener of young minds, and even helped him to recognize his real talent, not for the pictorial but for the verbal medium.

Edith Wharton's Newport was, probably, more exclusively of the summer-resort phase, for though not compelled by the summons of business her parents regularly returned to winter in New York. Nevertheless, some notes of the artistic and the critical may have lingered on for her in the Newport season of her later day. Perhaps it is only coincidence that made Newport the scene of her labors on her first book. To re-do the interior of "Land's End," the house purchased by the Whartons shortly after they were married in 1885, she called in a young architect, Ogden Codman, and in their discussions, practical and theoretic, about the design of interiors, she and Codman discovered that they had a message of taste and experience to pass on to others. So, she was launched on the writing of *The Decoration of Houses,* which, with its plea for an intelligent, informed use of the great styles of the past, was Edith Wharton's first statement of aesthetic principle. It was also her first disciplined exercise as a writer.

In the same breeze-filled place where James had listened to the urgings of John La Farge, she tackled the problems of professional writing. And for her, too, a helper was at hand. Walter Berry came down to visit at Land's End. He understood, as no one before had, how in earnest she was, and he took her writing in hand. Later she wrote: "In those weeks, as I afterward discovered, I had been taught whatever I know about the writing of clear concise English"—undoubtedly an exaggeration, but evidence, in any case, of the importance she attached to this beginning, and to the man who assisted her in making it.

Berry, too, belonged irrevocably to the Old America, out of which, as Edith Wharton said, she and James both came. When, some years after James's death, she showed him the manuscript of *The Age of Innocence,* he remarked to her, "Yes, it's good. But of course you and I are the only people who will ever read it. We are the last people left who can remember New York and Newport as they were then, and nobody else will be interested."

Actually, *The Age of Innocence* won a Pulitzer Prize in 1920 and next to *Ethan Frome* it is probably the most popular of her books. But few among its many readers could have shared its author's sense and Berry's—and James's—of poignantly mingled resentment and affection for that Old New York and Newport of their youth.

Another who shared with James and Edith Wharton the same Old New York and Newport associations was Mrs. Wharton's own sister-in-law. It was she who brought them together ten years after their abortive meetings in Paris and Venice. Mary Cadwalader Rawle had married Frederic Rhinelander Jones when his sister Edith was seven. This brother had not till then meant much to the child. He was already in college when she was born, and from those early years before his marriage she seems to have remembered best one rather nasty incident. When she was four, he forced her to swallow a glassful of claret, a joke no doubt amusing to a boisterous youth of twenty but so upsetting to the sensitive small girl that she remained unable to bear the taste of wine for the rest of her life. But he did do one compensating favor for her in the unusual person he married. Though she was to be divorced from him after a few years, the older woman attached herself indissolubly to Frederic's young sister. "To me she became closer than a sister of my own blood," wrote Mrs. Jones in summary of the long friendship they then began. Edith Wharton remembered in a letter to Mrs. Jones written in 1930 the circumstances of their early acquaintance when nineteen-year-old Minnie had been entrusted by her new little sister-in-law with the care of her pet rabbit, and had forgotten him in the park! "This incident," wrote Mrs. Wharton, "is the only blot that, after a microscopic scrutiny of the ensuing sixty years, I am able to discover in your perfect record as sister-in-law, friend and comrade."

Just as James placed it in his record of deepest appreciation that John La Farge had first introduced him to the poetry of Browning, so Edith Wharton remembered that it was Minnie Jones who gave her a copy of Browning when she was sixteen. Mrs. Jones had herself become a friend, by this time, of artists and writers, and her Sunday luncheons in her house on East Eleventh Street in New York soon became famous, for there regularly foregathered Brooks and Henry Adams, Theodore Roosevelt, the novelist Marion Crawford, the artists John La Farge, Augustus Saint-Gaudens, John Sargent—and Henry James. For James, she remained a constant friend whom he warmly welcomed whenever she came to him abroad in after years and with whom he maintained a faithful correspondence. Repeatedly in these letters his thoughts went back to younger days when he frequented her little salon.

He recalled his first visit: "Vivid to me still is that December night when, a weary & bewildered pilgrim, I scaled your stoop & invoked your welcome for the first time, & felt on the spot that I had come to the great good place. I don't know what I shld. have done without you then." And having mounted the brownstone steps and entered, in his imagination, once more, he recalled the "dear old Empire rooms, with their dimmish 'middle distance'." Often he remembered, he told her, "those Eleventh Street matitutinal *intimes* hours, those telephonic matinées, as the most romantic of [his] life." And again, "My New York of those dear East Eleventh Street 'first-floor-back' hours lives again for me as I write . . . it's astonishing, it's prodigious, how I find my spirit gratefully haunting them always—or rather how insidiously turning the tables they, the mystic locality itself, haunt and revisit my own departed identity."

All his feeling for Old New York seemed sometimes to concentrate upon his vision of Mary Cadwalader Jones. "I kind of make you out 'down there,' I mean in the pretty, very pretty as it used to be, New York Autumn, and in the Washington Square-ish region trodden by the steps of childhood, and I wonder if you ever kick the October leaves as you walk in Fifth Avenue, as I can to this hour feel myself, hear myself, positively *smell* myself doing. But perhaps there are no leaves and no trees now in Fifth Avenue—nothing but Patriotic arches, Astor hotels and Vanderbilt palaces."

2

Outre-mer

IN 1889, EDITH WHARTON began to write poetry again—something she had not thought of doing for ten years. But four years of marriage, of New York and Newport and the annual trip to Europe, then round again, were obviously not enough—or too much. There is a story, too, that S. Weir Mitchell, himself a novelist as well as a physician specializing in female neurosis, advised her to take up writing to ward off a breakdown. In July, 1889, at any rate, she experienced one moment of delirious happiness, as she recalled, when the editor of *Scribner's Magazine* mailed her a check of twenty dollars for a poem. "As long as I live I shall never forget my sensations," she said of the moment when she stood in the vestibule of her Madison Avenue house and opened this letter of acceptance. "I was to appear in print. I can still see the narrow hall, the letter-box out of which I fished the letters, and the flight of stairs up and down which I ran senselessly and incessantly, in the attempt to give my excitement some muscular outlet!"

She sent more poems, then stories to Edward L. Burlingame, the editor whom she called "my first and kindest critic" in the dedication of her third collection of tales published in 1904. Her first collection shaped up slowly under the patient encouragement of Burlingame and of W. C. Brownell of the Scribner book department whose critical judgment meant so much to her. Brownell, in particular, became a counsellor upon whom she relied long after she had stopped giving her books to Scribner, for he was not merely a practical teacher, like Burlingame, but a critic of literature whose own published writings she always admired, absorbing many of his principles as part of her critical creed. A warm affection developed between the two, although their relationship remained professional rather than personal. Brownell was something of a recluse, whose private life was shadowed by his wife's illness. "Though he became a dear friend it was chiefly by letter that we communicated," Edith Wharton recalled; it was "only on rare occasions that I could persuade him to come to our house." And she added, "I have always regretted that our friendly meetings were so rare, and so seldom occurred in a more sympathetic setting than his cramped and crowded office at Scribner's."

The years 1889 to 1899 were a time of lonely and hesitant growth. She continued to read omnivorously and her writing had now a definite place in her life; it became what she would call her "secret garden," to which her most private self could withdraw. But frequently in her letters to her editors she reported herself disabled by asthma or some other more vague malaise—ill and unable to write, unable to function, though she had a strong constitution and time would prove her capacity to grind the mill of her talent steadily through years of personal difficulty.

Something rather serious must have been the matter with her throughout 1895, for in December she wrote Burlingame from Newport, "Since I last wrote you over a year ago, I have been very ill, and I am not yet allowed to do any real work. But I have been scribbling a little, and I have sent you a few pages which I hope you may like." It is curious that so grave and prolonged an illness—during which she was "forbidden" to write—goes altogether unmentioned in her autobiography. The publishing house had thought of putting together a volume of her stories as early as 1893, but her collapse, of whatever sort it was, had put a stop to the project.

"Pray don't trouble yourself to answer this," her letter continued. "I only write it because it is such a distress to me to send such a waif instead of the volume that Messrs. Scribner were once kind enough to ask for that I cannot do so without a word of explanation. And I still hope to get well and have the volume ready next year."

An insight into her troubles may be found, perhaps, in one of her first short stories, "The Fulness of Life," which was published in *Scribner's* two years earlier. In the story, a woman is accosted on the threshold of eternity by the Spirit of Life to whom she confesses that her marriage has been unsatisfying. "His boots creaked and he always slammed the door when he went out, and he never read anything but railway novels and the sporting advertisements in the paper—and—in short we never understood each other." On the other hand, she has, she discloses, experienced the "Fulness of life," from time to time, through "the perfume of a flower or a verse of Dante or Shakespeare," and once through the spectacle of the church of Or San Michele in Florence at Easter. Understanding her problem, the Spirit then offers her the possibility of spending eternity with a real "soulmate."

But this was a solution which Edith Wharton, if she identified herself with her heroine and the husband of her story with Edward Wharton, was not yet ready to accept. Life with the gallant and generous if unintellectual "Teddy" was still supportable, even if it was perfectly true that he read only railway novels and sporting advertisements, and, for all we know, wore shoes that creaked and slammed doors. So, the lady of the story refuses the Spirit's offer and decides to wait on for her own dear bore of a husband. Still, it is obvious that she did not look forward with complete equanimity to an eternity—even a lifetime—in the sole company of Edward Wharton. It is interesting that this story was mailed from Newport a few weeks after Paul Bourget's visit. Afterwards she was embarrassed, perhaps, by its self-revelation, and refused to include it in her first book of fiction, *The Greater Inclination*. " 'The Fulness of Life' is one long shriek," she wrote Burlingame in 1898. "I may not write any better, but I hope that I write in a lower key."

The publishing of *The Greater Inclination* in 1899, she later wrote, "broke the chains which had held me so long in a kind of torpor. For nearly twelve years I had tried to adjust myself to the life I had led since my marriage; but now I was overmastered by the longing to meet people who shared my interests." There seemed one obvious answer—a broader acquaintance among the intelligentsia to be found in Europe. The only writer she knew was a Frenchman whom she had seen for no more than a week or two every year since their Newport meeting—each time with an increasing sense of all that was available to him in the milieu he inhabited. Bourget, in fact, was the first to suggest to her that foreign sight-seeing was not enough; she must alter her life to include regular and leisured relationship with the human stimulus available in Europe.

"He was always rebuking me for my apathy in continuing a life of wearisome frivolity, and telling me that at the formative stage of my career I ought to be with people who were thinking and creating," she recalled. Her old New York friend, Egerton Winthrop, who had lived for years in Europe, concurred, and urged her husband to take her to England that year for a visit of several weeks, "so that I might at least meet a few men of letters and have a taste of an old society in which the various elements have been found for generations."

Whatever her opportunities during this London trip, they were cut short. "My husband was bored in London, where he would have been amused only among the sporting set, while I wanted to know the writers," she remarked thirty years later, her bitterness still keen. "It is always depressing to live with the dissatisfied, and my powers of enjoyment are so varied that when I was young I did not find it hard to adapt myself to the preferences of any one I was fond of. The people about me were so indifferent to everything I really cared for that complying with the tastes of others had become a habit, and it was only some years later, when I had written several books, that I finally rebelled, and pleaded for the right to something better. Meanwhile we left London to take up again the Italian wanderings which we both enjoyed." The trip to Italy in 1899 was to prove more than usually enjoyable to her.

Mere "going abroad" in itself was nothing new to Edith Wharton. Like most wealthy Americans, her family tended to include travel to Europe in the schedule of regular entertainment—in fact, she had received a more than usually potent inoculation of Europe in her childhood. When she was four, she was already playing on the slopes of the Palatine in Rome, hunting for bits of precious colored marble from the rubble of the palace of the Caesars. The Joneses stayed on the Continent for five or six years after that, visiting Spain and Germany as well as Italy, and living mostly in Paris. With the outbreak of the Franco-Prussian War, however, they went home where they remained for the next eight years, renouncing, for some reason, the traditional summer trip to the European resorts and to Paris for clothes which continued to be the habit of her parents' friends.

They returned only in 1881 when she was nineteen, because of her father's illness—he died in Cannes that spring—and then she and her mother took up again their New York-Newport social life until her marriage in 1885. But during the long absence from Europe, the dream-world of her little-girlhood, she had begun to search in her reading for the scenes—particularly the Italian scenes—she had lost. "Ruskin fed me with visions of the Italy for which I had never ceased to pine, and Freeman's delightful 'Subject and Neighbor Lands of Venice,' Mrs. Jameson's amiable volumes, and Kugler's 'Handbook of Painting,' gave firmer outline to these visions," she later wrote. In the eighties her reading continued and broadened, and she read the favorites of the day— Pater's and John Addington Symonds' books on Italy, Shorthouse's popular novel, *John Iglesant,* with its Italian background, and two or three books on Italy by the mysterious Vernon Lee.

This taste for reading about Europe made a very special sort of traveller of her when the opportunity for actual visits came again. She would be, for the rest of her life, a tireless student of the architecture, landscape and local history of foreign countries. Somewhat to the amusement of her friends, her travelling trunks were always filled with books, and her curiosity in ferreting out some hidden treasure of art or some picturesque detail of landscape reported in her guides was formidable to behold. Tales are told of the Mrs. Wharton of later years descending upon some reluctant caretaker in a sleepy *paese* and effecting an opening of doors which would have stood fast to pope or army. As early as 1888, when she and her husband took a four months' cruise on a chartered yacht through the Aegean, their host, a cousin named James Van Allen, was somewhat staggered by her archaeological thoroughness. He let her follow the beckonings of the learned authorities whose books she had stowed aboard, and she reported that he allowed her "the necessary time, between Girgenti and Sunium, to see all but the most inaccessible Greek temples, and to explore nearly every one of the then little-visited Aegean islands." By 1894, she was bold enough to challenge the experts about some terracotta reliefs in an obscure monastery in the hills between Volterra and the Arno; these, she was convinced, were not by the minor seventeenth-century artist to whom they were traditionally attributed, but the work of an earlier and greater hand, perhaps one of the Robbias. She was enormously proud of her find, and it was, in fact, confirmed by the director of the Royal Museums in Florence. Her article on the subject, complete with photographs, was promptly sent to *Scribner's Magazine* and later reprinted in her book, *Italian Backgrounds*, making a curious item in the bibliography of this American novelist.

Henry James, whom she would later succeed in infecting with her enthusiasm for this sort of scholarly travel, once remarked that she had a "noble curiosity." Her appetite for the foreign became a more far-ranging, restless one than his, and she made her home eventually in the more completely alien environment of France whereas he was content in England with its greater ties of language and culture to the country of his birth. But in her reaching towards Europe for all the things her spirit craved—a landscape full of ancient suggestions, the sophisticated culture of the great European cities, the possibilities of friendship with persons of richly cultivated tastes, even with fellow-artists— she was really repeating James's own history. He, too, had experienced an early and deeply affecting experience of Europe as a small child. "The nostalgic cup," he wrote, "had been applied to my lips even before I was conscious of it." He had been, he said, "hurried off to London and to Paris immediately after my birth and then and there, I was ever afterwards to feel, that poison had entered my veins." The cup of Europe was always standing on the board of the James family, even at home; when Henry was only six his father began to consider a return to Europe so that his children could get "such sensuous education as they can't get here," and when he was twelve the family did go abroad for three years, and after a year home in Newport, returned again for another year. He went back again as a young adult of twenty-six, travelling alone in England, France, and Italy, a thorough, saturating experience that made his observant elder brother remark, "I fear his taste of Europe will prevent his ever getting thoroughly reconciled to this country and I imagine that he will end, when he becomes self-supporting, by spending most of his time there. Certainly with his artistic temperament and literary occupations, I should not blame him for the choice."

William's prediction proved exact. It had taken some years of restless self-questioning, of temporary adjustments to Cambridge or New York, but in the end James made his choice. In the seventies he had gone back for two long stays on the continent, mostly in Rome and Paris—making new friends not only American but foreign—and, most important of all, had entered the literary inner circle of Paris. Finally, in 1876, he settled in London.

The time had not yet arrived, however, for any permanent commitment to Europe on Edith Wharton's part. For some years she would attempt to combine both worlds, to live in America, yet go to Europe for yearly infusions of travel. When, at twenty-three, she married a man who was thirteen years her senior and contemplated the differences of taste which accompanied their difference of age, she felt compensated, she declared, "by his natural youthfulness, his good humour and gaiety, and the fact that he shared my love of animals and out-door life, and was soon to catch my travel-fever." Their mutual zest for travel took them back to her beloved Italy, promptly, and she began to track down the actualities behind the reading of the previous years. When Bourget visited her in Newport in 1893, he was surprised to notice examples of eighteenth-century Italian furniture in her house. There was nothing of the mode of Newport about her Venetian consoles. A specimen of this same sort of furniture had, as a matter of fact, originally aroused her interest in the whole period—a graceful eighteenth-century Italian armchair which she had noticed in the studio of the painter Julian Story as she sat to him for her portrait not long after her marriage. "What is it?" she asked him, and the painter answered, "Oh, eighteenth-century Venetian. It's a pity no one knows or cares anything about eighteenth-century furniture or architecture. In fact everybody behaves—the historians as well as the art critics—as if Italy had ceased to exist at the end of the Renaissance." So Edith Wharton and her husband, sometimes accompanied by Egerton Winthrop, undertook yearly rambles in northern Italy in search of this forgotten period before the *Risorgimento*.

Her Italian furniture at Land's End was the note most calculated to win Bourget's enthusiasm and interest. He had himself long been captivated by the same Italian glamour as she and had just written a travel book about his favorite haunts in Tuscany and Umbria, *Sensations d'Italie*. Their mutual discovery of a taste for eighteenth-century furniture may explain Bourget's dedication to Edith Wharton of his story, *Monique*, which tells of a modern cabinetmaker who worships the craftsmen of this period. *Sensations d'Italie* she would always love best of all Bourget's books, partly for the role it had played in her own development as well as for its enthusiastic charm, more than elsewhere in his writings like his own way of speaking, which caused James also to prize it above the rest of Bourget's work, and Robert Louis Stevenson, who had never met the author, to dedicate *Across the Plains* to him as a tribute.

She had already read the evocation of the Italian eighteenth century which Violet Paget (Vernon Lee) had written in 1880—the book which brought that remarkable woman sudden fame at twenty-four. James, too, had admired this work, and Edith Wharton was so enormously impressed as she studied it in her solitude in America that she developed her interest in *settecento* Italy into what was almost a ruling passion for several years, dictating the direction of her reading and, eventually, of her travels. Her first novel, *The Valley of Decision*, which was published in 1902, was an attempt at a panoramic historical romance dealing with Italy in this period; some of its tone and in particular its portraits of historical literary and musical figures stem from

Vernon Lee's description. By that time, they had become friends, and Vernon Lee, in fact, wrote a preface intended to be used with an Italian translation of the novel, which was never published.

Edith Wharton was proud to tell her own publisher that Vernon Lee and her half-brother, Eugene Lee-Hamilton, had warmly praised the novel's historical accuracy, "and they really know more about the Italy of the *settecento* than even the Italians themselves," she wrote Brownell. A few years later, she thought of composing an essay on *Studies of the Eighteenth Century in Italy*, and she wrote Miss Paget: "It will be a real pleasure to write an article on your delightful—if I were not torn by contending sympathies I would say most delightful of books; at any rate, the one specially dear to me as opening my eyes to that dear brilliant 18th century in Italy, which no one saw till you told us to look."

She owed the start of a personal relation with Vernon Lee to Bourget who gave her a letter of introduction to use when she went back to Florence, again, soon after that Newport meeting. She recalled that Bourget had warned her that his letter might not gain her entrance to Il Palmerino, the villa outside Florence where Miss Paget lived in semi-seclusion with the invalid Lee-Hamilton. Nevertheless, an invitation did arrive from the lady, who wrote that if Mrs. Wharton happened to be the author of a certain sonnet which had caught her brother's eye in a recent issue of *Scribner's*, they would be happy to make her acquaintance. Eugene Lee-Hamilton was a neurasthenic paralytic, confined to a wheeled couch, but he had a keen eye for sonnets, having just published a volume of them, called *Sonnets of the Wingless Hours*, in 1894. Edith Wharton praised this book perhaps too extravagantly in the obituary article she wrote when Lee-Hamilton died in 1907 ("it contains some twenty sonnets of exceptional beauty, and four or five which rank not far after the greatest in the language") but her tenderness for his memory is as understandable as her loyal praise of his sister—these two, after Bourget, were the first European intellectuals to become her close friends. Her expectation that Europe could furnish opportunities for intellectual concourse such as had been denied her till then was amply confirmed in this pair. "I look back gratefully to the moments spent at his bedside, talking of the things of the spirit," she wrote of her early acquaintanceship with Lee-Hamilton.

As for his sister—"Vernon Lee was the first highly cultivated and brilliant woman I had ever known. I stood a little in awe of her, as I always did in the presence of intellectual superiority, and liked best to sit silent and listen to a conversation which I still think almost the best of its day." Henry James, of course, had never thought anything else—it will be recalled that even at the height of his fury against Vernon Lee for her boorishness in writing "Lady Tal" he had had misgivings about warning off his brother and so depriving him of this lady's marvellous talk. Nothing, of course, is so perishable as conversation, and one can only guess the fascination of Vernon Lee's speaking presence from the oracular wit of her written prose. Here, for instance, is the way she expressed her view of Bourget as a writer, as she might have spoken it to James or Edith Wharton: "The psychological novelist traffics in people's ignorance, and men like Bourget and Maupassant manufacture individuals and types much as our earliest ancestors made up bird-women, bull-men and that magnificent human document, the bronze chimera of Arezzo."

Percy Lubbock has put down a poetic, if elusive, later impression:

So there was Edith, bright and alert, brisk on her feet after a winged glance; and beside her Vernon Lee, tall and angular vestal in her stiff collar and drab coat, fixed in rumination, absorbed and unheeding, her rugged face working in the coil and labour of her burrowing thought. She pondered, she reconnoitered as she talked; she wound her way through suggestion, sensation, speculation—she threaded a labyrinth, a branching forest of shadowy forms; and then again she slashed right and left, she broke into the open with a swinging cut—she thumped out with a judgment, a maxim, a paradox, on a croak or chuckle of her crusted laughter. It all took time, but it was worth while to wait for her. While she talked on, with her pungent and gutteral deliberation, a scene unrolled, brilliantly peopled and displayed—a drama was evolved out of all the admonitions, curious and lovely, grand and grotesque, of the genius of this place and this hour. Who will ever say, listening to Vernon Lee, that a thing of beauty is ever finished or an hour of time accomplished? She knew better; she talked on, planting her weight, as of an elemental earth-force, on any levity or futility of her companions, releasing them with a stroke of her grimly riotous wit—still she talked. Most surprising, most interesting, most exasperating of women, in her power and her humour, her tenacity and perversity—Vernon Lee holds her ground, to the eyes of memory, in the twinkling ilex-shade of that old garden.

Vernon Lee was only six years older than Edith Wharton, but in 1894 she must have seemed to possess a definition of self which the American woman could still only dream of achieving. She was already the author of a number of works on Italian culture besides the treatise on the eighteenth century, such as *Euphorion*, a study of the Renaissance which includes a chapter, "The Italy of the Elizabethan Dramatists," valuable even today. In addition, she had written and published poetry and fiction (among which was the novel, *Miss Brown*, dedicated to the unwilling Henry James, as well as the collection, *Vanitas*, published only the previous year, which contained the story that had so infuriatingly "drawn from life" his own person and character). Still more impressive to the wistful wanderer from America was the fact that this Englishwoman had been able to live for years in cosmopolitan Florence, enjoying the company of the sophisticated and talented of all nations who streamed through the city, and numbering among her friends writers such as Paul Bourget and—until lately—Henry James.

It was that spring that Edith Wharton made her little discovery of the terracottas of San Vivaldo, and she must have had a particular pleasure in, for once, reaching beyond the seemingly limitless knowledge of her new friend. "Even Miss Paget (Vernon Lee), who has lived so long in Italy and devoted so much time to the study of Tuscan art, never had heard of them or of

San Vivaldo," she boasted to Burlingame when she sent him her article. A few years later, however, Vernon Lee was able to help her substantially in her researches in the Italian countryside. With the publication of *The Decoration of Houses* in 1897, Edith Wharton had become something of an authority on domestic architecture, and after *The Valley of Decision* her knowledge of the Italian landscape was obvious; consequently, in 1903, the *Century Magazine* asked her to do a text for a series of water-colors of Italian villas by Maxfield Parrish. It was Vernon Lee who then conducted Edith Wharton to the principal villas in the Florentine region and directed her to others elsewhere, gaining her entrée among the Italian nobility who were the owners. When *Italian Villas and Their Gardens* was published as a book, it was dedicated to Vernon Lee, "who better than anyone has understood and interpreted the garden magic of Italy."

It is highly unlikely that Vernon Lee told Henry James about her new American friend, Edith Wharton. But Paul Bourget, with whom he was in constant touch, is sure to have gossiped to him about this increasingly interesting *américaine* and her European movements. James had known Bourget ever since the Frenchman's visit to London in 1884 when he had been charmed by the younger man's conversational brilliance and benevolently piloted him about the "great, grey Babylon" he now knew so well. Bourget, on his part, always approached James with something of a disciple's enthusiasm, and during that summer in London he wrote his first long work of fiction, *Cruelle Énigme*, which he dedicated to James "in remembrance of the time when I began to write it, which was the time, also, of our becoming acquainted. In our conversations in England last summer, carried on sometimes at one of the tables of the hospitable Athenaeum Club, sometimes beneath the shade of the trees in some vast park, sometimes on the Dover Esplanade while it echoed to the tumult of the waves, we often discussed the art of novel-writing, an art which is the most modern of all because it is the most flexible, the most capable of adaptation to the varied needs of each temperament. We agreed that the laws imposed upon novelists by aesthetics resolve themselves into this: to give a personal impression of

life." James may have been somewhat taken aback by the suggestion in this dedication that he had somehow given his approval to
Bourget's book. As a matter of fact, he disliked it; had he found
Bourget himself less charming he might have resented the dedication as he did Vernon Lee's dedication of her *Miss Brown* that
same year. James, indeed, had the same objections to Bourget's
writing that Edith Wharton felt in her turn—everything was too
prévu by the writer's habit of psychological analysis. To James,
to whom the action of the soul was everything, Bourget's analytic art seemed dead stuff.

He had serious reservations not only about Bourget's art, but
about his character. Yet the Frenchman's personal presence, his
excited, wide-ranging, always witty talk, were irresistible to a
man to whom the pure quality of intelligence was almost an
ethical virtue. Although they did not agree about how to write a
story, their instinct for material was often the same, and they
exchanged ideas for stories repeatedly, as James's notebooks
sometimes hint, and as the work of each gives evidence occasionally. In 1887, for example, when James was staying in Florence
while Bourget was also there, the Frenchman told him the true
episode which was transmuted into James's *A London Life*, later
dealing very differently with it himself, in his novel *Cosmopolis*.
However much they differed, they continued for a long time to
be mutually fascinated by the puzzle of their difference which
could exist along with so much common feeling for the mystery
of art and of life. Such, very exactly, as we have already noted,
would be the nature of the literary interest Edith Wharton and
Bourget also took in one another. They, too, would eagerly exchange themes for future work, though they had long concluded
that there could be no fundamental agreement on the art of fiction itself.

James and Bourget were to have frequent meetings during the
coming years, most often in Italy, and particularly in Venice,
where Bourget joined James's circle of American acquaintances
at the salons of Mrs. Bronson, the Curtises, and Mrs. Jack Gard-
ner, and in Florence, where he got to know other acquaintances
of James such as Bernard Berenson and Vernon Lee. In 1890, this
fellow-bachelor of thirty-eight was married, and the friendship

of two became a trio, with the elusive, fragile Minnie Bourget making a third in the holidays which they had got into the habit of taking together. Still on their honeymoon in 1892, the Bourgets joined James in Siena for the whole month of June.

In 1893, as we know, Bourget was in America, James having seen him off with much advice and a few letters of introduction, including one to his old Cambridge friend, Professor Charles Eliot Norton. But Bourget worked his connection with James a little too assiduously for the latter's taste, especially with William James—to whom he had not been given a letter of introduction; and Henry sent his brother a long, irritable letter expressing his many personal dissatisfactions with Bourget. "About Bourget himself I never had *any* delusions. He has, I think, a distinctly charming and affectionate side, but it loses itself in an abyss of which his unmistakable absence of 'early training' (as Aunt Kate used to say) never established control. Hélas, with all his brilliancy, all his literary mondanity, etc., he isn't a gentleman."

Edith Wharton saw only Bourget's "charming and affectionate side" that same August when he sat before her sea-fronting windows at Land's End. As with Vernon Lee, she was too grateful for his vivacious intellect, too intoxicated by the heady wine of his conversation, to be critical of his deficiencies. Though she shared James's dislike of his fiction, she remained affectionately attached to Bourget till his death, loyal to him, as to Vernon Lee, for being one of her first initiators into the illuminated world of international culture. James, however, drifted further and further away from Bourget as the years passed, increasingly repelled not only by his distaste for his work and his personality, but by his reactionary stand during the Dreyfus affair and his fanatic Catholic-royalist conservatism, while Edith Wharton, with a more feminine indulgence, argued with, but did not resent the views of her friend. Meanwhile, Bourget does not seem to have suspected how much Henry James at times disliked him, and they continued, for quite a while, to meet and communicate; there was so much, after all, that they had in common. From America, Bourget sent letters lengthily transmitting his observations on James's native land,

and, later, when James read the proofsheets of the book he was making of the experience, he admitted to Edmund Gosse that they were "singularly agreeable and lovely. It will be much the prettiest (and I should judge kindest) socio-psychological book written about the U.S. That is saying little. It is very living and interesting."

Only three of the letters Bourget wrote to James from America seem to have survived (there were at least five) and in these he does not mention his meeting with Edith Wharton though he does remark upon Newport "et ses beautés *smartly gowned*" and observes that Minnie Bourget had found "les upper terriblement lower" there. *Outre-Mer*, which was published the following year, contains a more detailed, but, of course, generalized report on his month at Newport. Bourget was a Frenchman of Frenchmen who considered himself an expert on feminine psychology and devoted most of his fiction to its analysis; hence it is not surprising that he concentrates with particular zest upon the description of American women, particularly those of the upper class whom he saw at Newport. Among the types he quite wittily characterizes there appear notes, now and then, that strike one as suggestively untypical—perhaps reflections of that meeting with the surprising Mrs. Wharton.

"Under the outward semblance of the woman of the world who is talking with you in a drawing-room amid lights and flowers, there is a resolute creature who, from the time she came *out* began to mould her own personality after some chosen model," he generalizes, describing one who wanted to be a great English lady, another a Parisian, another an actress, and "a fourth by way of being literary. Within a quarter of an hour you discover that in the midst of the whirlwind of society she had found time for a wide reading, and she keeps it up by talking to you with a singularly vigorous precision and particularity." Where, save at Land's End, could he have found such a "type" as this at Newport? And the love of the categorical of this student of Taine causes him to

note another "type," too, whom he calls "the intellectual tomboy." She

> has read everything, understood everything, not superficially,
> but really, with an energy of culture that could put to shame
> the whole Parisian fraternity of letters . . . Though like the
> others she gets her gowns from the best houses of the Rue de la
> Paix, there is not a book of Darwin, Huxley, Spencer, Renan,
> Taine, which she has not studied, not a painter or sculptor of
> whose works she could not compile a catalogue, not a school of
> poetry or romance of which she does not know the principles
> . . . She subscribes impartially to the *Revue des Deux Mondes*
> and the gazettes of the latest coteries of the Latin Quarter or
> Montmartre. Only she does not distinguish between them. She
> has not an idea that is not exact, yet she gives you a strange
> impression as if she had none. One would say that she has
> ordered her intellect somewhere, as we would order a piece of
> furniture, to measure, and with as many compartments as there
> are branches of human knowledge. She acquires them only that
> she may put them into these drawers . . . Before the intellectual
> girl one longs to cry:—"Oh, for one ignorance, one error, just a
> single one. May she make a blunder, may she prove not to
> know!" In vain. A mind may be mistaken, a mind may be
> ignorant, but never a thinking machine!

There is a bit of acerbity in Bourget's characterization of the
intimidatingly well-read "tomboy"—and one cannot help wondering whether Edith Wharton, who did not always charm on
the first encounter, may have been the model for this rather
specialized "type." The "smartly gowned" Mrs. Wharton may
have been a little over-eager, once her initial shyness passed, to
present her intellectual credentials to the famous visitor, and he
may be forgiven for a certain resistance. He could hardly have
met anyone else, in his travels, who could have supplied just the
details he sets down. Even the range of the "tomboy's" reading
list—from Darwin to current French criticism—exactly repre-
sents Edith Wharton's studies at that time.

It seems improbable, at any rate, that he did not give Henry
James some account, upon his return to Europe, of his encounter
with Edith Wharton. And soon he had further impressions to

transmit. The Whartons became regular visitors to the Bourgets when they arrived in Paris at the end of each winter, and in the Bourgets' apartment in the Rue Barbet de Jouy where James had so often sat and talked, the Whartons now took their place, the atmosphere full of the host's reminiscences of his great American friend. Soon they were meeting elsewhere—in the south of France and in Italy, in particular, where the Whartons' love of the road was communicated to the more cautious-spirited Bourgets, while Bourget led them into the scenes where he and James had often stayed together. Since little happened to Bourget that was not the stuff of conversation, each stage of this growing intimacy must have been described upon his next meeting with James.

At the end of the winter of 1896, the Bourgets bought an estate at Costebelle, near Hyères on the Riviera, which soon became a resort for their close friends—sometimes James, sometimes the Whartons, and perhaps on some occasion all three at once came to visit, for the Bourgets had intended it not only as a retreat for themselves, but for those choice few who would be invited to share with them its sylvan exquisiteness, so far from the bustle of Paris. Le Plantier was a walled park with 25 acres of wild pine and cedar woods along a terraced mountain-side overlooking the sea. The little villa above the peach orchards of Costebelle was peach-colored, and there was a second house which was to be set aside from the start, as Bourget explained to James that first spring, "for the use of any of my friends who would want to come there." James was invited to note, in particular, how his needs had been thought of in the provision of the little visitor's house; they were arranging a bedroom and study where he could work undisturbed. There were walks and carriage roads and even two saddle-horses on the place—mounted on the latter the host and hostess had fallen into the habit of a regular morning ride along the course (laid out by a nobleman of the past for the exercise of his race-horses) which ran along the rocky coast up to the Presq'île de Giens. James eventually responded to Bourget's invitation and Edith Wharton and her husband grew accustomed to stopping at the nearby hotel at Hyères every year until the time came, after the war, when she herself bought an old house, once a nunnery, Sainte-Claire le Château, on a *maquis*-covered hilltop overlooking Hyères. It was in this pleasant spot on the Mediterranean, full of memories of James and other friends, that she finally spent the winters of her old age.

In April, 1899, James paid a visit to the Bourgets at Costebelle on his way to Italy for the summer, where he planned to visit Rome and Florence and Venice after an absence of several years. "This little estate," he noted in his letter to William James, "is a precious and enviable acquisition. The walks are innumerable, the pleasant 'wildness' of the land (universally accessible) only another form of sweetness and light, the air, the noble graceful lines &c, all of the first order. It's classic—Claude—Virgil . . ."

But the mood at Les Plantiers was not exactly Virgilian at the moment. The Bourgets and the one other guest, the French writer Melchior de Vogüé, were oppressed by the Dreyfus affair. The crisis had drawn battle-lines across French intellectual life. Bourget was about to enter the political mêlée on the side of the anti-democratic forces who rose to the defense of the army, and his writing would henceforth bear the burden of his increasingly conservative political and social ideas. James found the thinking of Frenchmen like Bourget hard to comprehend; it seemed to him, as he wrote his sister Alice, that the Dreyfus case had cast a dark shadow over life and that at the verdict of the army officer's guilt, there would be convulsions throughout the world. At Les Plantiers, he tried to keep his counsel and talk of other matters, but the atmosphere was oppressive. "They make me homesick," he wrote his brother. "I treat the "Affaire" as none of my business (as it isn't) but is . . . It *is* a country in decadence."

Bourget, for the moment, was inclined to seek refuge from these agitations in the relaxation of travel, and now he and his wife joined the Whartons for an extended holiday in Switzerland and northern Italy. At the end of August he wrote to Henry James, who had already returned to Rye, about this wonderful tour. The Bourgets met the Whartons at Ragatz where they enjoyed each other's lively company amidst the worldly glitter of the resort hotel and the more refreshing glitter of the Alpine scenery. Ragatz had been chosen at the suggestion of Mme.

Bourget's doctors, and must have proved salubrious, for now they decided on a more adventurous and strenuous enterprise. After putting in a few days in Paris they returned, Bourget related to James, to Lugano, on the Swiss border, where the Whartons joined them again, and they then had gone from that well-known resort into the back country which lies east of Lake Como. The four travelled through the beautiful region known as the Valteline through which the little Adda river flows in the opposite direction towards the great lake. They had reached the "delicious Madonna di Tirano" and seen the great pilgrimage church of the region and afterwards turned into the more mysterious and wild country of the "Bergamasque alps" ("Quel nom!" wrote Bourget), which they had had to traverse by a travelling-carriage.

They had finally come to Lake Iseo to the south, stopped at Bergamo and Milan for a few days, and at last, to escape the heat, gone to Lanzo d'Intelvi up in the hills near Lugano, this place proving, as Bourget wrote James, "an adorable nook" only 950 meters and four hours from Como! Now they were at Brescia resting after their tour, and planning to see the city's artistic treasure, the painting in the palace by its sixteenth-century native artist, Alessandro Moretto. Bourget, who seldom, if ever, strayed from the beaten track in his frequent travels, had greatly enjoyed himself, and found some relief from his agitated thoughts about the fate of France. "These innocent joys are what I find best in this sad world of civil war in which we live," he wrote James.

James would get more details in time about this trip from both Bourget and Edith Wharton, for it seems to have been the occasion which arrives in every friendship which finally removes reserves and plants the seeds of a lifelong trust and affection. Before a later vision of these four intervenes, one should see them as they must have appeared on this happy occasion. Bourget, the dapper, somewhat paunchy little Parisian with the drooping moustaches and melancholy eyes that gave him the look of a wistful brown seal, was the most striking of contrasts to Teddy Wharton, the robust American who was still a "fine specimen" of his type of sportsman and bon-vivant, as competent in the outdoor aspects of their adventure as he was bemused inside museums and churches.

While Teddy bicycled ahead of the travelling-carriage, engaging rooms, ordering dinners, Bourget rode with the ladies. And these, too, were a study in contrasts—Edith, not yet the somewhat forbidding "grande dame" of later years but an elegant redhead about whom people asked, "Does she really write—with that figure?" and exquisite Minnie, a delicate "Tanagra madonna" as both James and Edith Wharton described her, with the dark coronet of braided hair.

When Mrs. Wharton came to give James her own account of this trip, it was full of further anecdotes. At Ragatz, she remembered, they had argued back and forth about the Dreyfus case and the trial at Rennes, Bourget insisting bitterly that the guilt of Dreyfus was of no importance whatsoever, only the dignity of the army. In the restaurant in the evening, his mood changed completely; he had identified the son of Balzac's Duchesse de Langeais in an old shrivelled gentleman seated in a remote corner, and Bourget, who worshipped Balzac, had sent him his card hoping to speak to a living souvenir of the master. Then they had gone down into Italy, lured by the words "Bergamasque alps" printed on a map, which reminded Edith Wharton of Verlaine's "Masques and Bergamasques" and suggested the antic figures of the commedia dell'arte. On the last day of their journey, after a "midsummer's week's dream," as she called it, "the most imperturbable member of our party"—Teddy, of course—had looked up from a guide book to announce that their route had taken them completely around, but never within the charmed region. "Though we agreed to make the real trip another year, we never dared, lest it should turn out to be less perfect," she later said.

"And in the evening, having entered the inn after a joyous day of healthy fatigue, of what did we speak, seated before the spaghetti and the chianti? Of everything, it seems to me, so open was the mind of Bourget, his culture so great, his memory furnished with recollections of his literary and worldly beginnings." She was surely happier, in this moment she describes, than she had ever been before. She had found her way, finally, into a rich European scene, replete with cultural suggestion, and she had a friend and guide.

3

The Mount

IN THE SPRING OF 1902 Henry James sat down with a fat, red-bound volume called *The Valley of Decision*. It was a curious, labored, and yet intensely intelligent book, a chronicle—hardly a novel—about eighteenth-century Italy, and it was dedicated to his good friends, Paul and Minnie Bourget, "in remembrance of Italian days together." That the Bourgets had spent many pleasant days with the author in Italy he was well aware; Bourget had been telling him lately about his *italianische reise* in the company, one might almost say under the spur of the spirited, talented, quite fascinating Edith Wharton.

James must have wondered a little about Mrs. Wharton, whom he knew only slightly. Was she an idealistic bluestocking like the heroine of the novel he was reading? Or did this daughter of Old New York speak for herself in the person of her hero, the Lombard aristocrat of whom she wrote: "None was more open than he to the seducements of luxurious living, the polish of manners, the tacit exclusion of all that is ugly or distressing; but it seemed to him that fine living should be but the flavor of fine feeling, and that such external graces, when they adorned a dull and vapid society, were as incongruous as royal purple on a clown"?

The novel itself told him she was studious and ambitious, that she had a taste for history and philosophy, a feeling for the aesthetics of landscape and art, and an obvious facility with language. As a novelist she had much to learn; her plot was shapeless

73

and her characters wooden. That famous resemblance to himself about which he had been hearing so much was nowhere in evidence; indeed, the reviewers who had chorused that she was his pupil when her early books had come out were now silent on this topic. Still, the book was a suggestive effort, for all its faults, perhaps the *Romola* of another George Eliot; it implied an interesting personality in the author.

He probably communicated his responses to his old New York friend, Mary Cadwalader Jones, whom he saw in London in August, 1902. Mrs. Wharton's devoted sister-in-law had long been eager to draw his attention to the author of *The Valley of Decision*. Now she felt bold enough to post him two earlier volumes of short stories, Edith Wharton's first, *The Greater Inclination*, and *Crucial Instances*, which had come out only the previous year. "Mary Cadwal," as James liked to call her, was fond of sending him small items for his comfort and amusement; the books were closely followed by a package of the new product, "Postum," and he acknowledged both in the same letter.

He was amusing about the "Postum," which tasted, he said, "like a ferociously mild coffee—a coffee reduced to second childhood," thereby according "but the better with my enfeebled powers of assimilation." "Mrs. Wharton," he went on more seriously, "is another affair, and I take to her very kindly as regards her diabolical little cleverness, the quantity of intention and intelligence in her style, and her sharp eye for an interesting *kind* of subject." He had not read—only heard about—these two volumes, and though he still thought *The Valley of Decision* was several notches above them, they had interested him greatly. He made a point apparently made before in his discussions with Mrs. Jones: "They've made me again, as I hinted to you other things had, want to get hold of the little lady and pump the pure essence of my wisdom and experience into her." And then came a sentence positively oracular. "She *must* be tethered in native pastures, even if it reduces her to a backyard in New York."

There are, of course, two things he may have meant. He may —and this is probable—have been making a judgment upon her use of foreign characters and settings, most conspicuously in the

74

novel he had just read, which was at times obviously "worked up" from her reading instead of being generated from personal experience. But also he may have been offering a comment on a subject already discussed with Mrs. Jones—Edith Wharton's growing preference for life abroad. Despite his own long-settled decision, he was not always ready to recommend that others should follow his course. Particularly with the young did he have this caution, and Edith Wharton, though actually forty, must have seemed comparatively young to him. For evidence, there is the advice he gave William James about the upbringing of his sons—in the same letter that we have looked at before, the letter written in April, 1899, from Bourget's little estate at Costebelle:

> Nothing you tell me gives me greater pleasure than what you say of the arrangements made for Harry and Billy in the forest primeval and the vision of their drawing therefrom experiences of a sort I too miserably lacked (poor Father!) in my own too casual youth. What I most of all feel, and in the light of it conjure you to keep doing for them, is their being *à même* to contract local saturations and attachments in respect to their *own* great and glorious country, to learn, and strike roots into, its infinite beauty, as I suppose, and variety. Then they won't, as I do now, have to assimilate, but half-heartedly, the alien splendours—inferior ones too, as I believe—of the indigestible midi of Bourget and the Vicomte Melchior de Vogüé, kindest of hosts and most brilliant of *commensaux* as I am in the act of finding both these personages. The beauty here is, after my long stop at home, admirable and exquisite; but make the boys, none the less, stick fast and sink up to their necks in everything their *own* countries and climates can give de pareil et de supérieur. Its being their "own" will double their *use* of it.

For some reason, 1899 was a moment for such second thoughts by James concerning his own development, for it was in the same vein, even more emphatically, that year, that he told the young Hamlin Garland, "If I were to live my life over again, I would be an American. I would steep myself in America, I would know no other land. I would study its beautiful side. The mixture of Europe and America which you see in me has proved disastrous."

He did not always view the matter this way, and the statement Garland remembered seems uncharacteristically flat and bitter. Mostly, he felt that his decision, which he had been long in making, had been the right, the inevitable one for him. On the whole, he accepted with trust and joy the conviction that he was uniquely fit to utilize the opportunities of a European viewpoint doubled upon an American one; "My choice," he wrote in his notebook in 1881, "is the old world—my choice, my need, my life. There is no need for me today to argue about this; it is an inestimable blessing to me, and a rare good fortune, that the problem was settled long ago, and I have nothing to do but act on the settlement." Yet others, similarly challenged, might—perhaps ought to—make an opposite choice.

It was in this light that he saw the career of a man he had known and admired for years, Professor Charles Eliot Norton of Harvard. At the latter's death in 1908 he wrote: "He had come to Italy and England early in life; he had repeated his visits to these countries with infinite relish and as often as possible . . . but he had been from the first incapable of doubting that the best activity and liveliest interest lay where it always, given certain conditions, lies in America—in a measure of response to intellectual and aesthetic 'missionary' labour . . . On the whole side of taste and association his choice was thus betimes for conscious exile and for a considerably, though doubtless not altogether irremediably, deprived state; but it was at the same time for a freedom of exhortation and a play of ironic comment less restricted, after all, in the clear American air." Clearly, there were two ways of looking at this matter of being an exile. Norton, as James saw it, had dedicated himself to a cultural task in his native land and accepted thereby an exile from his true home in Europe; this was his opportunity, his long-settled "good fortune," as James's species of exile was his own.

Edith Wharton was bound to be more impressed by the productive results, so abundantly present to her as an aspiring writer, of James's choice of life, despite the warnings he threw out. Yet her feelings about his writing were actually mixed, too, as can be seen by her reaction to the letter James wrote her just after he had read *The Valley of Decision*. She was amazed that the famous novelist had written at all, as she remarked to W. C. Brownell, to whom she forwarded the letter: "I am going to send you a long letter which Mr. James wrote me the other day about 'The Valley.' The letter was a great surprise to me, as I never send Mr. James my books, and should not have expected him to be in the least interested in 'The Valley.' " James's letter unfortunately is lost; one can only speculate as to its exact contents. But Edith Wharton was right in being astonished. It was certainly most unusual for Henry James to offer lengthy, unsolicited comment to a neophyte whom he as yet just barely knew, and it argues the intensity, already, of his curiosity about her. She, for her part, was armed with a certain resistance against his influence. "Don't ask me what I think of *The Wings of the Dove*," she ungraciously added in the same letter to Brownell.

She was also quite aware of the value of the choice of life that had been made by Charles Eliot Norton. Norton, indeed, had become a benevolent friend and guide during the writing of *The Valley of Decision*. And she was about to seek a firmer rooting in the American scene herself, partly because of his example. She had come to see the whole issue of life in America versus life in Europe as critical for her. As she came home from her trips abroad each year she had an increasing sense of what she was leaving behind and its contrast with her American life. Newport in particular must have seemed insupportable when she returned to it in September, 1899, immediately after the tour with the Bourgets in the Bergamasque alps. It was that spring that she began *The Valley of Decision*, which not only invoked her beloved Italy of her favorite past century, but depicted in the hero a fastidious and idealistic young nobleman who believed, as already noted, that the graces of luxurious life "when they adorned a dull and vapid society, were as incongruous as royal purple on a clown." Her summary of the years she had spent at Newport was more matter-of-fact, but no less crushing. "I was never very happy at Newport. The climate did not agree with me, and I did not care for watering-place mondanities . . . but the life suited my husband."

By 1900 she had succeeded in persuading Teddy that there was an alternative both to Newport and complete expatriation. That

June, upon their return from Italy, the Whartons went directly to Lenox in the Berkshire hills of western Massachusetts and stayed till December. Here was neither the Bergamasque alps nor Newport, but that native American countryside which James had wished his nephews to know. And happily it was an environment which appealed to both the Whartons, to the love of the outdoors, of natural landscape, country exercise, gardens and dogs which they happened to share, just as, in different ways, they both enjoyed travel. When they returned to New York that winter they had decided to sell Land's End and build a house of their own in Lenox.

At last, she exulted, she had escaped to the "real country." "If I could have made the change sooner," she later reflected, "I daresay I should never have given a thought to the literary delights of Paris or London; for life in the country is the only state which has always completely satisfied me, and I had never been allowed to gratify it, even for a few weeks at a time. Now I was to know the joys of six or seven months a year among fields and woods of my own, and the childish ecstasy of that first spring outing at Mamaroneck swept away all restlessness in the deep joy of communion with the earth."

Even as James wrote his letter to Mrs. Jones about Edith Wharton's need to "be tethered in native pastures," her new house was being finished. It was called "The Mount," after a house on Long Island that had belonged to her great-grandfather, a general in the American Revolutionary army, and a very American house she intended it to be. She moved into it in October, and Mrs. Jones, one of her first visitors, immediately sent off a description to James. James wrote in reply: "I assisted dimly, through your discreet page, at your visit to Mrs. Wharton, whose Lenox house must be a love, and I wish I could have been less remotely concerned." In exactly two years, to the day, he himself would be visiting the Whartons in their Lenox home.

For ten years, from 1901 to 1911, the Whartons were to spend part of every year at The Mount; until about 1909, from June to the end of December. Now a private school for girls, called "Foxhollow," the house can still be seen, standing on a slight rise above Laurel Lake with a perspective of the Hoosac Mountains and Tyringham Pass. Pencraig cottage and Land's End, the two houses the Whartons had used at Newport, had been purchased from previous owners, and imperfectly adapted to Edith Wharton's self-trained but exacting taste. The Mount was her own creation, built from her plans, a simple, foursquare, white building which seemed to float like a trim steamer upon the green expanse of gardens. On the first floor there was a library, a drawing-room, and a dining-room with French doors opening on a broad terrace shaded by a great, striped awning. From this terrace the Whartons and their guests could survey the formal garden laid out in parterres, like the Italian gardens she delighted in, and beyond this, lawn sloping to meadow up to the border of a pond framed with trees. On the other side of the house there was a kitchen-garden, a grape arbor, a small farm, and, surrounding the whole, a hundred and fifty acres of rolling woodland.

Like all Edith Wharton's houses, The Mount had creative significance for her. It is a curious paradox that this childless woman with almost no close family ties after her mother's death in 1901 —she seldom saw either of her two older brothers—had a passion and a genius for the building of homes. Her first published book, *The Decoration of Houses,* had been a by-product of her struggles to refashion Land's End into a living-place that suited her. Her attention to the perfection of every aspect of her houses and gardens was so thoroughgoing that one might be deceived into thinking them her principal interest.

"At Lenox," remembered Daniel Berkeley Updike, the founder of the Merrymount Press, "her writing was done early in the day, though very little allusion was made to it, and none at all to the infinite pains that she put into her work or her inexhaustible patience in searching for the material necessary to perfect it. By eleven o'clock she was ready for friends and engagements, for walking or garden-work." She did not mind at all giving the impression that her work was less important than these other preoccupations, as when she told another visitor, Judge Robert Grant, the novelist, that she hoped to pay for a new terrace with the profits of her next book. Certainly she was more comprehensible to her husband in this nest-building role; there exists a rather pathetic letter of his written to Charles Eliot Norton, a little note

79

of invitation urging Norton to visit The Mount, which he had not yet seen: "I should so like you to see 'The Mount,' to prove to you that Puss is good at other things besides her to me rather clever writing."

She was indeed "good at other things." If there was any criticism her visitors made it was that she was too good at this one—she made a studied art of housekeeping; she saw to every detail with a chilling exactness. Norton's daughter Lily complained of The Mount that "the sense of *home* was not there." Nor was it to be present, for all their exquisiteness, in the later dwellings she created in France, in the apartment in the rue de Varenne and the house built later in the suburbs above Paris, or in her final home at Hyères. A French friend's comment is the exact counterpart of Miss Norton's:

> The perfection of her taste, extending to everything, even to the smallest detail of her establishment, the arrangement of the flowerbeds, the symmetry of the hedges, the neat ranks of the trees in the orchard—sometimes . . . it chilled me . . . In nearly every French interior you will notice a clock that betrays the bad taste of the mother-in-law, or a woolwork chair-cover, touching relic of "bonne-maman." With Mrs. Wharton I was intimidated by the aesthetic perfection of everything about her.

Yet in the task of creating such perfection she would fling herself with a passion that was somehow revealing of the large energies her nature contained. Henry James understood this, when he remarked to Percy Lubbock: "No one fully knows our Edith who hasn't seen her in the act of creating a habitation for herself."

They were not only for herself, of course—and this was perhaps the secret of her devotion; they were houses created for the entertainment of friends, houses that could nurture those occasions of conversational communion, those festivals of wit which she had witnessed in Europe. Despite her devotion to "real country" she would have found it impossible to have remained content forever with unpeopled landscape. She had an instinct for intellectual society which had driven her to the "literary delights of Paris or London"; it was not these experiences which had created the appetite in her, as she claimed. So, she made her guestrooms marvels of appointment. "What a perfect desk— everything conceivably needed for writing is there," exclaimed Mrs. Gordon Bell, when Edith Wharton showed her to her room at The Mount. She laid out her terrace and made it spacious and inviting on its breezy knoll, picturing the guests, few but choice, whom she would assemble after dinner and invite to chat under her striped awning of all things in heaven and earth. She wanted, really, to create a *salon* there in western Massachusetts. Certainly on the occasions when Henry James was present at the center of her circle, she must have felt that she had succeeded as well as any Paris hostess.

In Lenox there lingered faint traces of the intellectual rurality of a former time. Fifty years before, Nathaniel Hawthorne had lived there and written *The House of the Seven Gables* and composed stories for his children to be called *Tanglewood Tales* because of a wild picnic spot nearby. And he had had Berkshire neighbors worth talking to. Herman Melville had lived for a wonderful year at Arrowhead, outside nearby Pittsfield, and had driven up often in between his sessions of work on his greatest book. Talk, the most vivid and inspiring for both men, had flourished in Hawthorne's red cottage or on the piazza of Arrowhead from which one could see Mount Greylock (Melville would call a later collection of stories *Piazza Tales*, in recollection of those hours). Others had joined them on outings in which ideas were assaulted and scaled along with the neighboring hills; there were several famous occasions in August, 1850, when Oliver Wendell Holmes, James T. Fields, and Evert Duyckinck came along. Duyckinck and Fields were visitors from the publishing worlds of New York and Boston, but Holmes lived every summer in Pittsfield. The Berkshires seem to have been full of literati in those days. At Broadhall, the old family house of the Melvilles' which had become a boardinghouse, Longfellow had spent a summer, with Charles Sumner and ex-President Tyler also in residence. The great Fanny Kemble, the Shakespearean actress, had also spent her summers in Lenox, as did the novelist Catherine M. Sedgwick. Indeed, the Sedgwicks were so numerous in the region that people said the very grasshoppers chirped, "Sedgwick, Sedgwick."

In 1862, the year Edith Wharton was born, one of the Sedgwick girls who had moved to Cambridge married Charles Eliot Norton, and two years later Norton bought Lilliput, an old farm at Ashfield, forty miles from Lenox, which he would use as a summer home for the rest of his long life. Like Edith Wharton, years later, he had sold his house in Newport in favor of this new rural haven, and he urged others to follow his example. "One could write Massachusetts idylls or a New England 'Arcadia' in this happy tranquil region of the world," he wrote George William Curtis, the American writer who had been at Brook Farm, and Curtis, in 1872, bought property separated by one field from Norton's.

With the exception of Norton, this generation had vanished from the Berkshires by 1901, though Edith Wharton met a few country neighbors of a similar quality, like Richard Watson Gilder, the editor of *Century Magazine*, who commissioned her to do the series of articles on Italian villas. She found in the Lenox neighborhood a haunting scent of that former New England flowering of minds among the peaceful hills. And so she began to bring down her own friends for house visits, those precious few whom she had sieved out of the New York-Newport dross— Robert Grant, Daniel Updike, Ogden Codman, Walter Berry, Egerton Winthrop, Robert Minturn, and others, including the playwright Clyde Fitch and some brilliant juniors, such as the poet, George Cabot ("Bay") Lodge. In addition to these visitors she soon had a few who came over from England one summer or another—her friends and James's, Gaillard Lapsley, Robert Norton, and John Hugh-Smith, who, with Berry, she called the "inner group." And of course, chiefest of all, Henry James.

Charles Eliot Norton, who was seventy-five in 1902, did not often travel the short distance between Ashfield and Lenox, but Edith Wharton was often at his place, like another one of his daughters who became her good friends, to listen to this "beaming little old gentleman with a note as sweet as an eighteenth-century organ," as John Jay Chapman described him. And as had been the case with Bourget, she found herself making a later discovery of a friend of Henry James, for Norton had befriended James years before when he was just such an aspiring writer as she now was. It was Norton, in fact, who had accepted James's first book review for the *North American Review* as long ago as 1864 and given him his first welcome to the career of literature, as James always remembered. Norton had asked him to Shady Hill, the gracious Cambridge house which he had filled with the books and objects of art accumulated in his years of European travel, and then had begun a friendship that had kept its continuous, never intense but always significant course. Norton helped James make his first acquaintances in London a few years later, introducing him to William Morris, Rossetti, and Ruskin. And in Italy Norton's writings, particularly his *Notes of Travel and Study in Italy*, had tutored James's responses, as he wrote the older man.

It had been Norton's lifelong mission to direct the youth of his nation into an ampler cultural inheritance. He had collaborated with Lowell in the founding of the *Atlantic Monthly* before he became editor of the *North American Review*, and he had helped to establish *The Nation*, thus taking a principal part in directing the publication of letters in three of the chief journals of the country. He had then assumed the professorship of Fine Arts at Harvard, and for twenty-three years he had carried out his intention, announced in a letter to his friend Carlyle, "to quicken, so far as may be, in the youth of a land barren of visible memorials of former times, the sense of connection with the past and of gratitude for the efforts and labors of other races and former generations." "I propose this afternoon to make a few remarks on the hor-ri-ble vul-gar-ity of EVERYTHING," ran a student parody of his lectures, but, in fact, this scholar and translator of Dante had affected a whole generation by his crusade in behalf of taste and the sense of tradition. James, as we have noted, saw a certain poignancy, peculiarly affecting to him personally, in Norton's career, a career carried out in the spirit of a letter written to Ruskin shortly after leaving England to undertake his duties at

Harvard: "For me life would doubtless be better in many ways in Europe; but I should be after all of less service there than here."

As a friend and advisor of young writers he had had an important influence, but he also showed his limitations, as both Henry James and Edith Wharton realized. The characters in American literature, he told William Dean Howells, should reflect not the average but "the ideal, that is the fully realized American man and woman—of whom there are some very few," and Howells deferentially accepted this counsel and renounced a plan to write a story about the Ohio village life of his youth, in the manner, he said, of the poet Crabbe. Norton read James's *The Better Sort* in 1903 with "repulsion and wonder," confessing to Howells, "If these people are his 'Better Sort' what can the Worse Sort be? How can he spend his days and himself on such an unredeemed lot, whom he, no less than you or I, would shrink from, at least would not wish to associate intimately with in real life?" If James heard this comment, it probably only amused him, and did not lessen his affection for Norton. Such, unquestionably, was Edith Wharton's reaction when Norton felt obliged to warn her, after the appearance of *The House of Mirth*, that "no great work of the imagination had ever been based on illicit passion." This—as she dryly commented, from the translator of Dante!

As Norton undertook to assist and guide her at the turn of the century, she might have been reminded particularly of the case of Henry B. Fuller, whose earlier *The Chevalier of Pensieri-Vani* was a kind of *Valley of Decision* in its capable description of the Italy Norton loved. Fuller, as a matter of fact, wrote Edith Wharton a letter of praise when her novel was out, and she observed to Brownell, "As I have always thought *The Chevalier of Pensieri-Vani* was the best 'sensation d'Italie' ever rendered in English, I am proportionally pleased by the author's superlatives." Fuller had gone on to write another novel with an Italian background, but then he had distressed and disappointed Norton by producing satirical studies of Chicago "high society." *With the Procession*, Norton wrote, "raises a somewhat serious question, whether such life is fit subject for literary art, and whether the record of it is the best work which you can do for Chicago

... I believe that your 'Chevalier' has done more for Chicago than any of the true Chicagoans whom you have given us, 'twice as natural' as life." Almost identical was the evolution of Edith Wharton when she turned, after *The Valley of Decision*, to a novel about the New York rich, *The House of Mirth*. And almost identical, apparently, was Norton's reaction.

But his help and encouragement, when she needed it most, at her earliest beginning, had been fully generous. She had already made his acquaintance during the formative stages of *The Valley of Decision*, and when she mentioned to Norton that she had been unable to find in library or bookstore copies of such rare works as the memoirs of Goldoni and Lorenzo da Ponte, he sent her crates of books from the treasure-house of his great library in Cambridge. Her notes for this novel survive, and they include several lengthy lists entitled "Books to Consult," many of which must have been supplied by the library at Shady Hill which had been for a quarter of a century the inspiration of Norton's students. Returning some of these books to him in the fall of 1901, she wrote, "If you ever have time and patience to wade through my story you will find the foot-prints of Moore, Barretti, and many of the other guides with whom you have so kindly provided me."

Lending books from his voluminous collection was one of Norton's regular acts of devotion to the cause of enlightenment; his bookplate bore the inscription, *Amici et amicis*—Friends and for friends. In the case of Edith Wharton, his pedagogic interest accompanied the books, and he discussed her novel minutely with her as it developed. To his daughter Lily she observed years afterward, "It is to your father I owe the encouragement and interest that made The Valley of Decision what it is. He lent me many books I could not otherwise have got, and the knowledge that he was interested and approved of my undertaking, made it possible for me to accomplish it." When the book was finished, Norton wrote enthusiastic letters to friends like Howells and Samuel Grey Ward, noting the deficiencies and also the promise of the new writer whom he had "discovered." To Ward he said,

A work of [a] woman of genius has been exciting my admiration during the last days and when you read Mrs. Wharton's "Valley of Decision," you will not, I believe, wonder that it has done so. She calls it a "novel," but it is rather a study of Italian thought and life during the latter part of the eighteenth century, in the form of a story. The material and spiritual scene and its significance are more interesting than the individual characters of the personages who are the actors in the drama. These are, indeed, not without interest, but they are not convincingly alive. The intellectual element in the book is stronger than the emotional and passionate, and Mrs. Wharton's imagination has fused her material of reflection, learning, and personal experience into a wonderfully complete and vivid picture of the Italy of the period, and exhibits its power in this more than in the creation of the men and women whose conditions and characters are the result of the long course of Italian history. Her knowledge of Italy is that of a scholar and a lover of "that pleasant country," and her book is one to be prized most by those who know Italy best and love it. It is a unique and astonishing performance, of which the style is not less remarkable than the substance. It is too thoughtful and too fine a book to be popular, but it places Mrs. Wharton among the few foremost of the writers in English today.

Today this still seems a completely just summary of the strength, as well as the weakness, of *The Valley of Decision*, and it is a measure of Edith Wharton's good fortune in meeting Norton at this point when the arcs of their careers—his ending, hers beginning—crossed in those meetings in the Berkshire hills. Whenever she was in Lenox, until his death in 1908, she found Norton waiting for her. He remained, though rarely present, a constant nearby reference for the group gathered at The Mount. Walter Berry, who had been his student at Harvard, frequently accompanied her on her visits to Norton. "It was he who opened my eyes to everything worthwhile," Berry said. The old scholar showed them the poet Gray's annotated copy of Linnaeus which he was preparing for publication, or read to them from Donne's love poems, which he was editing.

"I always evoke your dear father in his library [at Ashfield], or in the basket-chair outside, under the trees," Edith Wharton wrote his daughter, Sally, after his death. "Do you remember the day we sat on the verandah, and your father read Donne to us? And that evening in the sitting-room, he read Matthew Arnold. I think it was once when Walter Berry was with me, and I have always kept a specially charming memory of that afternoon and evening." There were other occasions, equally memorable, when her companion was Henry James, who had always kept in touch with Norton and his family.

James had looked forward to a further acquaintance with Edith Wharton with some eagerness after his discussions with Mary Cadwalader Jones, and his reading of her stories and novel. Early in 1903 she was back again in Europe, but she was mostly in Italy, busily collecting material for her book on Italian villas and gardens with the help of Vernon Lee. At the end of April, the Whartons returned to Lenox without, apparently, stopping in England, for Teddy was showing some signs of the illness which would become a source of trouble during the next few years. James had apparently invited the Whartons to visit him at Rye, and Mrs. Wharton had promised to come, and he expressed his disappointment to Mrs. Jones early that June. "Has Mrs. Wharton migrated to another planet or only returned to Lenox, Newport, or whatever? She promised herself to us here many, many weeks ago—I have her signed and sealed word for it. But darkness has since, to *my* vision, completely engulfed her, and silence to my ears."

That summer in Lenox Edward Wharton was apparently so disturbingly ill with what the doctors called "neurasthenia" that Edith Wharton had been unable, as she told her publishers, to do "any sustained work." It would be foolhardy to attempt to decide, today, just what the nature of his condition actually was. Still, it may be significant that the onset of his illness coincided with the emergence, after eighteen years of marriage, of his wife's ability to be a quite separate and manifestly able individual. One cannot think that this most recent visit to Italy can have had the same pleasurableness for him as previous ones, as he trailed after her up the dusty gravel paths of decaying gardens "like an equerry," it has been said, while she collected observations for her book. Now that she had published her novel, the stories were flowing fast from her pen and she had already started upon a sequel to "The Valley" and had ideas for other novels. It might be true, as he told Norton, that "Puss" could do other, more understandable, domestic things, but it was becoming clear that writing was something she could do in a fashion intellectuals and famous writers like Bourget, Norton, and James took very seriously. The company and conversation, moreover, that was beginning to give new life to Edith Wharton, whether in Europe or at Lenox, was, one can imagine, only death to him. James did not yet know much, if anything, about the domestic shadow that had appeared on her horizon with Teddy's illness. It would, however, soon become visible to him, and become a regularly observed part of his vision of Edith Wharton.

In December the Whartons did, finally, get to London and see James. He liked the lady more than ever, and reported to Mrs. Jones: "I mustn't omit to tell you though you probably by this time know it, that Mrs. Wharton has come and gone—gone, alas, more particularly, fleeing before the dark discipline of the London winter afternoon. I was in town for a day or two during her passage, and I lunched with her, with very great pleasure, and had the opportunity of some talk. This gave me much desire for more—finding her, as I did, really conversible (rare characteristic, *par le temps qui court!*) and sympathetic in every way. I count greatly on her return."

A little more drily, but with some slight pride, Edith Wharton, on her part, mentioned the meeting in her next letter to W.C. Brownell, who was not only her editor at Scribners, but James's also: "Mr. James came up from Rye and spent the day with us." She was struck forcibly by the change in his appearance; since she had seen him last, he had shaved off the beard he had worn since earliest young manhood and which had given him the look, as she said, "of a bearded Penseroso." And, of course, he had succeeded in charming her, as he almost invariably succeeded in charming intelligent women, though she may have been loth to admit this altogether to Brownell with whom she shared a dislike, much discussed between them, for James's late fiction. "He looks, without his beard, like a blend of Coquelin and Lord Roseberry,"

88

she remarked to Brownell, "but seems in good spirits, and talks, thank heaven, more lucidly than he writes."

The talk, it appears, had been about many things, among them about an old friend of James's who was also a friend of Edith Wharton's, Howard Sturgis. Sturgis had just written a novel, *Belchamber*, and James told Mrs. Wharton he thought the situation in the book very strong and original; when she left London for Paris she took with her the borrowed proofsheets of the novel. Now she added her own strong commendations and urged that Scribner secure the book for American publication. She was writing Brownell from Costebelle, where she had gone to stay for a while "amid the palms and the roses to be with the Bourgets."

Among other things discussed, James probably told her about his plans to make a long visit to the United States that autumn, and she had invited him to come to The Mount. He had been deliberating for months about this contemplated return to his native country, which he had not seen for nearly twenty years. "If I go at all I must go before I'm too old, and, above all, before I mind being older," he wrote his brother William in May. His reasons for desiring to make the trip were complex, both personal and artistic, and he explored them ruminatingly in his letter. He had no longer any real use for Continental travel, and no desire at all to write "*de chic*, little worthless, superficial, *poncif* articles about Spain, Greece, or Egypt." What interested him as an artist now was "human Anglo-Saxonism, with the American extension," and somehow he felt a need to recover his relation to that "extension." "If I *shouldn't* in other words, bring off going to the U.S., it would simply mean giving up, for the remainder of my days, all chance of such experience as is represented by interesting 'travel' . . . I should settle down to a mere mean oscillation from here [Rye] to London and from London here—with nothing (to speak of) left, more, to happen to me in life in the way of (the poetry of) motion." And his desire, his romantic longing for America was almost, now, what his longing for Europe had once been—he wanted to see it all, the places he had known in his earlier years and the great unknown regions of the West and South that he had never seen at all.

On the second of August he sailed for America. He remained

for ten months, revisiting the scenes of his younger days—New York, Newport, Boston, and Cambridge—travelling as far south as Florida and as far west as California. He re-explored the New England countryside. Late in October, 1904, he came for ten days to the Whartons at Lenox and the following June he was again at The Mount, for five days, having also spent some intervening time with them in New York.

For both Edith Wharton and her distinguished friend the visits to The Mount were feasts of rare new kinds of experience. For her here was the full revelation, finally, of Henry James's conversation. Howard Sturgis and Walter Berry had also come, and seated on her terrace in the company of this audience of old and new friends, stimulated and challenged by their affection and their own wit and humor, he talked and jested, grew reminiscent or philosophic, all in turn. Now and then poetry would glimmer like a silver light in the midst of the conversation; someone would walk to Edith's well-filled shelves and take down a book, and Henry James would read. One time, she relates, Emily Brontë's "Remembrance" was mentioned, and James, taking the volume from her hand, recited,

> Cold in the earth, and the deep snow piled above thee
> Far, far removed, cold in the dreary grave,
> Have I forgot my only Love to love thee,
> Severed at last by Time's all-severing wave?

"I had never before heard poetry read as he read it," she states. James was the sort of reader who was not afraid to chant verse; he did not slur and chatter in an effort to make poetry sound like ordinary spoken language, and as he read the Brontë lines there were tears in his eyes. An even more surprising disclosure was the latitude of James's responses. It was discovered one night that this novelist who had been judged so genteel and cerebral in temperament thought Whitman the greatest of American poets. All that evening, it seems, his audience sat rapt while he read from *Leaves of Grass*—"he wandered from 'The Song of Myself' to 'When Lilacs Last in the Door-yard Bloomed' (when he read 'Lovely and soothing Death' his voice filled the hushed room like an organ adagio), and thence let himself be lured on to the mysterious music of 'Out of the Cradle,' reading, or rather crooning it in a mood of subdued ecstasy till the fivefold invocation to Death tolled out like the knocks in the opening bars of the Fifth Symphony." The talk went on for hours after about Whitman, and then James, with a sudden flash of the humor that was always in wait behind his most exalted moods, tumbled the party into laughter with, "Oh, yes, a great genius; undoubtedly a very great genius! Only one cannot help deploring his too-extensive acquaintance with the foreign languages."

Another evening the stimulus to James's imagination came from a chance prompting of his own memories. Someone asked to hear more about his Albany cousins, the Emmets, the "Emmetry," as he called the vast flock of Emmets and Temples with whom he was related, and he began, says Edith Wharton, "forgetting us, forgetting the place, forgetting everything but the vision of his lost youth that the question had evoked, the long train of ghosts flung with his enchanter's wand across the wide stage of the summer night. Ghostlike indeed at first, wavering and indistinct, they glimmered at us through a series of disconnected ejaculations, epithets, allusions, parenthetical rectifications and restatements, till not only our brains but the clear night itself seemed filled with a palpable fog; and then suddenly, by some miracle of shifted lights and accumulated strokes, there they stood before us as they lived, drawn with a million filament-like lines, yet sharp as an Ingres, dense as a Rembrandt; or, to call upon his own art for an analogy, minute and massive as the people of Balzac." Recalling that night afterwards his audience wondered whether he had not been first inspired, then, to bring the Emmets and the Temples, and all his old and buried associations to life again in the autobiographical *A Small Boy and Others* and *Notes of a Son and Brother* that he undertook a few years later.

James's discoveries at The Mount were chiefly of the charm of the Wharton hospitality, its adroit grouping of guests and occasions, the fine opportunities for talk or for silence, as one pleased, the fine comfort of the house itself. He was a veteran houseguest, having enjoyed and endured the blandishments and exploitation of hostesses for years in England; and in a famous story,

"The Death of the Lion," he had savagely depicted the cruel, or at least callous, aspects of much of the hospitality he had enjoyed. In time he would glimpse something of this even in Edith Wharton, when her ambition to build a salon in Paris began to possess her. But at the moment, with this simpler and more intimate group at The Mount, his content was complete. "I need scarcely tell you that I am very happy here, surrounded by every loveliness of nature & every luxury of art & treated with a benevolence that brings tears to my eyes . . . Howard Sturgis is here, & the charming Walter Berry, & we are a very harmonious & happy little party," he wrote Mary Cadwalader Jones during the October visit.

Above all, he was captivated by the possibilities of motor-travel in the Whartons' commodious automobile which swept him through the countryside with dream-like ease. It was a charm that he would continue to find infinitely seductive, particularly when wielded by Edith Wharton, who would arrive in later years in Europe with her magnificent motor and her chauffeur and invite him to explore some loveliness of scenic interest or piquancy of human exhibition hitherto inaccessible to him. Travel, as he had noted to William James when contemplating the American trip, had become too costly in a number of senses for him in his later years; he felt himself too poor, and too tired, for all the tedium, and fatigue, and expense, of the old-fashioned railroad journey. And after all, one saw so little! So many by-paths seemed forever closed once one's youth had passed. Now, leaning back upon the leather-covered cushions of Mrs. Wharton's car behind the confidence-inspiring back of Cook, her massive chauffeur, he was conscious of the birth of a new joy, a new recourse giving him an augmented ability to see, extending that precious capacity of awareness and the opportunity of observation which the novelist in him prized above everything else and had feared to lose as age advanced.

In July, after the end of the second of his visits to the Whartons, he wrote his brother, "I greatly enjoyed the whole Lenox countryside, seeing it as I did by the aid of the Whartons' big strong commodious new motor, which has fairly converted me to the sense of all the thing may do for one and one may get from it. The potent way it deals with a country large enough for it not to *rudoyer*, but to rope in, in big free hauls, a huge netful of impressions at once—this came home to me beautifully, convincing me that if I were rich I shouldn't hesitate to take up with it. A Mrs. Wharton wrote to Norton about the return trip: "The 'bath of beauty' through which, as Mr. James said, we journeyed back to Lenox, rounded off most appropriately our few delightful hours at Ashfield. Mr. James left this morning, carrying away, I think, a real tenderness for this little corner of his big country, and rejoicing so much that he had been with you just before leaving."

Indeed, it was probably these motor trips with Edith Wharton in the Berkshires that enabled James to see New England in an almost visionary way, which he presents in a page or two of *The American Scene*, the travel-report written upon his return. He great transformer of life and of the future!"

At the very end of the visit which was still fresh in James's mind as he wrote William, the Whartons had taken him on a two-day trip that had included an overnight stop at Ashfield, to see Charles Eliot Norton. James saw again his old friend, whom he had already visited in Cambridge, "aged-looking & bent & delicate," as he told an acquaintance, "but with great vitality & character still," and then the party was off again in the car. was seeing his country, as he thought, for the last time, before returning to end his days in Europe, and there was a dream-like strangeness and beauty about the scenes that melted into one another as he rode by. He had been startled by the loveliness of the rural landscape as though he had never seen it before, by, as he told Edmund Gosse in a letter in October, his "intense impression (all this glorious golden autumn, with weather like tinkling crystal and colours like molten jewels) of the sweetness of the country itself, this New England rural vastness."

In *The American Scene*, he recalls, in his typically allusive way, the motor-trips that had taken him through the villages of Salisbury and Farmington, in Connecticut, Farmington where he mused upon the "conditions of life"—the real conditions—behind the great elm-gallery garnished with old houses, and reflected that it "was enough that the white village or the painted farm could gleam from afar, on the faintly purple slope, like a thing of mystery or of history; it was enough that the charming hill-mass, happily presented and foreshortened, should lie there like some beast, almost heraldic, resting his nose on his paws."

Behind the neutrality and commonality of the villages he passed, lacking as they did all the romance of costume, the "implication of vices, accomplishments, manners, accents, attitudes," lacking, as he said, "for evil or for good" all that a European landscape so amply provided, he sensed a mystery. Under the "smutch of imputation" the "village street and the lonely farm and the hillside cabin became positively richer objects . . . and borrowed, for dignity, a shade of the darkness of Cenci-drama, of old Greek legend, of old Greek tragedy, and thus helped themselves out for the story-seeker." That story-seeker, of course, was to be Edith Wharton, who, riding beside James, glimpsed the suggestion of her two novels of the New England landscape—*Ethan Frome* and the lesser known *Summer*.

James's own vision contained other elements. There was the Shaker settlement they had visited one October afternoon in the vast hollow of the Lebanon "bowl." Here his description is indeed extraordinary poetry; the scene has become a symbol of an aspect of American experience:

> The grimness, even, was all right, when once we had admiringly dropped down and down and down; it would have done for that of a Buddhist monastery in the Himalayas—though more savagely clean and more economically impersonal, we seemed to make out, than the communities of older faiths are apt to show themselves. I remember the mere chill of contiguity, like the breath of the sepulchre, as we skirted, on the wide, hard floor of the valley, the rows of gaunt windows polished for no whitest, stillest, meanest face, even, to look out; so that they resembled the parallelograms of black paint criss-crossed with white lines that represent transparency in Nuremberg dolls' houses. It wore, the whole settlement, as seen from without, the strangest air of active, operative death; as if the state of extinc-

94

tion were somehow, obscurely, administered and applied—the
final hush of passions, desires, dangers, converted into a sort of
huge stiff brush for sweeping away rubbish, or still more, perhaps, into a monstrous comb for raking in profit. The whole
thing had the oddest appearance of mortification made to
"pay."

And finally there was that "by-play" still more curious of the
house to which they returned after their ride, "a great new house
on a hilltop that overlooked the most composed of communities;
a house apparently conceived—and with great felicity—on the
lines of a magnified Mount Vernon, and in which an array of
modern 'impressionistic' pictures, mainly French, wondrous examples of Manet, of Dégas, of Claude Monet, of Whistler, or
other rare recent hands, treated us to the momentary effect of a
large slippery sweet inserted, without warning, between the com-
pressed lips of half-conscious inanition." Here was The Mount,
or another house like it, that provided James with a final vision of
leisure put to such uses as he had rarely seen in America before.
Here was something different from the crass relaxations of Newport—"the Massachusetts Berkshire—land beyond any other
today, as one was much reminded, of leisure on the way to legit-
imation, of the social idyll, of the workable, the expensively
workable, American form of country life."

And with this hopeful view of her achievement, James left the
Lady of Lenox, as he was afterwards fond of calling her, and
returned to England. He was to return again, seven years later,
when the American landscape would be scorched, for him, by
the death of his brother William. Visiting The Mount was then
to be a less pleasing revelation, for discord and madness had already darkened the inner life of this house; like the innocent
farm-houses he had touched in passing with a "smutch of imputation" it had revealed its capacity for Greek drama. By that
time, however, Edith Wharton was nearly done with her experiment in Lenox. It was to Europe, finally and irrevocably, that
she followed James.

4

English Hours

HENRY JAMES RETURNED HOME from his American trip in July, 1905, worn and wrung. It had been a barnstorming, wearying year; like a campaigning candidate he had gone up and down the country, he had lectured to crowds, given interviews, submitted to the business of "seeing people" till he could stand no more, for he had been determined, as he told a Paris friend "to get impressions." To Mrs. Jones he admitted that he felt himself, in the last weeks of his stay, "reduced to impotence by heat, fatigue, exhaustion, democratization, the snapping of the cord of my long tension." More trying than the merely physical strain of his American year, probably, had been the near-anguish of love and renunciation which underlay his experience. He had come to America to see it all again, all that he had known in his earliest, most impressionable years, to notice the changes time had made, and to see the parts of his country he was as unfamiliar with, almost, as a foreign visitor. He had needed, obscurely, to make sure, once and for all, of his satisfaction with his chosen life, for he did not expect to go back again. And he was satisfied. He returned to his English world, to Lamb House, in Rye, with completest conviction that no matter what others might choose, he had found his rest. Not for him was that life of Edith Wharton's which however skillfully built upon its comely site must always renew itself elsewhere.

She would soon be on her way to Europe again. Nothing

would suit, after the hospitality of The Mount, but that she must come to England (with her motorcar, of course) in the spring of 1906 and permit him to show her the English landscape, social and topographic.

Her first visit to England had been in 1899, when, after the publication of *The Greater Inclination,* she persuaded her husband to take her to London before their usual Italian adventure. That dip had been so brief, she recalled, that she had brought back from it hardly more than a list of names. At the dinners and large receptions to which she had gone that year she had glancingly encountered the thinkers and writers whom she longed to know better. George Trevelyan, the historian, and Thomas Hardy—whom she found, alas!, "remote and uncommunicative as our most unsocial American men of letters"—had sat next to her at Lady Jeune St. Helier's. At Lady Ripon's, she had matched literary quotations with Henry Cust, "one of the most eager and radio-active intelligences in London." At Bourdon House, Mayfair, her old New York acquaintance Adèle Grant, now Lady Essex, had introduced her to Claude Phillips, the director of the Wallace Collection, Sir Edmund Gosse, H. G. Wells, William Archer, and Max Beerbohm, and beside the incomparable Max she had felt herself "growing wings."

One Sunday her husband and she motored down for lunch to Cassiobury, Lord Essex's place near St. Albans, and found, scattered on the lawn under the great cedars, "the very flower and pinnacle of the London world," among whom were those great expatriate countrymen of theirs—John Sargent and Henry James! She had even entered those two famous English households of female literary fame—that of the novelist Mrs. Humphry Ward and of the poetess Alice Meynell, and observed with wonder and envy the domestic situation of these ladies: "I, who had been accustomed at home to dissemble my literary pursuits (as though, to borrow Dr. Johnson's phrase about portrait painting, they were 'indelicate in a female') was astonished at the prestige surrounding Mrs. Meynell in her own family; and at the Humphry Wards' I found the same affectionate deference toward the household celebrity."

But though some of these acquaintanceships gradually did deepen into friendships—with the Wards, for example—most of her encounters had been frustratingly fragmentary. At the lunch party at Cassiobury where she had found Sargent and James, the brilliant company, exhausted by the exertions of a long social season, had been capable of little beyond smiles and small pleasantries, and "meeting them in such circumstances," she remarked to her husband, "was like seeing their garments hung up in a row, with nobody inside." Somehow, in those vast mixed stews that were served up by the London hostess, no ingredient had its proper flavor or form. There was, above all, none of that conversation, intense and yet general, which would have been the product of a true *salon*. Much as she enjoyed these London plunges, they had not yet offered her what she always was in search of: "My idea of society," she said, "was (and still is) the daily companionship of the same five or six friends, and its pleasure is based on continuity, whereas the hospitable people who opened their doors to me in London, though of course they all had their own intimate circles, were as much exhilarated by the yearly stream of new faces as a successful shot by the size of his bag."

There was one English home where she found what she sought, however; by happy coincidence, it was a favorite haven, also, of Henry James. This was "Queen's Acre," in Windsor, familiarly called "Qu'Acre," where Howard Sturgis lived in easy eccentricity near the old park. Here is the description of one younger frequenter of the place, Gerard Hopkins:

> It was not, I suppose, a very lovely house. I seem to see it now as something in the Norman Shaw manner, with its wooden balconies and deep eaves and incised sunflowers on stucco placques. To modern eyes it would seem a period piece from an age not yet quite old enough to charm. Its rooms were full of chintz and cushions: there were tables covered with books and silver frames, walls huddled with water-colours, and everywhere the traces of dogs, all, when I came to know them, old, but cherished as life-long friends, comforted in their shortening journey to the row of little tombstones which marked the memory of

98

their predecessors. The point about Qu'Acre was that it was a *place*, existing only by individual right, a house in which one lived fully if only for the brief hours of a week-end. It tapped no country, served as a starting-point for no expeditions; it offered no games, no organized amusements. For the impressionable young it was a treasury of delights, a place where breakfast in bed was the rule and not the indulgent exception, a house where there were books in the lavatories. That, I think, was what struck my young imagination first . . . The fact in itself is trivial, but it stands out for me as setting the tone of the house, marking its independence, symbolic of the civilized standards which made a visit there so new, so delightful an experience.

Of the host of Queen's Acre it is less easy to offer a clear and just portrait, though he was full enough of easy, salient oddities for the caricaturist's pencil. His personality has been set out at length by two masterly hands—Edith Wharton's, in *A Backward Glance*, and George Santayana's, in *Persons and Places*—and between the tenderness of the one and the brilliant malice of the other one is left with the impression that this elusive man may be hiding, concealed by his geniality and his crotchets, from all observers.

His father, Russell Sturgis, was a Boston merchant who had become a partner of the banking firm of Baring Brothers, and had long lived in London as its English representative when Howard was born. In America, and in Boston in particular, the Sturgis family was prominent socially, and the rich and sociable Russell Sturgises of London entertained their visiting compatriots as well as English friends for many years both in town and at their country place near Leatherhead. James had known them all ever since he had begun to live in England, and he had formed a lasting friendship with Howard who was twelve years younger than himself. Edith Wharton had met this same friend at Newport, a few years after her marriage, when he had come to America for the first time to visit his American relatives. When she began to explore London society, she discovered him again, settled in bachelor domesticity at Qu'Acre.

Despite his American descent and connections, Howard Sturgis was an example of that sort of privileged strangeness which the English have occasionally tolerated in their wealthy classes; he would have been hopelessly lost and unhappy in Boston. He had been sent to Eton where his total unfitness for and dislike of "games" had somehow not produced the predictable persecution by his fellow school-boys; from the start, it seems, he was too charmingly poised, too at ease and witty and innocent of any sense of his own deficiency, to become anything but an object of affection to those around him. At Cambridge, he was intelligent and winsome and unambitious and he continued to bring out the amiability latent in the most unlikely natures. He was a sparkling conversationalist and an accomplished mimic, and he seems to have had what amounted to a gift for the making of friends.

Howard Sturgis may have been a homosexual or he may have been simply like the young Marquis whom he depicts in his novel, *Belchamber*: one of those who are cast in society's pageant to wear, because of the accident of sex, a garment of sturdy masculinity but who possess a nature full of feminine timidities and a taste for feminine occupations. Unlike "Sainty" in his novel, however, he was fortunate in being able to escape from the duty to "be a man" in any strenuous way. He never married; he had no position to maintain; he had a gift for the arts of hospitality, and he had enough wealth to live exactly as he pleased. His friends took him as he was with his limber humor and kindliness, and no one, apparently, was shocked, after the first visit, to see him at work at his dainty embroidery frame, a basket of brightly-colored silks always beside his low chair. As you contemplated this handsome, strongly-built man with thick black brows and moustache contrasting so dramatically with his wavy white hair, and listened to his engaging talk while his hands kept busy at their delicate activity, you were more likely, Gerard Hopkins found, to wonder why more men did not take up the hobby of needlework.

His psychological history would read too plainly today; he had been the last son left to his mother when her husband died and she had coddled and cossetted him and he had been devoted to her. After her death he had moved with some of the family servants to the house at Windsor. It was not far from Eton, where he still had friends among the masters and where he could enjoy the pleasant visits of the Eton boys who occasionally enlivened his gatherings with their presence. One of these was William Haynes Smith, a distant cousin who became a sort of adopted younger brother. This personage, generally known as "the Babe," far from producing embarrassment, appears to have added a touch of comfortable ordinariness to the scene at Qu'Acre.

Sturgis was, in a way, still another of those bachelor-dilettantes towards whom Edith Wharton was always drawn, a man—like Egerton Winthrop or Walter Berry—who preferred to live in a purely private world of his own, standing smilingly aside from the general press. He, too, had probably more talent than he chose to utilize, and his talent, a literary one, was not inconsiderable. It will be recalled that one of the topics discussed by Edith Wharton and Henry James at their first "real" meeting in London, in December, 1903, was Sturgis' novel, *Belchamber*, just about to be published. If her letter to Brownell is to be trusted, James had praised the novel, and she had felt able to cite his praise. She herself thought it "so remarkable in donné and character-drawing," that she had hastened to write immediately to recommend it to Brownell's attention. The matter was seriously taken up in the Scribner office, but the book was turned down. In answer to Brownell's letter of explanation, Edith Wharton wrote with some feeling:

> I have read with deep interest what you say about "Belchamber." I quite agree with your criticism as to its lack of proportion (I told him so when I read it, and found he was aware of it, though he had not the technical skill needful to remedy the mistake.) What completely surprises me is the objection on the score of *moeurs* in a book of such serious purpose and tragic import, and secondly the view that it isn't American enough to interest American readers. It isn't American at all, of course— It is an English novel, to all intents and purposes by an English novelist—but is that a reason why it shouldn't "take" in Amer-

ica? I don't think so—but no one will know now if I was right or if you are! I am sorry, though, for I think the book so far above the average that (as the author *is* American) I should have liked the U.S. to get the credit of it . . . I still think Belchamber would have sold in America as well as Red Pottage or Sir Richard Calmady (a filthy book that, par exemple!), and it deserves success far more than either of these flashy articles, which I name in connection with it only because both had what are called painful subjects—but not related from a high standpoint, as Belchamber is—Henry James agrees with me about it.

It is difficult to be certain, but Mrs. Wharton does seem to claim, in this letter, that James subscribed entirely to her view of *Belchamber*, which, despite admission of the book's weaknesses, was a strong plea for its high qualities. Many years later, however, in writing her autobiography, she gave currency to the idea that James had criticized the book so severely that Sturgis had lost all further interest in writing. James, she wrote in 1934, "pointed out with some truth that Howard had failed to utilize what should have been his central effect, and privately pronounced the book old-fashioned and feebly Thackerayan," though *she* had tried to comfort Sturgis with the reflection that it was "foolish to be discouraged by the opinion of a novelist who could no longer judge impartially any novel not built according to his own theories." She may at this much later date have been recalling events more exactly, or perhaps she was influenced by James's characteristic tirade which Arthur C. Benson recorded in his diary on April 29, 1904, and which Percy Lubbock included in his published selections from the diary in 1926:

H. J. and I talked of Howard's *Belchamber*. H. J. said that it was a good idea, a good situation. "He kindly read it to me: and we approached the dénouement in a pleasant Thackerayan manner—then it was suddenly all at an end. He had had his chance and he had made *nothing* of it! I tried, with a thousand subterfuges and doublings, such as one uses with the work of a friend, to indicate this. I hinted that the *interest* of the situation was not the *experiences*—which were dull and shabby and disagreeable enough in all conscience, and not disguised by the aristocratic atmosphere—not the *experiences,* but the *effect* of the fall of wave after disastrous wave upon Sainty's *soul*—if one can use the expression for such a spark of quality as was inside the poor rat—that was the interest, and I said to myself, 'Good God, why this chronicle, if it is a mere ante-chamber, and leads to nothing.' "

James intimates, of course, that he put his criticism to Sturgis himself more gently than this, and there is no such leveling of the whole, down to the last stick and stone, in the letter he wrote Sturgis just before he talked about *Belchamber* to Edith Wharton. In this he excused himself from comprehensive comment with the confession—usual to him in such cases—that he could not criticize the fiction of others without wanting to write the thing over his own way and "looking at it, so to speak, from within." "But even thus," he reassured his friend, "I 'pass' your book very—tenderly!" There was only one thing, he told him, that he was moved to say: he felt that Sturgis had complicated his task by situating his story at the least accessible social height—

I feel you have a great deal increased your difficulty by screwing up the "social position" of all your people so very high. When a man is an English Marquis, even a lame one, there are whole masses of Marquisate things and items, a multitude of inherent detail in his existence, which it isn't open to the painter *de gaité de coeur* not to make some picture of. And yet if I mention this because it is *the* place where people will challenge you, and to suggest to you therefore to expect it—if I do so I am probably after all quite wrong. No one notices or understands *anything,* and no one will make a single intelligent or intelligible observation about your work. They will make plenty of others. What I applaud is your sticking to the real line and centre of your theme—the consciousness and view of Sainty himself, and your dealing with things, with the whole fantasmagoria, as presented to him only, not otherwise going behind them.

It is somewhat baffling to discover James singling out for special praise Sturgis' emphasis on his hero's sensations, when he can also be heard deploring the absence of such emphasis in his remarks to Benson. To Sturgis, in this letter, at least, he certainly tempered his harsher verdict—if indeed he had it consistently in mind.

Whatever James and Edith Wharton had actually said about *Belchamber* in 1903, and however the author himself may have reacted to James's judgment, the fact remains that Sturgis did not undertake another book; he was seemingly content thereafter to continue to work dainty devices upon the embroidery-frame. It seems a pity, for *Belchamber* is a curiously moving and unusual book, a satiric study of upper-class English society in the nineties with a central theme of personal tragedy. It reminds one, indeed, of Edith Wharton's own novel, *The House of Mirth,* published the following year, which also exhibits the destruction of an individual by a pitiless and frivolous social world. Edith Wharton, unquestionably, was greatly impressed by Sturgis's example, and may have been actually influenced by it in writing *The House of Mirth. Belchamber,* it seems clear, figured in the argument—spoken or unspoken—she was always to have with James's view of the art of fiction, and the review of Sturgis's book which she wrote for *The Bookman* that same year clearly shows that she saw it as an example of a book whose excellences survived any strictures James might have applied. It has received other esteem as well. E. M. Forster, no incapable judge, wrote of *Belchamber* in 1934: "It seems to me now, as it did then, brilliant, amusing, unsparing, poised, full of incidents and characters, indeed well on the way to a masterpiece . . . Perhaps it was before his time. The public was not yet ready for that wide and yet careful canvass of aristocratic life." Certainly it was unkindly reviewed, and it was spurned by the Edwardian public as an "unpleasant" book. Sturgis, in any case, may have said his say on the one theme that he thought worth putting into novel form. He was by temperament, if not by lack of ability, an amateur, a dilettante, whose greatest achievement was the shaping of his own odd and graceful personality. As he grew old, he apparently lost some of this charm, as Santayana has rather mordantly described, but when Edith Wharton and James shared him between them in those early days of their friendship he was at his best.

Qu'Acre was to be the scene of some of their ripest moments together, for there foregathered, even more freely and frequently than at James's own Lamb House, that "inner group" which finally fulfilled Edith Wharton's dream of a perfect small club of congenial intellects and temperaments. "Our dear Howard," Henry James said, "is like a cake—a richly sugared cake—always on the table. We sit round him in a circle and help ourselves. Now and then we fling a slice over our shoulder to somebody outside; occasionally we draw our chairs closer together and make room for a new-comer." That newcomer might be Arthur C. Benson, for example, who reported, "Howard is observing, subtle, sensitive, smoothing over and adorning all social occasions with a perpetual flow of witty, unexpected, graceful talk that never palls or wearies." Yet Benson, a facile and charming conversationalist himself, sometimes wearied of the endless talk on which the Qu'Acre circle feasted, and once, when Sturgis and Lubbock visited him together, and talked for a whole weekend, confessed in his diary, "The truth is that a weariness, deadly, deep and inconceivable, fell on me. I felt as if I would never be able to talk again . . . It seems to me exactly like eating meal after meal . . .That is the worst of these great talkers, that they can't *stop*." Yet in such company, when James was added to it, Edith Wharton was seldom wearied. We need to look ahead only a short distance to see the rounding out of the group she evokes before the musing gaze of her last years: "This inner group I see now, gathered around [Howard] as the lamps are brought in at the end of a foggy autumn afternoon. In one of the arm-chairs by the fire is sunk the long-limbed frame of the young Percy Lubbock, still carrying in his mind the delightful books he has since given us, and perhaps as yet hardly aware that he was ever to put them on paper; in another sits Gaillard Lapsley, down for the week-end from his tutorial duties at Cambridge, while

John Hugh-Smith faces Percy across the fireside, and Robert Norton and I share the corners of the wide chintz sofa behind the tea-table; and dominating the hearth, and all of us, Henry James stands, or heavily pads about the room, listening, muttering, groaning disapproval, or chuckling assent to the paradoxes of the other tea-drinkers." It was, one realizes, a moment of perfect content for the one lady of the group.

Who and what were these other comrades of the spirit so prized by James and Edith Wharton? They all, even Percy Lubbock, with his "delightful books" still carried inside him, differed from these two in being less producers than persons; they were men of comparative leisure with no compulsive drive to do or make, content instead to be the recourse of their friends. They were not the less, they probably were the more valuable to the two real writers for that very reason. James and Edith Wharton came to them for refreshment and support which they might not have found save in these disinterested companions. Long after James and Sturgis were dead—in 1916 and 1920—Lapsley, Lubbock, Smith, and Robert Norton remained Edith Wharton's closest friends besides Walter Berry, who had also joined the group. Lubbock and Lapsley were, in a sense, memorialists of Henry James and Edith Wharton; Lubbock edited James's *Letters* and wrote *A Portrait of Edith Wharton* in 1920 and 1947, while his most famous book, *The Craft of Fiction,* is a skillful drawing forth into theory of James's technical principles; Lapsley was Edith Wharton's literary executor and the editor of her last unfinished novel, *The Buccaneers.* They were all bachelors, though Percy Lubbock did marry finally, when he was forty-seven. Edith Wharton's bachelor-dilettante type was with her at the last, for it was the younger men, Norton and Smith, whom she took with her on long motor-journeys and talked to in the mild Riviera winter evenings in her old age.

At the moment at which we have paused, however, the spring of 1906, when Edith Wharton was first to visit Qu'Acre in the company of Henry James, the circle was probably not complete. Smith and Norton, though they stayed to the last, had not yet entered it. But Lapsley and his young Cambridge friend Percy

Lubbock were already *de fondation* as Edith Wharton would say. Gaillard Lapsley, like James and Edith Wharton, and even Howard Sturgis, in a sense, was another transplanted American. He had gone to Harvard, where he obtained the bachelor's, master's, and doctor's degrees by the time he was twenty-six, in 1897; he had taught at a women's college in California, and then he had come to Cambridge, becoming a fellow of Trinity College and writing, in time, a learned treatise on the See of Durham. He had known, independently of one another, both James and Edith Wharton in America, and he remained in touch with American friends of theirs, so that he was for both a reminder of and connection with those earlier days; he was a representative, too, of a life finally settled upon a European basis, as James's had long been, as Edith Wharton's would be. Observing his bearing towards Edith Wharton, Percy Lubbock thought that he seemed "to know her as no one would who only beheld her as an event, a meteor from overseas, spreading her train. He appeared, by contrast, to know her quietly and privately, and when he talked of her the tone struck me; he seemed, even before he admired and applauded her, to be fond of her."

Sturgis, who was a frequent visitor to Cambridge, had found Lapsley there at his own old college of Trinity, and Cambridge had united them both with Percy Lubbock who was a student at King's College from 1898 to 1901, then a fellow at King's, and Librarian of the Pepys Library at Magdalene from 1906 to 1908. Lubbock had also been at Eton, and he may well have been among the Eton boys who strolled over to hospitable Qu'Acre during the nineties. There was a whole network of Eton-Cambridge connections these men shared. A. C. Benson, Lubbock's Eton tutor, for example, who had preceded his pupil to Magdalene, became Master of the College, and secured him the Librarianship. Benson had many literary friends, among them Henry James, and Lubbock remembered a dull summer evening when his tutor entered his little room with a visitor. The visitor was hesitant and Benson's star pupil felt unresponsive.

Who was it? Somehow between his hesitation and his massiveness the introduction was bungled; I didn't catch his name. He was sturdy and large-headed, with a close dark beard. He did his best, I am sure, to see an interest in the wretched little room and its inconspicuous owner; but it was a laborious proceeding, and I felt myself that there was none in either. We toiled at a few trivialities, where we could find them, but the chill and the gloom and the squalor were too much for us all; even my resourceful tutor was at a loss. I still had no idea who the stranger might be when he was released; with all courtesy but no particularity he said good-bye and was borne away. A chapter that was to develop so memorably never opened so tamely; for this was my first sight of Henry James.

Lubbock, the memorialist, edited Benson's diaries, as well as James's letters and the 35-volume *Novels and Stories of Henry James*. The Eton of his day he summoned from memory still later, in *Shades of Eton* which contains the account of the first meeting with James just given. It is here, also, that one may read Lubbock's description of the Vice-Provost of Eton, Francis Warre-Cornish and his wife, and their Pre-Raphaelite drawing-room with its tapestries and William Morris furniture, and of Arthur Ainger, the poet and the Latinist, a favorite and famous Eton master. These were Sturgis' friends of many years, too, and it was to Mr. Ainger or to Mrs. Cornish, noted for her salty intolerance of the inane, that Sturgis often took his guests for tea. Edith Wharton remembered the time when she came with Sturgis, promised to Mrs. Cornish as a friend of the Bourgets, whom the Vice-Provost's wife had met. Mrs. Cornish had seized a hapless Eton lad just then on the scene: "Have you read the novels of Paul Bourget?" she asked the bewildered child, who, of course, answered that he had not. "What, you've not read them? Not any of them?" shouted the terrifying Mrs. Cornish. "Then you should; you should read *all of them* immediately!"

Despite the first-rate and justly famous *The Craft of Fiction*, two novels, and his other books as well, Lubbock remains an amateur of letters compared to Henry James or Edith Wharton with their forty-odd volumes apiece, or A. C. Benson, with a total of over fifty. Surely a writer by more modest standards, it was his fate to live his life in the close company of these fertile and industrious workers who probably could never take his slender output quite seriously. Edmund Gosse—himself the author of over thirty books—who had known Lubbock since Benson had pointed him out at Eton as a school-boy of promise, was mystified by the paradox of an author whom he placed "in the front rank of living prose artists" who was so "modest and unenterprising." His constitutional self-effacement seems to have made him, as it did Sturgis, by preference an "occasional or desultory poet" and not "a soldier in the great army of constant producers," as James described Daudet.

Yet Lubbock's two novels, like Sturgis' *Belchamber*, have an overlooked merit. *Roman Pictures*, which was published in 1923, the same year that Lubbock edited the *Novels and Stories of Henry James*, is a social comedy narrated by a tourist in Rome, and a clever illustration of James's principle of consistent point of view. It also utilizes a formal device which attracted the admiration of E. M. Forster, who discusses it in *Aspects of the Novel*, the "grand chain" by which the narrator is passed from one group of persons to the next, finally ending again at the point where he began. But "what is so good in *Roman Pictures*," Forster writes,

is not the presence of the "grand chain" pattern—any one can organize a grand chain—but the suitability of the pattern to the author's mood. Lubbock works all through by administering a series of little shocks, and by extending to his characters an elaborate charity which causes them to appear in a rather worse light than if no charity was wasted on them at all. It is the comic atmosphere, but sub-acid, meticulously benign. And at the end we discover to our delight that the atmosphere has been externalized, and that the partners, as they click together in the marchesa's dining room, have done the exact thing which the book requires, which it required from the start, and have bound the scattered incidents together with a thread woven out of their own substance.

Like Sturgis' *Belchamber*, which, as we have noted, also won Forster's praise, *Roman Pictures* is an exceptional creative achievement in a life of only occasional effort. Lubbock did go on to write one other novel two years later, *The Region Cloud*, which is less brilliant yet still an interesting book with a theme that might have been used by James; it relates the story of a young worshipper's disillusion in a great painter whom he had credited with moral qualities to match his artistic powers. James was no longer alive to comment on either *Roman Pictures* or *The Region Cloud*, but the weaknesses of the novels, particularly of the second, were not unobvious—they lay in the slippery, vague style which, as one reviewer put it, "grips on nothing." Edith Wharton scored this criticism in her copy of the *Athenaeum* and wrote to A. John Hugh-Smith that she also agreed with the critic in the *Times Literary Supplement* who had called it "muse mellow." "Oh, les elderly jeunes," she rather cruelly remarked to Smith. It was unquestionably late in the day—Lubbock was forty-six—for this quiet observer of the performance of others to begin to learn how to write novels, but one cannot help feeling that Mrs. Wharton somehow resented his plunge into her own medium.

Lubbock was often to be found at Qu'Acre when she began to visit there. He recalled that she did not seem to notice him for a long time; the "long-limbed" young man she described was a diffident observer, content to listen and watch while the others performed their conversational feats. He had the habit and temperament of observation, the gift of immersing himself without egotism in the study of another personality. Whereas there are some writers who produce nothing at all but autobiography in one form or another—be it fiction, poetry or essay—Lubbock always seemed to be writing the history of persons other than himself. His first book, published in 1906, was a novelistic biography based on Mrs. Browning's letters, and after that he wrote a book about Pepys, which grew out of his work as Librarian of the Magdalene collection. In 1920, the year he edited James's letters, he published a biographical sketch of another personal friend who had died during the war, George Calderon. Two years later he wrote *Earlham*, which is about a house, the seat in Norfolk of the wealthy Gurneys from whom he was descended; this book, though not the history of a person, won the James Tait Black Memorial Prize for biography that year (the previous award had gone to Lytton Strachey for *Queen Victoria*). In later years, as we have mentioned, he devoted himself to memorializing Benson and Eton. He wrote a sketch of Mary Cholmondeley, another lady-writer friend of Sturgis and Lubbock (it was her *Red Pottage* that Edith Wharton indignantly compared to *Belchamber* in the letter to Brownell quoted previously). Finally, in 1947, he produced his *Portrait of Edith Wharton*, that delicate and graceful, if slight adumbration of the personality he had begun to watch so long before at Qu'Acre.

Towards the end of March, 1906, Edith Wharton arrived in Paris to stop for two weeks at her brother's apartment, and Sturgis went over to meet her and to accompany her across the Channel, like the visiting princess she so often seemed to be, the far-away princess who would alight from her dragon-chariot and dazzle her friends for a few brief moments. James, already practicing the language of gallantry which it always amused him to assume to her, wrote in mock-jealousy of his fellow-courtier, "How I envy you each other . . . I have been grilling sadly with the sense of my proved poorer style." But he added, "wait till I show you here!" He felt he could promise her an adventure. "Let me not deflower for you the fresh, the tropical bouquet that awaits you here. Come quickly and bury your nose in it," he urged, as he related a choice bit of conversation about the visit he had had with Mary Cholmondeley.

Miss Cholmondeley had held him in intense conversation about *The House of Mirth*, Mrs. Wharton's successful recent novel, *"dont elle raffole aussi bien que moi"* ("on which she dotes as much as I"), James related, and she had said at the end of a half-hour of talk about the book, "And you'd call her *subtle*, wouldn't you?" To which James replied, "demoniacally," as he said, "Ah, Miss M.C., there are others to whom I should so much *more* apply that sovereign last word of the higher criticism—!"

With the éclat of her new novel behind her and James's

chaperonage, Edith Wharton could expect a lively time among the literati on this visit. Of course, by the time she arrived, he warned her, London would be a place of "ethereal mildness," nearly emptied for the Easter holiday, a condition that perfectly contented him personally. "I myself, however unnaturally, don't abhor the London vacuum," he wrote. But she could "make ten Easter visits," if she hurried. "Do make them, so we can talk about them." And while they talked he would be able to guide her on a "motor-flight" through the countryside—a treat for the guide himself.

He welcomed delightedly her suggestion that he meet her and her husband at Dover and ride back with her in their automobile. His appetite for motor-touring had only grown stronger since she had first introduced him to such pleasures in Lenox. "*Bien sur que* I'll meet you at Dover on the 25th, or anywhere in the world—*this* world—you suggest, & motor with you as long as the machine consents to resist my weight . . . I really am exquisitely grateful to both of you for the motor-chance." And he gaily outlined an itinerary. "If we start from Dover on the 26th a.m.," he proposed, "I vote that we come southward through Kent & Sussex—we must keep south of London—and begin by lunching that day at Lamb House. In that case we might sleep at (I shld. think) Chichester, & make our way so, by Winchester to Salisbury, into the interesting Somersetshire of old houses (Montacute the beautiful!!) by *Wells*, on the way. Thence along the North Devon coast 1st, & then across Devonshire southward to wind up at Sidmouth on the south coast. (Ilfracombe is rather awful!) But this is a very rough hint. Don't resent the few monuments if thrown in & met—not sought & gone out of the way for; in this small country they come in (the occasional cathedrals &c,) of themselves."

They proceeded as he had planned. Edith Wharton long remembered that first ride from Dover to Rye, a revelation, comic and exasperating, of James's misguided compulsion to guide, now that he was on his own ground, and his utter lack of any ordinary sense of direction. James, having come down to Folkestone by train, insisted on seating himself next to the Wharton chauffeur,

Charles Cook, a superbly competent driver and route-finder, "on the plea that the roads across Romney marsh formed such a tangle that only an old inhabitant could guide us to Rye. The suggestion resulted in our turning around and around in our tracks till long after dark, though Rye, conspicuous on its conical hill, was just ahead of us, and Cook could easily have landed us there in time for tea."

But at last they were at Rye, at last they were at Lamb House. They turned the corner of the steep street and mounted between low brick cottages to the stately eighteenth-century house at the end, and perhaps the wide Palladian window of James's favorite room, the garden room, was lit in welcome. They entered the white-panelled hall, with its book-cases and prints, the oak-panelled morning-room. With murmurs of deprecation for the humbleness of his lovely dwelling, of which he was, in fact, quite proud, James made them welcome. Probably they did not motor on further that evening, having arrived so much later than their plan called for. Instead, they must have supped at James's, with much apology, again, from the host, for the plainness of his board. This last apology, according to Edith Wharton's account of things, would not have been unjustified. James had a morbid fear of being thought rich, worldly, and luxurious, and his kitchen was ruled on a principle of anxious frugality—quite a contrast, his visitors had cause to reflect, with the lavishness of Qu'Acre.

Probably they were off again, right after lunch the next day. There had never, Edith Wharton recalled after years of visits to James, been much lingering at Rye; she had not once even got to explore the quaint, old seaside town with its cobbled streets or more than glanced at the Norman church with its famous sixteenth-century clock. When she did, finally, it was years after James's death when Lamb House was tenanted by a much younger friend, Robert Norton. James loved to tease Edith Wharton about her passion for the road; indeed, he sometimes felt quite seriously that her restless craving for change of place was that of a possessed and driven being, a whirling fury, who would swoop him up in her golden claws and carry him away against his will. But Edith Wharton was quick to point out that his addiction to motoring was at least as great as her own. And— she added privately—at other people's expense! He might really have bought himself an automobile if he loved the thing so much, she observed, for they were not *so* expensive, even then, that he could not have afforded one. But no, "he took advantage to the last drop of petrol, of the travelling capacity of any visitor's car!"

But such wry thoughts were far from occurring to either of them that day in early April, the sweetest English time accord- ing to the poets, when James and the Whartons began to thread their way through the rural southwest of England. She did not, one can be sure, resent the "few monuments . . . thrown in and met"; her travels in Italy had trained her to seek out the architec- tural aspects of a landscape. So we can imagine her and James contemplating together Chichester and Winchester and Salisbury Cathedrals, if much distracted by conversation on the way. As for the old houses of Somersetshire—was she not the lady who had written a book on Italian villas and gardens? She must have quite fallen in love with the Elizabethan mansion of Montacute with its great formal gardens in the Italian Renaissance style— gardens that rivalled any she had seen even in Italy. Then, out beyond the beautiful cathedral city of Wells, she discovered the Devon landscape, the rugged shore on the Bristol Channel, with its cliffs and ravines, and, inland, the rolling moor country.

There were other fine trips that April and May in this spring- time moment of friendship, but on this first visit, as afterwards, James would find that entertaining the wonderful Edith could be something of a strain. On the fourth of May he reported himself to William James as having been "trying, under pressure, a three days' motor trip with the Whartons, much frustrated by bad weather and from which I impatiently and prematurely and gleefully returned." He had managed to dispose of the Whartons by passing them on to Gaillard Lapsley, to whom he wrote, only half-penitently, a few days later,

> Oh, it has all been very sad and clumsy and perverse. I left the rich, rushing, ravening Whartons under stress of most ill

weather (at Malvern) whereupon their luck quite changing, they went and threw themselves into your more or less obligatorily opened arms. Still my sense of loss is curable—but that is not quite how I want to put in my time with you—when I *can* put it. I see them tomorrow, however, and Mrs. Wharton will doubtless have the art of creating within me a temporary pang. Bear with me, meanwhile—and think of me even as pressing her for the pang. What she shall give me of you I shall take.

So now the Whartons were at Cambridge with Lapsley, and, probably Lubbock, too, though their return to Rye was imminent. Quite probably, there had been trips to Howard Sturgis at Windsor engineered by James with the same shrewd expectation of disposing of his charming, but sometimes wearying guests. "To tell the truth," Lubbock recalled, thinking back upon many visits of Edith Wharton to James in England, "he was not sorry to follow her away from Lamb House, to escort her on her flight and place her securely under another roof." At Qu'Acre he could stop to enjoy her society for a while, freer of care than when she was his sole responsibility—she even had the art of making him feel a temporary pang at his loss—and then he could return to Rye in blessed solitude.

It was a sort of joke, this characterization of them as the "rich, rushing, ravening Whartons," and yet not entirely so. Already at this starting point of their friendship James was disturbed by a spendthrift quality in Edith Wharton; she seemed to be willing to waste so much, less importantly of money than of self, of time, of personal energy, of feeling and thinking, even, in mere empty motion, like the American motorists of later years who would boast of their accumulated "mileage" as though movement were an achievement in itself. What did it mean?, he must have wonderingly asked himself, and confessed that as yet he did not know. He only knew that the intensely conserving nature which he himself possessed, a nature which extracted the most from every experience that came his way, was a different one from Edith Wharton's.

After her visit to England was over she returned to France, and then she was back at The Mount. To Mary Cadwalader Jones,

James summarized what he had seen: "They had, the W's, I thought, a rather frustrated, fragmentary, merely-motory time to have crossed the dreadful sea for—though it was what seemed to suit them best, and I daresay that after their more successful days in France they re-embarked with the sense of a rich adventure." As for himself, he "only rather thanked goodness, and during a few days here a little participated in it," that such fantastic wealth and freedom were not his portion—"such incoherence, such a nightmare of perpetually renewable choice and decision, such a luxury of bloated alternatives do they seem to burden life withal." After this magnificently crushing judgment, he added mildly, "However, I had some very charming and enjoyable, even if half weather-blighted hours with our friends."

Despite genuine pleasure in and growing affection for Edith Wharton, he had found a theme in her way of life; though he wrote "they," meaning Teddy, also, it is really just Edith he meant, or was soon to realize that he meant. "A nightmare of perpetually renewable choice and decision" he already called the principle of her being. How profoundly he struck at the heart of the matter! Not what Edith Wharton would do or not do, but the delusion that choices were "perpetually renewable," when the moralist in him declared that they were not. It was not mere physical restlessness, but the presumption of freedom, that disturbed him. As early as *The Portrait of a Lady*, he had suggested to his readers that great freedom was almost an illusion, that circumscription was inevitable. "A luxury of bloated alternatives" he termed a burden, a curse, not an opportunity. And so he began to watch his friend with some pity and fear, as much as admiration and affection.

She would come to England nearly every year. Each time, with a deepening intensity, James would enjoy her, despair for her. Comedy and tragic intuition would be strangely mingled in the comments he would make about her in letters to the little group of Lamb House and Qu'Acre. But though he may have made remarks enough even to her, to indicate his feelings, it is doubtful if she regarded them as anything beyond high humor, a crazy tower of nonsense which grew higher through the years. And surely they had many unforgettable times together in England.

She remembered the occasion when he had insisted on conducting her to Box Hill, to meet Meredith, whom the group at Qu'Acre had discussed one long evening, and whom James had masterfully dissected for them all. Meredith was old, ill, and rather deaf, but his greatness was visible. She watched the two faces, that of her own friend and that of his old literary brother—"Meredith's so classically distinguished, from the spring of the wavy hair to the line of the straight nose, and the modelling of cheek and throat, but all like a slightly idealized bas-relief after a great original; and James's heavy Roman head, so realistically and vigorously his own, not a bas-relief but a bust, wrought in the round by harsher but more powerful hands. As they sat there, James benignly listening, Meredith eloquently discoursing, and their deep regard for each other burning steadily through the surface eloquence and the surface attentiveness, I felt I was in great company and I was glad."

Then there was the time they went to see Castle Bodiam, in Kent. Again, Edith Wharton recalled a moment of rare exquisiteness. As they looked at the old ruined castle, mirroring itself in a moat filled with water-lilies, silent save for the hum of blue dragonflies in the pure sunlight, James said to her, "Summer afternoon—summer afternoon; to me those have always been the two most beautiful words in the English language." Afterwards, she wrote a poem to celebrate the occasion and the friend who had made it memorable with his words. Readers of *Scribner's Magazine*, where it appeared in March, 1911, could not have known how personal a cue was provided by the title—"Summer Afternoon (Bodiam Castle, Sussex)." Yet we can hear, among the vague phrases of rapture, not only a poet's but a woman's exaltation at a rare communion. "Not all the wasteful beauty of the years/Heaped in the scale of one consummate hour/Shall this outweigh," she began, and described the trancelike scene of castle and moat that lay before her and Henry James that day. It was, she wrote, one of those "moments that between the beats of time/May thus insphere in some transcendent air/the plenitude of being." She recorded an emotion for which, at last, only "love" is the word: "Thus we mused/And musing thus we felt the magic touch/And such a moment held us. As, at times,/

Through the long windings of each other's eyes/We have reached some hallowed silent place/That a God visits at the turn of night." Now she could say, "Suddenly/We took the hues of beauty and became/Each to the other all that each had sought."

Lamb House and Qu'Acre, even after she had made a home for herself in Europe, across the Channel, continued to be home of both the intellect and the affections for Edith Wharton, for in one place or the other there were to be found friends and in particular, one friend like no others. Her general English circle widened, too; she made other friends and became familiar with many corners of English society that gave her diversion; finally, in 1913, she even considered buying a house and settling in England. But perhaps she would never have done it; England had been too long a place of entertainment, by that time, and France had become home. In any case, the war settled the question for her the following year.

5

The Dance upon the Aubusson Carpet

JAMES WAS READY ENOUGH to admit that Edith Wharton's "luxury of bloated alternatives" often included better things than the "merely-motory" days he had spent with her in England in 1906. Such, for example, was her visit a few weeks later, during a tour through central France, to Nohant, the home of George Sand. She wrote him an account of it before leaving Paris for America, and after some delay, which he jestingly referred to his shock and envy, he replied, "I've really been for weeks in the disabled state, with the bleeding wound in my side, produced by the Parthian shot of your own last [letter]—your flinging back at me, over your departing shoulder, of your unutterable vision of the Nohant that I have all these (motorless) years so abjectly failed to enlighten my eyes withal (for I am indeed convinced that it *must*, as you say, enlighten & explain.)" Gladly would he have exchanged some of their recent English hours for this! "Oh, if we could only have been enlightened & explained to together! To think that that might (dreamily) have been even while we were splashing about Ross in the rain, or going up & down in the hideous Malvern lift!" He declared himself "lost . . . in the golden mist of your Nohant which I'm really almost capable of rushing over to Lenox to hear your story of—more capable than of starting next week for Dover, Paris, Chateauroux & La Châtre. To think you have seen La Châtre!—& that you might move me over to Ashfield again & tell me about it as we go!"

It is easy to understand James's feelings. George Sand had interested him ever since his own early days in Paris when he had listened to the talk of the men who had known her in her old age at Nohant—Gautier, Maupassant, Dumas *fils*, and Flaubert. Those visitors had descended from the Paris express at Chateauroux, stopping, no doubt, at the same inn where the Whartons had breakfasted, then taken a diligence along the road that skirts the Indre, the same road which the Whartons had followed in their car, and finally come to the big, plain house in the country where so much had happened. Departing, the Whartons had passed through the countryside where George Sand's earlier years had been spent—through La Châtre, the little town further on along the river, where she had lived for a winter, as she describes in the *Histoire de ma Vie*. James's essay on George Sand in *French Poets and Novelists*, published in 1878, quotes from the preface to *Isidora* in which she tells how a sudden recollection of her own little spot in provincial Berry had instructed her in creating the foreign personages of her novel. Of the secret of her style, he simply says, "she had picked it up apparently at Nohant, among the meadows and the traînes—the deeply-sunken byroads among the thick, high hedges." Yet he had never seen Nohant!

The javelin of Edith Wharton's Nohant experience was sticking in his side, he humorously declared, and threatened to remain, poisoning his blood,

> till you *write*—I mean till you *print*, till you "do" the place, the whole impression, for me under stress of imminent publication. For of course you are doing, you *have* done that. You can't *not*. I yearn and languish. Write to me that this act of piety is even already performed. I've no news for you comparable to that of my emotion on all that score. And there was, on my side—there had been before I heard from you—a strange telepathic intuition. A few days after you had sloped away to France I said to myself suddenly: "They're on their way to

The Dance upon the Aubusson Carpet

Nohant, d—n them! They're going there—they *are* there!" It came to me as a jealous, yet so tenderly sympathetic, conviction—out of the blue. You hadn't spoken of it. So you owe me the *récit*. There has been, you know, no *récit* (of the impression of the place) of any sort of authority or value but George's own. How you must have *smelt* them all!

She did write a description of Nohant and it appears in *A Motor Flight Through France,* which was published in 1908. It is a curious account, "enlightening and explaining" the woman writing as much as the woman about whom she writes. Edith Wharton had been startled to find George Sand's home so dignified and decent, an image of sober well-being "conscious in every line of its place in the social scale, of its obligation to the church and the cottages under its wing"—and yet,

When one recalls the throng of motley characters who streamed in and out of that quiet house—the illegitimate children of both sides, living in harmony with one another and with the child of wedlock, the too-intimate servants, the peasant playmates, the drunken boon companions—when one turns to the Hogarthian pictures of midnight carouses presided over by the uproarious Hippolyte and the somberly tippling Dudevant, while their wives sat disgusted, but apparently tolerant, above stairs, one feels oneself in the sinister gloom of Wildfell Hall rather than in the light temperate air of a French province. And somehow, unreasonably, of course, one expects the house to bear, even outwardly, some mark of that dark disordered period—or, if not, then of the cheerful but equally incoherent and inconceivable existence led there when the timid Madame Dudevant was turning into the great George Sand, and the strange procession which continued to stream through the house was composed no longer of drunken gentlemen-farmers and left-handed peasant relations, but of an almost equally fantastic and ill-assorted company of ex-priests, naturalists, journalists, Saint-Simonians, riders of every conceivable religious, political and literary hobby, among whom the successive tutors of the adored Maurice—forming in themselves a line as long as the kings in *Macbeth!*—perhaps taking the palm for oddness of origin and adaptability of manners.

Edith Wharton had expected, she confessed, that the scene of these confused goings-on would "wear the injured *déclassé* air of a house which has never had its rights respected." Instead it had, she liked to fancy, told her that it was the "image of those grave ideals to which George Sand had gradually conformed the passionate experiment of her life." The old house "so marked in its very plainness, its conformity" must in the end have helped to give George Sand, she thought, "that centralizing weight of association and habit which is too often lacking in the modern character."

How suggestive the whole experience obviously was to the visiting novelist, married to a husband whose interests and diversions were less and less her own! No "Hogarthian" scenes as yet—but was not Edward Wharton a Dudevant under restraint? If she thought of her future, of some impossible era of liberty still to reveal itself for another George Sand, she must have recognized in herself the secret energies that had seemingly disrupted the quiet habits of traditional life in the other woman's case. Could this happen to her? She may have both wished and feared such a history for herself, though knowing well that in the end, the "centralizing weight of association and habit" would order her life.

Before she composed her essay, her impressions were enriched by a second trip, this time in the company of Henry James, and it is impossible to tell how much her remarkable evocation owed to his company. He had written, "Perhaps if you have the proper vehicle of Passion—as I make no doubt—you will be going there once more—in which case *do* take me!" And in the spring he came to the Whartons in Paris, and, riding in the "vehicle of passion," toured all of the Midi and made the pilgrimage to Nohant with his hostess beside him. Edith Wharton recalled the visit—James,

> fascinated by every detail of the scene, deeply moved by the inscriptions on the family grave-stones under the wall of the tiny ancient church—especially in the tragic Solange's: *La Mère de Jeanne*—and absorbed in the study of the family portraits, from the Elector of Saxony and the Mlles. Verrier to

Maurice and his children. He lingered delightedly over the puppet theatre with Maurice's grimacing dolls, and the gay costumes stitched by his mother; then we wandered out into the garden, and looking up at the plain old house, tried to guess behind which windows the various famous visitors had slept. James stood there a long time, gazing and brooding beneath the row of closed shutters. "And in which of those rooms, I wonder, did George herself sleep?" I heard him suddenly mutter. "Though in which, indeed—" with a twinkle—"in which indeed, my dear, did she not?"

"I know of no such link of true interchange as a community of interest in dear old George," James would write to Edith Wharton nearly six years later when she sent him a new volume of Madame Karénine's *Life of George Sand.* "What a value it all gets from our memory of that wondrous day when we explored the very scene where they pigged so thrillingly together. What a crew, what *moeurs*, what habits, what conditions and relations every way—& what an altogether mighty and marvellous George! —not diminished by all the greasiness & smelliness in which she made herself (& *so* many other persons!) at home . . . It will be a joy when we can next converse on these & cognate themes."

The Nohant excursion was but one note in the general orchestration of James's visit to the Whartons in France in 1907, a visit that lasted from the end of March till the beginning of May. Edith Wharton at The Mount, Edith Wharton descending upon England, were still incomplete disclosures of her. In France she now found home ground, immersing herself in the fusions of culture and social life which were only possible there. She and her husband decided to give up their house in New York City for a flat in Paris—because the harsh native winters seemed to affect his health, for one thing, but also because the intellectual and social climate of Paris suited her. Their American base would henceforth be The Mount where they could return for the summer months. In the autumn of 1906 they sublet the spacious *hôtel* apartment of the George Vanderbilts, 58 rue de Varenne, in the old Faubourg Saint-Germain. It was a move James approved. "This is really charming & uplifting news," he wrote,

"& I applaud the free sweep of your 'line of life' with all my heart. We shall almost be neighbors." And he added, "I will most assuredly hie me as promptly as possible across the scant interspace of the Channel . . ."

He had some reservations, however, concerning the choice of France as a permanent milieu for a transposed American, particularly a writer. He had just read her latest story, *Madame de Treymes*, in the August issue of *Scribner's Magazine*, and he wrote: "All the same, with the rue de Varenne, &c, don't go in too much for the French or the 'Franco-American' subject—the real field of your extension is *here*—it has far more fusability with *our* native and primary material; between which & the French elements there is, I hold, a disparity as complete as between a life led in trees, say, & a life led in—sea depths, or in other words between that of climbers and swimmers—or (crudely) that of monkeys & fish."

Once again, as in the letter he had written in 1902, commenting to Mary Cadwalader Jones upon the subjects of Edith Wharton's first stories, he seemed to be making a comment both literary and personal. Then he had said, "she must be tethered in native pastures," suggesting at once both American themes for her future work and the choice of an American life. Now he accepted the idea that her writing—and her living—would involve the European scene, but he cautioned her against permanently involving herself with France in either sense. He urged that she adopt the English environment, as he had. He had tried France, himself, and long ago—in 1876, in fact—come to a point when, as he wrote his brother William, the last resistance to satiety with the French fell from him like a garment and his one wish was "to feed on English life and the contact of English minds."

In 1881, James analyzed his own development in an entry in his notebook. He had gone first to live in Paris, but that, he realized, "was not really what I wanted; what I wanted was London—and Paris was only a stopgap." Despite everything that year in Paris had meant to him—the friendship of Turgenev, and the acquaintance of Zola, Goncourt, Daudet—he had come to realize: "I should be an eternal outsider." So he now warned his friend that as an American she would find "the real field of her extension . . . here," i.e., in England, which had "far more fusability" with their native experience. In England the American did not feel cut off from his beginnings; rather he felt himself simply reaching back to earlier connections. The scene was familiar, even if one had never seen it before, and the language was still one's own—how important that was, for a writer! Had not Hawthorne called England "our old home"?

Certainly there was nothing final about the choice of Paris for Edith Wharton at this moment. England was to be part of her life from now on, in any case, because of her enlarging acquaintanceship there, and she would go over the Channel to pay visits as casually as ordinary persons cross a city street. Yet she was to remain in the rue de Varenne twenty years. After the lease of the Vanderbilt house expired in 1908, the Whartons took a flat in a modern house across the street, and there they remained. "Though I should have preferred London, I should have been hard to please had I not discovered compensations in my life in Paris," she recalled.

Her husband had always disliked London; that, until her divorce in 1913, had been determinant enough. But she had also grown to feel herself a part of Paris, to create a small world for herself within its great whirling sphere, as James never had. The Franco-American situation continued to be her chosen basis, as it continued to provide a basis for her fiction, too, despite James's suggestion that she relinquish it. As late as 1912, the year her novel *The Reef* was published, he commented on her choice of literary theme and personal environment. In the course of a long and delicately appreciative letter about her book, with its finely-drawn French scene, he remarked, "Your only drawback is not having the homeliness and the inevitability and the happy limitation and the affluent poverty of a Country of your Own (*comme moi, par exemple!*)." Perhaps his parenthesis, with its "par exemple!" may be ironic, for some might say that he of all people had no "country of his own." But James considered that he had found a country of his own across the Channel, as she had not among the French. He was, he felt, a successful "example" of what she lacked.

Edith Wharton found in France, more powerfully present than elsewhere, a quality which her innermost nature craved. That conscious continuity of custom and conformity which had revealed itself to her at Nohant as the order to which George Sand was ultimately obedient—this, to Edith Wharton, was the very essence of the French tradition she loved. As she drove with James in 1908 on the road to Arras beyond Boulogne, the very scene argued a philosophy:

> This part of France, with its wide expanse of agricultural land-scape, disciplined and cultivated to the last point of finish, shows how nature may be utilized to the utmost clod without losing its freshness and naturalness. In some regions of this supremely "administered country," where space is more restricted, or the fortunate accidents of water and varying levels are lacking, the minute excessive culture, the endless ranges of potager wall, and the long lines of fruit-trees bordering straight interminable roads, may produce in the American traveller a reaction toward the unkempt, a momentary feeling that ragged road-sides and weedy fields have their artistic value. But here in northern France, where agriculture has mated with poetry instead of banishing it, one understands the higher beauty of land developed, humanized, brought into relation to life and history, as compared with the raw material with which the greater part of our own hemisphere is still clothed. In France everything speaks of long familiar intercourse between the earth and its inhabitants; every field has a name, a history, a distinct place of its own in the village polity; every blade of grass is there by an old feudal right which has long since dispossessed the worthless aboriginal weed.

"Nature may be utilized to the utmost clod without losing its freshness and naturalness" is a way of saying that cultivation is the proper use of one's resources, that instinct and impulse become civilization only after they have submitted themselves to the plow and the pruning hook—or to discipline, tradition, standards. It was the presence in France of long-inherited habits and standards that made, Edith Wharton thought, for that social instinct which puts the rule above the person in essential matters, leaving the conscience happier and freer in unessential things. It was the acceptance of a time-approved order that lay at the basis of French manners and French taste.

Then, also, to the problem that had perplexed her since her youth, the problem of the relation of intelligence and social power, the French seemed long ago to have achieved a solution. She always contrasted her own country with France in the conviction that somehow, for the French, intelligence had a place in all aspects and ranks of life, that there was respect for its embodiment in books, science, or art even on the part of the most ignorant Frenchman, and that France, unlike America, expected this of peasant and aristocrat alike. It seemed to her that at home the leisure class into which she had been born had no contact at all with the world of intellectual creation. She had felt herself an incongruity among the members of her family and her family's friends; her only affinities were with men who, like the Lawrence Selden of her novel, *The House of Mirth*, lived stockaded against a barbarian society in a private "republic of the spirit."

"It is only in sophisticated societies," she wrote, "that the intellectual recognizes the use of the frivolous, and the frivolous know how to make their houses attractive to their betters." Such a sophisticated society existed in France. For France was the true home of the salon. There was no salon to be built in America, though she tried her best at The Mount; even in England, Society did not really know how to use the stray intellectual that wandered into one of its large social parties. Qu'Acre was something else—a private family of friends.

Edith Wharton turned to her life in the rue de Varenne with an eagerness born of long-felt, complex expectations. With an energy and interest that seem vulgar until we understand the motive behind them, she set herself to entering Parisian society. And to the rue de Varenne, even that first year, came new acquaintances from all of France's élites—the aristocracy of letters and the Academy as well as the old aristocracy of the Faubourg Saint-Germain which James's Christopher Newman, the hero of *The American*, had found so impenetrable. With the help of a few old Paris friends she conceived and attained the ambition of the Parisian hostess; she, a foreigner, built a salon.

The rue de Varenne, a narrow street on the left bank, which

runs from the busy Boulevard Raspail to the great mass of the Invalides with its golden dome, is not today very different from many old Paris streets, a little shabby-genteel, the old mansions cut into flats, with many new buildings. In that pre-war twilight of 1906, however, the old Faubourg in which it lies was still the geographic center of the most aloofly self-contained of aristocracies.

Renting a stately Louis XIV *hôtel* apartment did not guarantee, of course, that the Whartons would come to know the old families who were their neighbors. For this they needed the aid of several French ladies, now of the Faubourg, who turned out to be friends Edith Wharton had met years before when her parents took her to Cannes. These friends gave her entrée into the closed world of their families, and, perhaps more important, initiated her into the intricate protocol of French social relationships. One cannot help smiling at the obvious devotion with which, as her autobiography describes, she set herself to master the involved rules of precedence which governed the seating at dinner, for example, of one's French guests—that an Academician takes precedence over everyone but a Duke or an Ambassador, that the next-but-two most honored guest sits on the right of the lady who is on the host's right, and so forth. The bachelor James never had to worry about these rites of hospitality in his Paris days— but then, he had not begun by assailing the citadel of French society. He had begun with the boulevards, the cafés, the artists' studios, knowing at once a broader French world than she ever would, yet remaining only an occasional visitor within this guarded area.

Her greatest help in fashioning her French life came to her from the Bourgets, who lived nearby, in the rue Barbet de Jouy. Bourget, now a member of the French Academy, had a large and various acquaintance in French University and literary circles. The Bourgets were much in social demand, and James, calling on them one day that summer, heard Minnie complain that they were "more mondaine than ever," and that Paul had dined out every night for nine on end.

Bourget apparently took Edith Wharton in tow and brought

her into the houses where his success and his personal charm had long assured him a welcome. Most important was the salon of the widowed Comtesse Robert de Fitz-James, who, with the masterly hand of the great hostesses of French tradition, gathered and combined small groups of her friends at her weekly lunches and dinners. Among her staple social ingredients were members of the Academy like the Bourgets, the Comte d'Haussonville (grandson of Madame de Staël, and her biographer), popular playwrights like Paul Hervieu and the Marquis de Flers, the poet and novelist Henri de Régnier, representatives of the Institut like the scholars Comte Alexandre de Laborde and Gustave Schlumberger and the Baron Ernest Seillière, and diplomats like the Berlin Ambassador, Jules Cambon, an old Washington acquaintance of Edith Wharton's. Names like these, which read a little dustily today, were the most fragrant flowers of the social garden in the Paris of 1906, personalities and talkers as well as "men of distinction." "Rosa" Fitz-James herself was the born salon-mistress; though without any pronounced intellectuality of her own, this cosmopolitan daughter of Austrian Jews had an instinctive appreciation of the qualities of the most diverse persons, of the possibilities of affinity and disaffinity among them, and a creative joy in the spectacle of the big drawing-room in her apartment in the rue de Grenelle filled with her happily-conversing guests. To Edith Wharton, who became almost immediately a close friend of the affectionate Rosa, she was a model to be imitated, a colleague to be relied upon, an endless source of social introductions and information.

Yet it may be wondered whether the social interests of the Bourgets and Madame de Fitz-James were the happiest framework for an artist's observation. It is true that no one came to the rue de Grenelle who was dull, however great his rank or riches— but there was a barrier firm and fast against the intellect if it was not "polite." True, there were always the younger wits who sat at the *bouts de table*, the ends-of-the-table where the least of rank were placed, but they do not seem to have included any element that might have clashed with the Academicians and aristocrats seated at the center, beside the hostess. Mostly, it seems, they were the successful younger journalists of Paris, not the artists, writers, intellectual innovators of the coming time. But such are seldom to be found in fashionable salons.

Bourget was, perhaps, a false model for Edith Wharton, though she never seems to have realized it, for this son of a provincial scholar who had become a professor at the Lycée Louis-le-Grand and taken his family to Paris, had the small-town petit-bourgeois' worship of rank, and a ferocious disdain of the "unwashed." It was a limitation that Edith Wharton was herself unfitted to perceive, for she had her own aristocratic prejudices, inherited unconsciously from parents who dreaded personal contact with the shaggy monsters who produced art. Still, one may wonder what might not have happened to her if Paris, that city of liberation for so many too-properly reared Americans, had taken her into other corners of its bosom.

One looks almost in vain among lists of Edith Wharton's French acquaintances for the true makers of thought and art in the years just before the war. It is true, she often visited the studio of the fashionable portrait painter Jacques-Émile Blanche where one might encounter on a Sunday afternoon the playwright Henri Bernstein, and even George Moore and André Gide, and, as she says, "countless other well-known people, mostly of the cosmopolitan type," but we do not get the impression that Moore or Gide became frequenters of the Wharton apartment in the rue de Varenne. As for painters—surely she could have done better than Blanche! The great Impressionist fathers whom everyone now admired were dead or dying, but a new generation had emerged in Paris or had made its way there from the provinces since the century began—Rouault, Picabia, Utrillo, Delaunay, Vlaminck, Braque, Léger, Arp, Duchamp—and from other parts of Europe as well—Brancusi, Archipenko, Chagall, Kandinsky, Klee, Nolde, Franz Marc, Modigliani. There is no indication that she ever was interested in these fellow-residents of the city of light; indeed, the very nickname the critics had just given certain of them in 1905, "les fauves"—the wild beasts— would have been enough to frighten away Mrs. Wharton's polite friends. She seems never even to have encountered the giants of her time—Matisse or Picasso.

But what about the poets, whom a lady of letters would have perhaps heard about and looked about her to find? She seems to have known one poetess, Madame de Noailles, whose *Éblouissements* she attempted to translate into English, but even she was not to be found, Mrs. Wharton admits, at Madame de Fitz-James', although she was a countess, for "poets are usually shy of salons." Is it unfair to expect her to have known such contemporary poets as Paul Valéry and Paul Claudel, who were quietly at work in the Paris of her time; after all, Claudel ended up as an ambassador. She did, on the other hand, make friends with one young poet whom she met at the Blanches'—Jean Cocteau—who seems to have come often afterwards to the rue de Varenne, though in time she saw him elegiacally as one whose "light" had been effaced by Parisian life.

As for novelists, there were, of course, Gide and Proust, both of whom she had the opportunity to meet. But apparently the contact with Gide did not lead to any mutual interest. Marcel Proust was a friend of her own closest friend, Walter Berry, yet she never even tried to meet him. The case of Proust is particularly curious because she at once recognized the greatness of *Du Côté de chez Swann* when it appeared in 1913, and sent it to James, who was deeply impressed by the new master whose "protean" art was so unlike his. It was the reports of Proust's snobbery, so much more monumental than her own, that had caused her to neglect the opportunity to meet him, Edith Wharton later explained: "To be told that the only people who really interested him were Dukes and Duchesses, and that the only place where one could hope to find him was at the Ritz, after midnight, was enough to put me off." When she found out how great he was, and could have availed herself of Berry's connection with him, "his books were already the fashion in the very circles least capable of reading or understanding him—and on the whole I am glad I did not try to pursue him there," she says, her own snobbery asserting itself once more.

Yet it would be unjust to minimize Edith Wharton's relation

to certain sectors of French literary society. Bourget, after all, was a prolific writer of fiction at the very peak of his professional career, and he was able to assist her in gaining the most direct relation to French literary life; she herself began to be published in France. It was Bourget who introduced her to Charles du Bos, and Charles du Bos translated *The House of Mirth—Chez les heureux du monde*—which ran in installments in the *Revue de Paris* in 1908. She was thus immediately known to almost every literary person in Paris; her novel was much discussed and applauded, and in the editorial offices of both the *Revue de Paris* and the rival *Revue des Deux Mondes* there was an immediate demand for translations of her stories. Bourget himself had translated her "The Muse's Tragedy" for the *Revue Hebdomadaire* in 1900, but little notice had been taken of the unknown American author then. Now she was enrolled among the regular contributors to the French journals.

In July, 1908, she wrote to W. C. Brownell at Scribners, concerning the sales of *The House of Mirth* in book form in Paris, "I hear 'Les Heureux' is selling well. 'Souls Belated' comes out on Aug. 1st in the Revue de Paris, 'The Reckoning' shortly in the Rev. des 2 Mondes, 'The Verdict' in the Correspondant, 'The Confessional' in the Gaulois of Débats (I forget which), and another in the Temps! Marcel Ballot, the best critic they have now, is to do a review of 'Les Heureux' in the Figaro—the first time he has ever reviewed a translation." She even felt bold enough, after seeing herself so much in French translation, to contribute to the *Revue des Deux Mondes* an original "nouvelle" written directly in the French language, "Les Metteurs en Scène."

"I shall never dare look you or Henry James in the eye again; but shan't I take a high manner with the people who don't know French," she wrote Brownell. James did not, as a matter of fact, overlook the story. On her next visit to England she was with him when someone asked, "Well, Mr. James, don't you think it's remarkable that Mrs. Wharton should have written a story in French for the *Revue?*" James's eye twinkled and his lip twitched—"Remarkable—most remarkable! An altogether astonishing feat." And then, turning to Mrs. Wharton, "I do congratulate you, my dear, on the way in which you've picked up every old worn-out literary phrase that's been lying about the streets of Paris for the past twenty years, and managed to pack them all into those few pages." More seriously, it appears, he added afterward, "A very creditable episode in her career. *But she must never do it again.*"

She did not, for James's criticism was, no doubt, justified. But the "creditable episode" demonstrates more than the versatility she was fast acquiring in the use of French; all that year she had been practicing to perfect her command of the language, and *Ethan Frome*, curiously, was first written in a French version at this time. One can infer Edith Wharton's near-intoxication at her sudden emergence as a literary person in a world where literary persons were esteemed, in a society threaded through and through with cultural awareness. At home in America, no one in her family or social circle had ever even spoken to her about her stories, although they were certainly aware that *Scribner's* was publishing them. But now in Paris, Mme. Wharton, *l'écrivain*, was eagerly sought after.

So her salon grew and shaped itself. Salon-building is a strenuous activity, and James, preparing to visit the new Wharton establishment for the first time in the spring of 1907, was filled with his usual mixture of wonder and alarm at the promised revelation. As he wrote Mrs. Jones,

> I brace myself all appreciatively—for the prospect of the pilgrimage to the (to me) formidable Paris that this very interesting event opens up. It would still be interesting even if as only illustrating further, to my slightly troubled and bewildered eyes, the wild, the almost incoherent freedoms and restlessnesses of wealth, and its wonderful art when it's combined with ability, of harmonizing the same with literary concentration of so positive and productive an order.

He came, all eagerly, of course, and scattering cries of comic terror to left and right of him. "I know I shall (inevitably) be involved in the movements, the general rhythmic rush of my host and hostess—the latter especially—to say nothing (alas!) of that of their automobile; and they probably have plans," he told his American friend, Thomas S. Perry. To a friend in Paris, Lee Childe, he confessed that he had misgivings, having done "a rare & rash thing (for *me*)," that is, promised "to go to spend some 10 or 12 days with some friends, the Edward Whartons (58 rue de Varenne,) during which time I shall enjoy but imperfect freedom of movement & of circulation (always the precious penalty of staying with people in complicated capitals." He left for Paris on March 7. Once there, his groans (amid laughter) were heard in letters to England and America. His first impression to Howard Sturgis was: "Our friend is a great and graceful lioness, and I have come in for many odd bones and other leavings of the Christians (if Christians they can be called) who have been offered to her maw in this extraordinary circus. In fact I have an indigestion of Chères Madames and other like phenomena."

But the motor-trip through southern France on which the Whartons took him the following week won rapturous endorsement from James. The tour lasted three weeks and a day and took them down through Touraine, through Blois, Poitiers, and Angoulême as far as Bordeaux, then into the Pyrenees, through Pau. They ranged the entire Midi and returned to Paris through Provence and the valley of the Rhône and Burgundy. He had seen much of France in an intimate, fully exploratory way which only the automobile had made possible, he realized, and upon his return his letters poured from his pen to express his enthusiasm.

"My three weeks of really seeing this large incomparable France in our friend's chariot of fire has been almost the time of my life. It's the old travelling carriage way glorified and raised to the 100th power," he wrote Sturgis. To G. W. Prothero he repeated, "I am prostrate under my so big impression (so big yet so detailed as the magical monster the touring Panhard makes— the only way to travel with ease and power now) of the grand style and inordinate interest of this incomparable France." And to his nephew Harry he wrote, "It is a matter of travelling, when done *contemplatively*, with taste and discretion, and without the

awful brutality and vulgarity *generally* practiced here, which
utterly blights the train and the station and all those crowded
contacts and scrambles—only too utterly spoils one for *them*,
forever."

Unquestionably he had vastly enjoyed himself, and so, evidently, had Edith Wharton, though Teddy had been ill for three
days at Pau. But that pause at so picturesque a spot in the Pyrenees—the land-view at Pau, Lamartine had said, was the finest
in the world, like the sea-view at Naples—had proved a bit of
luck, "permitting Mrs. W. and me to make some extremely beautiful long excursions," James rather heartlessly informed his other
nephew, William. Altogether, as he told Harry, the trip was "one
of the most interesting experiences of my life."

As he had already discovered at Lenox, motor-travel provided
him, now past middle age and often ailing, with a wonderful
recovery of the power of reaching out for new and vast impressions, a power far greater than the young and robust could have
previously enjoyed. James's period of novel-writing now lay
behind him—the sensory enlargement had come too late to affect
his fiction. It was the craftsman of point-of-view, nevertheless,
who must have appreciated such a way of being a stationary
center in an unrolling panorama. And at least one late tale directly
found its setting in Paris as seen from Mrs. Wharton's automobile.
"One soft spring evening, after we had dined somewhere out of
town—possibly at Versailles, or at a restaurant in the Bois—knowing his love for motoring at night, I proposed a circuit in the
environs, which finally brought us home by way of Saint Cloud;
and as we hung here, high above the moonlit lamplit city and the
gleaming curves of the Seine, he suddenly 'held' his setting, as the
painters say, and though I knew nothing of it till long afterward,
'The Velvet Glove' took shape that night."

The Velvet Glove was not published till 1909, but two years
earlier James had plucked for this story its culminating bloom—
"poor John Berridge's" ride through the Paris night with a literary Princess. When the story was published Edith Wharton
felt a proprietary pleasure. "Read 'The Velvet Glove'—[James]
has done no nouvelle as good in years . . . [a] delightful little story

—a motor story!" she wrote Charles Eliot Norton's daughter, Sally, and a new young English friend, A. John Hugh-Smith, whom she had met at Qu'Acre.

To Edith Wharton also, James's 1907 visit had been rewarding. On the eve of her return to America she wrote Norton, "Well— we are returning to a country where the atmosphere is thin enough to permit my overcrowded sensations to 'settle.'" The quality of her enjoyment of this tour can be exactly traced in her account in *A Motor Flight Through France*, and in her own letters. Her eye is fresh; her information, historical and technical, is no doubt straight out of her guide-books, yet delivered with liveliness and humor. She cannot have been a dull companion to the ever-curious James. Pau, for example, where she and James had enjoyed their side-trips during Teddy's indisposition, was an

> astonishing balcony hung above the great amphitheatre of southwestern France. Seen thus, with the prosaic English-provincial-looking town at one's back, and the park-like green *coteaux* intervening beyond the Gave, the austere white peaks, seemingly afloat in heaven (for their base is almost always lost in mist), have a disconcerting look of irrelevance, of disproportion, of being subjected to a kind of indignity of inspection, like caged carnivora in a zoo. And Pau, on farther acquaintance, utterly refuses to be brought into any sort of credible relation with its great southern horizon; conducts itself, architecturally and socially, like a comfortable little spa in a plain, and rises only by a great deal of hoisting on the part of the imaginative sightseer to the height of its own dapper brick castle, which it has domesticated into an empty desultory museum, and tethered down with a necklet of turf and flowers. But Pau's real purpose is to serve as the hub of a great wheel, of which the spokes, made of smooth white roads, radiate away into every fold and cleft of the country. As a centre for excursions there is no place like it in France . . .

and she describes some of the excursions they took. In other parts of France, the human monuments—architecture and sculpture— dominated their impressions, as in Poitou, from which the Whartons and James had sent a postcard to Charles Eliot Norton. As she explained to Norton in a later letter,

the impression of those tormented, sinister capitals in the choir
of Chauvigny was so strange and haunting that we felt we must
share it with one of those "che sanno"—I only wish I could
have shown you the whole church on its proud fortified cliff.
Our whole journey through the Poitou was full of wonder for
me, and as for the return by the Morvan, when I saw for the
first time Avallon, Vézelay and Auxerre, there was a sense of
suffocation from the excess of suggestion received. This France
is so rich, so varied, so packed with old états d'âme and their
visible expressions!

But more memorable still had been her pleasure, never so full
before, in Henry James's company. He had proved "the most
enthusiastic and appreciative of travellers," she told Edward L.
Burlingame, and to Norton she wrote, "Mr. James left us last
week, after giving us two months of a companionship unfailingly
delightful, wise and kind. The more one knows of him the more
one wonders and admires the mixture of wisdom and tolerance, of
sensitiveness and sympathy, that makes his heart even more interesting to contemplate than his mind"—a remark in an already
characteristic vein, with its stress on the emotional quality of the
friendship she now felt, an experience transcending her appreciation of his intellectual greatness.

She added, "He has gone to Italy for a few weeks, and after
that he says he returns to England *for life.*" When he was back in
Lamb House in August he wrote, "I have drunk & turned the glass
upside down—or rather I have placed it under my heel &
smashed it—& the Gipsy life *with* it!—forever." For James,
much as he had enjoyed his long holiday, was suffering genuinely
from the sense of arrears accumulated. "Oh that House of Mirth—
58 rue de Varenne—has left me a piper to be paid—even as by poor
Lily," he wailed to Sturgis. For even the most generous hospitality demands its returns—as he had found out before in English
society, recording the lesson in "The Death of the Lion"—and as
Edith Wharton's own Lily Bart discovered in *The House of
Mirth.* He had explained to William James, while still in Paris, "I
have never found Paris so pleasant and nutritive, and have let
myself go to the absolute insistence of my good friends (of this
house) as to my staying on and on—because it has been simply

impossible not to repay kindness with kindness—and the kindness has too plainly been to give then the value . . ." To his nephew Harry he elaborated, ". . . in this house of the kindest and charmingest hospitality I am most agreeably 'located'; but the social complication, the general compromission of hours and times and free and independent motions, is very considerable and it is the price one pays for staying with friends in a very much organized and populated town-life . . ."

And so he vowed that no seduction would lure him again from his burrow at Rye. The vow (soon to be broken) could not have been more consideredly taken. Summing up the experience of his visit, its charms and its penalties, James wrote soberly to W. E. Norris:

> Last spring, I confess, I committed an act of comprehensive disloyalty; I went abroad at the winter's end and remained till the first days of July (the first ½ of the time in Paris, roughly speaking—and on a long and very interesting, *extraordinarily interesting* motor-tour in France; the 2d. in Rome and Venice, as to take leave of *them* forever) . . . I am not this year, however, I thank my stars, to repeat the weird exploit of a "long continental absence"—such things have quite ceased to be in my real moeurs . . . Nevertheless I was glad, last spring, to have been tricked, rather, into a violent change of manners and practices—violent partly because my 10 weeks in Paris were, for me, on a basis most unprecedented: I paid a *visit* of that monstrous length to friends (I had never done so in my life before,) and in a beautiful old house in the heart of the Rive Gauche, amid old private hotels and hidden gardens (Rue de Varenne) tasted socially and associatively, so to speak, of a new Paris altogether and got a bellyful of fresh and nutritive impressions. Yet I have just declined a repetition of it inexorably, and it's more and more vivid to me that I have as much as I can tackle to lead my own life—I can't *ever* again attempt for more than the fleeting hour, to lead other people's. I *have* indeed, (I should add,) suffered infiltration of the poison of the motor—contemplatively and touringly used: that, truly, *is* a huge extension of life, of experience and consciousness. But I thank my stars that I'm too poor to have one.

The Dance upon the Aubusson Carpet

From Edith Wharton, in December, 1907, came news of her contemplated return to the Continent, and the familiar summons. With the comic exaggeration that mitigated his rejection, James responded:

> I am immensely thrilled by your news of your prospective repatriation *là-bas*. It affects me as a most majestic maneuver—displaying in fact an almost insolent *maîtrise* of life. But your silver-sounding toot that invites me to the Car—the wondrous cushioned *general* Car of your so wondrously india-rubbertyred & deep-cushioned fortune—echoes for me but too mockingly in the dim, if snug, cave of my permanent *retraite*. I have before me an absolute year of inspired immobility—I am in short on the shelf. But, ah, how from the shelf I shall watch you on the Aubusson carpet! Dear old Aubusson carpet—what a more and more complex minuet it will see danced, with the rich Oriental note of Rosa flashing through (doubtless more closely still) & binding & linking the figures!

The metaphor of a dance upon the Aubusson carpet of the rue de Varenne apartment became one of James's favorite ways of describing the social activities constantly in motion there—activities he felt too old and too busy to share. He could picture it all from a distance—the Whartons and Rosa Fitz-James at the center of the figure. He could congratulate Walter Berry, her closest intimate of many years—perhaps, sooner or later, her lover—on joining "the sarabande of—well, of our dear great sarabandists in the Rue de Varenne," but insist, "I shan't be in it—I'm an aged and infirm *batteur d'entrechats* on the retired list." Mrs. Wharton would have to take it that his coming was "really de toute impossibilité—an all insurmountable impracticable thing. The truth is I shall never, never, never cross the Channel again—but live & die more & more encroûté Briton . . . !" And, with fewer metaphors, he related his decision to Mary Cadwalader Jones, to whom he always spoke with simple frankness:

> The Whartons must be at this moment on the windy wintry sea, and she informs me that the great Cook has already embarked with the great motor! I foresee *du tirage* when she and Teddy

really take in that in spite of their tender of the princeliest
hospitality it is insurmountably impossible for me to join them
either in Paris or in Italy. In fact they must have taken it in
already for I have written it large and bold, and so must leave
it. In fact I've told them *all* the rude truth—that it's never to be
again, and I've really and absolutely crossed the absurd channel
for the last time of my life. It's fantastic, it's grotesque—if you
or they will; but nothing can exceed henceforth my aversion to
"going abroad." It's dead and done with for me and I've no use
for it whatever. The prospect brings with it a peace that passeth
understanding. So I shall be here for you whenever you come—
which is an immense further beauty of the arrangement. The
energy of our friends meanwhile—of Edith's and Teddy's
(though I think in him it *must* wane) fills me with a deep and
solemn awe. Such an arrangement of my life would be to me the
grimmest of nightmares. But my conception of felicity is more
and more to crouch behind a Chinese wall; or at least behind
a good old English russet brick one.

James had particular need for immobility and seclusion that
winter of 1907. He was still at work on the massive New York
edition of his stories and novels. As he confessed to Mrs. Wharton, he spent the Christmas season finishing a job of writing
which he hoped would have "on my scant fortunes, a far-reaching effect." This was a play, *The High Bid.* He had been working
on it since October. During January and February it went into
rehearsal, and James was frequently in London for conferences
with the director, Forbes-Robertson, finally travelling with the
company for its Edinburgh opening at the end of March. The job
once done, however, he began to long again for the outer world
—even for the deplored distractions of the rue de Varenne.

In January, 1908, he already conceded—"I *don't* despair of
coming over to you for 15 days later on (steel-plated against
mondanités)." And he confessed to longings for the mondanités,
just the same, for the diversions of the dance upon the Aubusson
carpet with Minnie and Paul Bourget, Charles du Bos, Comte
Robert d'Humières, Morton Fullerton, and Paul Hervieu all taking part along with Rosa de Fitz-James—"It's horrible even
now not to know the Minnie Paul, the "Charley," the d'Hu-

mièers & the Fullerton-d'Hervieu last words &c—but *je me contiens;* I resign myself even not to knowing if you went to the Dounnay reception. Rosa, I trust, really plays up—not, I mean, in special deeds, but in *character,* candour & fidelity. I seem to feel she does. But even this pale immersion demoralizes yours, both, all too exposed, ever & always, Henry James."

It soon appeared that he definitely might come for a short while, though he insisted, jocularly, "when I come I must come masked and muffled"—and at the same time he was thirsty for the small gossip of the group. "I ache in particular for some new formulation of the Minnie-Paul truth"—whatever that was—he confessed, and to know whether Bourget's recent success with a vaudeville play would do anything to *gentil*-ize him. He was thrilled to discover that she had been to Nohant a third time, with her new young friend Morton Fullerton. "Cette douce France," he exclaimed in his extravagant way, "the wondrous flowers of personality it throws off in its wealth! No wonder it's miraculous & presumptuous & splendid & *insupportable.*"

And so, with more and more transparent pretense of reluctance, he continued in the letters that followed to declare that the impending cordialities of the rue de Varenne circle terrified him— "It is just those admirable & amiable inquiries for 'cher James' that profoundly terrify me in advance—I feel as if I couldn't in any degree face the Social Monster—so formidably irrelevant to me now. Let me come, please, utterly incognito & wholly masked in motor-goggles—." For a motor-trip was to be included even in this brief holiday, of course! Mrs. Wharton would meet him at the end of April on French soil and sweep him through Normandy, where, he confessed, "I've everything there to see." "At Amiens the most gracious of ladies and kindest of friends and most accomplished and *remuante* of women is to meet me in her chariot of fire and take a little turn about of 2 or 3 days through 'that part' of France," he contentedly told Sturgis.

And so he came, for what was, in fact, his last visit to the rue de Varenne. It was then that they motored from Boulogne to Amiens, and Edith Wharton observed and admired the "disciplined and cultivated" Normandy landscape. They looked at the great cathedral at Amiens and compared it with the English cathedrals they had examined together on that first motor trip in England in 1906. Finally, in Paris once again, the "mondanités" renewed themselves, to James's mingled entertainment and despair, as he had predicted.

That May, Edith Wharton took James to the studio of Jacques-Émile Blanche, and the painter, who had already painted Hardy, Dégas, Debussy, Aubrey Beardsley, George Moore, and Marcel Proust, undertook to set forth the complex personality of Henry James. James enjoyed sitting for his portrait; the painter's preoccupation released a flow of monologue in the relaxed sitter, and Blanche found unforgettable James's humorous talk, particularly the "side-splitting critiques of personality which he risked in the intimacy of my atelier," as Blanche recorded later, critiques even of his own brother, William, who was greatly admired in France, and of Edith Wharton, the friend who had just brought James and Blanche together.

As always, too, when contemplating the painter's *procédé*, James was stimulated to comparisons of his own medium with that of the pictorial artist. Interrupting himself for only a moment, he would sometimes exclaim to Blanche, "Well, *my good friend*, j'ai peur d'être bien bavard, un détestable modèle, je vous donne beaucoup de mal? Merci de votre *trop admirable* complaisance de fixer avec vos brosses *incomparables* mes traits *décadents!* Ne bougeons plus!" Conscientiously, he would resume his pose, only to burst out again after several minutes, "Je vous envie! Horreur d'écrire! Écrire? Oh! combien votre art est plus direct que le nôtre!"

The portrait first produced by Blanche as James sat before him during this last Paris visit to Edith Wharton did not entirely please the self-deprecating possessor of those "*traits décadents.*" He told his young painter-cousin, Ellen Emmet, that Blanche had made him "very big and fat and uncanny and 'brainy' and awful," painting him full-face with broadly-displayed expanse of portly body, and he privately implored Mrs. Wharton to urge Blanche "not to lay such stress on the resemblance to Daniel Lambert." It was with some apprehension that he went to the exhibition of his

The Dance upon the Aubusson Carpet

portrait at the New Gallery in London that autumn, and discovered, to his delight, that an altogether different painting was on display. Instead of the full-face Blanche had done in James's presence, the painter had sent over a profile. "The 'funny thing about it'," James wrote Miss Emmet, "is that whereas I sat in almost full face, and left it on the canvas in that bloated aspect when I quitted Paris in June, it is now a spendid Profile, and with the body (and *more* of the body) in a quite different attitude; a wonderful *tour de force* . . . consisting of course of his having begun the whole thing afresh on a new canvas after I had gone, and worked out the profile, in my absence, by the aid of fond memory ('secret notes' on my silhouette, he also says, surreptitiously taken by him) and several photographs (also secretly taken at that angle while I sat there with my whole beauty, as I supposed, turned on. The result is wonderfully 'fine' (for *me*)—considering!"

Really funny, however, is the fact that Blanche had an altogether different account to give of the origin of this second portrait. According to the painter, James had no reason to be so surprised at its creation, for he had proposed many of its features himself and consciously posed for the supposedly "surreptitious" preliminary photographs. Twenty years after the events, Blanche told his own version of the portrait's history:

Il ne me dit pas, comme certain grand statuaire français: "Je veux être représenté sublime"; mais je sentis qu'il ne lui aurait pas déplu de l'être comme un Gladstone, un Prime minister, fût-ce l'Honorable Mr. Balfour, qui n'était pas encore pair du Royaume. Mon deuxième portrait, le profil dont les lettres de Henry James nous font croire qu'il fut aussi enchanté que le premier l'avait attristé, pourtant je l'exécutai à l'aide de dessins stylisés, de photographies prises chez moi selon ses désirs; pose cherchée, discutée sans fin; c'est un poète-lauréat, au regard méditatif, lointain, se détachant sur un papier de William Morris à grappes de raisins et feuilles de vignes, dorées comme dans le cabinet d'un don d'Oxford ou de Cambridge. Toute la fantasie que je me suis permise, et qui le ravit, ce fut de lui mettre un gilet chamois qu'il n'aurait plus osé porter, à son âge.

143

Je savais, tout en le contentant, lui et ses admiratrices, ne pas m'éloigner de la ressemblance, ou de la vraisemblance morale, et même l'accentuer.
[He does not tell me, "I'd like to look sublime," like certain great French statuary; but I sense that he would not be displeased to look like a Gladstone, a Prime Minister, or even the Honorable Mr. Balfour, who was not yet a peer of the Realm. In his *Letters*, he makes it clear that my second portrait of him enchanted him as much as the first dismayed him. Nevertheless, I made it with the use of stylized sketches, and photographs taken in my studio according to his express wishes: a carefully studied, endlessly discussed pose. The result is a Poet-Laureate, with a faraway, meditative look, against a William Morris wallpaper of gilded vine leaves and grape clusters—the sort you'd find in the study of an Oxford or Cambridge don. The only imaginative touch I allowed myself—and which ravished James —was a yellow chamois vest which, at his age, he would never have dared wear. I knew that to please him and his admirers, I had to stick to appearances, or at least to moral appearances, and even to accentuate them.]

James and his "admiratrices"—particularly Edith Wharton— were contented with the results, however achieved. Mrs. Wharton observed that Blanche's profile portrait is "the only one that renders him as he really was."

James was to resist further attempts to pry him out of England —only the illness of his brother William would later require of him a melancholy departure for Germany, then for America. As he told his other correspondents and Mrs. Wharton repeatedly, he was through with *douce* France. Mrs. Wharton, whom he called "our great and glorious pendulum" for her easy swings from country to country, from continent to continent, continued to demonstrate a mode of being that astonished him for its utter unlikeness to his own craving for peace, immobility, seclusion.

The end of 1908 came, and he was able to refuse her new invitation to come to Paris. ". . . though she has kindly asked me to come to them again this month or spring I have had to plead simply abject terror—terror of the pendulous life. I am a *stopped* clock—and I strike (that is I caper about) only when very much

144

wound up," he wrote Mrs. Henry White. "I've had to decline a visit to the rue de Varenne and to funk another go at the grande vie. The grande vie has, yes, too sensibly ceased to be my affair," he reported to Walter Berry early in 1909. Sally Norton came to Europe in February and he congratulated her on her opportunities for studying "the wonderful, the unique E. W. in her Paris setting," an opportunity now closed to him—"for I am aged and broken and can't lead the life. The way she does is prodigious." To Sally's sister Elizabeth Norton he remarked that he was glad that this daughter of Cambridge would bathe for a moment in the tropic waters of Mrs. Wharton's salon: "I am glad . . . that she has floated into those deep and alien waters of the rue de Varenne (in which I have gently splashed, myself, a little) because the adventure will have been worth the trouble to her."

1910 was less a year for such visits than any. James was himself ill for months; then his brother's illness and death gravely preoccupied him. He lingered on in America for the summer of 1911 and did not return to England until September. Mrs. Wharton's suggestion that he come to Paris at long last only again elicited from him the familiar protest: "London is better for me, during these months, than any other spot on earth, or of pavement; & even here I seem to find I can work—& n'ai pas maintenant d'autre idée." Nor would he come the following summer of 1912, either. "It is written, dearest Edith, (& I myself have written it twenty times, I think) that I shall never (D.V.) again leave the shores of this island . . . the Continent is an utterly & finally closed chapter: that book, sharply & inevitably padlocked, stands now on the highest thinkable shelf, far out of my reach."

6

The Eagle and the Worm

WHEN PERCY LUBBOCK PUBLISHED the two-volume edition of the letters of Henry James in 1920, Edith Wharton reviewed it in the *Quarterly Review* with a curious hint to the reader about the basis of selection:

> One of the things impossible to preserve because so impossible to explain, with whatever fullness of footnotes, was the quality of fun—often of sheer abstract "fooling"—that was the delicious surprise of Mr. Lubbock's task . . . From many of his letters to his most intimate group it has been necessary to excise long passages of chaff, and recurring references to old heaped-up pyramidal jokes, huge cairns of hoarded nonsense—Henry James's memory for a joke was prodigious; when he got hold of a good one he not only preserved it piously, but raised upon it an intricate super-structure of kindred nonsense, into which every addition offered by a friend was skillfully incorporated. Into his nonsense world, as fourth-dimensional as that of the Looking Glass or the Land where the Jumblies live, the reader could hardly have groped his way without a preparatory course in each correspondent's private history and casual experience.

What she did not reveal was that of all the "pyramidal jokes" ruthlessly excised from Lubbock's edition, none was piled as huge as the family joke about herself.

In intimate letters unpublished until now James had regaled

their social circle of mutual friends with wit-play about Edith
Wharton's social life, her automobile, her life in general, so over-
loaded with accoutrements, so perpetually, nevertheless, in a constant dance of change. For each new aspect of her existence, his
comic imagination constantly generated new images, each more
extravagant than the last. Although he steadfastly refused to visit
her in Paris after 1908, or travel with her on the Continent, again
and again she was at his door, and he did not fail to enjoy her
company—and to shudder at her "devastation."

All generosity and golden brilliance, she would invite him to
leave his dull study and to take a spin with her through the
country, to pay some delightful week-end calls, to visit here, dine
there. Often as not, he accepted, amid the moans and laughter
that would echo in his letters. As her visits to him became more
frequent, he built up a prolonged chain of wonderful comic variations upon the theme of her restless energy and her shattering
intrusion. One could make an amusing list of the epithets he
created for "the most *remuante* of women"—the Princess Lointaine, the whirling princess, the great and glorious pendulum, the
gyrator, the devil-dancer, the golden eagle, the Fire Bird, the
Shining One, the angel of desolation or of devastation, the his-
toric ravager (like Attila)—each more hilarious than the last.
Should such a sequence be dismissed as a "cairn of hoarded nonsense"—as Mrs. Wharton seems to imply? Even were it merely
this, non-initiates might have mastered the comic code more
easily than she allowed. Lubbock's "delicious surprise" might
have been experienced by later readers if he had so chosen.

The truth is that Lubbock and Edith Wharton, old friends of
each other as well as of James, did not want to share these jests
with outsiders because they were not quite so nonsensical, so
innocent, after all. James, in the height of comic appreciation,
held a serious judgment in mind. And he did not always jest. He
might speak in a letter to her own dearest friend, Walter Berry,
about the social "sarabande" at the Wharton apartment in Paris,
but in sober plainness also tell Mary Cadwalader Jones that life in
the rue de Varenne seemed to him "the grimmest of nightmares."
Mrs. Wharton's visits to him in England were, in plain fact, often

sources of scandalized astonishment to the patient, saving, intensely concentrated spirit inhabiting the urbane James known to the world. He was amused, charmed beyond measure, but the jests he made were often as not half-earnest, and it is possible to reduce the hyperbolic extravagance, the poetic abandon of his mockery, to a sober judgment.

Beneath the jest there may have been another serious note. There was something not truly sober and normal, something hectic and desperate about Edith Wharton's life from about 1907 on. That year her husband suffered what can only be described as a severe mental breakdown. As we have seen, Teddy Wharton had previously experienced a similar attack of "neurasthenia" as the doctors called it, which lasted through the summer and fall of 1903. Now, in the winter of 1907-1908, he had a painful attack of gout which was soon complicated by symptoms that recalled his previous breakdown. By March, he was somewhat improved and off to Hot Springs, chiefly for the lingering gout, while Mrs. Wharton remained in Paris. But gout was only the beginning of his trouble. At The Mount, in June, he appeared in deceptively good physical health, but suddenly collapsed again, and in September was seriously ill. All through that winter he suffered what Mrs. Wharton described to W. C. Brownell, as "a real *crise* of neurasthenia such as he had five years ago at Lenox." His condition grew steadily worse, with deceptive remissions, as months and then years began to pass.

There seems no question that Edith Wharton was herself a sufferer from these events. Her relation with her husband, never, one gathers, a deep and passionate one, became hardly bearable under the strain of his invalidism that exhibited symptoms not so much pitiable as exasperating to the inexpert eye. Her letters to her publisher show how seriously she found her work as a writer impeded by his condition. She frankly complained to John Hugh-Smith, the young English friend who would be a mainstay of her later years, "I'm an eclipsed planet," when she was compelled to accompany her husband during "weary weeks" of treatment in southern France. It seems plain that her chief desire from then on was to get away from him if she could—to delegate his care to capable hands and continue living as before. "Living as before" was, however, bound to be a somewhat unnatural pleasure, snatched rather hysterically between intervals of misery when her husband returned from one "cure" or another. Her visits to England, her motor trips with James or other friends, her restless gyrations which were such a source of amusement to them all may well have been animated by the frantic energy of escape. Heretofore she had been able to control the phenomena of her life with an imperial hand, but now she was encountering a difficulty not so easily subdued. She did subdue it, finally, in the most drastic way, by divorcing Wharton in May, 1913.

The year 1908 was the time of greatest crisis in Edith Wharton's life for a reason still more hidden from the eyes of all but the closest witnesses to her affairs. In that year, when she was forty-six, her love for Walter Berry became completely clear to her and avowed to him. He had been the most closely cherished of her friends for many years. He had helped her with nearly all of her books from the beginning, and even at the time of their first meeting, before she was married, she had felt a unique accord between them. There is no reason to believe, however, that she had previously been able to admit to herself the intensity of feeling that now seems to have surged to the surface in this woman of middle years. It may be that her husband's disintegration made her finally realize how little love for Edward Wharton she was able to command. In any case, in a notebook diary, some extracts of which have been published, she began to make entries in German (possibly because it was the language least likely to be understood by other members of her French- and English-speaking household) which describe the anguish of longing, ecstasy and desolation which wracked her during these months.

In January, she set down the phrase "unvergessliche Stunden" —"unforgettable hours"—in the notebook. Then weeks followed during which, while Teddy's condition simmered and slightly improved, the social dance of Edith Wharton's Paris life continued to weave its familiar patterns; Henry Adams came to tea, the Bourgets to lunch, Jacques-Émile Blanche and the playwright Henri Bernstein were entertained. On February 21, she set down one of a series of confessional passages that read like excerpts from letters addressed to the man who now dominated her thoughts—though whether these declarations were ever actually sent to him it is impossible to tell. In this "letter" she recalls an evening they had lately passed together. In a tranquillity almost connubial they had sat together in the rue de Varenne apartment, now emptied of all other guests, and he had read to her from an article on George Meredith by a French critic she admired, André Chevrillon. She had rejoiced in the acute discrimination of Berry's comments, which interspersed the reading; he had seemed to catch up so much she herself had overlooked in the article; she had rejoiced in the perfect meeting of minds which the moment crystallized. And suddenly she surrendered to a dream of a life in which such happy evenings were a daily habit; in this hour she called him in her mind not merely "lover" but "husband."

Did she voice any part of these longings? Her diary does not say, but somehow, it seems, Berry responded with word or gesture that shattered her dream. Perhaps his attitude suggested that mistress rather than wife was his conception of her future with him. Or perhaps, bored, he had simply got up and left her with no offering at all, no intenser agreement than that of literary talk. Whatever had happened, she recorded only that she was sunk in bitter disappointment and that she was more than ever in love with this man. And the next day brought further chagrin. She had been looking forward to a drive with Berry to Montfort L'Amaury, the beautiful little village near Versailles where they might be alone again in each other's company. All the previous week she had dreamed, she tells him (or imagines herself telling him), of spending a whole day with a companion to whom everything at last could be said, of grasping for one day a woman's perfect hapipness, she who had never known it. Berry sent word that he could not come.

Some weeks later, however, there were to be moments of the bliss she longed for. One evening in March, while she was at the theater, Berry came in and took a seat beside her when she had not expected him—and she was at once convinced of an unexpressed oneness with the elusive man silently close in the shadowed box. There had been another such mood the previous Sunday when the two had driven back from St. Cloud in the snow and the thick curtain of falling flakes had shut them away from the outer world. There, in the seclusion of the car, she had felt at last that all that might once have baffled and irritated him in her personality and her life was now understood and forgiven, and that he had opened at last his own guarded mind and heart. And she told him, in her diary, that she was content. She asked no more than this fugitive harmony which vibrated between them at such moments.

All this while, of course, Edward Wharton had been dimly, but nonetheless positively, present in the rue de Varenne, and occasions of secluded intimacy such as those just described must have been rare accidents. But now, no longer showing any symptoms of neurasthenia, although still suffering from gout, he left for America to try a "cure" at Hot Springs, Virginia. "The doctors," she explained in a letter to Edward L. Burlingame, had "advised him to do so, rather than wait till it was warm enough to go to Aix." She was alone. Under the date of April 18th Edith Wharton recorded in her diary simply that she and Berry were together and that it was the "sweetest hour" she had ever enjoyed.

During the following week her journal addressed itself to Walter Berry in a hymn of rapture and gratitude. Like the most romantic of young lovers she marvels that they are never apart in mind, even when separated for an hour or a day. She rejoiced, it is plain, in the surrender of her own proud reserve, her fierce privacy and her inherited and self-imposed habit of restraint. Even her well-trained mind, so long content with purely intellectual occupations, was carried from its old moorings of daily reading and writing. She could concentrate on neither. She was surrendered to love's obsession. Correctly enough she was moved to compare her exaltation to the ecstasy, the leaving of the self a religious worshiper can feel.

It was just at this climax of self-knowledge and liberation for Edith Wharton that Henry James, after holding out all winter, as he told Gaillard Lapsley, arrived in Paris "to beguile the interval" of her husband's absence. He was to find that little beguiling on his part was needed, for there is no doubt that the situation was soon to clear to so acute an observer and so close a friend as James. He stayed the ten days he had promised, and left, shortly before Edith Wharton set sail for America on the 23 of May. Teddy, who had reported cheerfully that Hot Springs had "given him new feet and new hands," was waiting for her.

And Edith Wharton went to him in a state, judging from her journal, of near hysteria. She records the unbearable oppression of her unwilling journey across the ocean away from the man she loved toward the man she nearly loathed. As she rode out of New York on the train with the oblivious Teddy she buried her face in Locke's *Heredity and Variation*, but lifted it once to read out a passage to him and to receive the expected smirk at her interest in "such things." It seemed now that she could not draw another breath as Wharton's matrimonial captive.

How tragically she must have contemplated her situation! Not only could she foresee no change in her relationship with her husband, but she knew that Walter Berry had accepted a post as Judge of the International Tribunal at Cairo, Egypt, a position that would keep him out of Europe, save for brief holiday returns, for several years. In the diary in which she had already addressed him so often, she "spoke" to Berry again of her despair. She tried to believe that she was willing to end all connection between them once and for all rather than watch the slow weakening of the thread that must stretch over such time and space. To wait for a reunion unpromised, a date never to be named—this she recognized would be worse than surrendering at once all hope of a new life to replace the old. And yet, like any lovesick girl, this mature —past mature—lady of the great world could only wail for her lover and declare herself unable to give him up.

It is difficult to say for what she still hoped when Berry returned from Egypt three years later. By that time she already contemplated a permanent separation from Edward Wharton and in 1913 she made herself absolutely free by divorcing him. There seems no doubt that she was willing to accept whatever Berry was willing to offer her, though it was still to be short of marriage, in after years. She made no secret to her friends of her devotion to this friend who, she often declared, was an unfailing counselor and intellectual guide until his death in 1927. To him she also owed, as only a few knew, the belated emotional awakening that surged in her still as he departed from France late in 1908.

She was to see Berry before he left for Egypt, however, for in October she was on her way back to Europe, and she made plans to visit England for an extended stay, alone. Teddy, once more ill, was undergoing another "rest-cure" at home. James was quite aware, now, as he waited for her, that her efforts at self-entertainment were hardly animated by a normal gaiety. He must have understood that the dance of her restless being was almost, indeed, as "wild," as he jokingly called it. A note of such diagnosis can be perceived, beneath the bantering descriptions of her comings and goings with which he regaled her own intimate friends as well as his.

Her zest amazed him, as always. "Her arrangement of life is to me one of the prodigies of time. I don't 'keep pace' . . . when it comes to creatures with rue de la Paix wings," he told Lapsley. On the same day, however, he wrote a letter to Mrs. Wharton which sounded a different string. Obviously replying to a somber letter from her describing her current difficulties with Wharton, he sent her the following philosophic advice:

I am deeply distressed at the situation you describe and as to which my power to suggest or enlighten now quite miserably fails me. I move in darkness; I rack my brain; I gnash my teeth; I don't pretend to understand or to imagine . . . Only sit tight yourself *and go through the movements of life.* That keeps up our connection with life—I mean of the immediate and apparent life; behind which, all the while, the deeper and darker and unapparent, in which things *really* happen to us, learns, under that hygiene, to stay in its place. Let it get out of its place and it swamps the scene; besides which its place, God knows, is enough for it! Live it all through, every inch of it—out of it

153

something valuable will come—but live it ever so quietly; and
—*je maintiens mon dire*—waitingly! . . . what I am really
hoping is that you'll be on your voyage when this reaches the
Mount. If you're not you'll be so very soon afterwards, won't
you?—and you'll come down and see me here and we'll talk *à
perte de vue*, and there will be something in that for both of us
. . . Believe meanwhile and always in the aboundingly tender
friendship—the understanding, the participation, the *princely*
(though I say it who shouldn't) hospitality of spirit and soul of
yours more than ever, Henry James.

This emotional passage still mystifies most readers of the Lubbock "Letters" where it is printed without explanation of any
kind. Knowing what we now do of Mrs. Wharton's problems
just then, it is not hard to imagine the news that was contained in
her original letter. She was at The Mount with her husband.
Only a few days earlier she had written Charles Scribner that she
was glad to have withdrawn her novel, *The Custom of the Country*, from *Scribner's Magazine*, "for I have suffered so much from
insomnia for the last two months that my work has been para-
lyzed by it." The situation was one she could not cope with,
except by flight. And James advised, "go through the movements
of life," keep on living and doing in your normal fashion; keep
the dark subwaters of life deep in their underground channel lest
they overflow and ruin you. Live and wait. Modern psychiatry
would probably not approve of this prescription, but it was in the
most immediate sense practical. It was the advice she followed,
and that he continued to prescribe throughout the course of her
troubles.

One cannot help thinking of how much it reveals about James's
own attitudes towards what he called the "deeper psychology."
André Gide complained that James's characters "are only
winged busts, all the weight of flesh is absent, all the shaggy,
tangled undergrowth; all the wild darkness . . . I hardly ever feel
behind his figures, which are lighted from every side, that cone
of unexplicable shadow where the suffering soul lies hidden, but
his characters have no need of shelter—they have no souls."
Many will disagree, feeling that the cone of shadow is really

present in James's fiction, but it is present by only the most subtle indications, as it is, indeed, in ordinary experience. The surface of his stories maintains the propriety of conscious thought, of the "immediate and apparent life," uninvaded by the "deeper and darker and unapparent."

In this letter, also, James offered something more precious even than his wisdom, justifying what Edith Wharton was always saying about the superior greatness of his heart. Despite all the mockery and impatience she could arouse in him, he could promise her "the aboundingly tender friendship—the understanding, the participation, the princely . . . hospitality of spirit and of soul" of Henry James. Here was a glimpse of the depths of his feeling for Edith Wharton. Yet on the surface was the old laughter, and actual trepidation at her advent: Sturgis was warned that on the fifth of November she would arrive,

> (these whirling Princesses!) and I go on there—to Dover on that a.m. or afternoon to attend her (these obedient admirers!) She rather likes, I gather, the idea of spending some little time in England—and I have asked her to come down *here* for a jabbering *week* (!)—*j'ai été capable de ça!* But I am sure she would also be glad to come to you for a little—no art that I could employ would avail to dissimulate to you, on my part, that conviction. Do be kind to her then (I needn't say it for you'll be *l'ange de l'hospitalité* full feathered and with an aureole that it would take all the gilt paper in the kingdom to represent or imitate.) If you *can* entertain her for a little I *might* be able to look in then— . . . What an incoherent life! It makes me crouch more dodderingly than ever over my hearth-stone.

And to Mrs. Jones he observed, "I shall be delighted to see her—and shall wonder more than ever again at such organized incoherency of life which would break *me* up in three months. However, one man's bale is one woman's bliss—"

Dear reliable old Howard, "l'ange de l'hospitalité," did entertain the Princess in appropriate fashion after her brief stay at James's. And James approved it all—from a distance.

Delightful your letter with its wondrous glittering *reflex* of the most brilliant of women and of all the lights she sheds—in the form of the myriad far-scattered paillettes—as well as in others. Truly you too are caught up, and the chariot of fire, I gather, causes you to flash, almost consort-like, at her shining side! . . . It all sounds glorious and godlike—almost too insolently Olympian, and I rejoice in it save for squirming a little over the sight of what the mighty machinery of Qu'Acre is able to do for our friend—after the lean yield of my tenth of an acre and no cow!

She was "going through the movements of life" with undiminished elasticity, it would seem. He wrote her: "I gather from Howard that you are making as many *gestes* as possible, for which I heartily applaud & commend you, and only wish I could make more of them with you. Keep at them, keep at them, and when you've made a great, *great* many—well you'll see! So I rejoice that circumstances make for a multiplication of them."

Her stay in England lasted a month and a half, during which her "*gestes*" were as free and numerous as possible. On the 21st of December, James informed Henrietta Reubell: "Mrs. Wharton has just been for a couple of months in England, leading an immensely répandue life and having a great success—she left this very house, in her motor, only this a.m.—without any of her keys, the malheureuse, on her general way to Paris . . ."

To Walter Berry, already in Egypt, he gave a fuller account in which the old astonishment is tempered by a pity for her private circumstance:

. . . I should like to tell you *par le menu* the entire sequel to that poignant hour of our loss of you, mine and the Lady of Lenox's, as it would indeed be much a matter of the *menu* with the part every sort of furious feasting has played in it. But the theme is too large, and the whole thing defies, by volume and quantity, my lame epistolary muse. She has been having, indeed, after a wild, extravagant, desperate, detached fashion, the Time of her Life. London, and even the Suburbs have opened their arms to her; she has seen everyone and is even now the occasion of some great house party away off in the midlands (at Stanway—the Elchos!) whence she comes back to more triumph and will, I imagine, be kept up here, in one way or another, till the New Year & the arrival of Teddy. She has really been much amused and pleased, and, with her frame of steel, it has been remarkably good for her. But what a frame of steel, and what a way of arranging one's life. I have participated by breathless dashes and feverish fits, but then had to rush back to recuperate or meditate. Here I hope, between honest toil, *la promenade et la lecture*, to stick fast for the next two or three months. But I envy you great livers . . .

Some time after she left he summarized to Gaillard Lapsley, who had departed for America,

I have been motionless in this place [Lamb House] ever since I came back to it finally or after episodes on our wondrous friend E. W.'s eventual (at the end of five or six weeks) departure for Paris—the prodigious devil's dance of which you saw but the first pass or two. I daresay no at all adequate reflection or reverberation has reached you—or very well could from any near witness; I having been so ignobly dumb. But it's too late now to pick up *those* smashed pieces before you & I meet again (heaven speed the day;) when you shall have them *all* set out in a row. Suffice it that she had a social "time" worthy of her general eagle-pounce or eagle flights, of her devouring or desolating, ravaging, burning or destroying energy. Lady——, awfully good and helpful to her, Howard Sturgis, Chauffeur Cook and I bear the brunt, and the angel of desolation was the mildest name we knew her by.

One of her "gestes" was a new friendship, seized with ready impetuosity one November afternoon at Qu'Acre, during this visit, and retained for life. Percy Lubbock remembered that it was he, who had so far lounged in his corner nearly unnoticed by the great Edith, who had asked Howard to invite A. John Hugh-Smith, a Cambridge classmate of his own, to meet her at Qu'-Acre. As Lubbock watched, the spark was struck, and Edith Wharton, thoughts of the distant and despised Teddy and the distant and adored Berry equally behind her, threw back her head in delighted laughter at her discovery. "That," recalled Lubbock,

157

"was the sort of young Englishman she needed, a most unusual sort, for the ideas that thronged in his brain weren't imprisoned there, they streamed out in lively order; and he knew so many books, and so much life as well, that in a very short time they were talking at each other as though they couldn't stop." There appears to have been no need for them to stop, for Smith was as captivated as she; "not only was her conversation the most entertaining I had ever heard, but she seemed to stimulate those who were with her," he recalled.

Apparently she took him off with her from Qu'Acre that very day, for company while she made other visits. "I saw much of her during the next weeks at Clivedon, in London, and at Stanway; the more I saw of her, the more there was to learn and to enjoy—it seemed endless," Smith declared. A few weeks later, she wrote him from the south of France, "I'm afraid I always go with outstretched hands towards any opportunity for a free and frank exchange of ideas, and am too much given to omitting the preliminary forms where I find a fundamental likeness of mind! It was a great pleasure to wander over the cosmos with you in that easy fashion, and if you liked it too, for whom are you concerned, and why do you plan better things for our next meeting?" They would, indeed, meet many times again, and correspond with affectionate frequency for years to come. Meanwhile, her abduction of Smith amused James greatly, and he demanded an account of it all on her next trip to Lamb House.

She had need of amusement, he would have conceded, for now she was returning, in January, 1909, to Paris, where her husband was joining her after his supposedly recuperative delay in America. He was still ill. She wrote Sally Norton a gloomy description. Teddy, on landing, had had an immediate attack of gout, and was distressing in his distress—"He's the worst 'patient' I've ever seen," Edith Wharton remarked. Then he came down with grippe, headaches, and neurasthenia once more, "a real 'crise' of neurasthenia such as he had five years ago at Lenox, also after grippe—fatigue, depression, inability to decide any question, however trifling, morbid preoccupation with his own symptoms." Change of scene was prescribed, and, rather reluctant, he was driven down to Avignon, where she was soon to join him. "It is very wearing and I am utterly tired," she told Miss Norton. She disliked the prospect of going to the Riviera with her ailing husband even more than she expressed to this old American friend of theirs. To A. John Hugh-Smith she frankly complained before setting out from Paris, "I'm so utterly sick of the Riviera that my heart fails me at the thought."

The lustre of the "Shining One" was dim indeed at this moment. To Smith, in this same letter, she confessed: "I wish I were the unclouded luminary you imagine, describing serene curves through the seventh heaven; but I am, as you see, a shabby, close-to-the-ground, and frequently eclipsed planet, and just now I'm exceptionally dim, and need to have the 'optick glass' of sympathy fixed on me to be at all visible." In March, the Whartons were back in Paris, Teddy hardly improved. Again she wrote Smith, "I have had weary weeks to live through since I wrote you." They had gone, as scheduled, to the Midi, "but it did not do my husband any good, and he was so anxious to come back that I yielded. He's now under treatment by a specialist with a course of massage, electricity, etc . . ."

James himself had been ill meanwhile. He had had "a bad and worried and depressed and inconvenient winter" followed by a "tolerably ominous cardiac crisis," which had manifestly made it impossible for him to consider another Paris visit. "The grande vie has, yet, too sensibly ceased to be my affair," he remarked to Berry in his letter to Cairo, adding, "I am afraid it's rather to be poor Teddy's though I do suspect in him resources of Ptolemaic duration." But he continued, despite his own illness and worry that winter, to follow Edith Wharton's affairs with the "hospitality of spirit and soul" he had promised, and he wrote once more with finely perceptive sympathy, and an offer of the same advice as before—"sit loose and live in the day":

So much mainly to explain to you my singularly unsympathetic silence during a period of anxiety and discomfort on your own part which I all the while feared to be not small—but which I now see, with all affectionate participation, to have been extreme . . . Sit loose and live in the day—don't borrow trouble, and remember that nothing happens as we forecast it—but always with interesting, and, as it were, refreshing differences. "Tired" you must be, even you, indeed; and Paris, as I look at it from here, figures to me a great blur of intense white light in which, attached to the hub of a revolving wheel, you are all whirled round by the finest silver strings. "Mazes of heat and sound" envelop you to my wincing vision—given over as I am to a craven worship (*only* henceforth) of peace at any price. This dusty village, all deadening grey and damp (muffling) green, meets more and more my supreme appreciation of stillness—and here, in June, you must come and find me—to let me emphasize that—appreciation!—still further. You'll rest with me here then, but don't wait for that to rest somehow—somewhere *en attendant.* I am afraid you won't rest much in a retreat on the Place de la Concorde. However, so does a poor old croaking barnyard fowl advise a golden eagle!

To Gaillard Lapsley, a week or so later, he wrote, a little more coolly:

I fear she has had a baddish anxious, overclouded winter in Paris. Teddy is worryingly, nervously, a bit ominously ill—and the best "advice" now is that he may be cerebrally compromised. This is the first "cross" I really imagine, that she has had to bear, and I seem to make out that it comes terribly hard. He has gone back to America for the time, but they have *let* the Mount this summer (for a million or two!) or are to drift or "board," or whatever, according to his condition. She intends, I believe, to be in England next month, and though we are all bracing ourselves a bit I shall be truly delighted to see her. She begged me to Paris, of course, very kindly, during the winter, but my going was wholly out of the question for me. All of which—in its essentials—you of course may more or less know —but I have felt her a fond reference, and subject of interest, with you, that I couldn't on the chance neglect . . . I go up to London 4 or 5 days hence to put in such time as I can in a quick way. Breaking the spell of this extremity of sequestration —when the angel of desolation is at work on another planet— seems, after an enormous quantity of it during the last 4 or 5 years, rather sharply indicated for me.

And so she planned to come to them all in England again, her husband once more "packed off"—if that is not too harsh an expression—to America. Possibly his family had begun to criticize her management of him. She wrote Sally Norton: "I get poor reports from America where Teddy has been (naturally!) *completely reassured* about business, but seems no better in consequence. The family seem annoyed with me for having sent him (they behaved exactly in the same way when he was ill before); and he writes he will probably return in two weeks ... My own plans are—that I have none. I live from hand to mouth ..."

But she knew where refreshment was to be found and in June she was again in England to visit Lamb House and Qu'Acre. At the latter, she stayed, comfortably resting and writing, "reviving slowly in this green refuge," as she told Smith. She also did a little of the usual touring with "le cher Maître" who seemed "unable to tear himself away from the charms of the new motor." James, however, wrote in the old vein, to Lapsley:

> The Angel of Devastation has become a mere agitating memory, but nothing could have exceeded the commotion and exhaustion produced by her actual prolonged stay. Devoted as I am to her I feel even as one of those infants of literary allusion whom their mothers trust to terror by pronouncing the name of the great historic ravagers of their country, Bonaparte, or Attila, or Tamurlane. She is actually in Paris, waiting from day to day to hear from the absent Teddy ...

But tedious waiting was not her way, after all. Walter Berry was back for a holiday, and James, declining, of course, to join them, remarked to him, "besides, your cup is full-held and by so fair and firm a hand; why should I pretend to make it overflow!" Then Berry left, and, at no loss for means of distraction even for this blow, she took a trip to Germany in the late autumn. "You are my ideal of a dashing woman, and you never dashed more felicitously or fruitfully, for my imagination, than when you dashed at that particular psychological moment, off to dear old rococo Munich," observed James.

And then Teddy was back. His behavior was becoming increasingly alarming, though to the casual eye he was in better health than ever. It is questionable whether even Mrs. Wharton realized at the time how sick he actually was. Psychotic behavior often appears to be simply "bad" behavior, to pardon which one must have either professional discernment—or extraordinary sympathy. And Teddy, engaged in various irrationalities (business and money were particularly on his mind, as hinted in the May letter Edith Wharton wrote to Sally Norton), probably found little of the latter in his wife. It may be chiefly upon her report, at any rate, that James went, when he wrote Lapsley on New Year's Day, 1910:

> I wish I had better impressions of this particular phase of the Angel of Paris; but those I have are bad—in respect, I mean, to the influence of the unspeakable Teddy on the state of affairs. I seem to divine that that influence has been sinister, even very sinister, in a financial way—inasmuch as having lately come from N.Y. after running some sort of speculative rig there, he has been packed off back on some ground that I don't imagine a ground of health at all, but one of urgent practical connections—or in other words I fear that something has *happened* and that he has pretty grossly misbehaved—and not at all neurasthenically, but with a great deal of fatuous and misapplied energy of ambition. But please know nothing from me as I only gather that poor Edith has been through some rather dreadful weeks. Kindly, however, allude to nothing but what you may hear from myself. I have only heard very partially—but I greatly pity her. I can't help regretting however that an *intellectuelle*—and an Angel—should require such a big pecuniary basis. How much more consistently intellectual and angelic are *we* in our unmoneyed state.

It is impossible to tell from this just what mess—obviously involving money—Edward Wharton had got into. Even James only "divines" and "fears" whatever may have been the miserable facts. What is worthy of note in this letter is its detachment, though he greatly pities her. And the last sentence, whatever the nature of the prompting occasion, is still indeed the sober summary of his criticism of her way of life. Somehow, James felt, a votary of the Gods of Thought should be less concerned about money than was Mrs. Wharton.

But a serious money loss might have endangered her ability to move with the celerity and splendor that James deplored but she found necessary. The following year, 1911, saw the beginnings of her break with her old publisher, Charles Scribner's Sons, over issues fundamentally connected with her desire to earn greater returns on her books. In 1912, she gave *The Reef* to D. Appleton & Co., who offered her an advance of $15,000, three times what she had previously received on her novels. It was at this time, or possibly in 1910, that the Wharton house in New York was sold. Economy may have been one of the causes, though Anna Bahlmann, Mrs. Wharton's companion and secretary, wrote W. C. Brownell: "With regard to the sale of the New York house, it does not mean at all that the 'last links with America are cut,' but simply that the doctors have advised both Mr. and Mrs. Wharton to avoid the New York winters. Mrs. Wharton feels that she is a different being since she got away from the intense cold and violent changes of temperature."

"You will be sorry to hear," Miss Bahlmann continued, "that Mr. Wharton has had another bad nervous breakdown, and Mrs. Wharton is now awaiting the advice of his doctors, who are to decide whether she is to join him in America (where he has been for the last month), or whether he is to return here." Apparently it was decided that Wharton would come to Paris, where arrangements had been made for taking a new apartment in the rue de Varenne—number 53—across the street from their old address. They moved into it with little joy, it can be imagined. "Teddy's condition is very serious, but he is delighted with the apartment, and glad to be here (if gladness can be associated with such a state!), and the doctors think he will improve gradually," she wrote John Hugh-Smith. "Meanwhile he cannot be left alone a moment, and my days are terrible. He is quite 'lucid' but has acute melancholia. I don't know a much worse combination."

James himself was under the shadow of illness for all of 1910, an illness "mainly nervous," as Lubbock puts it, but one which deprived him almost completely of his precious powers of work and caused immense depression of mind. He could participate but

distantly in Mrs. Wharton's own troubles. The paying and receiving of extended visits was out of the question. Yet during this
period of his own darkness, he maintained his sympathy with his
harassed friend. She was full of delicate attentions during his
illness, and acknowledging some of these early in February, he
wrote the words she quoted with such pride years afterwards in
her memoirs: ". . . the great thing is that we always tumble together—more and more never apart; and for that happy exercise
and sweet coincidence of agility we must trust ourselves and each
other to the end of time."

He had begun to see the entire design of things for her and to
accept the inevitability of certain features—particularly her
permanent and complete residence abroad. To Sally Norton he
wrote, "Your allusion to dear E. W. opens up a big subject but one
that has cleared up for me greatly this last winter. I now realize
that she has adopted the only habitat (and with its consequences
—many very interesting ones) that is really possible for her.
That she must have a winter home, that New York is without
form . . . and that the Mount will eventually go. Teddy is cerebrally and nervously bad (I fear very bad) again; and a catastro-
phe is sooner or later due there."

It was in the summer of 1910 that James joined his beloved elder
brother and his sister-in-law in Germany. He was hardly well
himself yet, but William James was truly and mortally ill. He
decided to go back to America with them, and wrote Edith
Wharton from Germany a letter to which he added the following pathetic remembrance of her difficulties: "And now I simply
fear to challenge you on your own complications. I can *bear*
tragedies so little. *Tout se rattache* so *à the* thing—the central
depression. And yet I want so to know—and I think of you with
infinite tenderness, participation—and such a large and helpless
devotion. Well, we must hold on tight and we shall come out
again face to face—wiser than ever before (if that's any advantage!)" James himself began to mend as the gloomy summer
wore on, but William was sinking, and then news came to the
two brothers that their younger brother, Robertson, had suddenly died in America.

In August they returned together, after a stop in England where Edith Wharton met James for a brief hopeful moment, but at the end of the month William died at Chocorua, New Hampshire, leaving Henry James to that unutterable grief which he yet so beautifully expressed in letters to many friends. To Edith Wharton, he wrote of his "sense of what he had still to give, of his beautiful genius and noble intellect at their very climax, never having been anything but intense, and in fact having been intenser than ever all these last months. However, my relation to him and my affection for him, and the different aspect his extinction has given for me to my life, are all unutterable matters." He intended to stay on in America for a while, now that he was back again in so grimly unexpected a fashion.

Edward Wharton, meanwhile, had come around again to that illusory recovery which deceives the observer of such illnesses as the patient gradually takes the descending spiral path. "Dr. K. finds Teddy *much* better since his rest-cure of last summer and so does William Wharton, who has been staying with us, and helping me arrange for the trip," Mrs. Wharton wrote Sally Norton in October. She had been with her husband for two months in America, and she was able to declare that she herself saw distinct improvement. Plans were being made, accordingly, for him to take a long holiday in Japan! A companion had been found, who she wrote "is full of tact, good sense and discretion, and has made himself so companionable to Teddy that there is no doubt of things working well on that score." Mrs. Wharton, who was not going along, was full of cheer—life was again responding to the management of her expert hand. "Dr. K. thinks a return to normal conditions probable, and considers the journey and especially the two long sea-voyages, the best preparation for complete recovery."

Relieved of her burdens temporarily, she was able to return to Paris to her work, "putting in the pent-up energy of lots of wasted months in a new opus," as she informed John Hugh-Smith, and "trying gradually to get back my lost balance." In January, she was able to announce to him, "I am just finishing my short novel." It was *Ethan Frome*. If we consider the circumstances of Edith Wharton's life during the time she was writing it, the famous short novel of rural New England will seem much closer to her intimate experience than has generally been supposed. True, she had only glimpsed her "types" and background from the comfortable seat of her motor when driving through the Berkshire country, and had merely guessed at the possibility of tragedy in the lonely farmhouses she passed. But a moment's reflection will suggest that for Ethan's tragedy she had no further to go than her own.

She had found herself married to Edward Wharton as Ethan Frome was married to the mean-spirited Zeena, without love, understanding, or inspiration. Was Walter Berry her Mattie in whom she saw, having not before realized its existence, the possibility of another life? Now, like Ethan, she found herself chained to the querulous, neurasthenic Teddy for life. As he had with others of her books, Walter Berry is supposed to have carefully read the pages of *Ethan Frome* before it was sent to her publisher. For he was back, now, from Egypt, and was about to open a law office in Paris in the Avenue de l'Opéra.

She was also at work on other projects. *The Reef* is probably the book James meant when he wrote her, "I take unutterable comfort in the thought that two or three months hence you'll probably be seated on the high-piled and *done* book—in the magnificent authority of the position, even as Catherine II on the throne of the Czars . . ." She had never been, professionally, in better shape. She took thought, with particular feeling, for James, whose year had been almost a fruitless one.

The consequence of such non-production was, for James, loss of income. This was serious for him, more serious by far than it would have been for her. She had watched with sympathy the public hostility towards his late novels make it gradually impossible for him to count on their royalties. The failure of the great New York Edition of 1907-1909, the crowning *oeuvre* of his career, was not only a blow to his pride but to his pocketbook, for he had relied upon a recoup with its sales. He would remark a year later: "A dismal document from the Scribners flanked by an appalling one from the Macmillans this a.m. tells me that the sales

166

of my Edition, on which I had counted for the bread of my vieux jours, is rapidly & hopelessly falling to derisive figures." His attempts to lay siege to the stage once more with "The High Bid" —that work which he had hoped would have "on my scant fortunes a far-reaching effect"—had come to nothing much financially. When all this is considered in the light of the cost of his American trip itself, it is readily understandable that James must have felt altogether too "unmoneyed" as 1911 came into view, much as he had congratulated himself and Lapsley upon their condition of superior intellectual and moral grace the year before. In January, 1911, a one-act play, "The Saloon," was produced in London, with no particular improvement to his fortunes. "Have you seen the unhappy James play at the Little Theatre? He read it to me two or three years ago, and I thought it doomed to certain disaster. Alas!" Edith Wharton wrote John Hugh-Smith.

At the time the New York Edition appeared, Mrs. Wharton had hoped that public understanding of his work might be dispelled by an article by Morton Fullerton in which, as she told Charles Scribner, she had "had a hand—or at least a small finger." It was this article, probably, which did finally appear in the *Quarterly Review* in April, 1910. But the interest of the general public was hardly to be aroused by Fullerton's refined analysis. James was a difficult man to help in any direct material way. We shall see presently what disaster met the attempt, engineered by Edith Wharton, to present him with a cash sum as a gift from his American friends upon his seventieth birthday in 1913.

In 1911, she tried to do what she could to create a movement for giving the next Nobel Prize in Literature to Henry James. In February, she wrote to William Dean Howells:

> I don't know if you have heard that there has been for some months past a desire on the part of many Englishmen of letters to ask that the next Nobel prize be given to Henry James. Mr. Edmund Gosse and one or two other members of the English committee have already voted for him, and I believe that Mr. Kipling, who has a vote, is prepared to give it to him. But the English committee can of course do nothing effective without the support of public opinion in America, and it is certainly

time that Mr. James's countrymen should show themselves not
less appreciative than his European readers.

Mary Cadwalader Jones also wrote Howells a week or so
later enclosing letters collected by Mrs. Wharton from various
English supporters of the plan. Mrs. Jones observed: "As you
know, he has never been a 'best seller,' and his personal property
has dwindled in value, as property will if one lives in Europe and
has less than no business ability."

Howells replied: "Of course I think the notion of getting
James the Nobel prize is wonderfully good and fit, and I am only
vext that Gosse should have thought of it first." He suggested the
idea be put before the Chancellor of the Academy of Arts and
Letters, and promised himself to write to Henry Holt, President
of the Author's Club, and Henry Van Dyke of the Institute. "All
and singular the authors of America will favour getting the prize
for James," he said.

But nothing came of this promising plan. The Nobel Prize for
Literature in 1912 went to Gerhart Hauptmann. James, the expatriate, was not as popular with American readers as he may
have been with fellow-authors. What the "reading public" might
have thought of as a likelier candidate is indicated in Edmund
Gosse's letter to Edith Wharton, which she forwarded to Howells.
Gosse, while urging that James be pressed as an American candidate for the prize, warned that "a strong effort has been (and
perhaps is still being) made to secure it for Winston Churchill,
the American novelist."

Care was taken to keep James ignorant of the move to secure
the Nobel Prize for him until there should be definite promise of
success. As the plan did not materialize, it is probable that he
never knew of the effort made for him by his friends, or the part
Edith Wharton had played in it. While the negotiations were
going on, he was in the United States enjoying the warmth of
relatives and friends in the homeland he was now visiting for the
last time. To Edith Wharton, still in Europe, he wrote: "A
report even reaches me to the effect that there's a possibility of
your deciding to come over and spend the summer at The

Mount and this is above all a word to say that in case you should do so at all betimes you will probably see me here . . ." In June she sailed from Cherbourg.

Edward Wharton had been briefly back in Europe, and then had gone again to Hot Springs. From Salsomaggiore, where she took her annual asthma-cure, his wife wrote Sally Norton: "The three weeks with Teddy were a strain . . . He is very well physically, and if people see him only for a short time, they generally think there is nothing amiss. But the money idea has become an obsession, and is likely to be productive of painful difficulties in the future." She was absorbed, in this interval, in reading and writing. "I hope to finish my novel by the autumn," she remarked to Miss Norton, "—hope, but don't expect, seeing what I see ahead." James saw it also, and he wrote to the same correspondent: "I am afraid E. W. comes back to great difficulties and miseries, of sorts, here—and I confess I am not anxious for a nearer view of them." She insisted on his visiting her at Lenox, and James admitted that the prospect seemed "so thankless a privilege when one can play so little of a repairing or a preventing part."

This visit to The Mount in 1911 was to be quite different from James's previous visits in 1904 and 1905 when a domestic harmony had been reflected in the mellow Indian Summer of the Berkshire landscape. As though to represent the alteration of human emotions, the weather was at its worst—the sultry heat of a New England July. Edith Wharton humorously described, years later, the great man's prostration by the torrid atmosphere:

> Like many men of genius he had a singular inability for dealing with the most ordinary daily incidents . . . During a heat-wave this curious inadaptability to conditions or situations became positively tragic. His bodily surface, already broad, seemed to expand to meet it, and his imagination to become a part of his body, so that the one dripped words of distress as the other did moisture. Always uneasy about his health, he became visibly anxious in hot weather, and this anxiety added so much to his sufferings that his state was pitiful. Electric fans, iced drinks and cold baths seemed to give no relief; and finally we discov-

ered that the only panacea was incessant motoring. While we were moving he was refreshed and happy, his spirits rose, the twinkle returned to lips and eyes; and we never halted except for tea on a high hillside, or for a "cooling drink" at a village apothecary's . . .

Mrs. Wharton must have remembered, though she does not mention them, other reasons for James to have found the air at The Mount oppressive. She had hoped to have Teddy off the scene, if possible. On the third of July, she wrote to Sally Norton, "Teddy decided at the eleventh hour to go fishing with his brother, and will be away about two weeks longer. This enables me to get settled quietly, and perhaps have H. J. a little quietly to myself; though he threatened not to come till the 17th." But before James left, Teddy was back, and James, at Mrs. Wharton's urging, departed for cooler—and calmer—Nahant, writing Lapsley:

> Teddy had arrived Thursday p.m.—very "well" (for *him*) and that evening passed more or less normally. But he is impossibly and excitedly futile and foolish—and I left her to him with a pang. She would have nothing else—very naturally; however she is to write me what will have passed—and I hope to hear tonight, but my general sense is that his futility and inconsequence can only simplify the whole. Physically well and active as he is, he is incapable of a minute of continuous real reason. She has only to take her course—quietly, patiently and firmly; he can hold or follow no counter-proposal, no plan of opposition, of his own, for as much as a minute or two: he is immediately *off*—irrelevant and childish. But I didn't mean to go into this—one's pity for her is at the best scarce bearable. I am so glad you go back there—even if only to be near her, and I hope you will then write me another word.

The visit cannot have seemed a success to anyone concerned. James wrote again to Sally Norton of his eight torrid days at Lenox which "came to an abrupt end with Teddy W.'s return." He concluded: "The domestic situation makes my presence too officious. That situation can only have got worse—but talking

(that is writing) of it is impossible." This must have been the
feeling of the other friends assembled there that grim season—the
young Englishman John Hugh-Smith and Gaillard Lapsley. To
Smith, Mrs. Wharton wrote wistfully: "I am so glad you left
America feeling that it is a problem not to be solved in three
weeks. May I hope that you were generous enough to suspend
your judgment of our weather also? Because really it was almost
as unnatural as some of our other recent phenomena! Things
were rather bad after my husband got back. He is much better
physically, but very nervous and excitable." And she was able to
add a less personal observation:

> America can't be quite so summarily treated and so lightly
> dismissed as our great Henry thinks; but at the present stage of
> its strange unfolding it isn't exactly a propitious "ambience" for
> the arts, and I can understand his feeling as he does. Balzac
> would not have! I am so glad you saw Mr. James as you did. I
> never knew him more completely and lavishly himself; and that
> *greatness* in him is just the all-enclosing fact . . ."

There must have been little time for discussion of the arts in
America while Teddy was present at The Mount. The great
topic of debate was The Mount itself, which Edith Wharton
wanted to sell so that they might live in Europe the year round.
Teddy was attached to the gracious and familiar place, but Mrs.
Wharton felt that the American ambience in general was not "exactly propitious," and that the time had now come for her to abandon her American home. She had been coming towards this
decision gradually, but inevitably, ever since she had given up her
winter house in New York for the rue de Varenne. On the practical level, the sale of The Mount also seemed called for because
of Teddy's condition. He was not well enough to manage the big
country estate as he had done in the past; it was becoming clear
that he never again would be.

James advised: "She has only to take her course—quietly, pa-
tiently, and firmly; he can hold or follow no counter-proposal, no
plan of opposition, of his own . . ." But on August 6, Mrs.
Wharton told Smith, "I have decided not to sell The Mount for

the present, on the chance that he may improve and really benefit by the life here . . ." Then, at the end of the month, she announced to Sally Norton:

> We have suddenly decided to sell The Mount. The reasons are partly economic and partly based on Teddy's condition. The place is *very* expensive, so much so that it requires constant care and adjustment to keep it from being too much so; and with a big country place you know how hard it is to maintain that balance! —Still, I was prepared to do it if Teddy had been disposed to manage the place as he was eager to do at one time . . . He is so much better mentally and morally that we were able to survey the whole field quietly and impartially and I left the decision entirely to him, except that I was rather on the side of keeping the place *if possible.*

Somehow, one cannot help feeling that nothing might be more cruel than to leave the decision up to Teddy, to "let him decide" that he was unable to take the responsibility of keeping the place. Yet Edith Wharton also deserves one's sympathy; even the talented and strong can suffer. So, at least, James seems to have seen it. To Lapsley, who had watched and reported as he had begged, James wrote:

> Your letter is intensely welcome, interesting and luminous— also of course awfully harrowing as emphasizing so one's inability to help or hinder—to do anything but make vain gestures and futile remarks. The violent and scenic Teddy is negotiable, in a measure, but the pleading, suffering, clinging, helpless Teddy is of course a very awful and irreducible quantity indeed —and Edith's problem in face of him is such as to make one howl with an almost equal pity for both of them. You put it all most vividly and intelligibly—and I thank you with all my heart for your gallant generosity in writing to me of that which I've longed not to lose the so terribly twisted clue to. And I say that even though rather moved to wonder what more of distressful and tormenting one can really bear to have "put on" one— . . . I have written no word to the lady of The Mount since I got back—partly because I've been so floored by the

nonrefreshment here that is so much the contrary of what I had fondly looked for after the American horrors, and partly by reason of not having at my disposal any word that I could feel so opportune or relevant to the particular phase of her kaleidoscopic dilemma at the moment it might reach her. The swing of the pendulum over the sale of The Mount is of itself baffling to mere affectionate approach—the pendulum hits you in the eye just when you thought it was off at its opposite career! But your letter makes me awfully want to write to her—and I shall make her a fond confused sign; hanging *on* the pendulum myself even like a brilliant trapezist. Seriously, I feel abject before it all.

To Mary Cadwalader Jones, James observed: "Teddy is 'well' enough—perfectly sane so far as it suits him, but wholly quarrelsome, abusive & impossible. Definitely, I think, after going through some rather dreadful scenes, Edith has decided, *really* decided, to both sell The Mount and separate from him absolutely—making him an allowance but demanding that they live apart. The 'family' denounce her—but God grant she carries it through. *It is the only thing to save her life.*" Repeating the substance of these remarks in a following letter to Mrs. Jones, he added, "I believe that with a separation she would very much come up. But *basta*—it's all difficult & deadly. Such a marriage originally! But who knows what other she might have made?"

The Whartons' dilemma was complex even for so skilled an analyst of complexities as Henry James. But one knot was soon cut. "The Mount *is* sold, and Teddy, described as 'much better,' is at western gout-waters, *French Lick* (lick not sick) Arkansas —while she is at Italian Lick Lombardy! What a dividing abyss!" wrote James to Sturgis the following month.

In the retrospect of old age Mrs. Wharton summarized this decision to sell The Mount in a passage which gives only a hint of the anguish and disorder of those days.

. . . much as I loved [The Mount], the glowing summer weeks, and the woodland pageantry of our matchless New England autumn, it was all darkened by my husband's growing ill-health. Since the first years of our marriage his condition, in spite of intervals of apparent health, had become steadily graver. His sweetness of temper and boyish enjoyment of life struggled long against the creeping darkness of neurasthenia, but all the neurologists we consulted were of the opinion that there could be no real recovery; and time confirmed their verdict. Such borderland cases are notoriously difficult, and for a long time my husband's family would not see, or at any rate acknowledge, the gravity of his state, and any kind of consecutive treatment was therefore impossible. But at length they understood that he could no longer lead a life of normal activity, and in bringing them to recognize this I had the help of some of his oldest friends, whose affectionate sympathy never failed me in those difficult years.

The care of The Mount had been my husband's chief interest and occupation, and the place had now to be sold, for much as I loved it the burden would have been too heavy for me to carry alone. It was sad to leave that lovely country, and for the moment I did not feel like making another country home for myself; so I lingered on in the rue de Varenne during the last two or three years before the war, going away only for a few weeks now and then, to visit friends and to travel.

And now she was off to Italy with Walter Berry. They were to tour through all of upper Italy, with good stops in Florence and Rome. James had been asked to come along, and had refused. To Edith Wharton he wrote:

Alas it is not possible—it is not even for a moment thinkable. I returned, practically, but last night to my long abandoned home, where every earthly consideration, and every desire of my heart, conspires now to fix me in some sort of recovered peace and stability; I cling to its very doorposts, for which I have yearned for long months, and the idea of going forth again on new and distant and expensive adventure fills me with—let me frankly say—absolute terror and dismay—the desire, the frantic impulse of scared childhood, to plunge my head under the bedclothes and burrow there, not to "let it (i.e. *Her!* [the motor]) get me!" In fine I *want* as little to renew the junketings and squanderings of exile—*time*, priceless time

squanderings as they are for me now—as I want devoutly much
to do something very different, to which I must begin immediately to address myself—and even if my desire were intense
indeed there would be gross difficulties for me to overcome. But
enough—don't let me pile up the agony of the ungracious—as
any failure of response to a magnificent invitation can only be.
Let me simply gape all admiringly, from a distance, at the
splendour of your own spirit and general resources—or rather
let me just simply stay my pen and hide my head (under the
bedclothes before-mentioned.) My finest deepest sense of the
general matter is that the whole economy of my future (in
which I see myself reviving again to certain things, very definite
things, that I want to do) absolutely lays an interdict (to which
I oh so fondly bow!) on my *ever* leaving these shores again.
And I have no scruple of saying this to you—your beautiful
genius being so for great globe-adventures and putting girdles
round the earth. Mine is, incomparably, for brooding like the
Hen, whom I differ from but by a syllable in designation; and
see how little I personally lose by it, since your putting on
girdles so quite inevitably involves your passing at a given
moment where I can reach forth and grab you a little. Don't
despise me for a spiritless worm, only *livrez-vous-y* yourself . . .
with all pride and power, and unroll the rich record later to
your so inevitably deprived (though so basely resigned) and
always so faithfully fond old Henry James.

To Walter Berry, the same day, James, the most fluent of
letter writers, also wrote:

The Angel of Devastation writes me that if I will join you
within a day or two in Paris you will very kindly lead me forth
into Lombardy for magnificent operations—up and down the
Italian Kingdom! This is a hurried word (I found her letter here
but last night—coming home from the first stay since I returned
from the Belmont!) to say that as no such "great time" can
now be in question for me, you are not to have me on your
mind for a moment as to restrict for that space your freedom of
actions. I really am entirely unable to start for any such glorious frolic—I have only within these 24 hours got Home (and
there is no place, as we know, like Home!)—and got there with

the most passionate determinations to stick fast for the rest of my life. I have the most urgent necessities here. I have written our incomparable friend—as the worm may write to the eagle. That is the Eagle's only fault that she exposes one often to wormlike consciousness. (I like to do my worming in private and feel as if I am doing it now in the eyes of all Italy.) For you it's different; you're of aquiline race (your nose betrayeth you) your spirit is attuned to great gyrations. So go and girare —be bold and free and happy—and tell me later all about it. Now that both she and you have so boldly put your affairs in order là-bas, I feel that I can count on your brave beaks (for I maintain I am a toothsome worm) to come and peck at me once in a while. Vada pure! I do feel deprived—but not of the grand tours (I have absolutely no use for them more;) only of the genial, the generous jaw . . . I charge you with no message —it would kind of have the air of an aggravation; but I bless you both and envy you well—and await your appearance here. Does that aggravate? Well, I do hold on to you *de toutes les forces* of your faithful Old Henry James.

It must have been with a certain relief that James, having had to deal so recently with Edith Wharton in the light of pity, could again deal with her in the light of his inimitable satire. She herself hardly seemed to require anyone's sympathy at the moment, "in a splendid 60 h.p. car with Walter Berry for bon camarade—which he admirably is," as James observed to Mrs. Jones. "She most kindly appealed to *me* to meet her also at Milan for that purpose (or to join Walter in Paris and come down with him;) but such a feat and flight was not possible then to any of my powers— perhaps least of all my pecuniary. *Her* power to go and to consume and to enjoy—her incomparable restlessness—leave me more and more abasourdi." And he was quite, quite sure about it. To a regretful declaration from Mrs. Wharton upon her return that he might have come, he firmly rejoined: "Don't dream . . . that I 'might' have come—I so utterly mightn't!" though he also observed, "You must indeed have had a Bacchic tuscan time."

He was again hard at work, never to go far again from Rye or his little retreat in Chelsea where Miss Bosanquet's typewriter clicked away at the two volumes of his reminiscences. He made a few weekend forays from time to time; to "Hill," the hospitable

home of Mary Hunter, and to Howard Sturgis' Qu'Acre he paid
visits, and sometimes, as in December of 1911, to both in succession in the company of Edith Wharton. But he was wary. When
she came to meet him in London for these visits, he wrote,
"Don't bring the Motor, dearest cunning cosmopolite, no matter
what lassitudes, of the ends of—anything, or even of all things,
you may foresee; for it is absolutely impossible your poor
'Jammes' should return to Paris with you—dut il (or dut—anyone else!) en mourir! But it isn't a question of dying; sticking fast
is what helps him exactly to live—that & that only. You won't
miss the car at all—the taxis here are as excellent as they are
numerous, & if you will trust me I will *take* you on a Saturday to
Hill." "Our great Edith has been with us—come and went, with a
great flap of her iridescent wings, some three weeks (or so) ago.
She seemed very brave and bright and did, in her ten days, exactly 9000 separate and mutually inconsistent things; but she
liked it all. . . . She has every way great success in England and
could easily flourish here—save for gasping, herself, for the right
conversational air, not only à la longue, but in a very brief
space," James observed to Mrs. Jones.

But her holiday was over. After the trip to Italy and her visit
to England, she returned home to Paris; and Teddy was also
coming "home" there. There was no longer any question, it
seems clear, that any real recovery could be expected for him.
Edith Wharton must have already begun to think of divorce, or
at least of some kind of permanent separation which would enable her to delegate his care to others. Her friends had begun to
think of this prospect with her. So James, from his "tabernacle"
of literary seclusion in London, remarked, "take refuge in your
like Tabernacle when Teddy comes—which I am very sorry to
hear of. However, the case will settle itself—there must be so few
questions now—save only the final or compulsive one; & you
need lose no inch of the ground you have gained . . . yours
tenderly without a grain of cruelty, Henry James."

What *was* going on? Even James was not quite sure. To Lapsley,
who had been at the Whartons', he appealed:

I pant and ache for your news of 53 r. de V . . . But the mysteries and ambiguities (and may I add illegibilities?) of your note stretch me on the rack—and I yearn to know if Teddy is *there*—and what this new (I can't make out your word . . . "hellishness"?) *is*. Can you, oh *can* you, make just a very brief statement of the essential facts—as on a postcard? 1) as to whether he *is* there in person. 2) as to whether there is any definite "new fact" (of hellishness—promising thereby action and a relief;) any new proposal or possibility of his specially marking the occasion? Make it as brief as you will—30 words well used!

One perceives that Edith Wharton's friends had begun to hope that Teddy's behavior—whatever it was—would become utterly and sufficiently bad to make their case simple and clear. The trouble seems to have been that Edward Wharton was never *legally* insane; he was a "borderland case," entitled still to life among the normal. To Edith Wharton herself, who was complaining of spells of vertigo, James gave his old advice: sit still and let the evil spend itself about you, "go through the motions of life," "bear in mind that all these phenomena essentially contain the germ of their own evanescence, & if he comes but to destroy he destroys his own duration, his own application, his own continuity or consistency even more than anything else." Stay on the main road, he told her. "Don't deflect into by-paths or wander into wilds—stick to the firm Macadam and the firm Macadam will stick to *you* . . . What has Teddy to propose? . . . If he has nothing better to propose than your proposing to be quiet, one seems to make out that that itself must minister to quietude. You will say that *j'en parle à mon aise:* still, hold out— hold on, hold on.—"

This was more than mere philosophy just now; it was policy. James explained to Lapsley:

I believe Teddy to be in the very act of reaching 53 about this time . . . He had been on the point of going to Bermuda—but a malencontreux optimistic word of Egerton Winthrop's soothingly cast upon the breeze ("Oh I'm sure Edith would be glad to see you!") had switched him straight off and directed him upon his victim. *But,* dearest Gaillard, I can't all the same, brood over it, hang about it, helplessly and too luridly consider of it. The great thing seems to be that *all* Teddy's motions enclose within themselves the germ of immediate disintegration and evanescence, and by the time he will have come anywhere, by that time he will almost have gone—his possibilities spend themselves like burnt brown paper. Temporizing, sitting tight and letting him flounder—that is her nearest possible solution . . . Walter B. tells me that his outward seeming gives no colour to K-n-tt's theory of confinement; he's unconfinable on present *appearances.* All of which doesn't make me less all sorely and sorrowfully *wonder!*

But it was more than James, personally, could bear to contemplate. As he told Sturgis:

> . . . I can't think of Teddy's victim when I'm myself down and *affaibli.* I need *all* my resources—physical, moral, and financial—to look the situation in the face at all, and even then I don't stare at it very hard, but give it every chance to cut me if it will. I can neither do anything, write to her or be written to, about it—and ask myself why therefore cultivate, in the connection, a mere platonic horror—which permits me neither to hold her hand nor to kick his tail.

Unquestionably her friends rallied around her. There was no sympathy for Teddy now. Walter Berry, staying with the Whartons as what he called a "shock-absorber," sent an account of things to James, who relayed to Sturgis:

> . . . he says that Teddy is extraordinarily well and strong and normal—but only the more helplessly futile and arid and *énervant,* and that though it be true that with his restlessness he can't "endure," so on the other hand, and from the same cause, he can't *be* endured, or scarcely; and that he does last long enough, each time, to make one feel there's no issue, and that with these renewals he may go on and on. It sounds rather bad—and why do I torment you with it? It only comes as a piece of definite news just after my letter of two days since—

and *with* your beautiful and bountiful one of this A.M. Don't be harrowed by it—stand with me resolutely from under the harrow.

And then he asked the question of questions:

What comes to me most is the thought of how it must come to poor Edith, in these dark vigils, that she did, years ago, an almost—or rather an utterly—inconceivable thing in marrying him. As how superfluous, irrelevant, incoherent an act (with all its futility in its face—or in *his!*) it must now press upon her! And there is the intolerable pressure! Her bed is so made—and such a great big uncompromising four-poster!

But there were, again, as always, her periods of escape, her far-flung motor-trips which she called, with unconscious aptness, "motor-flights." In March, 1912, Edith Wharton was in Spain with Rosa Fitz-James and their young French friend Jean de Breuil. "May your 'fugue' with Rosa bring you (*be* for you) a big diversion & refreshment; & after that the better months come to you promptly," wished James. He sent his messages of admiring envy, but he was not to be tempted to go along—not even to Nohant, the home of George Sand, once more, not even to Italy:

I seem to get the side-wind of great adventures, past, present, and to come, from you, tout de même—not counting the chronic domestic one; which keeps my heart in my mouth. "And did you see Shelley plain?"—and did you three times go to Nohant ("coloured",) retour d'Espagne too? All of which plunges me into yearnings & broodings ineffable, abysses of privation & resignation. It's all right for you to go—by which I mean it's all right for *me* not to; but it's all wrong for me not otherwise to participate—& I shall sit gaping, watch in hand, till I do. And you go to Salso again—& you "motor in Italy"—& you're ready for anything prodigious; as such *are*, obviously, the sublimities of the sublime. It is the grande vie, don't deny that—for which I was so little framed, ever—& am so much less so than ever now.

Nor to the Thuringian forest, he insisted in July, as he told Sturgis: "I am *not* going to meet the Greater Angel than any of us at Boulogne and be motored to the Thuringian Forest by her—there to dally a month in her spirited society, after she shall herself have motored up from Naples to keep the tryst . . ."

But there was no escaping, after all; she was winding up these months of angelic flight by alighting in England. At which prospect, James was in his usual half-serious, half-laughing terror at her energy and her presumption. The high-piled jest was piled higher still:

> *Lamb House, Rye*
> *Reign of Terror*
> *le vingt juillet, 1912*

My dear, dear Howard, This is a sort of signal of distress thrown out to you *in the last confidence,* at the approach of the Bird o'freedom—the whirr and wind of whose great pinions is already cold on my foredoomed brow! She is close at hand, she arrives tomorrow, and the poor old Ryebird, with the majestic Paddingtonia no longer to defend him, feels his barnyard hurry and huddle, emitting desperate and incoherent sounds, while its otherwise serene air begins ominously to darken. *Bref,* the Angel, ("half-angel and half-bird," as Browning so vividly prefigures her,) has a *plan,* of course; which is that, struggling in her talons, as you will say, I am yet to be rapt off to Qu'acre on Tuesday in order to proceed thence that evening, as soon as we shall have hastily gulped down tea, to dine in her company with Lady Ripon at Combe. But from that plan I, in my tenderest consideration of *you,* dearest Howard, which exceeds the molehill, utterly dissociate myself in advance, and this is a word equally in advance to tell you so; just as I have emphatically wired to the Angel in Paris to tell her so—and that I absolutely refuse to make use of so large a slice of your noble hospitality for such purpose. I will, if she insists on Lady R., go from London from her for that night, and proceed to Combe from *there;* but I don't alight chez vous as at an hotel and simply give notice on arriving that I won't dine at the table d'hôte, but am dining (liking it so much better) at the café round the corner. I foresee that on Edith's arrival the battle will be engaged—and that she probably won't easily agree either to give up Lady R. (whom she appears indeed to have closed with) or to go to an hotel in London for the night. In that case we shall come to you on the morrow for the day and night (by the morrow I mean Wednesday,) or else not come at all, alas, if I have died fighting. I scarcely know what is before me, but I gird my loins for the worst (I am just settled here to urgent work;) I shall give your further, and perhaps lurider, news; and I am tout évènement yours all devotedly, Henry James.

One wonders how Lubbock could have borne to keep such a comic gem out of his published collection! But of course, what James meant under all the laughter was not altogether flattering to Edith Wharton. She came and she went, she went and she came; one might enjoy oneself greatly with her, but she would direct the course. To his sister-in-law, Mrs. William James, Henry James related three days later:

I have got back to work again after a good many final adversities in London, and I now feel that it, the work, will go on as it hasn't at all yet. There is only this sorry circumstance, that the Angel of Devastation (as Howard Sturgis and I unanimously dub her), Mrs. Wharton, who arrived day before yesterday by motor-car from Paris and Folkestone, departed this morning, after 36 most genial hours here, only with the pledge that I will join her at Windsor (Howard S.'s) on Thursday (this is Tuesday) to motor with her up to Wimmergill, the Charles Hunter's Yorkshire Place, there to spend 4 or 5 days—motoring again, so far as we can, over that region.

But even Mrs. Wharton sometimes weakened, and the following week he was able to tell his sister-in-law that he had had an unexpected reprieve:

I was on the point of uprooting myself (most reluctantly,) from L.H., in which I had just got settled again after London, in order to let Mrs. Wharton whirl me in her car (she arrived in for the purpose from Paris,) up to Wimmergill in Yorkshire and to a few days of the inexhaustible Hunter hospitality intermixed as much as possible with a few North-Country ruins. I rejoice to say that the project broke down after we got to Windsor (Howard Sturgis's) which was to be for the 24 hours our 1st *étape*. Mrs. W. gave out at the 11th hour, before the arduous Yorkshire programme, and I, only too delighted to abbreviate and simplify, (not because the thing wouldn't have been intrinsically interesting, but because I've no use for it *now*, when it is quite mistime for me,) fell back with relief on 3 or 4 days at the admirable Windsor (with 3 or 4 beautiful motorings thence,) and then a speedy home to my blest home and my much more urgent business . . . Mrs. W. returns tomorrow to Howard S.'s and then soon (I believe and even hope!) back to the continent . . .

Poor James could hardly sustain this much, however. He was more literally not "up to it" than Mrs. Wharton may have realized. On one of "3 or 4 beautiful motorings"—to the Desboroughs' at Cliveden—he suffered what seemed a slight heart-attack and Chauffeur Cook had to speed him home in Mrs. Wharton's automobile. He explained to Mrs. Wharton: "There was something in the conditions of excitement and tension, of having to reckon simultaneously with the whole time-scheme & social chaos, & also with the very *emotion* of our impressions, that for the hour tipped the balance the wrong way." It was not a serious *accès*, his doctor assured him, but there it was, and Mrs. Wharton was all humble regret.

And now that she was with him again, he could write to Sturgis with that mixture of love and censure which were compounded into matchless humor:

The fire bird perches on my shoulder while I bend, all eagerly, to acknowledge your delightful letter—yet, luckily, not to the point of my having to deprive that beautiful record of a response as free as itself. She has been with me since last evening, and was to have remained till tomorrow, but within this afternoon the horoscope has not unnaturally shifted, and Frk. Schuster and Claude Phillips having been with us, from Folkestone, for a couple of hours, she moves off, as soon as we have had tea, to rejoin them there for the night—they have just dashed away in their own car—and I retreat upon my now forever inexpugnable base, after wriggling out of every net cast to draw me into the onrush. She embarks tomorrow morning to all appearance—in order to arrive, at tea, at 5, with the Jacques Blanches in Normandy—after which my comprehension sinks exhausted in her wake. She had held us, F.S., C.P., and I, spell-bound, this pair of hours, by her admirable talk. She never was more wound up and going, or more ready, it would appear, for new worlds to conquer. The only thing is that none at this rate will soon be left to a lady who consumes worlds as you and I (don't even) consume apples, eating up one for her luncheon and one for her dinner. That is indeed, as your charmingly, your touchingly vivid letter so expresses, the terrible thing about (and *for*) a nature and life in which a certain saving accommodation or gently economic bias seem able to play so small a part. She uses up everything and every one either by the extremity of strain or the extremity of neglect—by having too much to do with them (when not for *them* to do,) or by being able to do nothing whatever, and passes on to scenes that blanch at her approach. She came over to us only the other day in order to help herself (and us!) through part of an embarrass-ing and unprovided summer, to put in a block of time that would bridge over her season; but she has already left us in raggs (as they used to, and I inadvertently happen to, write it—I shall recover my orthography, and other powers, only little by little!) and she with her summer practically still to somehow constitute. That is what fairly terrifies me for her future, possessed as I am, as to the art of life, with such intensely economic, saving, sparing, making-everyone-and-everything-go-as-far-as-possible instincts—doubtless in compar-ison a quite ignoble thrift. I feel as I shouldn't know where I might be if I didn't somehow or other make every occasion serve—in some degree or other. Whereas our firebird is like an extravagant dandy who sends 30 shirts to the wash where you and I (forgive, dear Howard, the collocation!) send one; or indeed even worse—since our firebird dirties her days (pardon again the image!) at a rate that no laundry will stand; and in fact doesn't seem to believe in washing and still less in the ironing—though she does, rather inconsistently in the "man-gling"!—of any of her material of life. Well, let us hope that a Divine Chemisier will always keep her supplied straight and to a sufficiency with the intimate article in which he deals!

All thanks for your wishes and inquiries about my pectoral botherations. They will be better enough, I feel sure, when a sordid peace again reigns. All I want for the improvement is to be *let alone*, and not to feel myself far aloft in irresistible talons and under the flap of mighty wings—and about to be deposited on dizzy and alien peaks. "Take me *down*—take me home!" You saw me having to cry that, too piteously, the other day to the inscrutable and incomparable Cook—rescuer as well as destroyer.

I am really inditing these remarks *after* our friend's departure: the after-dinner evening has now closed about me—and the sight of poor heroic Gross [Mrs. Wharton's maid] (who had again, for the millionth time, polished off her packing and climbed to her forward perch, but with the light of near Folkestone and fresh disintegrations in her aged eye,) has already became a pathetic memory. They are all—the Firebird, Frank S., Claude P., and their respective cars to cross from Folkestone together tomorrow, as I understand, Schuster and Phillips proceeding then by that means to a Strauss festival at Stuttgart. In a wonderful age—for the Firebirds, Claudes and Shoos—do we verily live! I have as much as I can do to live at my own very advanced one—and to that end must now get me to a belated bed; where you must take me for dreaming of you with all the devotion, dearest Howard, of your faithfullest, Henry James
P.S. *Please* destroy all this gross profanity.

But how could Howard bear to destroy this masterpiece of art and analysis, of humor and tragic insight!

James became painfully, though not dangerously, ill that autumn of 1912 with a visitation of the skin disease known as "shingles"—medically *herpes zonalis*—which prostrated and depressed him. While Edith Wharton "whirled" onward on what James called (in a letter to Mrs. Humphry Ward) "her dazzling, her incessant braveries of far excursionism," he followed her movements with a melancholy admiration. "I do rejoice that you're leading the great life in your great way, for the mere rushing side-wind of it enlarges for the hour the horizon of one who seems more & more condemned to a mere fine farscanning wistfulness." She travelled into pockets of France he had always wanted to know better; in Auvergne she looked out upon the magnificence

of the Massif du Cantal. "I always wanted to handle that massif—
& shall never again come so near it," he wrote. And now that she
was no longer a threatening presence, but a far-away legend—the
Princesse Lointaine—he could not hear enough about her, besieg-
ing Berry and others for news of her, reading her letters with
intense appreciation.

Finally she was back in Paris. "Dear Princesse Rapprochée," he
addressed her, "I'm really glad you're back there—it makes me
feel less lonesome." In Paris she was engaged—she had been for
some time—in definite negotiations with Edward Wharton's
family for the purpose of gaining a formal divorce. Howard
Sturgis had an account of it all from her one day in December
and relayed it faithfully to James, who replied:

Very lucid and liberal and, as we say, (or rather don't when we
can possibly help it) lovely, your letter this morning received in
our dear Firebird's interest, and which I have deeply digested.
As a mere warning or red flag earnestly waggled on the line, I
hadn't strictly been requiring it; with rockets from poor mad T.
himself lately much streaking my darkness; though not in a
way that I couldn't more or less successfully deal with. My
darkness has all these weeks been deep and is but a dreary
dimness still; yet I didn't want it, if lighted at all, flushed with
the particular lurid rays emitted by such a visitor. Edith has
written me a little—and had moreover prepared me for your
letter; so that I feel in full possession of the horribly distressing
facts. If indeed the ground *could* be taken for him by *les siens*
that he is a pearl of sanity and sense, the case in favour of his
wife's divorcing him would be simple and manageable. His
great physical salubrity and activity give the matter at the least
a different colour from what it appeared to have a couple of
years ago. He writes me from Paris with the last and crudest
extravagance—but just that, however, argues in a manner
against one's willingness merely to throw him upon the world.
It's a peculiarly damnable case—that he's so impossible for
intercourse and yet so possible for circulation (or at least
would be were there only people, victims, subjects of devastation, enough, to go round.) I think she is very wonderful—to
have been able to write the exquisite "Reef" (for I hold what is

186

finest in The Reef to be really exquisite, and haven't scrupled to try inordinately to encourage her by putting that faith in the most emphatic way) with that amount of harum-scarum banging about her ears.

A closer view of the ultimate Teddy is given in James's report to Mary Cadwalader Jones, a sort of comic-grotesque vision of madness:

> He is truly as slatedly, and swaggeringly, and extravagantly mad as he can be . . . Every sound of him is the maddest possible swagger and brag about his exploits and conquests, the first with his prodigious and unique American motor-car—100 miles an hour—in which it is quite open to him to kill himself; the second by his effect on the ladies, especially of the variety theatres, wherever he goes, and among whom it is probable that he will soon find himself, pecuniarily speaking *nu comme un ver*. The Walter Gays gave me the most extraordinary account of his dashing out to them in the country from Paris (for he *was* in Paris for a few days, unseen of E.) for very calumnious, but above all childishly, or rather crazily, swaggering purposes; during which one of the first things he did was to say: "Have you seen my gold garters?" and then to whisk up his trousers and show them in effect his stockings held up with circles of massive gold!

To Edith herself, at this final hour, his advice was still—soar serenely above it all on outstretched wings—*planez!*

> The facts you communicate are surpassed in interest only by their dreadfulness; yet, too, I think their dreadfulness really surpassed by their futility, as it were—their general weakness and negligibility. Of course they are superficially sickening— but they don't go down deep—I mean into the soil of consequence or the fine large substance of the Whole; which may strike you perhaps as an airy way of treating them! But no, it won't, for you will see and feel what I mean—being about the only person who ever does, in general; which fact doesn't at the same time, prevent me from almost blushing for my incapable situation, my state of inability to contribute by any act of

187

presence or stroke of inspiration to your greater ease. However, you really are all the while and *quand même* taking care of that yourself, and *je conçois bien que vous planez—il n'y absolument que cela à faire. Planez, planez*—to find how one can is a magnificent resource.

In late April 1913 Mrs. Wharton obtained a decree of divorce. James sent the news to the circle. To Sturgis: "Of course you know in respect of our great Edith that Teddy is now definitely and legally 'put away' (I mean divorced—and *incomed*) by formal process of French law: the whole business terminated and consummated. And now I both long and shudder (though that's a rude word) to see the great author, or authoress, of the deed!" "Teddy," he wrote to Percy Lubbock, "is now howling in space."

To Edith Wharton, James sent his congratulations on her "definite liberation," and in the same letter he added a word for Walter Berry, who had just recovered from a siege of illness. "I address this, you see, a bit confusedly & economically—for Edith is my gage of your improvement, just as you are that of her *épopée*."

7

The Real, Right Thing

IN READING THE LETTERS Henry James wrote to Edith Wharton and about her at the time of her divorce one is struck by the extremity of his participation. James, the witness of life, the outsider, the bachelor guest, the emigré, the novelist who had loved to situate his heroes and heroines among strangers and foreigners and to tell his stories from the point of view of detached observers, had lived quite intensely through his friend's experiences. Imaginative involvement was perhaps the secret of his great knowledge of the variety of human relationship he dealt with in his fiction. He knew that the life of art, the life of the mind, could, if lived fully enough, incorporate all other kinds of life. James's answer to Hawthorne's "The Artist of the Beautiful"—the tale of an artist who fashions his ideal only at the price of renouncing life—is Strether's discovery in *The Ambassadors* that he has lived after all, he, the contemplator, as keenly as any of the others.

In another year war would bring before everyone's consciousness its demonstration of gigantic "doing"—and never would mental and emotional part-taking be brought to such a pitch as James would bring it as he stood, old, infirm, and breathlessly interested, at the battle-side. In the midst of the clashing scene he would observe with admiring attention the figure of Edith Wharton. His skepticism about her personality expressed in many letters of humorous burlesque in earlier years, had, of course, always allowed for the qualities that held his faith and affection. In 1908 or 1909, shortly after A. John Hugh-Smith had met her at Howard Sturgis', James told him, "Ah, my dear young man, you have made friends with Edith Wharton. I congratulate you; you may find her difficult, but you will never find her stupid, and you will never find her mean." How else, indeed, could she have held the fidelity of Henry James? At the last he was to see a new revelation of her which put a sometimes ridiculous, sometimes deplorable restlessness in the service, as he felt, of her intelligence and nobility. She would be, again, but in a different fashion, the focus of his own projection into the trampling active life.

By the end of 1912, after several years of intermittent illness, James found himself able once more to take up regular habits of work in a little London flat in Cheyne Walk. He finished the first of his autobiographical volumes, *A Small Boy and Others*, which he had begun in the autumn of 1911 upon his return from his American visit, and was at work on the second volume, *Notes of a Son and Brother*. He had undertaken this task with the intention of re-invoking the early life of William James, but now as he shaped his story his real purpose took hold—the final view, clear-sighted and yet tender, down the long path which had led him away from those beginnings. In the confidence of his vision, his work went happily. "I have got back to a sort of regular *besogne* much more steadily than at any time since—awful interval—1909," he wrote Mrs. Wharton.

After the tumultuous experiences that had been her portion during the same period, Edith Wharton considered for the first time the possibility of settling down to a quieter existence in England. Her English friends were full of encouragement, and as soon as her divorce was achieved, Mrs. Charles Hunter, a devoted friend of James's and now of Edith Wharton's, offered to place "Hill," her house in Essex, at her disposal for a stay of rest and recuperation. Actually it was in another house, secured for her by Robert Norton, and not far from Rye, that she settled in July of 1913, only to drive out house-hunting with Percy Lubbock and Gaillard Lapsley and inspect an old estate in Essex with a view to buying it—an interesting place with walled gardens and great cedars that might well have challenged the creator of homes.

In September she was in England again and looked once more at this or another house, and seemed to be weighing its purchase so seriously that James wrote to Mrs. Jones that the house was "slowly closing around her—slowly, but surely, I think; & a jolly good thing, too, probably, for it's a wonderful fit to her case and her need." Yet she temporized, and instead of purchasing an English home decided to rent Stocks Tring, the country-place of the Humphry Wards, in Berkshire, for the summer of 1914. James thought this, too, "a very wise and comfortable thing for her to do," writing to Lapsley about it in June. But they were only a month away from the monstrous eruption of human unwisdom which would overturn everyone's settled plans.

On April 15, 1913, James was seventy years old, and a group of his English friends wished to make him an appropriate birthday gift. They therefore presented the author of *The Golden Bowl* with a piece of gilt plate, and they asked him to sit to John Singer Sargent for his portrait in oils. Naturally his close friends—the little circle of Edith Wharton and Walter Berry, Percy Lubbock and Sturgis and Lapsley—were all involved, although only the English friends contributed and signed their names, Percy Lubbock penning the birthday letter itself. James insisted nevertheless on inserting Berry's and Edith Wharton's names along with the rest in his letter of thanks.

A month earlier Edith Wharton had written to a number of American friends of Henry James:

> April 15 next is Henry James's birthday. His English friends and admirers have raised a fund to present him with a portrait. We believe that his American friends will be at least as eager to ask him to accept a gift commemorating this date.
> In view of the shortness of time, such commemoration, we think, might most appropriately take the form of a sum of money (not less that $5,000) for the purchase of a gift, the choice of which would be left to him.

This circular is addressed to a restricted number of his personal friends and admirers. The success of the plan therefore depends upon their immediate and generous response.

You will no doubt agree with us that this proposal should be kept *strictly confidential* for the present, so that it may not reach Henry James prematurely.

News of the plan did somehow reach James, and he did not like it. The American birthday plan, therefore, had to be abandoned, and Mrs. Wharton wrote to those who had already subcribed: "Owing to an unfriendly misrepresentation of the nature and intention of the Birthday Gift which Mr. James's friends had planned to offer him, he has made known that he prefers not to accept it." The money already contributed was returned to the donors. To one, publisher Charles Scribner, she wrote more fully:

I know how sorry you will have been to hear of the failure of the Birthday plan. I was not its originator, as it happens, but as the circular, for lack of time to form a committee in America, had to be sent out with my signature alone, Mr. James's family apparently represented to him that I was trying to raise a fund for the support of his old age. It is difficult to understand how any one can have so maliciously misrepresented the circular, which was certainly explicit enough—and the net result has been to cause great distress to Mr. James when he learned the facts, and to put his compatriots in the rather sorry position of making no sign on his birthday, while his English friends have offered him the equivalent—or more—of what we proposed to ask him to apply to the purchase of some birthday remembrance.

It seems possible that "malicious misrepresentation" had really not been needed to make James look askance at the proposal to honor him. It was too patently an offer of assistance to an old and failing worker who could no longer earn his own living. James had the delicate pride that suspects condescension in the gift-giver. From the English group he accepted the bowl, but not the portrait; that, he insisted, was to belong to the givers themselves—and today it hangs in the National Gallery.

Mrs. Wharton herself might have anticipated his reaction. James had accepted many small tokens from her—books, for example—always with elaborate gratitude. A gift that was in the least expensive, however, embarrassed him. The single letter to Walter Berry included in the Lubbock volumes—James's acknowledgement of the gift of a leather dressing-case—illustrates, comically and yet half-seriously, his reaction to what seems to have been a costly specimen of its kind. "I have been truly overwhelmed by the princely munificence of your *procédé*, and I have gasped under it while tossing on the bed of indisposition," he wrote to Berry, and he was, it may be, only half exaggerating. Mrs. Wharton herself had tried, at almost the same time, to give him a Sargent charcoal drawing for which he had posed under the impression that she had ordered it for herself. He had refused it, as he was to refuse the Sargent painting. "I am moved to distress as well as to the deepest confusion by your offer to me of so valuable a trophy," he had written her.

And now he wrote her again, explaining his feelings about the various birthday gifts being tendered him:

> The Golden Bowl is a most charming thing, & I accepted it with emotion, but I have not accepted the gift of the portrait, & shall in no way possess or retain or enjoy it: I shall simply sit—*le reste les regarde* (I don't say it ungraciously.) And I know the modest value of the (silver-gilt) Bowl; which will have cost my 250 subscribers about 10/apiece. *That* I shall beautifully have faced. Of the impossibility of my lending myself to the American scheme I will tell you more when we meet if you will ever so kindly listen. There would have been depths within depths of impossibility—as to the form (the Dread form) the movement seemed capable of. A Fifty Pound piece of plate (forgive the vulgar specification) I would radiantly have thanked for—& that is all I have practically thanked for here. *Basta!*

It must have tickled his sense of humor to make Mrs. Wharton and Berry (a man of considerable private wealth) "come in on the cheap," as he put it, by having themselves acknowledged publicly by him as contributors to the English gift!

193

In the autumn of 1913, Edith Wharton was off on another of her "world-swings," as James called her travelling-jaunts. She had gone on a trip to Germany in the company of the art critic and connoisseur Bernard Berenson, whom she had known since 1909. She was, for once, able to put away her guide-books and histories as she followed the learned Berenson about the great Museums of Berlin, where they spent eight days, and they went in the evenings to the opera, hearing not only Wagner's "Ring" but an enchanting performance of the new *Der Rosenkavalier*, which neither had heard before. Yet, despite these distractions, which would once have floated her spirits clear of her sorrows, she wrote John Hugh-Smith in the midst of it all, "You would give me a scolding if you knew at what a low ebb I am just now—no heart for anything, and what's considerably worse (since there's no demand for *that* organ), no head for books! I can't read—and I've never got as low as that before. Don't scold, though: wait till you're my age first. Not that I mind the number of my years: not a bit! Only, on the road to them, one goes through some things— at least I have—that turn everything bitter."

In the early spring of 1914, she took Gaillard Lapsley and Percy Lubbock with her on a motor-tour in North Africa, as though to seek in its remoter foreignness some balm that she had looked for in vain in her own civilization. Percy Lubbock, in his somewhat poeticizing way, recalls the impression she made upon her companions,

When she sat in the dusk (as I see her) at our inn-door, in the winding of the pass, watching the white-robed figures that now and then came swinging silent and stately down the road, she sat still and intent—as if she could have sat for ever, alone in the night, breathing some relief, some pacification that she hadn't found in the world she knew so well. And presently she made a discovery that quaintly struck her—it was fresher to her than to most. Small incongruous lump of visibility that we were, descending into the desert with our books and our maps and our imperturbable Cook at the wheel, we seemed now to be dissolved—to float as a thin light over space and time: a very odd sensation, no doubt, if you have never worn the cap of darkness in your life before. That is what it is to be for once completely isolated in an unknown world that doesn't know you, a world too old to be moved, too vast to be touched, beneath your hand yet out of reach.

On the day that her tenure of Mrs. Ward's "Stocks" began, in July, 1914, she had set out for a final adventure to Majorca with Walter Berry, "even like another George Sand and another Chopin," as James commented to Sturgis. They prolonged their stay through brilliant days in the Pyrenees and Catalonia. "Even the transparent summer air had never seemed so saturated with pure light. I remember a day when we picnicked in the scant shade of a group of cork-trees above a vineyard where an iridescent heat-shimmer hung visibly over the fiery red earth," she later recalled. But Barcelona was sultry and the little boat that was to take them to the Balearics would not be crossing, it turned out, for another three weeks, so the pair wandered back to the Pyrenees and then to Bilbao, on the shore. The days were long and shining and international politics seemed remoter than the stars of the summer evenings.

The morning they had left Paris the newspapers had carried the bulletin of the assassination of Archduke Ferdinand at Sarajevo. Now, as they lingered in Spain, the rumbles of world repercussion began to reach them. They turned their automobile north and on July 30th they were at Poitiers, where all night long there were crowds singing the *Marseillaise* in the square in front of their hotel. They went on the next morning towards Paris, stopping to lunch by the roadside, under some apple-trees, and gazing at the "sober disciplined landscape" all around them, which Edith Wharton saw again as the symbol of the vigilant habit of generations of the French. Two days later war was declared.

Stocks, guarded by her faithful butler, Alfred White, was waiting, but she was not to occupy it as she planned. Overnight, France was mobilized, and it was not possible to get a permit to leave for England immediately. She stayed on in the rue de Varenne, finding herself irresistibly held by the spectacle of Paris in its first weeks of war—the conscripts already marching off, the streets flooded with pedestrians and emptied of motor-traffic, all vehicles having been commandeered by the War-Office, the closed restaurants and shops, and, finally, the first German flag— from an Alsatian regiment—hung out on the balcony of the Ministry of War. Her English friends began to worry about her, and advised her, she recalled, to get to England as soon as she could, and to stay there, "till the war was over," a matter, presumably, of six weeks or so.

James, with his keen intuition of her state of mind, and his anxiety for her final achievement of the English haven he had hoped for her, wrote on the sixth of August, "Enormous must be your frustration, your dislocation, your painful dividedness— over which I lose myself in desperate conjecture when not in lurid evocation. *Ci vuol' pazienza*—you *will* get over, by some abatement of the congestion unless your heart incalculably declares for preference of the whereabouts, the actual, of your body, & you are conscious of greater interests to guard *là-bas* than here—where White must be so gallantly guarding those that do exist. Mine are intensely in your getting over at the 1st moment you can do it with any comfort."

On August 19th, James replied to a letter of Edith Wharton's from Paris:

> Your letter of the 15th has come—& may this reach you directly, though it probably won't. No I won't make it long—the less that the irrelevance of all remark, the utter extinction of everything, in the face of these immensities, leaves me as "all silent and all damned" as you express that it leaves *you*. I find it the strangest state to have lived on and on for—and yet, with its wholesale annihilation, it *is* somehow life . . . Mary Cadwalader Jones gives me a sense of the interest of your Paris which makes me understand how it must attach you—how it would attach me in your place. Infinitely thrilling and touching such a community with the so all-round incomparable nation. I feel on my side an immense community here where the tension is proportionate to the degree to which we feel engaged—in other words up to the chin, up to the eyes, if necessary. Life goes on after a fashion, but I find it a nightmare from which there is no waking save by sleep. I *go* to sleep, as if I were dog-

tired with action—yet I feel like the chilled vieillards in the old epics, infirm and helpless at home with the women while the plains are ringing with battle. The season here is monotonously magnificent—& we look inconceivably off across the blue channel, the lovely rim, toward the nearness of the horrors that are in perpetuation just beyond. I can't begin to think of exerting any pressure upon you in relation to coming to the "enjoyment" of your tenancy—your situation so baffles & beats me that I but stare at it with a lack of lustre! At the thought of *seeing* you, however, my eye does feel itself kindle—though I dread indeed to see you at Stocks but restlessly chafe.

It is difficult for a later generation, so long out of sympathy with "that other war" of 1914-1918, to realize what a profoundly moving event it at first seemed—the naked confrontation of "civilization" and "barbarism" in the form of victim and assaulter. To James, as to Edith Wharton, no event in their lifetimes had ever seemed so stirring, had ever brought them into so close a sense of connection with the old verities of honor and valor and beauty and intelligence held so dear that they are worth dying for. Engagement was instantaneous for both of them, though for Edith Wharton, it meant, as James already feared, that she would remain in France. For himself, he felt engaged "up to the chin, up to the eyes," right where he was.

While she lingered in Paris, waiting for her visa and for her Paris bank to release her usual remittance so that she could send money to her servants at Stocks, a French friend, the Comtesse d'Haussonville, President of one of the branches of the French Red Cross, asked her to set up a workroom for women in her *arrondissement*. She collected about 12,000 francs from American friends, rented an empty flat, and organized about ninety skilled seamstresses to make *lingerie* to be sold on order. Then her visa to England was granted.

She went to pay up her bills in Tring and hand Stocks back to the Wards, but already she had determined that her proper place was in Paris. James met her at Folkestone and took her to Lamb House for the night, and then she hurried on to the big country house now waiting so pointlessly for her. As she got there, a letter from James followed: "I hope with all my heart that with Stocks really spreading its generous umbrage about you, you are feeling something of a balm—if we can talk now of balm." But she found Stocks frustratingly remote in that day before the "wireless," though Lapsley and Lubbock and James came up to visit, and she yearned to get back to Paris "and the blessed drug of hard work."

She could not, at first, obtain permission to leave England, and she arranged to take the Wards' London house meanwhile, to be closer to the center of news and action. There she remained until some weeks after the battle of the Marne. James, more than most of her friends, understood her impatience:

> . . . your disposition to go back to Paris . . . I think a very gallant and magnificent and ideal one, but which at the same time I well understand, within you, the urgent force of. I feel I cannot take upon myself to utter any relevant remark about it all; any plea against it which you wouldn't in the least mind, once the thing *determined* for you, or any in favour of it, which you so intensely don't require. I *understand* too well—that's the devil of such a state of mind about everything. Whatever resolution you take and apply you will put it through to your very highest honour and accomplishment of service; *sur quoi* I take off my hat to you down to the ground, and only desire not to worry you with vain words.

Three days after this letter was written, the battle of the Marne opened, and then came the news of the bombing of Rheims. James wrote Edith Wharton:

> Rheims is the most unspeakable & immeasurable horror & infamy—& what is appalling & heart-breaking is that it's "*forever & ever!*" But no words fill the abyss of it—nor touch it, nor relieve one's heart nor light by a spark the blackness; the ache of one's howl & the anguish of one's execration aren't mitigated by a shade even as one brands it as the most hideous crime ever perpetrated against the mind of man. There *it was*—and now all the tears of rage of all the bereft millions & all the crowding curses of all the wondering ages will never bring a stone of it back! Yet one tries—even now—tries to get something from

saying that the measure is so full as to overflow at last in a sort
of vindictive deluge (though for all the stones that *that* will
replace!) and that the arm of final retributive justice becomes
by it an engine really in some degree proportionate to the act. I
positively do think it helps me a little to think how they can be
made to *wear* the shame in the pitiless glare of history . . .

This passage by James on the bombing of Rheims was translated
into French by Mrs. Wharton's arrangement, and was read at a
meeting of the Académie Francaise and printed in the *Journal des
Débats*. She herself was back in Paris a few days after she received the letter.

Upon her arrival, she returned to the operation of her
ouvroir, the workshop for seamstresses that she had organized in
August. James warmly followed every stage of her efforts, full of
a wistful admiration, feeling again and again, as he said, "like the
chilled vieillards in the old epics, infirm and helpless at home with
the women." He wrote: "I rejoice more than I can say in the way
the *ouvroir* leaps and bounds and booms, blessings on its head; if I
were but capable of physical action I see I should leap and bound
and in fact boom almost to a like tune; it's the curse alas of my
years and my compromised cardiac state that I can't!" She also
organized an American committee of the *Accueil Franco-Belge*
(afterwards the *Accueil Franco-Américain*) to carry on various
charities in aid of the Belgian refugees, and James participated by
forwarding French newspapers to the Belgians who had been
domiciled at Rye; it turned out that they were humble folk who
spoke and read nothing but Flemish!

However physically incapable, James was indeed emotionally
enrolled among Mrs. Wharton's war-workers. And her great
energy, which had so often struck him as futilely expending itself
in mere physical motion, now was fully justified in his eyes: ". . .
the tremendous pitch of Paris is all mixed, in my consciousness
with yours, so that the intensity of yours drums through, all the
while, as the big note. With all my heart do I bless the booming
work (though not the booming anything else) which makes for
you from day to day the valid *carapace*, the invincible, if not
perhaps strictly invulnerable armour. So golden-plated you shine
straight over at me—and at us all."

Both James and Edith Wharton, the expatriated Americans, were perhaps more agitated by the war than some of the English, feeling it all the more keenly because their country had not yet to their mind done the "decent" thing and recognized that all humanity was implicated in the struggle. Both of them found it almost impossible to write fiction. James had been forced to put aside his novel about America, *The Ivory Tower*, and Edith Wharton, a novel about an American writer, called "Literature." In both instances it was impossible for the authors to believe in the reality of the world that had so violently been changed within a few months.

On August 5th, the day after Britain declared war on Germany —and President Wilson had announced the neutrality of the United States—James wrote Howard Sturgis: "The plunge of civilization into this abyss of blood and darkness by the wanton feat of those two infamous autocrats is a thing that so gives away the whole long age during which we have supposed the world to be, with whatever abatement, gradually bettering, that to have to take it all now for what the treacherous years were all the while really making for and *meaning* is too tragic for any words." And to another friend he wrote a few days later, "I find it such a mistake on my own part to have lived on—when, like other saner and safer persons, I might perfectly have not—into this unspeakable give-away of the whole fool's paradise of our past."

In the face of the great, belying facts of the moment, it was impossible to attempt to represent life as he had understood it, in particular the modern scene of *The Ivory Tower*, and when he returned to the writing of fiction after a while, he took up the pointedly unrealistic *The Sense of the Past*, which he had begun and abandoned as far back as 1900. As he wrote Mrs. Wharton in December, 1914, he had sent his secretary down to hunt it up out of an old drawer at Lamb House, "as perhaps offering a certain defiance of subject to the law by which most things now perish in the public blight."

Meanwhile he had had a conversation with their old friend and fellow-novelist, Mrs. Ward:

"Are you able to work?" I am asked.
"Oh dear no, alas—are you?"
"Ah yes—I have already finished half a novel."
"That seems to me very wonderful: how *do* you manage?"
"Well, you know, it's so preponderantly for America, they"—
they—"mind the war so much less." And then as I, stupefied at
the account of the process, but mumbled something about my
own lack of *any* receipe, came the triumphant light: "Oh but I
shouldn't be able to do it in London, you know!" And yet after
all I doubt—I think she *would* be able! . . . I am going really, I
think, to try that precious solution of our friend's: I mean
making it, and thinking of it as, so preponderantly for America,
where they don't care, that their belle insouciance will infect
my condition and perhaps even my style.

In a later letter, James continued: "I try myself to get back to
work—but it's of a stiffness of uphill—a sheer perpendicular. I
crawl like a fly—a more or less frozen fly—on a vast blank
wall. It's impossible to 'locate anything in our time.' Our time has
been *this* time for the last 50 years, & if it was ignorantly and
fatuously so, the only light in which to show it is now the light
of that tragic delusion. And that's too awful a subject. It all
makes Walter Scott, him only, readable again."

Edith Wharton had begun to write "Literature" late in the summer of 1913, while on the trip to Germany with Berenson—in
fact the first page of the manuscript bears the inscription, "Dres-
den, August, 1913." In February, 1914, she let her publishers
know that she was undertaking a big book about modern life of
about forty-five chapters which she estimated would take until
January, 1916, to complete. But by December she admitted to
Scribners that she had had to lay the project aside. Yet a month
later she was still hopeful of getting back to it and meeting her
original deadline. "I am beginning now to want to get back to
work, and am kept back only by the steady drudgery of the
charities in which, like everyone else here, I am involved. At first
I could not *write*, and it was maddening to think I could have
made a little money for the charities I wanted so much to help,
and yet to be absolutely pen-tied," she wrote in January, 1915.

But her return to this task was to be less readily accomplished than she anticipated. She became interested in war-reporting, and visited the various fighting fronts, bringing back impressions which were put into a series of articles for *Scribner's Magazine*. She undertook the editing of a lavish anthology of literary pieces and prints contributed by famous intellectual figures in France, England, and America for the purpose of raising funds for the Belgian refugees—*The Book of the Homeless*. By the end of March she was forced to take a long rest in the south of France.

Still feeling incapable of tackling "Literature," she started a short novel which does, indeed, read more as though it were written to make money than anything else she ever produced—*The Glimpses of the Moon*. She now wrote her publisher, "I have every hope of finishing "Literature" after the war, but it is on too large a scale to be taken up now." Three months later, during another short vacation at Fontainebleau, she did something much finer than *The Glimpses of the Moon*—her companion-piece to *Ethan Frome*, the novelette, *Summer*. This book, she recorded later, as remote as it was from everything that had been occupying her for many months, "was written at a high pitch of creative joy, but amid a thousand interruptions, and while the rest of my being was steeped in the tragic realities of the war."

Summer, that brief and elemental tale of a country girl's passion, had come from some deepest depth of herself; for the broad, panoramic novel of society that "Literature" was intended to be, her powers continued to fail her. As she admitted to her publisher, she found its subject "impossible to treat, with the world crashing around one." Even when the war was over the book would not revive under her hands. "The war dealt that masterpiece a terrible blow," she told Brownell. "I still 'carry' it about with me, and long to make it the dizzy pinnacle of my work; but *when* did it all happen?"

The contemplative occupations of the writer seemed particularly out of key with the general emphasis on action, which was, to both James and Edith Wharton, the necessary tone of everything worth-while in such a time. James, especially, was oppressed by his inability to do what younger and stronger men were able to. His thoughts must have dwelt on the fate that had kept him long ago from marching to battle with those of his own American generation who had gone into the armies of the Civil War. In that distant time he had read the letters of his younger brothers, Garth Wilkinson and Robertson James, written from the front, "seeing, sharing, envying, applauding, pitying, all from too far-off," as he observed in *Notes of a Son and Brother.*

He had become a fascinated reader of war-letters and war-memoirs, perhaps in search of a nearness to the life of physical action that his imagination and sympathy could win only from the experiences of others. When Field Marshal Viscount Wolseley sent him his two-volumed *Story of a Soldier's Life* in 1903, James wrote him, "To a poor worm of peace and quiet like me—yet with some intelligence—the interest of communicating so with the military temper and type is irresistible—of getting close (comparatively!) to the qualities that make the brilliant man of action . . . I would give all I have (including Lamb House) for an hour of your retrospective consciousness."

Now, past seventy, he found he had the same wistful eagerness to know and to participate in the deeds of others. He could not stand being "sequestered" at Rye, and moved in October, 1914, into his Cheyne Walk flat so that he could be closer to the throb of London. The tension there was great. "Immensely do I understand," he told a friend, "the need of younger men to take refuge from it in *doing*, for all they are worth—to be old and doddering now is for a male person not at all glorious. But if to *feel*, with consuming passion, under the call of the great cause, is any sort of attestation of use, then I contribute my fond vibration." And so he questioned and listened to everyone who could tell him about the war—to wounded soldiers in the hospital or even met in the streets, to the accounts of friends in the army or close to the field. He followed with ardent attention the activities of Charles Eliot Norton's son, Richard, who had organized the American Volunteer Motor-Ambulance Corps in France, and he wrote an "appeal" to be used for raising funds for the Corps. But, above all, his emotions and imagination fed upon reports received from Edith Wharton.

Early in 1915, Mrs. Wharton, having had occasion to investigate the conditions of military hospitals for the French Red Cross, decided to do a series of "reports from the front" that would bring the realities of war to her still-stolid countrymen. With the cooperation of the French General Staff, she was permitted to visit portions of the war zone from Dunkerque to Belfort. To James, even before the articles were written, her reports of her experiences arrived in the form of letters which he received with eager homage.

She wrote him several letters describing her two trips into the Argonne in February. She had gone to Châlons-sur-Marne, the little town with its Romanesque church that had suddenly become the headquarters of an army, crowded with soldiers and vehicles and long lines of the *éclopés*, or battle-shocked, and then she had driven into the desolated country between the Marne and the Meuse. In ruined Clermont-en-Argonne she stopped to see a Hospice, originally for old men but now sheltering injured infantrymen, run by a little band of nuns who had taken her into a garden from which she had glimpsed the rush of men and the puff of smoke of the battle of Vauquois. At a village called Blercourt she looked into abandoned cottages which had been turned into hospital rooms, and, finally, into the church, which was filled with wounded, behind whom the curé was officiating at his altar while a few women, the only "civil" inhabitants left in the village, stood between the rows of cots.

"It was a sunless afternoon," she wrote, "and the picture was all in monastic shades of black and white and ashen grey: the sick under their earth-coloured blankets, their livid faces against the pillows, the black dresses of the women (they seemed all to be in mourning) and the silver haze floating out from the little acolyte's censer. The only light in the scene—the candle-gleams on the altar, and their reflection in the embroideries of the curé's chasuble—were like the faint streaks of sunset on the winter dusk."

By way of contrast, there was another field hospital in a church. "In the doorway our passage was obstructed by a mountain of damp straw which a gang of hostler-soldiers were pitch-forking out of the aisles. The interior of the church was dim and suffocating. Between the pillars hung screens of plaited straw, forming little enclosures in each of which a dozen sick men lay on more straw, without mattresses or blankets. No beds, no tables, no chairs, no washing appliances—in their muddy clothes, as they come in from the front, they are bedded down on the stone floor like cattle."

Finally, she came to Verdun, having obtained permission to pass from a General in charge of the area who had happened to read *The House of Mirth*! Another lucky recognition—on a freezing night when no beds were to be had in Châlons—came when a staff-officer who turned out to be Jean-Louis Vaudoyer, the poet and novelist whom she had known in Paris, turned over his lodgings to her. She must have been, even as she describes herself, "an eager grotesque figure," a "prosaic Valkyrie," as she hurried into these scenes, this woman no longer young, in the elegant long skirt and large hat of the fashion, riding behind her "Cook" as she had ridden on so many trips of pleasure. Yet there is something moving about the spectacle. And perhaps it is true, as Lily Norton thought, that she became in those days a warmer person than she had been heretofore, "her rather starved heart expanded . . . human sympathies were no longer hidden behind a social veneer . . . social values were no longer of much importance, her outlook widened."

James was enormously moved by her accounts. Early in March he wrote her:

How can I welcome & applaud your splendid thrilling letter—in which though it gives me your whole spectacle & impression as unspeakably portentious I find you somehow of the very same heroic *taille* of whatever it was that gave the rest at the monstrous maximum. I unutterably envy you these sights and suffered assaults of the *maxima*—condemned as I am by doddering age & "mean" infirmity to the poor mesquins *minima*, when really to find myself in closer touch would so fearfully interest & inspire & overwhelm me (as one wants to be overwhelmed.) However, since my ignoble portion is what it is, the next best thing is to heap you on the altar of sacrifice & gloat over *your* overwhelmedness & demand of you to serve me still more & more of it. On this I even insist, now that I have tasted of your state & substance—for your impression is rendered in a degree so vivid & touching that it all (especially those vespers in the church with the tragic beds in the aisles) wrings tears from my aged eyes. What a hungry *luxury* to be able to come back with things & give them then and straight into the aching voids: do it, *do* it, my blest Edith, for all you're worth: rather, rather —"sauvez, sauvez la France!" Ah *je la sauverais bien, moi,* if I hadn't been ruined myself too soon!

This was his response to her first letter from the Verdun region. Later in the month, after her second visit, she wrote James another letter, giving further descriptions, and telling him, too, about the death of her friend Jean du Breuil de Saint Germain, described to her by a fellow-officer. James told her: "Your whole record is sublime, and the interest and the terror of it all have again and again called me back to it. I have ventured to share it for the good of the cause and the glory of the connection (mine) with two or three select others—this I candidly confess to you— one of whom was dear Howard, absolutely as dear as ever through everything, and whom I all but reduced to floods of tears, tears of understanding and sympathy. I know at last, your incomparable pages, by heart—and thus it is I really feel qualified to speak to you of them."

James wrote her of the state of mind and emotion of the people he talked to in London, his response to the daily news from the front. One sees him, in his own account, a little comic sometimes in his eagerness and helplessness—as he did not fail to emphasize —and yet touching in the genuine fervor of his feeling. "The thing that most assuages me continues to be dealing with the wounded in such measure as I may," he confessed, and instanced, "my having turned into Victoria Station, yesterday afternoon, to buy an evening paper and there been so struck with the bad lameness of a poor hobbling convalescent that I inquired of him to such sympathetic effect that, by what I can make out, I must have committed myself to the support of him for the remainder of his days—a trifle on account having sealed the compact on the spot. It all helps, however—helps *me*, which is so much what I do it for."

James suffered, none the less, from his inability to do anything but contribute money from his slender purse. As he wrote Edith Wharton the following week,

> One is surrounded in fact here with more affirmations of energy than you might gather from some of the accounts of matters that appear in the *Times*, & yet the paralysis of my own power to do anything but increasingly & inordinately *feel*, feel in a way to make communication with almost all others impossible, they living & thinking in such different terms—& yet that paralysis, *dis-je*, more & more swallows up everything but the sore & sterile unresting imagination. I can't proceed upon it after your sublime fashion—& in fact its aching life is a practical destruction of every other sort, which is why I call it sterile. But the extent, all the same, to which one will have inwardly & darkly & drearily & dreadfully lived!—with those victims of nervous horror in the ambulance-church, the little chanting country church of the deadly serried beds of your Verdun letter, & those others, the lacerated & untended in the "fetid stable-heat" of the other place & the second letter—all of whom live *with* me & haunt & "inhabit" me. And so does your friend du Breuil, & his friend your admirable correspondent (in what a nobleness & blest adequacy of expression *their* feeling finds relief)—& this in spite of my having neither known nor seen either of them; Seguier creating in one to positive sickness the personal pang about your friend & his, & his letter making me feel the horror it does himself, even as if my affection had some stake in that.

As she sent him letters from other scenes of action, he continued in the same vein:

> What wondrous wafts of the real right thing the post gathers from you *à mon adresse*, & how these, reaching my comparatively dim corner here, move me to admiration & gratitude & the sense of being unsurpassedly distinguished! You're magnificent & I am thrilled, & can't sufficiently rejoice in you and be proud of you. The only thing is that you make my life on these

dim terms of my own not worth the living, when there are such possibilities of vision . . . I do find myself intensely enough in presence, I profess—in presence of the whole monstrosity—till I hear from you, & then I shrink to nowhere and nothing, learning from you what it really is to live . . . I myself have no adventures of any sort equal to just hearing from you of yours —apart I mean from the unspeakable adventure of being alive in these days, which is about as much as I can undertake at any moment to be sure of . . . I am learning to take for granted that I shall probably on the whole *not* die of simple sick horror— than which nothing seems to me at the same time more amazing.

On July 26, 1915, James became a naturalized British subject. His feeling for England, the country not of his birth but of his choice, had become still stronger during the two years of her crisis, and he had ached for some way of demonstrating his gratitude to the home he had found there for forty years. The slight, precipitating cause was his discovery that, while the United States was neutral, he was classified as a technical alien, able to go down to Lamb House only under police supervision. But his impulse was more fundamental. As he told his nephew Harry, the son of his beloved brother William, and the American, above all, by whom he wanted most to be understood, "Hadn't it been for the war I should certainly have gone on as I was, taking it as the simplest and easiest and even friendliest thing: but the circumstances are utterly altered now, and to feel with the country and the cause as absolutely as I feel, and not offer them my moral support with a perfect consistency (my material is too small a matter), affects me as standing off or wandering loose in a detachment of no great dignity . . . My practical relation has been to this [country] for ever so long, and now my 'spiritual or sentimental' quite ideally matches it."

His indignation at American non-participation in the military struggle had most to do with his decision. Throughout his letters to Edith Wharton he gave expression to his impatience with American inaction. As early as October 1914, he had written her:

The Real, Right Thing

"Very wonderful, your having assisted at those Tuileries bombs —but what I want of Fate is that the American Ambassador be offered up on the altar of the Union of the 2 (more or less) English-speaking peoples: if a German bomb could but painlessly extinguish him in order to precipitate the American relation to the Kaiser's general undertaking." In May 1915, shortly after the *Lusitania* was sunk, he related to Mrs. Wharton:

> I lunched today with two American officials . . . & got from them the impression that though they find no positive forecast of the German answer to the American Note possible, their apprehension doesn't exclude a virtual flouting of the same— such a flouting as will test the President's true sticking up to the pitch at which the Note so admirably placed him. I can't be sure they are sure he *will* stick—they stick so themselves, up, up, up! (It's of an enormous effort for them to be here, & to have been in France—and in Germany!) But I may do them (or the President himself) injustice, & I am only afraid Germany may not flout us *enough*.

The President did not yet think us sufficiently flouted for a declaration of war, however, and so, two months later, James himself, so to speak, declared war on Germany by assuming membership in a nation that had already done so. He could no longer wait to take action. But now, almost at the very end of his life, Edith Wharton failed him in her sympathy, for, like many Americans, she could not see any real need for his alienation from his birthplace. She felt his act was a mistake. "It seemed to me rather puerile, and altogether unlike him," she later admitted, and she refrained from writing him the word of understanding he might have appreciated.

One of his final acts was to assist Mrs. Wharton in getting together the materials for *The Book of the Homeless.* The proceeds from the book went to the Belgian refugee agencies; the original manuscripts, paintings and drawings were later auctioned in New York for the same purpose. James helped by soliciting contributions to the book from writers of his acquaintance such as William Dean Howells and William Butler Yeats. Yeats contributed his "A Reason for Keeping Silent" which seems to reproach the verbosity of the other contributors with its

I think it better that at times like these
We poets keep our mouths shut, for in truth
We have no gift to set a statesman right;
He's had enough of meddling who can please
A young girl in the indolence of her youth
Or an old man upon a winter's night.

Only one other contribution had something of this same modesty —James's "The Long Wards." In this essay, specially written for the book and probably the last piece of writing James did, he speaks for the purely contemplative mind made humble before the soldier, the man of deeds.

He may well ask himself what he is to do with people who so consistently and so comfortably content themselves with *being* —being for the most part incuriously and instinctively admirable—that nothing whatever is left of them for reflection as distinguished from their own practice; but the only answer that comes is the reproduction of the note. He may, in the interest of appreciation, try the experiment of lending them some scrap of a complaint or a curse in order that they shall meet him on congruous ground, the ground of encouragement to his own participating impulse. They are imaged, under that possibility, after the manner of those unfortunates, the very poor, the victims of a fire or shipwreck, to whom you have to lend something to wear before they can come to thank you for helping them. The inmates of the long wards, however, have no use for any imputed or derivative sentiments or reasons; they feel in their own way, they feel a great deal, they don't at all conceal from you that to have seen what they have seen is to have seen things horrible and monstrous—but there is no estimate of them for which they seek to be indebted to you . . . The case thus becomes for you that they consist wholly of their applied virtue, which is accompanied with no waste of consciousness whatever.

Such was James's humility before the life of action. It was a feeling that tinged his last relations with Edith Wharton, whose daily "doing" during those years was to him the only appropriate response called for by the times. Almost gone, from these last letters, is the old mockery at her ceaseless, restless stirring and overturning of the world.

As autumn deepened into winter in 1915, James seemed to grow visibly more tired to observant friends, as though his participation in the general cause, howsoever he had deprecated it, had been taking more of his strength from him daily. In December he suffered a stroke, followed shortly by another, and on February 28, he was dead.

Edith Wharton was at Hyères, where she received news of his first stroke from his secretary, Theodora Bosanquet. She came back to Paris and waited through the weary weeks for news of the end which was deemed inevitable. The thought that this supremest votary of the value of consciousness might survive with impaired brain struck her as the most horrible of possibilities. "Consciousness," he had once said, "is an illimitable power, and though at times it may seem to be all consciousness of misery, yet in the way it propagates itself from wave to wave, so that we never cease to feel, though at moments we appear to, try to, pray to, there is something that holds one in one's place, makes it a standpoint in the Universe which it is probably good not to forsake." And now he was soon gone, taking out of the world that extraordinary light of awareness that had shone for so many years, illuminated so many objects, among them his friend Edith Wharton.

PART TWO

The Literary Relation

8

The Continued Cry

IN THE LANDSCAPE of Edith Wharton's life the figure of Henry James is of almost too-distracting importance. He was the greatest man she knew. James himself had many friends and acquaintances who stood equal beside him; he moved among his peers from youth to old age. The son of a remarkable father who deliberately exposed his children to the constant encounter and recognition of what was distinguished in art, in scene, in personality, he went to Paris and made the acquaintance of Flaubert and Turgenev when still a young man, and in time he knew literary London with the familiarity of an intimate. He had lifelong friends as gifted as himself; Howells and Stevenson were brothers in equality of powers and his own brother William was one of the most remarkable Americans of his generation. Edith Wharton, on the other hand, had few close friends who were her intellectual equals—and none who towered into that elevation where James stood alone. In her maturity, if not in her youth, her familiar company was composed, as we have seen, of many talented writers such as Paul Bourget, Howard Sturgis, and Percy Lubbock—but no other genius. One tends to see James in a mountainous scene, among many firm-planted contemporaries including Edith Wharton herself, but the topography of her experience is a different one; she seems to rise from the plain with only his overmastering bulk in sight.

Consequently, no discussion of her work can avoid contemplating the effect of his example; the danger, really, is that we will assume more of a one-way transfer than we have a right to. Although James's own work was almost complete before their friendship was under way, we may tend to underestimate Edith Wharton's impact on his last stories; there is actually some indication that *The Ivory Tower*, for one, may have borrowed something from her distinctive tone. But no one has ever been able to overlook the possibility that James greatly influenced this younger writer who might be supposed to have had a feminine willingness to accept his masculine tutelage and dominance.

The expectation that she be in some way "Henry James's heiress," to use Q. D. Leavis' phrase, has resulted in the too-easy assumption that she simply took her art out of his generous pocket. That there was a connection between their works was sensed with some justification by her earliest reviewers. Then ensued the friendship which was conspicuous in the literary and social worlds in which they moved, and lasted for the years in which she emerged from obscurity to fame while James rounded out his long career. Naturally enough, the reviewer's formula— "She is one of Mr. James's most faithful followers"—continued in use, however complex the resemblance or great the divergence of her mature art. Even in later years, when her own work was over, the same bald statement was invariably invoked whenever her fiction came up in literary discussion, and few of her critics since have troubled to establish the actual degree and nature of the artistic relationship.

But as Henry James and Edith Wharton were themselves aware, even if their critics were not, personal and literary affinities are quite different matters. Until 1914, Mrs. Wharton had made no remarks in print about her great friend's art of fiction and James had commented upon her work only once, briefly reviewing her novel *The Custom of the Country*. But private letters, still mostly unpublished, contained enough scattered comment to reveal what each thought of the other's writing through the years. We now are able to trace a curious and often amusing evolution of attitude on the part of each in regard to the other's productions—an evolution quite independent of their growth of

216

friendship. In James we witness the first interest of the would-be teacher giving way to a resigned recognition of her fundamental difference. In Edith Wharton, correspondingly, an early desire to emulate yields to an irritated sense of the need to assert her distinctiveness, and then, having made her point, she again finds uses, in altered ways, for the example of James.

As we have already related, the wistful young society woman who first glimpsed him at a dinner party in the 1880's was hardly able to muster anything beyond silent awe in James's presence. She could scarcely call herself a writer, having done little besides some verses of amateur quality. There was little in these efforts to forecast the future writer of fiction, beyond possibly a preference, after Browning, for dramatic monologue and for situations of romantic renunciation and resignation of the sort that appear later on in the older woman's sophisticated stories. "Some Woman to Some Man," beginning, "We might have loved each other after all . . . ," which was included in the 1878 *Verses* privately printed in Newport when she was sixteen, is a pale, poor little poem. Nevertheless, it anticipates a mood of pessimism and "might have been" which emerges in her later fiction, and which could have been influenced by the example of James, whose heroes and heroines so often accept defeat and renounce happiness. But one can't really speak of a literary influence on this childish writing. All we know is that by her own admission, a few years later, she was agog with admiration for *Daisy Miller* and *The Portrait of a Lady*, and too aware of her own insignificance to tell the author so when they met.

During the nineties Edith Wharton sold stories as well as poems to *Scribner's Magazine* regularly enough to furnish a collection, *The Greater Inclination*, in 1899. If James had hardly been aware of young Mrs. Wharton's existence heretofore, the reviews of this book must have brought her to his attention. From the *Boston Congregationalist* to the *San Francisco Argonaut*, the reviewers voiced remarkable unison. "The author has been a faithful student of Henry James" (*Springfield Republican*); "One cannot help feeling that she has read James deeply and affectionately" (*New York Outlook*); "plainly modelled on the methods of Henry James" (*Hartford Gazette*) are sample statements. The *Philadelphia Telegraph* called her stories "a tracing through transparent paper" of the James model, and remarked, "If imitation is indeed the sincerest form of flattery, Mr. Henry James must regard himself complimented in the highest degree in the appearance of this book."

In many of the reviews an invidious comparison was made with James. "Her nearest affinity is Henry James," wrote critic Harry Thurston Peck in the *New York Commercial Advertiser*, "and we are free to say that Mrs. Wharton has no cause to shrink from this comparison." The monthly *Bookman* agreed, but discriminated, saying that it was the later James, who had "suffered just the least perceptible deterioration as a moralist," whom she unfortunately resembled most. Only the merciful critic of the *New York Musical Courier* was moved to remark, "I shan't imitate the rest of the critical chain gang and speak of Miss Wharton's close study of Mr. James's style; in reality she has a very neat, telling style of her own."

Edith Wharton never took pleasure in the verdict that she was James's imitator. There is evidence that she resented this judgment even at the start of her career, when the charge had some basis in fact. The remarks of one early critic, John D. Barry of the Boston *Literary World*, she remembered for a lifetime, recalling the smart of a particularly stupid jibe when she came to write her autobiography over thirty years later. Barry's observations were in substance the same as those of other reviewers of *The Greater Inclination*, but were more odiously put: "The author, Miss Edith Wharton, has evidently studied Henry James very closely. In several of her stories in this volume she not only shows that she has been influenced by his method of developing a motive but by his style as well. Some of his worst faults of style she reproduces with a skill that after a time becomes very amusing, notably his trick of repeating words, which in James himself is at times exasperating, and his habit of spoiling the formation of his sentences by inserting parenthetical clauses." Barry then went on to criticize her openings, remarking, "Take the first sentence in the book—Henry James to the life!" The sentence in question,

which begins her story, "The Muse's Tragedy," was certainly
long, and it might well be called Jamesian: "Danyers afterwards
liked to fancy that he had recognized Mrs. Anerton at once; but
that, of course, was absurd, since he had seen no portrait of her—
she affected a strict anonymity, refusing even her photograph to
the most privileged—and from Mrs. Memorall, whom he revered
and cultivated as her friend, he had extracted but the one impressionist phrase: 'Oh, well, she's like one of those old prints
where the lines have the value of color.' "
    There are many points about the sentence, not least the
egregious estheticism of the last bit, which might have annoyed
the Boston critic, but he merely remarked crankily that Mrs.
Wharton "apparently does not believe in the principle that a
writer should always begin his story or his article with a short
phrase—an admirable principle, by the way," recalling that
Thomas Wentworth Higginson had advised Louisa May Alcott
always to begin her stories with conversation. Years later, ordering her recollections of that early critical assault, Mrs. Wharton
spoke of her first reviews as "unbelievably kind" with one exception. "At length I came on a notice which suddenly stiffened
my limp spine. 'When Mrs. Wharton,' the condescending critic
wrote, 'has learned the rudiments of her art, she will know that a
short story should always begin with dialogue.' " Though her
quotation is inexact and the name of the writer may have slipped
from her memory, it is undoubtedly Barry's article she recalled
at that much later date.
    Curiously, she does not say anything in her memoirs about
Barry's principal charge of Jamesianism, the burden, as we have
seen, of most of her first reviews, which were not so unbelievably
kind as she preferred to remember. Even in an earlier account of
her experiences at the hands of critics, the essay called "A Cycle
of Reviewing," which was published in the London *Spectator* in
1928, she lists various charges laid late as well as early at her
door—but not this one. Perhaps she preferred not to give any
recognition to this most persistent as well as most resented criticism of her work. The full grounds of her immediate annoyance
with reviewer Barry in 1899 must, however, have become known

to him. Some weeks later he wrote again (having learned that she was *Mrs.* Wharton, meanwhile): "She is said . . . not to relish the frequent references made by her readers to her indebtedness to Henry James, so her next book will probably not be marked by slavish adherence to the methods of a very questionable literary model."

She did not relish them. During the next five years she wrote industriously enough. *The Greater Inclination* was followed by a novelette, *The Touchstone* (1900), by another volume of short stories, *Crucial Instances* (1901), by a two-volume historical novel, *The Valley of Decision* (1902), another novelette, *Sanctuary* (1903), and still another volume of short tales, *The Descent of Man and Other Stories* (1904). On the whole, the critics were not inclined to change their opinion of her indebtedness to Henry James. With the exception of her novel, which received some mild praise as an evocation of the past more to be compared with *Romola* or *Marius the Epicurean* than with anything by her fellow-American, her productions were still labelled "of the school" of James.

She found herself caught, moreover, in the current of a considerable critical antagonism to James which had begun to prevail, particularly in America, and her works, whether praised or censured, were used in the attack upon her Master; she was approved for supposed superiorities and differences, warned against the peril of resembling him. Reviewing *The Touchstone*, the *Atlantic Monthly* critic condescendingly advised: "There is one distinguished contemporary writer, indeed, whose influence is too plain to be overlooked. Mrs. Wharton has sat at the feet of Henry James, and in the way of her art she has unquestionably learned much from him. But she would now do well to rise from her deferential attitude. Better things than he can inspire are, we believe, within the scope of her still widening powers." The critic of *The Independent* beat James with a stick fashioned from the offenses of his pupil: "The reader receives the impression that Mrs. Wharton has made a literary art of casuistry. Her characters have conscientious scruples that rarely deal with the real issues of life . . . no one except perhaps Mr. Henry James can present a revolting scene with more social delicacy."

Returning this and other reviews of her third collection of stories, *The Descent of Man,* which had been sent in a batch by her editor, W. C. Brownell, she wrote in exasperation: "I have never before been discouraged by criticism because when critics have found fault with me I have usually abounded in their sense, and seen, as I thought, a way of doing things better next time; but the continued cry that I am an echo of Mr. James (whose books of the last ten years I can't read, much as I delight in the man) . . . makes me feel rather hopeless."

There were numerous paradoxes in the situation. James, it will be recalled, was at this very moment becoming a personal friend —"I delight in the man" expresses her amazed discovery in 1904 of the boundless resources of his personal charm. In January of that year she had written Brownell about her meeting with James in London, and had reported that the great man "talks, thank heaven, more lucidly than he writes." And it was that autumn, as we have seen, that he came for the first time to the Whartons in their Lenox home, there to reveal the full wonder of his personality and conversation. In a way that must surprise the modern reader who tends to see James as a man whose essence was his books, Edith Wharton recorded afterwards: "I had never doubted Henry James was great, though how great I could not guess till I came to know the man as well as I did his books." At that time she "could not read" the works of the decade 1894-1904.

Yet think what that decade included! It had begun with those somber, characteristic tales, "The Death of the Lion," "The Altar of the Dead," "The Figure in the Carpet," and included *The Spoils of Poynton, What Maisie Knew, The Awkward Age, The Turn of the Screw* before the century closed; then *The Sacred Fount* in 1901, *The Wings of the Dove* in 1902, *The Ambassadors* in 1903, and *The Golden Bowl* in 1904. Contemporary criticism has tended, of course, to regard this last harvest as James's culminating triumph, his "major phase," as F. O. Matthiessen named it. But in 1904 Edith Wharton found herself one of many of James's early admirers who were unable any longer to enjoy the author who had first captured their notice with *Daisy Miller* and *The American.* Her friend and adviser Brownell was himself another such reader, and the correspondence between them indicates a mutual confession of distaste for James's last novels.

In the course of a letter written to Brownell in 1902 she exclaimed, "Don't ask me what I think of *The Wings of the Dove!*" In 1904, then, we find him writing to her, "It's a relief to know you can't read H. J. The efforts I made to read *The Ambassadors!* I broke one tooth after another on it." And in this same letter, written in reply to her complaint over the *Descent of Man* reviews, he sympathetically acknowledged that it must indeed be unpleasant for her not to have her "uniquity" recognized. But sometimes, he reminded her, she had come out better than James himself did. "Do you remember the paper that called you 'a masculine H. J.?'" he chuckled, recalling another review which had used her work to deprecate James's. The following year, Brownell wrote an article for the *Atlantic Monthly* which was severely critical of James's later style, and he won unqualified applause from Mrs. Wharton: "You have certainly said the most penetrating thing ever said of him—every line so exactly expressed my own feeling about him, and the last shade of a shade, that I feel as if I had had the article celestially written for me—like which saint—while I slept! Only you have seen lots more—at least more reasons why."

W. C. Brownell had been Edith Wharton's trusted friend and literary counsellor ever since Scribners began to publish her six years before. He was himself a critic of ability whose books as well as personal advice had already profoundly influenced her, and would continue to until his death in 1926. In 1924 she wrote him, calling him "cher maître," upon the occasion of the publication of one of his last books, "Well—it is rather lonely at times on the Raft of the Survivors, but not when I think of you, and of what I owe to you, and what I am still going to learn from you, and how, best of all, you have been my friend and guide for so many, many years."

In many respects Brownell's thinking was in harmony with Henry James's. With James and Edith Wharton he shared a common desire to raise the standards of literary criticism in a period of its nearly complete inconsequence. They were at one in wanting to give to the writing of fiction a particular canon of principles, a sense of form. All three were fascinated as well by the problem of standards and manners in social life; Brownell in his essays, Edith Wharton and James in their stories and novels, were occupied in examining the contrasts of class and culture between America and Europe during the years before the First World War.

Yet in certain ways, Brownell's influence worked counter to James's. His early work, *French Traits*, may have assisted Mrs. Wharton in coming to view France as her spiritual home, the country, as they both felt, where nature was truly "cultivated." As we have seen, she did finally choose to live permanently in France—against the advice of Henry James. Brownell's literary essays, published between the years 1900 and 1909 and collected in the two notable volumes, *Victorian Prose Masters* and *American Prose Masters*, helped her to find her own critical principles and choose her models, and some of these choices strengthened, at least temporarily, her resistance to James's mastering influence. Brownell's most important effect upon her during these early years was his strengthening and rationalizing of her resistance to the example of Henry James by means of arguments finally expressed in the James essay.

The firm of Charles Scribner's Sons, was, of course, Henry James's as well as Edith Wharton's publisher, and Brownell, as its editorial chief, had a constant view of James's evolving art. He utterly disliked his later productions, and when *The Sacred Fount* came to him in manuscript in 1900, he had thrown up his hands altogether. "It is like trying to make out page after page of illegible writing," he declared in his confidential report to Charles Scribner. But despite his chief editor's objections, Scribner continued to publish James's books; Brownell, publicly silent, was quite free in communicating his views to such friends as Mrs. Wharton (it was not until five years later that he wrote the article in the *Atlantic Monthly* which so delighted her). His views were an embarrassment to Henry James's publisher; the James essay is the only piece in *American Prose Masters* that had not made its appearance first in *Scribner's Magazine*.

Edith Wharton's views would not be expressed in print for many years, until, in fact, they had lost some of their early impulsion. Personal loyalty to James always made her reluctant to draw attention to their artistic differences. Even in 1928, in a memorial essay on Brownell, she does not mention this critique which had seemed "celestially written" for her, though she praises the whole book as his best and finds her "one quarrel" with it to be the essay on James Fenimore Cooper.

As she read Brownell's essay in the pages of the *Atlantic*, Mrs. Wharton noted one observation after another which prompted her applause. In the letter already quoted from, she reported:

> It's all so good that I can only dash breathlessly from "we have the paradox of an art attitude, etc." (p. 497) to "He has reversed the relation between his observation and his imagination" (p. 498); thence to column 2 of p. 503: "Disinterested curiosity is, however, itself a very personal matter, etc., etc." on to p. 511; all the part about his curiosity, and especially your summing-up of the prying and "snooping" in the Sacred Fount; then every word of part VII; especially the "Lilliput without Gulliver"—and the whole paragraph it occurs in; rejoicing next in "the chevaux-de-frise of his later style," and the 3rd paragraph of this part most particularly—oh, and then (p. 518) "It is simply marvellous that such copiousness," etc.

It is easy to follow her footsteps through the essay. "We have the paradox of an art attitude that is immaculate with an art product that is ineffective," Brownell had written, describing what seemed to him to be James's over-meticulous reporting of the insignificant. "It is not because he is a man but because he is an artist, that nothing human is foreign to him . . . Thus it is due to his seriousness that a good deal of his substance seems less significant to his readers than to him."

For Brownell, James's observational faculty had, indeed, flourished at the cost of other gifts: "He has reversed the relation between his observation and his imagination, and instead of using the former to supply material for the latter, has enlisted the latter very expressly—oh! sometimes, indeed, worked it very hard—in the service of his observation." What Brownell missed in James, apparently, were ideas and judgments; he found the Jamesian reserve about the pathos of Maisie's situation, for example, quite insupportable: "It is an excellent illustration of an order of art that *must* be radically theoretic, since it could not be the instinctive and spontaneous expression of a normally humane motive." Edith Wharton thought the point well-taken.

She also, it seems, accepted Brownell's insistence that "disinterested curiosity is . . . itself a very personal matter. Carried to the extent to which it is carried by Mr. James . . . it becomes very sensible, a very appreciable element of a work of art. It is forced upon one's notice as much as an aggressive and intrusive element could be." Brownell went on to point out with considerable force that we are altogether too much aware of the absence of the author for his abnegation to be effective. "We see him busily getting out of the way, visibly withdrawing behind the screen of his story, illustrating his theory by palpably withholding from us the expected, the needful, exposition and explanation . . ." To view events through what James called "some more or less detached, some not strictly involved, though thoroughly interested and intelligent witness or reporter," was to Brownell, as to Edith Wharton, often to get at the story by unnecessary indirection.

Basic to these points is a fundamental suspicion of James's formalism, his attachment to theoretic principles. Mrs. Wharton would always see this as a weakness. When, in 1920, she reviewed Percy Lubbock's collection of James's letters, she paid testimony to his qualities as pathbreaker and theorist, but went on to say, "Henry James, as his years advanced, and his technical ability became more brilliant, fell increasingly under the spell of his formula. From being a law almost unconsciously operative it became an inexorable convention; and to turn the difficulty created by his growing reluctance to shift the consciousness he invented the 'chorus' of unnaturally inquisitive and ubiquitous hangers-on, the Assinghams and others, who, oddly, resuscitated from the classic drama (*via* Racine and Dumas *fils*) snoop and pry and report in 'The Wings of the Dove,' 'The Sacred Fount,' and 'The Golden Bowl.' " Despite other remarks in this review that indicate the depth of her final appreciation and conscious debt to James, these sentences are directly traceable to Brownell's hostile essay of 1905.

James's characteristic inspiration, Brownell observed, was a rather unphilosophical one—curiosity. For lack of a more fundamental prompting, each of his works seemed "an independent illustration of some particular exercise of his talent," instead of an expression of his view of life. Consequently, his personages tend less and less towards the typical, the representative, the significant, since there is little or no insistence upon what they typify or represent, or signify to humanity generally. Brownell felt that James was less interested in his characters than in the puzzle of their situations—Densher's or Maisie's, or Vanderbank's or Chad Newsome's. And yet, if "curiosity is James's one passion," it is a passion pursued with what Brownell felt to be a pathologic devotion. The results, in at least a few instances, he thought, were distinctly distasteful. "The most conspicuous instance of this is undoubtedly 'The Sacred Fount,' which for this reason is an unpleasant as well as mystifying book. The amount of prying, eavesdropping, 'snooping,' in that exasperating performance is prodigious, and the unconsciousness of indiscretion combined with its excess gives one a very uncomfortable feeling—a feeling, too, whose discomfort is aggravated by the insipidity of the fanciful phenomena which evoke in the narrator such a disproportionate interest." The "snooping" and "prying" of James's *ficelles* —as he called these confidants and witnesses so conveniently placed in his fictions—would always annoy Edith Wharton. In *The Writing of Fiction*, she complained that the Assinghams of *The Golden Bowl* were "forced into it for the sole purpose of acting as spies and eavesdroppers."

Part VII of Brownell's "Henry James," which particularly met with her approval, makes the surprising charge that James's culture was limited—if not in mere acquaintanceship, certainly in active awareness—to the thought of the modern period. "A writer interested in 'Antigone,' and imbued with the spirit of its succession, would naturally and instinctively be less absorbed in what Maisie knew." *The Awkward Age* struck him as "Lilliput without Gulliver," a phrase that obviously tickled Edith Wharton. What *The Awkward Age* lacked, Brownell explained, was the implication of another scale than its own. "If the futilities and *niaiseries* of 'The Awkward Age,' instead of being idealized by the main strength of imputed importance, were depicted from a standpoint perhaps even less artistically detached, but more removed in spirit by knowledge of and interest in the sociology of the human species previous to its latest illustration by a wretched little clique of negligible Londoners, the negligibility of these *dramatis personae* would be far more forcibly felt."

Brownell's final strictures concerned James's style. Edith Wharton appears to rejoice in the sweeping declaration that opens this section of Brownell's discussion: "We could readily forego anything that he lacks, however, if he would demolish for us the chevaux-de-frise of his later style." It was here that the two met in mutual admission that they couldn't read the James of the late period. She admired Brownell's analysis of James's leisurely obscurity: "It is simply marvellous that such copiousness can be so elliptical. It is usually in greater condensation—such as Emerson's—that we miss the connectives. The fact attests the remarkable fulness of his intellectual operations, but such plenitude imposes the necessity of restraint in direct proportion to the unusual extent and complexity of the material."

"Are the masterpieces of the future to be written in his fashion?" Brownell finally asked. "If they are, they will differ signally from the masterpieces of the past in the substitution of a highly idiosyncratic *manner* for the hitherto essential element of *style:* and in consequence they will require a second reading, not, as heretofore, for the discovery of 'new beauties,' or the savoring of old ones, but to be understood at all. In which case, one may surmise, they will have to be very much worth while."

In 1905, the same year that she read the Brownell essay, Edith Wharton had her own answer ready. She produced her first important novel, *The House of Mirth*, which made her at once a considerable figure in American letters and was as far as could be conceived from the late or even the early Henry James. The critics were not slow to see the significance of the new work; it seemed to some at the time, that she had put James's example aside. As Edward Clark March wrote in *The Bookman*, "It was not for nothing that she was proclaimed the disciple of Mr. Henry James. Perhaps the persistent attribution of this discipleship stung her to escape into a different field. Whatever the reason, the marks of her former master's influence have wholly disappeared . . ." It almost seemed that the James influence had operated again by producing a defiantly different style, in this instance, a determined opposite. Nevertheless, the accusation of sedulous imitation was to return and persist.

But how accurate was the label so securely fastened to Edith Wharton prior to the publication of *The House of Mirth*? The admiration which had once choked her with shyness in James's presence had certainly had its effect upon her early experiments in the short story. Many filaments of theme connect her first efforts with his work. She was evidently attracted by James's kind of story, one involving subtleties of moral responsibility. Egotism, which James, like Hawthorne before him, viewed as the master-sin, is often at work in her chief characters too; like both Hawthorne and James she had a particular horror of the subtler forms of human exploitation.

Like James, she was stimulated by that peculiar conflict of claims which is involved in the guardianship of the past, of reputations. James's attitude may be seen in such a story as "Sir Dominick Farrand," in which a struggling writer comes by chance upon some compromising letters by a dead statesman and is tempted to sell them. His temptation is the greater because he has fallen in love with a poor woman. By selling the papers to the editor whom he has unsuccessfully besieged hitherto with his own compositions, he may gain entry for his own work, and the purchase price itself may enable him to marry. He resists the opportunity and is rewarded by the discovery after his marriage —which takes place nonetheless—that his wife is Sir Dominick's daughter.

The Continued Cry

This story must certainly have come to mind as readers studied the dilemma of Glennard, the hero of Edith Wharton's novelette, *The Touchstone*. He, too, has some letters to sell, and he, too, needs money to marry on. But unlike James's hero, he succumbs to the temptation, and his crime is the more heinous in that the letters he sells are no stranger's. Margaret Aubyn, the famous writer, had once written them to him, and they are not merely love-letters, but, as someone in the story remarks, "unloved letters"—the heartbreaking eloquence of a gifted woman whose passion was not returned. Essentially, both stories have the same moral center. James, by concealing from his protagonist the knowledge that his action involved anyone known to him, makes his temptation more tenuous and abstract. Edith Wharton preferred to make the issue cruder and her protagonist's egotism a completer case, for Glennard had first taken without returning the love of the living woman before he thought of using the letters of the dead one.

Another pair of companion-studies dealing with the responsibilities of the present to the past, the living to the dead, and of the recipients to the givers of love is provided by James's "The Aspern Papers" and Mrs. Wharton's story "The Muse's Tragedy" in *The Greater Inclination*. Over both stories broods the spirit of a dead poet—James's Jeffry Aspern, Mrs. Wharton's Vincent Rendle—and both concern the encounter of one of his literary worshippers with the still living woman who had supposedly inspired his famous poems—"the Juliana of some of Aspern's most exquisite lyrics," "the Silvia of Vincent Rendle's immortal sonnet-cycle." In both, romance triangulates the relation of poet, critic, and inamorata—though in James's story it is actually the niece of the celebrated Miss Bordereau who becomes emotionally engaged with the literary pilgrim, while in Mrs. Wharton's it is Mary Anerton herself with whom Danyers becomes involved.

James and Edith Wharton each selected a somewhat different question posed by these elements. James's interest lay in the psychology of the young man; it is he who as the narrating consciousness exposes himself to the reader as he coldly lays siege to the celebrated literary remains, gaining instead an unanticipated and unwanted victory over the heart of one of the guardians of the treasure. Edith Wharton's interest was aroused by the situation of the aging Muse who, being so eminent a priestess, could never be anyone's divinity. And she added a further irony. What if even the grand friendship itself were more legend than fact; what if the woman were to find herself trapped forever in the splendor that she alone knew to be a literary invention? Yet though each saw a different "story in it," James and Edith Wharton had a similar kind of interest in the situation. Each asked, in effect: at what cost to the human may the cause of art be pursued?

The conflict between art and life was, of course, one of James's favorite themes. And Edith Wharton's "The Portrait," also in her first collection, must have been classed by early readers with James's studies of artists. Mrs. Wharton, like James (and again like Hawthorne, earlier, in "The Prophetic Pictures"), was interested in the moral problems arising from the portraitist's privilege of perception and disclosure. George Lillo has the master artist's seemingly occult power to penetrate into the innermost character of his sitter. Unlike Oliver Lyon, who in James's story "The Liar" paints the hideous truth he discerns, Mrs. Wharton's artist "expurgates" his portrait of the corrupt Vard. He does so from a humane motive, to spare Vard's daughter the harrowing revelation a real portrait would have made. Yet the difference in outcome once again seems to prove the stories to be related. James's hero makes the un-humane choice; he deliberately plans to expose the character of her husband to Mrs. Capadose, hoping to make her regret her previous rejection of his own suit. Mrs. Wharton seems to have then asked: "But what if love persuaded an artist to withhold his destructive truth?" In both stories we are asked to consider how far the artist's powers may be permitted to operate without reference to ordinary moral limits.

Mrs. Wharton's early readers were struck by resemblances less significantly thematic than these. Similarities of scene and cast as much as of situation seemed to link her work to James's. In "The Angel at the Grave," in *Crucial Instances*, her second collection

of stories, the granddaughter of a dead writer is another of those
guardians of reputations who confront the callousness or oppor-
tunism of publics and publishers. Like the widow of Warren
Hope in James's "The Abasement of the Northmores," or the
sister of the dead and misestimated genius in his "John Dela-
voy," she is posted to observe the ironies of fame and obscurity.
In "Copy," in the same collection, a pair of famous writers resolve to burn the love letters each had once received from the
other to keep the vulgar world out of their sanctuary. And in
"The Quicksand," in *The Descent of Man*, the public press is
again the representative of exploitive egotism. *The Radiator*, a
popular organ which thrives on scandal, compromises the moral
position of those who draw their incomes from it. Mrs. Quinton,
who married its publisher thinking she might avert her face from
the sources of her refined existence, finds herself requited by a
son who continues his father's occupation and expects that the
idealistic girl he has fallen in love with will make his mother's
adjustment.

James had remarked in 1887 upon "that mania for publicity
which is one of the most striking signs of our times." He had a
particular horror of the menace of democratic curiosity about
the personal lives of the wealthy or the famous which was fanned
to consuming fire by the popular press. In Henrietta Stackpole, in
The Portrait of a Lady, and in Matthias Pardon, in *The Bostonians*, he had drawn unflattering portraits of the American news-
hound, a species related ultimately to that more diabolic and yet
more highly-motivated "publishing scoundrel" who is the "hero"
of "The Aspern Papers." In *The Reverberator* (how reminiscent
of this name is Edith Wharton's *The Radiator!*), James based his
story upon a real instance of journalistic indiscretion. He created in George Flack, the Paris correspondent of the American
society newspaper, a representative of the new press—ruthless
and at the same time quite unblushing—which aimed to give the
millions the "news" they wanted, at whatever cost to the few
who happened to be the objects of curiosity. "That's what the
American people want and that's what the American people are
going to have," Flack says.

Edith Wharton obviously shared this view of the menace and immorality of journalism. The desire to protect their own privacies from such exploitation made them both excessively cautious about the disclosure of personal matters. James destroyed many of the letters written to him, including Edith Wharton's; at her death, her own collection of correspondence went into a thirty-years' "cold storage" so that all the persons whose affairs might be revealed in letters she had received would be safely in the grave before they became public. The writers who burn each other's letters in her early story "Copy," are not unlike Edith Wharton and James themselves, separately pondering the disposition of their mutual revelations.

An uncertain privilege separates the artist who draws his materials from living persons, their tragedies and embarrassments, from the mercenary newspaper scribbler. We have seen how such stories as Edith Wharton's "The Portrait" and its analogue, James's "The Liar," are related explorations of the moral perils of the artist's role. James considered the artist's case—the *American* artist's case in particular—in many different respects. No American writer before him—not even Hawthorne—had explored the special problems of the artist so fully and variously. Thus, the mere presence of artists in Edith Wharton's stories gave them a Jamesian flavor for many. Nine of the fifteen stories in her first two collections deal in some way with writers or painters, while the two early novelettes, *The Touchstone* and *Sanctuary*, concern the problems in one case of literary publication, in another of artistic rivalry.

One story in *Crucial Instances*, "The Recovery," expresses a particularly Jamesian situation, for it concerns an American painter who finds in Europe, with its treasured greatness, a revelation of his native barrenness. In finding out his own limitations when measured by the great scale of the old masters, he reminds us of young Lance Mallow in James's "The Tree of Knowledge." His "recovery" is indicated in another of James's stories. One may recall the dialogue between the old Yankee painter who has lived out his years in Florence and the young narrator of James's "The Madonna of the Future." "We're the disinherited of Art!"

232

James's painter cries, to which the narrator replies, "Nothing is so idle as to talk about our want of a nursing air, of a kindly soil, of opportunity, of the things that help. The only thing that helps is to do something fine." Edith Wharton's Kenniston suffers the shock of Europe but also perceives the remedy James had prescribed. "Nothing left?" he replies to his wife who has seen his self-satisfaction crumble before the force of European art, "There's everything! Why, here I am, not much over forty, and I've found out already—already!"

It is possible to find other correspondences between Edith Wharton's first stories and James's fiction. It is time, however, to take the measure of such evidence. An author's "materials"—his theme or narrative or, in the roughest sense, the characters he proposes to deal with—all these are only significant in a certain way because of a certain handling of them, because of his treatment. It is technique, it is style that may make different buildings altogether of two stories seemingly built of the same lot of bricks and mortar.

The situation in "The Aspern Papers," to consider this model once more, is only James's starting-point. It was really no one's property, in any case; James had based his tale on a well-known anecdote concerning Jane Clairmont, Shelley's sister-in-law and the mother of Byron's daughter Allegra, which Vernon Lee's brother, Eugene Lee-Hamilton, had related to him and later, again, probably to Mrs. Wharton. But the scope, the studied evolution of "The Aspern Papers" (which occupies 140 pages in the New York Edition of James's works) is quite different from the form Mrs. Wharton gave her brisk little "The Muse's Tragedy." There are some touches of James's method in the Wharton tale. Like James, Mrs. Wharton employs a *ficelle*, a mutual acquaintance particularly in the confidence of her hero— Mrs. Memorall, who, like James's Mrs. Prest, drops out of the narrative once she has brought the young investigator to his object.

This is obvious—and unimportant. But how deliberately James records the transitions in his narrator's consciousness, making meticulous use of the reader's opportunity to look through and beyond his protagonist's vision. There are ironies, but no cheap surprises in what happens to James's manuscript-hunter. Mrs. Wharton's third-person account moves rapidly; in a dozen pages she disposes of Danyers' acquisition of Mrs. Anerton's friendly collaboration; then there is a blank, an unwritten chapter during which the two are together in Venice—not to write their book on Vincent Rendle, but to try love for themselves. Finally, there is a letter in which the lady suddenly is heard speaking for herself, confessing to her tragedy and its insolubility. The letter is a surprise because the point of view is a new one and nothing in the man's apprehensions has prepared us for what the woman now discloses. Edith Wharton's story is a much slighter thing than James's. It is also aimed differently. James's elaboration and his consistency of point of view would not serve the anecdotal turnabout which Mrs. Wharton evidently prized.

James's preference, particularly in the short story and in his later novels, for posting his reader at the side of a single strategically-placed character, restricting him to a single "center of consciousness," is, of course, the most famous of his artistic principles and has affected the writing and criticism of fiction ever since his day. Edith Wharton accepted James's principle in theory—she would repeatedly declare her subscription in later years—though she insisted that it should not be rigidly applied to all conditions and circumstances of fiction-writing.

Among her early stories about half are written entirely from the point of view of one character. But her use of the limited point of view is not James's. Even in the early stories that are seemingly built according to his dictum, we often miss the quality that is the object of James's restriction. He was interested always in the reverberations of character. His central consciousness itself is inevitably the most deeply felt element in his tales; his revelations are always the revelations not merely of what happens, of circumstance, but of how the consciousness in question receives its portion of experience. Even though she acknowledged in her own critical apologue, *The Writing of Fiction*, that James's "unity of vision" made for greatest "compactness" in the short story, Edith Wharton never seemed to realize that his choice of reflecting mirror is actually itself his choice of story in terms of character.

She found the essence of the short story, she declared, in "situation." She saw it as a legitimate descendent of the epic or ballad, "those earlier forms of fiction in all of which action was the chief affair, and the characters, if they did not remain mere puppets, seldom or never became types." It is not surprising, therefore, that her choice of a point of view is no more than a matter of narrative convenience. Her interest is in an event, a "crucial instance." This makes the real difference between her "The Portrait" and his "The Liar." James wished his reader to be in unbroken contact with the mind of his character so that his action might be seen not as the result of a single conscious decision, but as a gradual unconscious growth. In Mrs. Wharton's story another voice is heard first asking the question which is then deliberately answered in the section of the story given over to the hero's reply. We are not, therefore, dramatically saturated in a mind in crisis, as is so often true in James's stories.

Another interesting example is Mrs. Wharton's "The Moving Finger," in *Crucial Instances*. The *donnée* of this story was truly one James could have exploited. Claydon, a painter, creates a remarkable portrait of the lovely Mrs. Grancy, and one of the little group of Grancy's friends says that "Claydon had been saved from falling in love with Mrs. Grancy only by falling in love with his picture of her." Some time later, Mrs. Grancy dies, and the narrator again visits Grancy and the portrait and finds that *both* have changed; the man has aged and saddened and so has the pictured lady, the latter alteration having been done by Claydon at Grancy's request. For ten years or more thereafter Grancy and the portrait alter with one another in order, as Grancy explains, that his wife should follow him, as she would have wished, into age and decline. When Grancy is stricken with serious illness, the portrait is found to wear a foreboding look. Grancy seems about to recover, but the portrait seems to forbid hope. In a fortnight Grancy is dead. In a final conversation with the narrator, Claydon reveals his crime and his motive. Grancy's strange request that he alter his own work had proved the painter's opportunity. He had hastened Grancy's death by means of the evolving portrait, only later to restore it to its original appearance when he could in solitude contemplate Mrs. Grancy's youthful loveliness once more.

The story, as Mrs. Wharton tells it, is a series of changes of voice. The narrator is an observer merely; he cannot see into the inner character of either Grancy or the painter. Instead, he hears one revelation after another; first, Grancy's explanation of his peculiar reasons for having the portrait altered, then Claydon's explanation of his use of the opportunity. There are, in a sense, three "posts of observation"—the observer's own, Grancy's, and Claydon's, for the chosen narrator is so far outside the drama that he can only record it through the explanations the other two offer him.

Reviewers often called Mrs. Wharton's early stories "clever," and this seemed to imply that they were clever and not something else, not profound or moving. The witty cream of the jest was often her chosen end, so she favored situation over character and relished the effect of unexpectedness, the joke on the reader which reveals life's capacity for paradox. She enjoyed the snap of dénouement achieved by passing the story from the hands of one narrator to another. But she could achieve this in other ways also—by deliberately controlling the narrative so that the outcome springs upon us almost without warning like the ending of a piece of detective fiction. Her stories often sound like tales told aloud after dinner by some worldly guest at one of her own elegant parties. In such a story the appetite for the curious and paradoxical is best satisfied by a technique which resembles not a lens gradually brought into focus but a window whose blind is suddenly rolled up.

There is, nonetheless, enough of the James tone in many of Edith Wharton's early stories to justify the critics in overlooking these subtler differences. What one is surprised to note is that they overlooked the stories she was writing which bear no particular relationship with his. Some of these deserved attention, we now can see, because they asserted an individuality she would later develop. "The Pelican," in *The Greater Inclination*, for example, is thoroughly satirical in a way that anticipates her novel, *The Custom of the Country*. This story demonstrates her talent for the satiric definition of social types—here the familiar lady lecturer whose shallow effusions represented culture before lecture audiences throughout nineteenth-century America. James, of course, is often satirical also. Many of his minor characters from *The American* to *The Portrait of a Lady* are almost as summarily categorized as is Edith Wharton's Mrs. Amyot. But in these books, as in his short stories, satire is not James's chief end, and it stops short before the characters through whom he expresses his central themes—Christopher Newman or Isabel Archer. Even in those two experiments in social analysis, *The Princess Casamassima* and *The Bostonians*, his satiric imagination is harnessed to a concern with the tragic and the moral. Miss Birdseye is marked out with a genius for the characteristic that Mrs. Wharton may well have attempted to emulate, but James has made her ancillary rather than central to the human drama of his book.

Another story in her first volume, "Souls Belated," also anticipates a distinctive Wharton quality. It explores the social ironies in a situation which is repeated and amplified in *The Gods Arrive* published in 1932. Its heroine, in defiant flight from an unsatisfactory marriage, travelling in apparent freedom with her lover from one European resort to another, discovers, like Halo Tarrant of the later novel, that convention is indeed what she does crave after all. Like so much of what she later wrote, this early story shows Edith Wharton's competence in the ironic arithmetic of manners. She understood the uses of situations which juxtaposed differing social attitudes; one of her favorite themes became that of the cost of personal deviation from the dominant code of behavior. James's primary concern is seldom so sociological. A Daisy Miller interests him because she illustrates not only the immediate conflict of manners her story involves, but the permanent issue of innocence and experience.

It is this strain of social satire and irony that becomes predominant in Edith Wharton's later stories. Her third collection, *The Descent of Man and Other Stories*, contains such studies almost exclusively. The title story is another "instance" out of the world of publishing, but Mrs. Wharton is not concerned with Jamesian moral issues. Her humor is local. Prof. Linyard, who thought he had written a burlesque of the popular works which "reconcile" religion and science, found (like Samuel Butler after writing *The Fair Haven* in 1873) that he had actually written a best-seller specimen of the thing he meant to expose. Another comic treatment of the paradoxes of popular reading taste is "Expiation," which relates how Mrs. Fetheral's novel, *Fast and Loose*, became a success only after her cousin the Bishop obligingly denounced it. The humorous contradictions of manners created by divorce are what engage Edith Wharton's attention in "The Other Two," in which a man marries a woman twice divorced and appreciates his wife's peculiar pliancy when he finds her able to pour tea for all three husbands at once. A related discovery is made by Mrs. Westall, of "The Reckoning," who marries under the new dispensation, "Thou shalt not be unfaithful—to thyself" only to discover appallingly that the rule she followed in divorcing one man is now invoked against herself by another.

Social criticism is also the goal of *The House of Mirth*, published in 1905. To the reviewers the novel may have seemed a decisive act of liberation, but as we have seen there were loomings of the same quality in her earliest fictional efforts. Some of her stories had already defined the peculiar dilemmas of the rich, and here, given the dignity of full-length tragedy, was the story of Lily Bart, the product and the victim of those conditions. In telling of Lily Bart's struggle in the cross-currents of "high" society, Mrs. Wharton was led to depict the specific habits of Fifth Avenue and Newport and Tuxedo Park, to expose a layer of the American scene with a sociologist's sense for the characteristic. With a Balzacian thoroughness she surveyed the circles impinging upon circles in this layer—the Trenors and Van Osburghs and Dorsets who were "in," the Wellington Blys and Simon Rosedales and Norma Hatches who were still outside, and the dynamics of social change that moved these circles upon one another. Her interest was in milieu and her technique was satiric, the definition of social types rather than the exploration of individual variability, the selection of instances crucial for a general rather than for a special problem.

Even her heroine became a case in illustration rather than a singular case. Despite a moral fastidiousness that proves to be an eccentric weakness in the struggle for survival, she is viewed rather coolly by her creator as a subject of forces greater than herself. *The House of Mirth* is thus an early example of American naturalism. It is impossible to say how much Edith Wharton knew in 1905 about the theories of French naturalism, or even if she had read Frank Norris' *The Pit* which had been a best-seller in 1903. But she did have a decided interest in the post-Darwinian biology, and it is illuminating to notice how repeatedly Lily Bart is described by means of biological symbols. She is thus conceived of as the exact sum of heredity and environment, unable any more than the "water-plant in the flux of the tides," as Mrs. Wharton puts it, to choose the direction of her growth.

The House of Mirth was not accused of being Jamesian by its reviewers; neither its realism nor its scientific determinism of viewpoint bore resemblance to James's fiction. Yet James had worked in the same garden-plot of types—the leisure class. Lawrence Selden, the refined dilettante who fails to save Lily from her overdose of a sleeping-drug, is the first example of a recurrent type of male figure in Edith Wharton's novels, and a type closely resembling certain heroes of James. Gifted with every faculty but the power to act passionately, they repeatedly fail the women who need them. James's incarnations of such men are numerous and vary from the most forgivable to the most criminal, so that Isabel Archer is let down by the entirely noble Ralph Touchett as well as by the quite evil Gilbert Osmond. His favorite theme of renunciation, the last mark of virtue in Christopher Newman, merges imperceptibly at times into its opposite, the inability to accept the gift of love which is the coarse defect of a Morris Townsend, in *Washington Square*. At his most typical, the protagonist is an observer, almost an artist, in whom reflection has usurped the power of feeling and doing. There is Winterbourne in James's early *Daisy Miller* and Longmore, in *Madame de Mauves*, a book Edith Wharton took for a conscious model in her next work, *Madame de Treymes*. Among James's late stories, the great illustration of this theme is Marcher, in "The Beast in the Jungle," which influenced Edith Wharton's characterization of the hero of *The Age of Innocence*.

Perhaps, as we have already speculated, there was something in James himself, or in his personal experience, that made him come back again and again to situations in which a richer feminine nature is betrayed by a man of equal or superior cultivation and inferior heart. Edith Wharton was herself familiar with this type, whether exemplified by Walter Berry and the other "dilettante-observers" she had as friends or by James himself. Whatever the reason, both knew and depicted a masculine personality who may simply have been the recognizable product of a wealthy society affording no opportunity for worth-while dedication to the occasional individuals of sensitivity and intellectual ability arising in its midst. Edith Wharton's instances of the type are distributed large and small in her work—not only in Lawrence Selden and in Newland Archer of the *The Age of Innocence* and in Darrow of *The Reef*, but in such a tiny acid study as that of Thursdale in the early story, "The Dilettante." It is not impossible that James's precedence in setting down this character may have helped her to place him so centrally in her fiction. There may even be, in the case of Lawrence Selden, a particular relation, as Marcia Davenport has suggested, with Vanderbank in James's *The Awkward Age*, a man whose selfishness or inhibition also keeps him from commitment to a woman unjustly placed in a dubious situation.

James had also found subject-matter in the identical problem that confronts the heroine of *The House of Mirth*. Kate Croy of *The Wings of the Dove*, which had appeared three years earlier, was, like Lily, a girl of "good" family without a fortune and so forced to make shift with her beauty and wit. Living with a wealthy aunt who expects her to acquire a rich husband, Lily's position is exactly like Kate's at the start of James's novel. She can no more afford to marry Lawrence Selden than Kate can afford to marry Merton Densher. Her dilemma was one that continued to interest Edith Wharton, and in Sophy Viner of *The*

Reef and Susy Branch of *The Glimpses of the Moon* it is again her central focus.

James placed many of the ladies of his stories, particularly those he called his "bad heroines," in this situation. Madame Merle, of *The Portrait of a Lady*, and Charlotte Stant of *The Golden Bowl* are both seen, retrospectively, as girls of "society" origins who had been too poor to marry as they would choose. Again, the theme and situation may have its source for both Edith Wharton and James in biography and observation of the same social scene. It seems probable that Mrs. Wharton was herself a victim of the compulsion to "make a good marriage"; her mother had been a poor relation of the immensely wealthy Rhinelanders until her marriage into the prosperous Jones family, and she probably urged upon her daughter the necessity of such choices. James, though a member of a family of some inherited wealth and certainly of social position, probably could not have afforded marriage. Among all the explanations for his celibacy that have been offered by biographers, this simple reason tends to be overlooked. Lawrence Selden, to come back to him again, is Lily's counterpart, and in this, too, a Jamesian figure—he cannot afford to retain his tastes and leisure except by bachelorhood.

But neither in *The House of Mirth* nor in her later treatments of the theme does Mrs. Wharton really suggest James. Kate Croy is not the heroine of *The Wings of the Dove*—any more than Madame Merle is of *The Portrait of a Lady* or Charlotte Stant is of *The Golden Bowl*. James was not interested in externally determined choices, the preoccupation of the naturalist; his attention was always fixed upon freedom, the condition of moral responsibility, its possibilities and its perils. Thus his imagination was captured above all by Isabel Archer and Milly Theale and Maggie Verver. And he was able also to depict as a final adumbration of masculine integrity the figure of Lambert Strether, in *The Ambassadors*, who, though he is also too poor to marry, does not reject his happiness with Maria Gostrey for so simple a reason as this. Strether remains, in the end, as free in action as Christopher Newman, the wealthy American whose renunciation of happiness is also his proof of freedom.

Design no less than viewpoint made *The House of Mirth* completely unlike the products of James. Nothing could have differed more from the architectured balance of one of his novels than the episodic proliferation of Lily Bart's career. The story of Lily, most delicate and pathetic of rogues, is picaresque; Lily passes from one experience and social group to the next in a series that might be shortened or prolonged without altering the total effect. Edith Wharton subsequently used the phrase "chronicle-novel" to describe her technique in *The Custom of the Country* and it applies to this earlier work as well. James, she acknowledged, had no use for fiction of this form, but "cared only for the elaborate working out on all sides of a central situation."

Significantly, "chronicle-novel" is a term that may also be used to describe her earlier, unsuccessful attempt to establish herself as a novelist. *The Valley of Decision*, published in 1902, was a weak pastiche of eighteenth-century Italian scene and history which she herself was later to condemn as "not, in my sense of the term, a novel at all, but only a romantic chronicle, unrolling its episodes like the frescoed legends on the palace-walls which formed its background." Certainly it was unlike James—and even the reviewers omitted the usual reference to his influence applied so insistently to her short stories. It was compared, instead, to *Romola*, but was recognized to be even less of a true work of fiction than George Eliot's splendid failure. Most critics praised it for what it was, a philosophical romance, and occupied themselves with pointing out its graceful use of eighteenth-century sources—the way the trip along the Brenta, for example, is adapted from Goldoni's account of his flight from Rimini to Venice. It was, of course, a false start, yet its formal pattern, "a romantic chronicle unrolling its episodes," makes it a precursor for the linear design of her next long work of fiction. That work, *The House of Mirth*, established Edith Wharton's claim to independent consideration. It was the production of this second novel in 1905, she declared, that "turned her from a drifting amateur into a professional." Yet *The Valley of Decision*, unpropitiously enough, was the first specimen of Edith Wharton's writing that James actually read.

The House of Mirth was deliberately, aggressively un-Jamesian, and it seems to have had some relation with Howard Sturgis' *Belchamber,* which James and Edith Wharton had discussed together the previous year. In a review she wrote for *The Bookman* in May, 1905, she clearly reflected her disagreement with James on the importance of form and asserted the pre-eminence of subject in terms that fitted either Sturgis' novel or her own. *Belchamber,* it was to be admitted, had "faults of construction and perspective such as the hack writer could easily have avoided," but it had, for compensation, "the quality of the 'thing in itself;' with something of the desultoriness, the irregularity, of life caught in the act, and pressed still throbbing between the leaves of the book." And with a defensiveness that surely had grown out of the personally-felt challenge of James's ordered art, she went on, "Form is much—so much that, to the plodder through the amorphous masses of Anglo-American fiction, it sometimes seems all in all—but when it is the mere lifeless reproduction of another's design, it is of no more artistic value than any other reproduction; whereas the *chose vue,* the thing personally felt and directly rendered, asserts itself through all accidental difficulties of expression."

It seems that Sturgis' very *chose vue* had influenced her own choice of subject in the novel she wrote immediately after reading his. She defends *his* subject—artistocratic and "unpleasant"— as though she were speaking of *The House of Mirth:* "Books dealing with the adventures of idle and fashionable people do not generally make for edification . . . But there is a noble way of viewing ignoble facts; and that is the view which Mr. Sturgis has taken of the world he depicts. He has shown us, in firm, clear strokes, the tragedy of the trivial: has shown us how the susceptibilities of a tender and serious spirit . . . may be crushed and trampled under foot in the mad social race for luxury and amusement. A handful of vulgar people, bent only on spending and enjoying, may seem a negligible factor in the social development of the race; but they become an engine of destruction through the illusions they kill and the generous ardours they turn to despair." It is impossible not to suspect that the fate of Sturgis'

243

sensitive hero was consciously paralleled by Edith Wharton in the history she imagined for her Lily Bart. Of her intentions in her own story, she wrote, years afterwards, echoing her description of *Belchamber*:

> The problem was how to extract from such a subject the typical human significance which is the story-teller's reason for telling one story rather than another. In what aspect could a society of irresponsible pleasure-seekers be said to have on the "old woe of the world" any deeper bearing than the people composing such a society could guess? The answer was that a frivolous society can acquire dramatic significance only through what its frivolity destroys. Its tragic implication lies in its power of debasing people and ideals. The answer, in short, was my heroine, Lily Bart.

In the coincidence of her view of her own and Sturgis' accomplishments in 1905 we can read the quality of her conscious resistance to the example of Henry James.

9

Correspondences and Differences

In 1902 a new apartment building was built in New York City and named the *Henry James*. William Dean Howells posted the news to James and received the following wry reply:

> Your most kind communication . . . in respect to the miraculously-named "uptown" apartment house has at once deeply agitated me and wildly uplifted me. The agitation as I call it, is verily but the tremor, the intensity of hope, of the delirious dream that such a stroke may "bring my books before the public," or do something toward it—coupled with the reassertion of my constant, too constant conviction that no power on earth can ever do that . . . The *Henry James*, I opine, will be a terrifically "private" hotel, and will languish like the Lord of Burleigh's wife, under the burden of an honour "unto which it was not born." Refined, liveried, "two-toileted," it will have been a short-lived, hectic paradox, and will presently have to close in order to reopen as the Mary Johnston or the Kate Douglas Wiggin or the James Lane Allen. Best of all as the Edith Wharton.

James's irony was prompted by the fact that his supposed follower was a decided success while his own giant efforts—*The*

Wings of the Dove was a failure in 1902—were now shouldered out of the way by an impatient public. It seemed that his over-commodious, refined art must yield place to something more popular. Although he probably had not yet read anything by Edith Wharton he was already aware of the existence of her first books of stories, so insistently credited to his influence—and, to enlarge the humor of it, so preferred by the fickle reader. The charge of Jamesianism had not, apparently, done any harm to her sales, for three months after the publication of her first volume, Charles Scribner was able to report to his brother Arthur, "Of the newer books the most successful is *The Greater Inclination*. The reviews have recognized it as an exceptional book; the first edition is gone."

A few months after his letter to Howells, James discovered that Edith Wharton had published a novel, *The Valley of Decision*, and curiosity finally pricked him sharply enough to make him get hold of and read the odd, rambling, most un-Jamesian chronicle. He was sufficiently impressed to write the author his views, which she in turn communicated to W. C. Brownell, as has been previously noted.

The exact quality of James's interest must remain obscure since the letter itself seems to have been lost. Although Mrs. Wharton was not apparently disposed to make much of this unlooked-for nod from greatness, his response, as we have seen, did impress her sister-in-law, James's old friend Mary Cadwalader Jones, who had been telling him for some time about her remarkable young relative and who now sent him two other volumes by the same author. These books—*The Greater Inclination* and *Crucial Instances*—tempted him to take up that role of Edith Wharton's teacher which the critics had already assigned to him. He picked up and turned about her small products in his great, experienced hand, and wrote Mrs. Jones:

> . . . I take to her very kindly as regards her diabolical little cleverness, the quantity of intention and intelligence in her style, and her sharp eye for an interesting *kind* of subject. I had read neither of these two volumes, and though the "Valley" is, for significance of ability, several pegs above either, I have

246

extracted food for criticism from both. As criticism, in the nobler sense of the word, is for me enjoyment, I've in other words much liked them. Only they've made me again, as I hinted to you other things had, want to get hold of the little lady and pump the pure essence of my wisdom and experience into her. She *must* be tethered in native pastures, even if it reduces her to a backyard in New York. If a work of imagination, of fiction, interests me at all (and very few, alas, do!) I always want to write it over in my own way, handle the subject from my own sense of it. *That* I always find a pleasure in, and I found it extremely in the "Vanished Hand"—over which I should have liked, at several points, to contend with her. But I can't speak more highly for any book, or at least for my interest in any. I take liberties with the greatest.

He respected, plainly, the conscious intelligence at work in these stories—the author's sense of object and style. "The Moving Finger" in *Crucial Instances* (which is probably the story he incorrectly recalls as "The Vanished Hand") has, as we have seen, a subject particularly attractive to him. Others, too, it will be recalled, exploited material he had shown a predilection for. Yet he challenged some of her choices of subject with "she must be tethered in native pastures even if it reduces her to a backyard in New York." The remark may be taken to mean that James urged her to restrict herself to the American scene, and if this is the case, the advice is curious, for James was even then occupied himself with so "international" a work as *The Ambassadors*. But one tends to forget that James's international subject was compound and comparative and not exclusively foreign. *The Ambassadors* is "tethered" in Woollett, Mass., however far it ranges; it is concerned with the encounter of Woollett and Europe, the challenges and transmutations effected. It seems likely that James's advice to Edith Wharton in 1902 was that she avoid the *completely* foreign subject—the second-hand Italy of *The Valley of Decision* or of the story "The Confessional." However the remark be interpreted, it was certainly true that Edith Wharton did not discover her potentialities as a writer of fiction until she wrote a novel literally located in New York's backyard, *The*

House of Mirth. And then, ironically, she stood forth from his shadow.

Meanwhile, her short stories showed likenesses to his own, and his impulse was to increase the resemblance. His pedagogic urge made him want to see the student's work done over "from his own sense of it."

What he might have been ready to do for Mrs. Wharton is illustrated by two letters written to an older feminine follower, Mrs. Humphry Ward, in 1899 concerning her novel *Eleanor.* In the first of these letters, James earnestly and passionately goes into minor details with Mrs. Ward, offering corrections in regard to the American background of one of her characters, but also making larger suggestions on how best to enter a subject such as hers (he suggests that the reader must approach it by an "ante-chamber or two and the crooked corridor before he is already in the Presence"). He urges her to relocate the "centre" of her subject more logically, to choose the right consciousness, and "make that consciousness full, rich, universally prehensile, and *stick* to it—don't shift—and don't shift arbitrarily—how, other-wise, do you get your unity of subject or keep up with your reader's sense of it?" And as he multiplies these comments he ruefully catches himself to admit, "I can read nothing, if I read it at all, save in the light of how one would *one's self* proceed in tackling the same *data!*", ending his letter, "Do let me have more of 'Eleanor'—to re-write!"

It appears that Mrs. Ward protested James's seeming insistence that there was only one way to handle a subject. He replied that he believed nothing of the sort, that there was, in truth, not one "hard and fast rule of presentation" in his view, but "five million . . . or as many as there are subjects in all the world." Yet though he was ready to declare that it was the subject itself that dictated its treatment, it was obvious that he was confident that he knew the one treatment a subject dictated. He had to confess, "I am a wretched person to *read* a novel—I begin so quickly and concom-itantly for *myself,* to write it rather—even before I know clearly what it's about!" These letters were written after Mrs. Ward had shown him only the opening portions of the novel; when it was finished he again commented, hinting irrepressibly his disapprovals amid various notes of praise, but adding, "I can't 'criticize'—though I *could* (that is, I *did*—but can't do it again)—rewrite."

It was a teaching system with some limitations; a pupil might not appreciate a master who knew no other way than to "pump the pure essence" of his particular wisdom into the waiting vessel. James had received something of a snub from Mrs. Ward for attempting to do so, and possibly Mrs. Wharton's reaction was the same. In any case, he did not seriously undertake the task of refashioning Edith Wharton's art. He was no more her deliberate instructor than she was his conscious pupil.

Yet he continued to watch her development with the greatest interest. One move in which she seemed to have followed him was her decision in 1907 to establish a home in Europe. For James, the dedicated artist, such a choice was, exclusively, a *writer's* choice of foothold. In Europe he found not only the conditions of life that suited his tastes, but the medium of his artistic investigations, a source of inspiration and materials. Edith Wharton's need for Europe may have been more diffuse than this, but to James, seeing her as a young writer, the question remained simple: where would she most surely find substance and inspiration for her writing? His own choice, made years before, had been for England rather than for France or another country, as providing a more native environment of language and morality while adding the old world richnesses. He was no longer as interested in extremes of international contrast as he had once been, but in a briefer, more vibrant space that separated the English from their American cousins, where he could locate contrasts less specifically national.

He had done this in two of the novels in his final "trilogy"—*The Wings of the Dove* and *The Golden Bowl*, and he would not have considered even *The Ambassadors*, with its locale in Paris, a return to his earlier kind of interest in the French difference from the American. All of his late "international" studies dramatize his great theme of innocence and experience, even of American innocence and European experience, rather than of particular national misunderstandings. On the whole, one was safer, he now thought, in dealing with differences more subtle, more moral, than those blatant distinctions of nearly everything which had attracted him when he had written so early a work as *Madame de Mauves.* And yet these were precisely what had caught Mrs. Wharton's eye and stimulated her to write a novel which closely resembled it, *Madame de Treymes,* in the same year in which she took up residence in the rue de Varenne. He wrote her there from London:

> I think I have had no chance to tell you how much I admired your single story in the Aug. *Scribner*—beautifully done, I thought, & full of felicities & achieved values & pictures. All the same, with the rue de Varenne &c, don't go in too much for the French or the "Franco-American" subject—the real field of your extension is *here*—it has far more fusability with *our* native & primary material; between which & the French elements there is, I hold, a disparity as complete as between a life led in trees, say & a life led in—sea depths, or in other words between that of climbers and swimmers—or (crudely) that of monkeys & fish.

Madame de Treymes, unlike *The House of Mirth,* was very Jamesian. It seems almost as though she felt free, now that she had demonstrated her individuality, to express the influence she had feared to admit. She invited comparison almost deliberately, with her echo of James's title, and some of the critics seized the bait. H. G. Dwight, the reviewer for *Putnam's Monthly,* wrote, "Yet, after granting the unfairness of comparisons which Lily Bart's successor would inevitably be compelled to undergo, it was positively exasperating for *Mme. de Treymes* to hark back to Henry James. If a slightly different twist were given to her adventures, the machinery of them, her nationality, her setting, her case, her very name reminded one of Madame de Mauves."

Actually, James's *The American* is a closer analogue than *Madame de Mauves.* In *Madame de Mauves,* as in *Madame de Treymes,* there is an American woman married to a corrupt French aristocrat and loved by a possible rescuer, an American.

But the American, Longmore, only toys with the idea of taking Euphemia Cleve away from the Baron de Mauves, while Edith Wharton's hero nobly undertakes to rescue Madame de Malrive. Euphemia's virtue is more than the baron can cope with; closing her door both to a lover and to him, she finally, and rather improbably, one must say, drives him to suicide. At home in America, Longmore learns that Euphemia is free—and does nothing about it.

A more fruitful comparison can be made with *The American.* The hero of *Madame de Treymes*, John Durham, is an illustration of American scrupulosity strikingly like James's Christopher Newman. Durham and Newman both boldly engage themselves in conflict with a French aristocratic family for love of one of its members, and both show themselves superior to their opponents by a capacity, in the end, for noble renunciation. There is nothing particularly noble, on the other hand, in Longmore's retreat from the problem of Madame de Mauves.

Of course there is a great difference between the heroines of *Madame de Treymes* and *The American.* Madame de Malrive, Edith Wharton's lady, is really an American, Fanny Frisbee, who has married a Frenchman she now loathes—like Madame de Mauves—while Newman's Claire de Cintré is French, a member of the redoubtable Bellegarde clan. But this difference is less important than it seems. Just as James's Newman is engaged with the Bellegardes as a close-ranked force, indeed with all that they represent as traditional Europeans, so Mrs. Wharton's Durham is shown in relationship not so much with his lost little American as with the Malrives who control her through their hold on her son. It is significant that Edith Wharton's title leads us to locate the center of the story not in Fanny (née Frisbee) de Malrive, but in her sister-in-law, Madame de Treymes, who is the representative of that antithetic European quality with which Durham comes to grips. To understand this quality with its different sense of virtue, admitting it nevertheless to be a sense of virtue, and to reject it, finally—this is the sum of Durham's experience as it is that of Newman's. And Madame de Treymes, like the Bellegardes, is taught by her encounter with this American to appreciate his native height of pride.

Thus *Madame de Treymes* is a study in cultural comparison, an exploitation of that same "Franco-American" subject which had once so powerfully attracted James. But in 1907 James must have felt like crying: "But that is only the way I *was!* Keep up with me now!" For now he was engaged upon the retrospective ordering of his works in the monumental New York Edition and looking back upon *The American* over thirty intervening years. His own final exercise in the international theme had been *The Golden Bowl* in which the scene had been English, a medium of "far more fusability with *our* native & primary material." The discrepancy, on the other hand, of French life, French character, now seemed to him so absolute as to reduce itself to a banal formula, if one were not careful. That, indeed, is Strether's precise error, in *The Ambassadors,* to think, first, that he understands perfectly what Paris is likely to have done to Chad; then, in an equal error, to think that he understands what Paris has done *for* him. It is his discovery that nothing of great importance has happened to Chad, only to *him,* and not because he has been abroad so much as because he has consented to experience whatever has been given him.

Mrs. Wharton's literary preoccupation with the Franco-American subject persisted in *The Reef, The Custom of the Country, The Mother's Recompense,* and other works. Only in her final, unfinished novel, *The Buccaneers,* and in a few late short stories does she employ an English background. The comparison of French with American traits is, indeed, one of the dominant motifs of her fiction, the result of a lifelong conviction, shared by her friend Brownell, about the particular difference in tastes and manners. It is a difference which is nowhere so compactly and clearly presented as in *Madame de Treymes* where, indeed, it can be said to be her entire theme. And in this simplicity of intention she outdid even James at his earliest and most "international." Her John Durham's discovery of the French depth of difference seems to resemble that of Christopher Newman, but Mrs. Wharton's study is more ethnological and less ethical than *The Ameri-*

can. In the end she does not decide upon the superiority of either side, but merely arranges her tale so that each finally understands the quality of the other. The American says "You poor, good woman" to the French lady of the title, who replies, "Ah, you poor, good man," though each had managed previously to misapprehend the other.

In finding James's interest to be in all his work more exclusively moral than Edith Wharton's, one touches upon the fundamental difference between them in the use of international comparisons, the "international theme" altogether. As time went on, Edith Wharton's writing became almost exclusively focused upon the description of social relationships. Within the play of the comedy of manners, her characteristic tone, the contrasts of national as of class behavior provided her with the means of definition and analysis and the opportunities for comedy and pathos, though seldom for tragedy. As one looks down the list of her stories and novels it is amazing, in fact, how few fail to use the device of national comparison. James, for his different ends, found the international comparison useful but not in the end necessary; the characters of his last novels could have been made all American or all European without substantially changing his meaning.

A few months after *Madame de Treymes* appeared in *Scribner's*, a new, full-length novel by Mrs. Wharton, *The Fruit of the Tree*, began its run in the magazine. This work made no use of James's precedent in any important respect. It was an ambitious attempt to write a modern "problem novel" and it tackled problems of the kind James would have found unusable, tackling them, moreover, in huddled succession. Would John Amherst, idealistic young factory manager, be able to bring reform to the Westmore Mills and the town of Hanford? Can marriage reconcile natures so different as Amherst's and the luxury-loving, unintellectual Bessy Westmore's? Is nurse Justine Brent justified in administering a lethal "mercy" dose of morphine to Bessy, now hopelessly injured by a riding accident? May Amherst find happiness, finally, with Justine? There was stuff here for a dozen novels. The multiplication of dramatic occasions and the appalling shifting of thematic center in this book must have bewildered readers, and the critics pronounced it a failure. Edith Wharton never attempted anything like it again. One can see, however, that it may have been prompted by her renewed desire to assert an individuality which she had seemed to surrender in the novelette *Madame de Treymes.*

She had great difficulty in doing the book. As often, the writing of a successor to a best-seller had proven a paralyzing challenge. *The House of Mirth* had been a phenomenal success. It had been reviewed with enthusiasm and copies flew out of the booksellers' hands faster than they could order them—100,000 were sold in the first two months; then the Curtis Publishing Company got out a special cheap edition of 10,000 more to distribute as a premium to magazine subscribers. Edith Wharton knew that part of this success was attributable to the reputation of the book as an exposé of high life written by an insider—the very sort of interest she and James would have been ashamed to cater to. At the same time, she was accused, as James had often been, of writing about the small coterie of wealth and privilege while all of democratic America waited for its portrait.

She determined that her next book would be less narrowly focused. It would include "life in New York and in a manufacturing town, with the House of Mirth in the middle of the block, but a good many other houses adjoining," as she wrote her publisher. And her hero would be of a different sort. It would seem that the characterization of Selden, a frail Jamesian note in a predominantly un-Jamesian book, was smelt out for criticism by some readers of *The House of Mirth.* Charles Scribner had been moved to write her, "In your next book you must give us a strong man for I am getting tired of the comments on Selden." And Edith Wharton resolutely declared to him as she set to work on *The Fruit of the Tree,* "As for the hero, he is going to be a very strong man." John Amherst is intended to be a very different hero indeed from Lawrence Selden; unquestionably Edith Wharton had resolved upon a new masculine idea; during the presidency of Theodore Roosevelt the passive aristocrat may well have begun to seem passé. She had also obviously decided to meet the criticism that she could deal only with the frivolous concerns of a small particle of the social mass; this was to be a story that would encompass areas and human varieties never before introduced into her fiction.

It is interesting, however, that her hero is not so much an opposite to Selden as a Selden who has accepted an alternative never considered by Lily Bart's friend. Though he is the Assistant Manager of a textile mill in a small town in western Massachusetts, he is not a workman who has risen from the ranks but the grandson of a "gentleman," whose reduced family fortunes and idealism have combined to bring him to his role. Justine Brent, the nurse he finds attending one of the hospital workmen injured at the plant, is, again, a Lily Bart who has found another way of meeting her circumstances. It turns out that she is actually a schoolmate of Bessy Westmore, the owner of the mills, a girl, like Lily, whose family has lost its money and who retains the manners and tastes of her original background.

Justine is animated, like her counterpart, Amherst, by a desire to make some contribution to the alleviation of human suffering; as he has learnt his trade at the factory, she has gone beyond Lily—who was a failure at trimming hats in a shop—and has been trained as a competent surgical nurse. So, by the slenderest of threads, Justine and Amherst have a relation to James's own favorite types—the dilettante-observer and the Kate Croy-Charlotte Stant "bad heroine," but Edith Wharton has translated them into a new medium.

There is a curiously distorted relation, in fact, between the situation that ensues after Amherst's marriage and the story of *The Wings of the Dove*. When Bessy becomes a hopeless invalid whose death will free her husband to marry Justine, and incidentally bestow upon him her millions, she becomes a debased counterpart of James's Milly. Justine's noble "mercy-killing" of Bessy, though prompted by nothing except pity, does, in the long run, serve this end. Edith Wharton has made hero and heroine of James's conniving pair, and his "dove" has become her empty-headed and shallow-hearted canary. Yet there is a certain rela-

255

tionship between the shape of the triangular situation in each novel. And a very odd thing, in fact, seems to have occurred. There is a strangely unconvincing quality about the plot of *The Fruit of the Tree*. It is as though the new characteristics of Edith Wharton's three chief characters have failed to disguise completely their original foundation, as though, wanting to describe the new man and the new woman, she had secretly been unable to sympathize with them and drawn them so coldly that their nobility becomes suspect; few readers, I think, feel complete confidence in Justine's disinterested "mercy-killing" of Bessy. As though revenging herself upon the false intentions of her creator, Bessy emerges as the most successful and vivid character of the book—alive and attractive for all her putative contemptibility.

The Fruit of the Tree has more obvious sources of weakness, however. In her desire to take into her scope the House of Mirth and "a good many other houses adjoining" as well—to include, possibly, areas where her actual interest was slight—Edith Wharton strained the unity of her novel. It is a chronicle that moves on and on not only from episode to episode but from interest to interest. Some of the "other houses" she knew too little about. Although notable examples exist—*Ethan Frome* among them—to prove that a writer need not have experienced at first hand what he describes, Edith Wharton simply did not know enough about factories and factory-workers. She even made technical errors, which readers hastened to point out. But more important than her difficulty in "working up" the scene was the fact that her unfamiliarity with its human conditions made it impossible for her to develop a dramatic story that seriously involved the issues of such a world. It was inevitable that, beginning with the Westmore Mills and the bedside of an injured workman where factory manager John Amherst stands with Nurse Justine Brent, she shifted to the drawing-room of the owners and finally to the Long Island estate of Bessy Westmore, taking Amherst and Justine into a new environment in which the author, if not her characters, felt more comfortable.

The book must have shocked James, who was at that very moment contemplating a critical article on his friend's work. Late

in the summer of 1907 he forwarded to Mrs. Wharton a letter
from a journalist by the name of Markeley who proposed that
James do a "personality paper" about her for his "International
Press Service." Markeley apparently declared that she had "expressed a wish" that James might do such an essay, and James was
eager to comply: "I only want a hint from you to the effect that
he *did* gouge out of you some allusive preference for my ancient
hand—I only want this (it will make me feel not only more
inspired but more comfortable), to proceed to my little étude . . .
On that little word in short I shall be able, I think, to "picture
you up" as not even he could do. And the attempt will greatly
charm me. (*Me*, I say; I speak not of Others)." Although she
must have answered that she had given no encouragement to the
editor's solicitation, James still thought the idea a good one and
wanted to make her current fiction the occasion for his "étude."

> . . . the seed having been dropped, by however crooked a *geste*,
> into my mind, I am conscious of a lively & spontaneous disposi-
> tion to really dedicate a few lucid remarks to the mystery of
> your genius; & I am writing today to the inquirer whose letter I
> sent you that if he can explain so highly imaginative a state-
> ment about your wish (really, evidently, a barefaced, & as I
> judge, common trick of the trade), I will send him his 3,000
> words; waiting however for the appearance of *The Fruit of the
> Tree* to do so. I trust their appearing in his organ—which I
> have had an opportunity of asking about (to learn that it's
> recognized)—won't displease you. The organs all seem to me
> much of a muchness. So I shall sharpen my pen. I lost the
> sequence of the F. of the T. while abroad those 4 or 5 months
> —it was inevitable—& then decided to *wait*. And I am intensely
> waiting. It has been cruel.

Upon receiving this letter Mrs. Wharton at once dispatched a
note to Charles Scribner asking that a copy of *The Fruit of the
Tree* be posted to James. "He has just written me that he wants
to write an article about me, and wants to read 'The Fruit' first—
having mercifully waited till the volume should appear . . . He
says he 'wishes to say a few mild words on the mystery of my

genius'—which looks to me as if he meant to make mince-meat of me," she wrote. James had no desire to make mince-meat of her, however, at least not in public. But over a month later, having studied *The Fruit of the Tree,* he wrote her,

> I haven't yet thanked you for the copy of *The Fruit of the Tree* (admirable work!) nor told you—since indeed this has just become apparent—that I shall probably *not* find myself at all well-advised to do that paper on your Personality for the mendacious Markeley . . . He wrote me such a very lame and unattenuated explanation of his preposterous statement that you had "expressed a wish" &c that I felt I must cause inquiries to be made about him and his mysterious periodical—as I was able to do; & these have eventuated in nothing reassuring. I don't feel I can "enthuse" over you in a hole & corner publication—it doesn't seem to me the proper place for either of us. Yet—apart from this—I am embarrassed as I am in no intimate relation at present with either the Atlantic or the N.A.R. . . . If Scribner had *deux sous* of inspiration (left over from what it employs in getting you to write in it) *it* would invite me to wrestle with your Personality in the bright Arena of its pages; but I am not, for particular reasons, by way of *offering* anything to ces messieurs at all. I *want* to enthuse over you, I yearn to, quite—but I must wait for the right & harmonious occasion for so doing. Ne craignez rien—so to speak (as if you cared!) I say to myself at least that the thing won't lose or spoil by keeping or waiting. I have read the *The Fruit* meanwhile with acute appreciation—the liveliest admiration & sympathy. I find it a thing of the highest and finest ability & lucidity & of a great deal of (though not perhaps of a completely) superior art. Where my qualifications would come in would be as to the terrible question of the composition & conduct of the thing—as to which you will think I am always boring. About this side I think there are certain things to say—but as against it the whole has intensely held & charmed me, & Dieu sait si je suis (in my blighted age), a difficult reader (of "new fiction"). The element of good writing in it is enormous—I perpetually catch you at writing admirably (though I do think here, somehow of George Eliotizing a little more frankly than ever yet; I mean a little more *directly* & avowedly. However, I don't "mind" that—I like it; & you do things which are not in dear

old Mary Ann's chords at all). However, there are many more things to say than I can go into now—& I only attempt to note that you have to my mind produced a remarkably rich & accomplished & distinguished book—of more *kinds* of interest than anyone now going can pretend to achieve.

Buried among the flutter of compliments in this letter is a severe judgment. James questioned—ever so diffidently—nothing less than the essential qualification of the book as a novel—"the terrible question of the composition & conduct of the thing." He did not expect that Mrs. Wharton would appreciate his insistence upon form "as to which you will think I am always boring," and this is a measure of the distance he perceived between their attitudes towards the art of the novel. He generously conceded that "the element of good writing in it is enormous" but even here catches himself to murmur that the writing of *The Fruit of the Tree* is too "directly and avowedly" after George Eliot. He concludes with a barbed compliment. She has produced, he tells her, a book "of more *kinds* of interest than anyone now going can pretend to achieve." More kinds, indeed! The multiplicity of interests was precisely the source of the book's trouble.

To Mrs. Jones soon afterwards he explained himself more bluntly: "I have read the book myself with great admiration for the way much of it is done—there is great talent all along. But it is of a strangely infirm composition and construction—as if she hadn't taken thought for that, and two or three sane persons here who have read my copy find it a 'disappointment' after the H. of M. That is not my sense—I find it superior—and I think the admirers of the 'House' will stultify themselves if they don't at least equally back it up."

It certainly seems that James's dissatisfaction with the "occasion" for comment upon Edith Wharton just then presented was not merely due to his investigations of Mr. Markeley. In October he had already decided that the "mendacious Markeley's" organ would do; by November he thought differently, at the same time finding various obstacles to lifting his voice from any other platform. He preferred to wait, perhaps, for an opportunity of a different order than this "strangely infirm" novel.

Edith Wharton did not produce another full-length novel for five years. There were two volumes of short stories, meanwhile, and one long tale destined to become her most famous production— *Ethan Frome*. The *Hermit and the Wild Woman and Other Stories*, put together the year after *The Fruit of the Tree* was published, told nothing new about her capacities. The two stories of decided merit in it were "international" in Mrs. Wharton's only half-Jamesian way upon which we have already remarked. "The Last Asset" is another of her exercises in satire in which a discarded American husband proves to be a belated "asset" when his presence becomes necessary for his daughter's marriage to a French nobleman. "The Pretext" brings a European to America for a change, recording the effect upon an American woman of the advent of a cultivated English visitor. Of the other stories in this volume nothing need be observed beyond the fact that most of them are concerned with the choice—made by artists, a philanthropist, a politician—between pursuit of the ideal and worldly reward. Possibly her own artistic problem posed itself to her in such somewhat trite terms at this time.

Tales of Men and Ghosts, which followed in 1910, seems at any rate to have settled upon a program. The stories are neater, "snappier," than most of her previous short fiction. These are studies in situation rather than in character which have moved decisively out of the penumbra of James into a lighter element. There is little of his brooding submersion in the intricacies of consciousness; instead, each tale is a pointed anecdote with an ironic, often a startling climax. "The Bolted Door" illustrates a man's inability to convince others of his guilt when he confesses to a long-concealed crime. "His Father's Son" shows that a talented and refined son is more indebted to his crude parent for what he is than he thinks. "The Daunt Diana" explains that a collector's passion for a piece of statuary is only really rewarded when he is unable to afford to own it. "The Debt" relates how a young biologist discharges the debt he owes to the teacher who fostered him by refuting his mentor's theories. "Full Circle" describes still another turn-about, as its title hints—how a successful writer stoops to maintain his pride before his secretary by the

260

same means the secretary employs to hold on to his job—the composition of bogus fan-mail. "The Legend" tells how the great Pellerin is unrecognized by the votaries of "Pellerinism." "The Eyes" is a psychological ghost-story which ends with the revelation that the eyes that have haunted a man are actually his own. "The Blond Beast" uncovers the uncalculated spring of altruism in a man who is determined to be a perfect opportunist. And even the simple ghost-tale, "Afterwards," makes use of a surprise ending—the shock of the heroine who realizes much later that she has seen a ghost. In each of these stories the conclusion is sprung upon us deliberately to reveal the paradoxical nature of experience.

Among the stories written in this period, one has special interest, for it was directly based upon a suggestion given to Edith Wharton by Henry James. He had related to Mrs. Wharton some gossip about an English friend of his, and Edith Wharton had asked his permission to use the anecdote for a story. James replied:

> Je vous le donne, je vous le donne indeed, our petite donnée, which I perfectly remember every word of our talk about, & which I applaud to the echo the fructification of in your rich intelligence! Sharp & vivid came back to me the crown and consummation we formulated (for the original, limited anecdote;) the voyage *d'enquête* by the Englishwoman relative or reporter, & the remarkable—the *startling* (they must *startle* her!) constatations she was to be led to on the spot. I think it as beautiful & âpre (as Bourget would say of your faculty for it!) a little ironic subject as ever—&, no, I *don't* feel, on interrogating myself, that there is any objection that *counts* to your using it. My sense of the whole matter is a little *coloured* today, no doubt, by the fact that oddly enough I am more or less surrounded (as it were) by the English actors in the affair: that is the Sidney Waterlows, Jack Pollock's brother-in-law & sister have taken a house here for the winter, & Jack himself, who is most charming & sympathetic, comes down sometimes to see them—and is even soon to spend a Sunday with *me*. (I meet, at rare intervals, Gladys Holman Hunt in town—the said Jack's massive Ariadne; but *her* side of the drama is less present to

me.) My own impression that the "impossibility" of "Mrs. Professor Joy" (textual) has been in no quarter (not even by the youth!) fully *realized*, & that the postulate of the "pretext" hasn't therefore been brought home, affords a sufficient *cover* or protection: which is still further afforded moreover by the fact that your "free hand" rests on your complete personal ignorance of everyone concerned—in the midst of which you have picked up, & been struck by, that anecdote as you'd have picked up, & been taken by, any other. It's *inevitable* of course the youth shld. be English—& it doesn't matter! I give you all my "rights" to it (all *honestly* come by—not a word of authentic light from anyone,) & I wish you a happy issue! Art is long & everything else is accidental & unimportant.) Only give false scents all you can & *appuyez* on the English relative, who doesn't exist in the original. She might be Mary Cadwalader's acquaintance Miss Warrander (if you've seen the latter.)——

The result was "The Pretext," already mentioned, which relates how an American matron imagines herself to be the *inamorata* of a young Englishman only to discover that he has merely used his connection with her as a "pretext" for breaking off his engagement with a girl at home.

It is worth our while to dig in and explain the little real-life drama that forms the germ glimpsed by James and bestowed upon Edith Wharton, for nothing better illustrates the way their respective imaginations worked. Fifty-five years have passed, moreover, since the events in question and we need not share James's always excessive caution about the disclosure of personal mysteries. It is not difficult to identify the actual persons concerned. The chief actor, "Jack himself," seems to be the late Sir John Pollock, whose sister, Alice Isabella, married Sidney Philip Perigal Waterlow in 1902. The resemblance between actual events and Edith Wharton's rendition in "The Pretext" can hardly be traced with confidence now, but obviously James refers to a relationship between Pollock and Gladys Holman Hunt, the daughter of the Pre-Raphaelite painter, a relationship presumably broken off since she is termed "the said Jack's massive Ariadne."

Edith Wharton's Guy Dawnish does indeed play the role of Theseus to an unnamed British fiancée in the story. Dawnish's visit to the American college town where he meets Mrs. Ransom (who is to furnish "the pretext") may have its basis in Pollock's actual visit to Cambridge in 1903-4, when he attended Harvard Law School. The son of the famous jurist Frederick Pollock, to whom Harvard had given an honorary L.L.D. and who was a friend of Justice Holmes and William James, young Pollock would have found many friends in the Harvard community. The originals of Professor and Mrs. Ransom are not clearly defined by the cautious James and the visiting English aunt who brings Mrs. Ransom the disillusioning revelation of the use to which she has been put, is, obviously, James's improvisation, for which, however, he suggests a real-life model in a friend of Edith Wharton's sister-in-law, Mary Cadwalader Jones. Jack Pollock himself, however, may well have been described thoroughly to Edith Wharton, if she did not know him, and he would seem to have been an excellent specimen of the young English upper-class intellectual, with ability as well as the benefit of "fine breeding," who was calculated to dazzle the wife of an American professor. In later years he became a prominent journalist, the author of many books and plays.

This *donnée* is certainly one that James might have been glad to turn his hand to, for the intrusion of Old England into a New England community is full of the possibilities for contrasts he had explored in *The Europeans*. And the inner theme of exploitation, with a woman as its victim, is one that is echoed many times in his work. That the exploiting man should be a European gives the situation an even more direct connection with some of his fiction. Nevertheless, the contrast of Edith Wharton's way of developing an idea and James's characteristic treatment is obvious. The story, for all its debt to James's suggestion, is distinguishably Edith Wharton's own, crisper, more anecdotal than James's version might have been, while still showing a kinship of subject—which is hardly surprising this time, for the subject had been plucked for her by James himself.

This is the only instance, though never publicly admitted by either Edith Wharton or Henry James, of a direct "gift" of this sort from the elder to the younger writer, although the idea has persisted that there were many such transfers. It was rumored, for example, that James had advised her to make an English tale out of a little narrative exercise in French which was her first version of *Ethan Frome*. "That legend," she later found it necessary to assert, "must be classed among the other inventions which honour me by connecting my name with his in the field of letters." Certainly it does not seem likely that James would have sensed an opportunity in the relations of Mattie, Zeena, and Ethan, those New England primitives whose tragedy she traced in *Ethan Frome*. The "historian of fine consciences," as Conrad called him, required for his kind of drama natures more sophisticated and expressive than these. Mrs. Wharton herself admitted: "They were, in truth, these figures, my *granite outcroppings;* but half-emerged from the soil, and scarcely more articulate."

Possessed as she was of a sensibility trained like James's own in the practice of fine discriminations, Edith Wharton had set herself a task of peculiar difficulty in this work. As she said, "The theme of my tale was not one on which many variations could be played. It must be treated as starkly and summarily as life had always presented itself to my protagonists; any attempt to elaborate and complicate their sentiments would necessarily have falsified the whole." Yet she does not, because she cannot, quite adapt her presentation to the perspective of her actors. She must invent a narrator who is an adventitious "fine conscience" through whom Ethan's experience is related, and more than one reader has complained that this reflective engineer, idling in Starkfield while a strike holds up a "job," comes uneasily into the story.

James laughed rather unkindly at Mrs. Wharton's fictitious "I" because he really resembled the author so little; once at their friend Howard Sturgis' he read aloud the passage in which she, or rather he, says, "I had been sent by my employers"—and snickered at the preposterous image of the imperious Edith *sent,* and by *employers!* One wonders whether James was not putting his finger on a crucial critical point at the same time. Surely he would have noted the implausibility of the narrator, which is due not to his lack of resemblance to the author but to his inadequate connection with the story and his lack of individual interest.

Yet *Ethan Frome* is a brave *tour de force*, an experiment in consistent point of view. Mrs. Wharton mentioned Balzac's "La Grande Bretèche" as providing a clue to her method, but James, we know, had contributed to her conviction that so short and intense a tale must be reflected in a single and adequate consciousness. Only the method was here applied to materials from which the master would have drawn back. As John Crowe Ransom has observed, "Henry James himself would have failed in this particular undertaking; or if not, it is because his sense of tactics would not have permitted him to try it." Perhaps not. Yet in Edith Wharton's hands, and despite an inescapable taste of artificiality about it, the thing became a success. Though she grew to dislike the common assertion that *Ethan Frome* was her best composition, she declared that when she wrote it she felt for the first time the artisan's full control of his implements.

She particularly resented the charge that the tale was clumsy in structure. "Though I am far from thinking 'Ethan Frome' my best novel," she declared, rejecting at the same time the extravagance of its admirers, "I am still sure that its structure is not its weak point." For the obvious fact about *Ethan Frome* is that the author has concentrated on structure above all and that it is the challenge of a problem in formal design that stimulates her. These are what she chiefly discussed in her own introduction to *Ethan Frome* written for the Modern Student's Library edition in 1922. She defends her narrator:

It appears to me, indeed, that, while an air of artificiality is lent to a tale of complex and sophisticated people which the novelist causes to be guessed at and interpreted by any mere looker-on, there need be no such drawback if the looker-on is sophisticated, and the people he interprets are simple. If he is capable of seeing all around them, no violence is done to probability in allowing him to exercise this faculty; it is natural enough that he should act as the sympathizing intermediary between his rudimentary characters and the more complicated minds to

265

whom he is trying to present them. But this is all self-evident, and needs explaining only to those who have never thought of fiction as an art of composition.

"Self-evident" Mrs. Wharton's argument may no longer appear in an age of such varied formulations of the recording, narrating consciousness as those of Joyce and Faulkner. We are no longer so convinced that "simple" and "complex" constitute valid descriptions of different kinds of minds—all minds now appearing to be more complex than any writer of fiction can possibly represent. But surely it is because Ethan and Mattie and Zeena are, indeed, so "simple"—so far removed from the mind observing them—that we are horrified, not moved, by their fate. There is, as Lionel Trilling has pointed out, something cruel, as well as factitious, about this book. It is a book in which we are aware of "scarcely any moral reverberation, that strange and often beautiful sound we seem to hear generated in the air by a tale of suffering." Edith Wharton's impulse in creating it was not that "of moral experimentation," he says, but "a purely literary impulse, in the bad sense of the word 'literary.' "

Trilling finds a theme in *Ethan Frome:* that moral inertia, the *not* making of moral decisions, constitutes a large part of the moral life of humanity—but surely this is a theme by default. The truth of the matter is, I think, that *Ethan Frome* has very little theme at all. And why is this so? One says at once: because crass accident has determined an outcome—the survival of Ethan and Mattie—which, as some of the reviewers felt, is not "necessary." But more essentially, it is because the characters are only postulated—Ethan with his thwarted sensitivity, Mattie with her groping young gift of feeling, Zeena with her narrow bitterness—and not realized with the fullness and elaboration of human complication. Mrs. Wharton, like her narrator, condescended to them.

They were the stuff of an exercise, begun, appropriately, as an exercise in writing in a foreign language. Then, several years later, she began the story again in English—"reading my morning's work aloud each evening to Walter Berry, who was as familiar as I was with the lives led in those half-deserted villages before the coming of the motor and the telephone." That Berry was really very familiar with New England village life may be doubted; *Ethan Frome*, as has already been suggested, may actually have more to do with the tragic frustration of Mrs. Wharton's own life than with those other lives she claimed to know so well. And in its hopelessness, its themelessness, it probably reflects her own bafflement at her personal situation rather than any insight into the conditions likely in Starkfield. Hence, possibly, the factitiousness Trilling speaks of, the empty formal competence.

James was undoubtedly pleased to see in *Ethan Frome* precisely that high degree of formal control, so different from her laxity in *The Fruit of the Tree*. He respected in particular the story's strong and economic use of symbolic detail growing out of the simple notation of facts. "I exceedingly admire, sachez Madame, Ethan Frome," he wrote. "A beautiful art & tone & truth—a beautiful artful Rightdowness, & yet effective cumulations. It's a 'gem.'" She seemed to be accepting, finally, his doctrines of fictional control. That it was an exercise in Jamesian method empty of the Jamesian moral energy he did not need to say.

In the full-length *The Reef*, published the following year, 1912, Edith Wharton presented James with a still more impressive demonstration of technical discipline. *The Reef* was also a novel whose very materials were of the kind he deemed fruitful. Here, in contrast with *The Valley of Decision*, *The House of Mirth*, and *The Fruit of the Tree*, was a long work of fiction which made consistent use of the restricted "post of observation" that James favored. *The Fruit of the Tree*, with its uncertain anchoring of theme, was also a chaotic compound of points of view. "As if she hadn't taken thought for that," Mrs. Wharton leaned over the shoulders of major and minor characters each in turn according to the wanderings of the plot and the shift in focus. Among the titles she had considered for the novel was the name of one character, "Justine Brent," but the story was actually no more Justine's than it was Amherst's or Bessy's. Her two earlier novels had concentrated more exclusively upon the adventures of a single character, but in neither case had the novelist made use of the opportunities for intensified inner drama that the limited viewpoint provides.

Though told very nearly entirely from the hero's vantage point, *The Valley of Decision* casts few inward glances upon the mind of Odo Valsecca; it is all "long-shots" of landscape and human spectacle, a travelogue through eighteenth-century Italy related in an unvarying tone of elegant detachment. *The House of Mirth*, while it does keep more or less to the story of Lily Bart, avails itself of the traditional chronicler's freedoms in describing and commenting upon her career, adding further objectivity to the naturalist's taxonomic interest in types. *The Reef*, however, had been planned in a different way. Viewpoint is faithfully limited to the observations and reflections plausible for either George Darrow or Anna Leath who form the alternating "reflecting mirrors" in which the story is made visible. A deliberate symmetry controls this alternation. The opening eight chapters are all Darrow's, the closing eleven all Anna's, and the story is assigned to one or the other in the remaining twenty chapters, each of which is the undisputed property of its narrating consciousness.

In *The Writing of Fiction*, published a dozen years later, Mrs Wharton asserted that it is best to shift the point of view in the novel "as seldom as possible, and to let the tale work itself out from not more than two (or at most three) angles of vision." She goes on to say that verisimilitude was hindered by "the slovenly habit of some novelists of tumbling in and out of their characters' minds, and then suddenly drawing back to scrutinize them from the outside as the avowed Showman holding his puppets' strings." She credits James along with Conrad with making "the most interesting experiments" in achieving verisimilitude by the control of point of view. *The Reef* was her first long work of fiction which attempted such control and it achieved it with a strictness that certainly indicates subscription to James's principle.

The Reef was as Jamesian in materials as *Madame de Treymes*, published five years earlier, but what should have pleased the

Correspondences and Differences

Master still more, also Jamesian in technique in his own latest sense. It was not a chronicle of linked episodes like *The House of Mirth*, nor, like *The Fruit of the Tree*, a succession of dramatic occasions lacking even a common significance. Rather it was a case of "the elaborate working out on all sides of a central situation." Like many of James's books, early and late, it was a study of moral comparisons established by situating an American conscience—a female American conscience—in an alien environment.

Anna Leath, its heroine, is a still un-Europeanized American, an older Isabel Archer who has survived her Gilbert Osmond (whom the dead Fraser Leath seems to have resembled) to face a profounder test of her original virtues in her love of George Darrow. The novel has one pivot only—Anna's adjustment to the discovery that Darrow had had a love affair with a girl who is now the fiancée of Anna's own stepson. Diagrammatically, *The Reef* bears a decided resemblance to James's *The Golden Bowl*. Each novel concerns a quartet of characters—in Mrs. Wharton's work they are Darrow, Anna, Anna's stepson, Owen Leath, and the girl, Sophy Viner. As in *The Golden Bowl* we witness in *The Reef* the effect upon one couple of the connection already established between the other two. Anna and her stepson, like Maggie Verver and her father, plan to marry without realizing that the mates they have chosen have themselves once been mated. Anna, like Maggie, must accept and assimilate this knowledge before her own union can be achieved.

What is more significant than this, however, is the fact that the method of *The Reef* approaches that of *The Golden Bowl*. As we have seen, the point of view is shared by just two characters, just as *The Golden Bowl* is divided between the Prince and the Princess. In neither novel is there a crowd of minor characters to give a sense of social density, a Balzacian perspective of milieu such as James had aimed for in *The Bostonians* and Edith Wharton in *The House of Mirth*. And neither novel makes use of the cultural contrasts available in the fact that its characters are Americans abroad. The action of *The Reef* is played upon a European stage and concerns Americans who have lived long in England and France, yet its theme is not "international" in the fash-

269

ion of *The American* or *Madame de Treymes*. The alien environment which envelops Anna Leath is not national; it is rather a universal dimension of passionate experience for which her training has not prepared her. What seems to interest Edith Wharton in this instance is not so much the cultural encounters involved in her story as the more abstract conjunctions of moral attitudes. The foreign scene, in fact, has become simply an isolating medium, like the clear fluid which surrounds James's four principals in *The Golden Bowl.*

All this is somewhat curious when one recalls that it was precisely such features of *The Golden Bowl* that Edith Wharton told James she had found objectionable. "What was your idea in suspending the four principal characters in 'The Golden Bowl' in the void? Why have you stripped them of all the *human* fringes we necessarily trail after us through life?" she asked him once, feeling that the late James fictions were "more and more lacking in atmosphere, more and more severed from that thick nourishing human air in which we all live and move." It is impossible to tell just when this conversation, which is recorded in the autobiography she published in her seventies, took place. It might have occurred quite soon after *The Golden Bowl* was published in 1904, for we have seen how much she disliked James's late novels when they first appeared. But she showed a readiness to deprecate this particular novel throughout her lifetime.

In *The Writing of Fiction* her appreciation was qualified, for after praising James for establishing the canon of point of view, she went on to criticize his "pursuit of an impossible perfection" which led in *The Golden Bowl* to the awkward use of "coordinating consciousnesses." Speaking of the Assingham couple, who serve this function in James's book, she wrote, "The author created them for the sole purpose of revealing details which he could not otherwise communicate without lapsing into the character of the mid-Victorian novelist chatting with his readers of 'my heroine' in the manner of Thackeray and Dickens. Convention for convention (and both are bad), James's is perhaps even more unsettling to the reader's confidence than the old-fashioned intrusion of the author among his puppets."

Judging from the way she stated her views in her reminiscences, which appeared in 1934, her final attitude was still more unsympathetic; she seemed to have forgotten, in fact, how closely one of her own books fitted the description she gave *The Golden Bowl*, its "characters isolated in a Crookes tube for our inspection" and engaged in just such subtle repositioning as Maggie and her father and their *sposi*. However it happened, she did not go to this model again. Her later novels are generally looser in form, less observant of Jamesian principles. When the "international situation" is again employed it is, as in *Madame de Treymes*, a means of sociologic analysis.

It seems possible that between writing *The Fruit of the Tree* and *The Reef* Edith Wharton reopened those later books by James which she had once declared she couldn't read. She was sympathetically aware at this time that James had suffered severely in reputation and pocketbook because of the general unpopularity of his last productions, and aware, certainly, of how little the public who rejected him understood his aims. The great, definitive edition of his tales and novels on which James was spending such labor began to appear in 1907, and, as we know, it refused to sell. Early in 1908 Edith Wharton tried to persuade *Scribner's Magazine* to publish an article on James by Morton W. Fullerton of the London *Times*, an old friend of James and herself. In January she wrote Edward L. Burlingame, the editor of the magazine: "I am trying to get Mr. Morton Fullerton to finish and send you an admirable article on Henry James which he has been writing, because I thought it would come out in the magazine so opportunely just now. He says just what I have always been wanting to say about the great man." "The article has struck me very much, and I thought it might come à propos just now, coinciding with the appearance of the 'definitive' . . . I want very much to have a ringing word said for H. J. just now, and I think this would attract a great deal of attention," she added the following month. Charles Scribner informed her in March that the "definitive" was doing badly: "The reception of James's new edition has been disappointing and shows again to what a low ebb we have fallen in our American reviews. The prefaces of the earlier volumes interest readers but they are frightened by the false impression that the older novels have been rewritten in the later style." Again she urged that the Fullerton article be used by *Scribner's*, this time adding the information, "I have had a hand —or at least a small finger—in the article, and I think it's good. (Admire my modesty!) I *long* so to have someone speak intelligently and resolutely for James."

For some reason, *Scribner's Magazine* did not use this article in which she confessed to having "had a hand—or at least a small finger." It may be this very essay by Fullerton that appeared, however, two years later in the English *Quarterly Review*. "The Art of Henry James," an extended review of the completed New York Edition, seems indeed the "ringing word" Mrs. Wharton wanted said. It defends the evolution of James's art and declares that in the last novels James's power to create plastic reality had been brought to new heights. "It is this achievement which makes them, in spite of the more accessible charm of his earlier novels, the significant and the original part of his work," Fullerton declared. He contrasted the scientific precision of James's projection of round reality upon the flat map of his narrative with the procedure of novelists who ignore the problem altogether "and go on *ad infinitum* mapping out longitudinally"—examples of the latter including *Anna Karenina, The Charterhouse of Parma, Harry Richmond, Vanity Fair*—and *The House of Mirth*! Of these masterpieces Fullerton says, "There are none but purely artificial reasons why [they] should ever end."

If Fullerton's article may be taken as representing Mrs. Wharton's views at this time, it shows a marked increase in her appreciation of the late James. It is true, there is another method of writing fiction—that of *The House of Mirth*, etc., the "chronicle-novel" in which, as she was to note herself, James "had long since lost all interest." But his final experiments may now have won her sympathy. She certainly had come some distance from the view she held in 1905 when she complimented W. C. Brownell on his severely critical article on James, declaring, "Every line so exactly expressed my own feeling about him." *The Reef* may represent her new interest in James's ripest works. It was as close as she would ever come to the model of James. In the novel that was published after it (and on which she had been working during the same years) she successfully returned to a form more natural to her.

When James read *The Reef* he was excited by the way she had made progress towards his current ideal. He noted with enthusiasm some of the characteristics we have mentioned in his brilliant letter of analysis written in December, 1912. But he could not restrain some mild complaints against features that still resisted his example:

There remains with me so strongly the impression of its quality and of the unspeakably *fouillée* nature of the situation between the two principals (more gone into and with more undeviating truth than anything you have done) that I can't but babble of it a little to you . . . It all shows, partly, what strength of subject is, and how it carries and inspires, inasmuch as I think your subject in its essence [is] very fine and takes in no end of beautiful things to do. Each of these two figures is admirable for truth and *justesse;* the woman an exquisite thing, and with her characteristic finest, scarce differentiated notes (that is some of them) sounded with a wonder of delicacy. I'm not sure her oscillations are not beyond our notation; yet they are so held in your hand, so felt and known and shown, and everything seems so to come of itself. I suffer or worry a little from the fact that in the Prologue, as it were, we are admitted so much into the consciousness of the man, and that after the introduction of Anna (Anna so perfectly named), we see him almost only as she sees him—which gives our attention a different sort of work to do; yet this is really I think but a triumph of your method, for he remains of an absolute consistent verity, showing himself in that way better perhaps than in any other, and without a false note imputable, not a shadow of one, to his manner of so projecting himself. The beauty of it is that it is, for all that it is worth, a Drama, and almost, as it seems to me, of the psychologic Racinian unity, intensity and gracility. Anna is really of Racine, and one presently begins to feel her throughout as an Eriphyle or Bérénice; which, by the way,

273

helps account a little for something *qui me chiffonne* throughout; which is why the whole thing, unrelated and unreferred
save in the most superficial way to its *milieu* and background,
and to any determining or qualifying *entourage*, takes place
comme cela, and in a specified localized way, in France—these
non-French people "electing," as it were, to have their story out
there. This particularly makes all sorts of unanswered questions
come up about Owen; and the notorious wickedness of Paris
isn't at all required to bring about the conditions of the Prologue. Oh, if you knew how plentifully we could supply them in
London and, I should suppose, in New York or Boston. But the
point was, as I see it, that you couldn't really give us the sense
of a Boston Eriphyle or Boston Givré, and then an exquisite
instinct "back of" your Racinian inspiration and settling the
whole thing for you, whether consciously or not, absolutely
prescribed a vague and elegant colonnade or gallery, with a
French river dimly gleaming through, as the harmonious *fond*
you required. In the key of this, with all your reality, you have
yet kept the whole thing: and, to deepen the harmony and accentuate the literary pitch, have never surpassed yourself for
certain exquisite *moments*, certain images, analogies, metaphors, certain silver correspondences in your *façon de dire*
examples of which I could pluck out and numerically almost
confound you with . . . There used to be little notes in you that
were like fine benevolent finger-marks of the good George Eliot
—the echo of much reading of that excellent woman, here and
there, that is, sounding through. But now you are like a lost
and recovered "ancient" whom *she* might have got a reading of
(especially were he a Greek) and of whom in *her* texture some
weaker reflection were to show. For, dearest Edith, you are
stronger and firmer and finer than all of them put together; you
go further and you say *mieux*, and your only drawback is not
having the homeliness and the inevitability and the happy limitation and the affluent poverty, of a Country of your Own
(*comme moi, par exemple!*) It makes you, this does, as you
exquisitely say of somebody or something at some moment,
elegiac (what penetration, what delicacy in your use there of
the term!)—makes you so, that is, for the Racinian-sérieux; but
leaves you more in the desert (for everything else) that surrounds Apex City. But you will say that you're content

with your lot; that the desert surrounding Apex City is quite enough of a dense crush for you, and that with the *colonnade* and the gallery and the dim river you will always otherwise pull through. To which I can only assent—after such an example of pulling through as The Reef. Clearly you have only to pull, and everything will come.

James gave *The Reef* warmer praise than any of her other novels. Earlier in the letter just quoted from he said: "The whole of the finest part is, I think, quite the finest thing you have done; both *more* done than the best of your other doing, and more worth it through intrinsic value, interest and beauty." He had, as even this statement shows, his reservations about those other portions than its "finest part," but he preferred to emphasize what he could fullheartedly approve. Not the least of Edith Wharton's triumph in writing it, he knew, was the fact that she had written it at all in a period of serious personal difficulty. "I think she is very wonderful—to have been able to write the exquisite "Reef" (for I hold what is finest in The Reef to be really exquisite, and haven't scrupled to try inordinately to encourage her by putting that faith in the most emphatic way) with that amount of harum-scarum banging about her ears," he wrote Howard Sturgis a few days after he had sent his letter to Mrs. Wharton.

Unquestionably, much in *The Reef* seemed to James a closer approach to his own ideal. He was favorably impressed by the exhaustiveness of her exploration into the situation between Anna and Darrow. Plainly she was not interested merely in the turnabout of episode, the trick of fate by which Darrow is made to pay for his moment of indiscretion, but in the interior dynamics of her characters' souls. It is delightful to hear James accuse Edith Wharton of oversubtlety—"I am not sure her oscillations are not beyond our notation" he says of Anna—for she does seem almost to caricature his own preoccupation with minute mental movements. He approved, after some hesitation, the author's use of two centralizing consciousnesses, rather than one; after all, had he not shifted his own camera from Amerigo to Maggie in *The Golden Bowl?* He praised her handling as now being full of metaphoric touches, her style as having outgrown the merely imitative George Eliotism he had disliked in her earlier efforts. And he finally produced the perfect word for *The Reef;* it was "Racinian." In its unity, intensity, its complete economy of means it was like classical French tragedy; in these qualities, again, like *The Golden Bowl.*

One sentence of his praise carries a wealth of suggestion about James's most essential recommendation to a writer of fiction. "It all shows," he wrote Mrs. Wharton, "what strength of subject is, and how it carries and inspires, inasmuch as I think your subject in its essence is very fine and takes in no end of beautiful things to do." Some years later, when she reviewed the posthumous collection of James's letters edited by Percy Lubbock, she remarked, in summarizing James's views, "For him, every great novel must first of all be based on a profound sense of moral values ('importance of subject'), and then constructed with a classical unity and economy of means." And she herself, in *The Writing of Fiction,* laid down, "A good subject . . . must contain in itself something that sheds a light on our moral experience. If it is incapable of this expansion, this vital radiation, it remains, however showy a surface it presents, a mere irrelevant happening, a meaningless fact torn out of its context."

It is perfectly true that James valued in a given story or idea the possibilities latent in it for the realization of high human significance—which must be ethical. But Edith Wharton curiously simplified his view, as expressed in "The Art of Fiction": "There is one point at which the moral sense and the artistic sense lie very near together; that is, in the light of the very obvious truth that the deepest quality of a work of art will always be the quality of the mind of the producer." Edith Wharton herself was not always capable of selecting subjects that gave forth "this vital radiation." Perhaps the cause lay in the "quality of mind" of which James spoke. Certainly she lacked, as *Ethan Frome* shows, James's passionate conviction about the value of life, perhaps because her own heart was a more bare and hopeless place than his. *Ethan Frome* fails to radiate with moral significance for all its "classical unity and economy of means."

In *The Reef,* however, she wrote a finer novel, and one with a great theme. It is a theme deeply in the American grain, a theme

276

integral to Hawthorne as well as James, that of the relation of innocence and experience. As James had posed the question in *The Portrait of a Lady*, as well as other works, Edith Wharton asked it in this novel. *The Reef* probes the "innocence"—symbolically American—of Anna Leath, and contrasts it with the "experience" of Sophy Viner, who is after the fall, has tasted of the apple, and in the end inherits a paradise fairer far within. Nothing is as interesting and as infrequently remarked upon as the warmth of Edith Wharton's portrait of Sophy; almost despite herself she has given this representative of "experience" a strength which raises her to Anna's level and makes the contrast intensely dramatic. One is strongly reminded—as one often is in the case of James, also—of Hawthorne's *The Marble Faun*. Anna is a sort of Hilda, of that unspotted and insufficient innocence which must be enriched by at least a knowledge of the darker side of experience. Sophy is a "dark heroine," like Hawthorne's Miriam. And Darrow, who must mediate between the two? He distinctly reminds one of Hawthorne's own rather irresolute hero, the sculptor Kenyon.

James, of course, had inherited much of Hawthorne's preoccupation with this theme and devised, in the "international" situation, a way of symbolizing it. Edith Wharton at her greatest moments found her moral subject here, too. *The Age of Innocence* is given a depth of significance it would not otherwise have by means of the play upon the title that the story manages to convey. Ellen Olenska, in this later novel, is principally the representative of what has been gained from an older civilization, more liberal manners, more cultivated tastes. But her "knowledge" is also, ambiguously, a knowledge of sorrow and sin, an awareness of the human possibility which the "blonde heroine" of that book, May Welland, must learn, at least by sympathy if not by act.

James had questioned in *The Reef*, as he had in *Madame de Treymes*, Edith Wharton's choice of a French rather than of an English medium, her lack of what he had found, but he acknowledged that her very distance from the background she employed assisted the Racinian elevation of her drama. For other kinds of action the landscape might be rather too bare. By "Apex City," outside of which she had hitherto preferred to situate her stories, he meant the average American community which neither of them knew well but which Edith Warthon would regard from afar until in *Hudson River Bracketed* she even attempted to depict it. This is the name Edith Wharton chose for the birth-place of her heroine of her next published book, and undoubtedly James and she had conversationally used this same name as a symbol of that inland U.S.A. which both viewed with a some-what uninformed repugnance.

The Reef was, in the long run, hardly so characteristic of her real propensity as *The Custom of the Country*, which traced the career of Undine Spragg of Apex City. With this novel Mrs. Wharton returned in 1913 to the line begun with *The House of Mirth*. This, too, was a loose but vigorous chronicle of a woman's career. The story of Lily Bart had been a tragedy, for it had exhibited its heroine in a descending series of views from her beginnings as a legitimate member of elegant society to her pa-thetic death in a New York rooming house. Undine Spragg, the barbarian invader from the Middle West, rises, however, as she penetrates successive social elevations, and picaresque comedy emerges from her history (though there is subordinate tragedy resulting for her victim, Ralph Marvell). Yet there is only the difference of direction between these two plots. Each serves to take the reader with the heroine in exploration of the social scale as much as to set into motion the inner forces of character. There is consequently "no reason why it should ever end," as Fullerton had said of the type, no reason, that is, dictated by the inner requirements of the personal drama at its center. Edith Whar-ton's powers of social observation are at their most brilliant in *The Custom of the Country*. Dialogue and description are the notations of an imagination richly alert to the play of appear-ances. And nothing could be more unlike the delicate psycholog-ical probing of *The Reef* than this succeeding novel's bold ex-posure of the surfaces of life.

The Custom of the Country, begun as early as 1908, bore no resemblance in form to a James novel. Because her purposes were this time so different from his she could afford to ignore James's injunctions concerning a single limited point of view and adopt a method almost Thackerayan in its freedom, "tumbling in and out of [her] characters' minds" in the fashion she herself theoretically condemned. Her own intelligence as the showman of Vanity Fair is always present; indeed its corruscating illumination lights the book with its informed scorn, enabling us to remain outside the illusioned minds of her characters and yet to understand them. Perhaps in the case of Ralph Marvell, her second principal character, she affords a view of the story in his own terms, for Ralph is sufficiently percipient to furnish us with much that his creator wishes us to know and feel. But Undine Spragg could be defined as she is by no one but her sharp-tongued creator; her own observation is too limited and her thinking too primitive to cast the necessary dry light upon herself and surroundings.

Yet the book interested James at first for its use of his own old favorite subject, the "international situation," in the whole second half which chronicles the heroine's marriage to a French nobleman. Only, somehow, Mrs. Wharton had missed the beautiful Jamesian opportunity presented there. She recalled that James had said to her: "But of course you know—as how should you, with your infernal keenness of perception, *not know*—that in doing your tale you had under your hand a magnificent subject, which ought to have been your main theme, and that you used it as a mere incident and then passed it by?" He meant, she understood,

> that for him the chief interest of the book, and its most original theme, was that of a crude young woman such as Undine Spragg entering, all unprepared and unperceiving, into the mysterious labyrinth of family life in the old French aristocracy. I saw his point, and recognized that the contact between the Undine Spraggs and the French families they marry into was as the French themselves would say, an "actuality" of immense interest to the novelist of manners, and one which as yet had been little dealt with; but I argued that in "The Custom of the Country" I was chronicling the career of a particular young woman, and that to whatever hemisphere her fortunes carried her, my task was to record her ravages and pass on to her next

phase. This, however, was no argument to James; he had long
since lost all interest in the chronicle-novel, and cared only for
the elaborate working out on all sides of a central situation, so
that he could only answer, by implication—if not openly:
"Then, my dear child, you chose the wrong kind of subject."

Certainly, their difference is well defined here. For him the
central, significant situation filling the confines of an exact and
limited form; for her the constantly changing interest of the
rogue-errant's adventures, and a form of continuous chronicle
open at either end. One of Undine Spragg's phases would have
been enough for James. He would have extracted the last drop of
"actuality" from it. For Edith Wharton there was no landfall she
would not willingly make with her heroine in search of new
revelations of effect.

Yet he knew that she had produced a work of first-rate skill, a
work which demonstrated a high degree of control, though of a
different sort from his own. He admired, in its unfolding, the
finesse with which the novel's successive chapters were formed.
"I hang on the sequence of the Custom with beating heart & such
a sense of your craft, your cunning, your devilish resource in the
preparation of them. It's done and arch-done, & something to live
for if other things fail," he declared after reading the first installment in *Scribner's* in January, 1913. "Let me not omit definitely
to say that I *have*, and have *englouti*, the second installment, with
all sorts of yearning reactions and admirations. It takes care of
itself, all, *to* admiration, and one has to the highest and happiest
point the sense of a full-orbed muchness to come—the large
mass of the orb hanging and looming there, with all the right
dimness, in the light actually forecast," he wrote next. "It *is*,
indeed, the best story Scribner has published for many years—
since *The House of Mirth*, in fact. You will have done it again
this time—but with a much finer asperity still, & with no end
of representative arts & graces that I wonder at—or should, if it
wasn't you," he pronounced when the novel was halfway
through the magazine.

It was in the spirit of these kindly approvals that he finally
wrote his only public comment on Edith Wharton's work in the

course of a survey of "The New Novel" done for the *Times Literary Supplement* in 1914. In this essay, which was a plea for form, selectivity, a sense of governing principle in the novel, he leagued her with himself. Others—H. G. Wells, Arnold Bennett, D. H. Lawrence among them—he accused of being votaries of the naturalist theory of the "slice of life," who abdicated the novelist's responsibility of "selection and intention." Edith Wharton, on the other hand, was an instance to him of "some state over and above the simple state of possession of much evidence." If Mrs. Wharton had herself "too clearly a saturation" of evidence, even as have the advocates of the famous "slice," we have it from her, he concluded, "not in the crude state but in the extract, the extract that makes all the difference for our sense of an artistic economy." Carefully and justly, he distinguished the characteristic excellence, the tone, of *The Custom of the Country:*

Mrs. Wharton's reaction in the presence of the aspects of life hitherto, it would seem, mainly exposed to her, is for the most part the ironic—to which we gather that these particular aspects have so much ministered that, were we to pursue the quest, we might recognize in them precisely the saturation as to which we a moment ago reserved our judgment. "The Custom of the Country" is at any rate consistently, almost scientifically satiric, as indeed the satiric light was doubtless the only one in which the elements engaged could at all be focused together. But this happens directly to the profit of something that, as we read, becomes more and more one with the principle of authority at work; the light that gathers is a dry light, of great intensity, and the effect, if not rather the very essence of its dryness is a particular fine asperity. The usual "creative" conditions and associations, as we have elsewhere languished among them, are thanks to this ever so sensibly altered; the general authoritative relation attested becomes clear—we move in an air purged at a stroke of the old sentimental and romantic values, the perversions with the maximum waste of perversions, and we shall not here attempt to state what this makes for in the way of esthetic refreshment and relief; the waste having kept us so dangling on the dark esthetic abyss. A shade of asperity may be in such fashion as security against waste, and in the dearth of displayed securities we should welcome it on that ground alone. It helps at any rate to constitute for the talent manifest in "The Custom" a rare identity, so far should we have to go to seek another instance of the dry, or call it perhaps then the hard intellectual touch in the soft, or call it perhaps even the humid temperamental air; in other words of the masculine conclusion tending so to crown the feminine observation.

As on at least two previous occasions, James had written a "partial portrait," both incomplete and favorably biased, of a younger fellow-writer who was a woman and his close friend. In 1887 he had published an essay on the work of Constance Fenimore Woolson which was included in *Partial Portraits* along with articles on Maupassant, Turgenev, Emerson, George Eliot, Trollope, Daudet, and Stevenson. That he was willing to put her small talent into such a gallery is itself remarkable; that he was gracefully kind, ingenious in the discovery of virtues and otherwise vague, is undoubtedly due to the affection he felt for Miss Woolson. In 1893, he performed a similar service for another novelist and lady—Mrs. Humphry Ward, and of this essay he wrote an acquaintance, "I have written no article on Mrs. Ward —only a civil perfunctory *payé* (with words between the lines) to escape the gracelessness of refusing when asked."

James's remarks on Edith Wharton in "The New Novel" (reprinted in *Notes on Novelists* in 1914) have just a little flavor of being a complimentary gesture. Edith Wharton was, of course, a writer of true distinction, and worth his august attention; James's interest in her work does not really need special explanation. But she was, also, his very dear companion, now, of many pleasures and tribulations mutually shared, and in this particular year just following her divorce he must have felt like doing her a good turn. His statement, if not a mere "civil perfunctory *payé*," is purged of the rather devastating judgment ("you had under your hand a magnificent subject, which ought to have been your main theme, and . . . you used it as a mere incident and then passed it by") which he had delivered to her privately.

That he could be serenely crushing his conversation had often taught her before. Of another occasion she recalled, "it would be a mistake to imagine that he had deliberately started out to destroy my wretched tale. He had begun, I am sure, with the sincere intention of praising it; but no sooner had he opened his lips than he was overmastered by the need to speak the truth, and the whole truth, about anything connected with the art which was sacred to him." She must have feared, consequently, what he might say in print—as she had when he thought of making *The Fruit of the Tree* the occasion of a critique of her work, and she had written her publisher half-humorously that she expected him to "make mince-meat" of her.

She underestimated James's kindliness. He had shrunk from the task altogether when the gravely defective *Fruit of the Tree* presented itself; now, though on her own terms still, she had written an immensely superior novel, and he was glad to speak aloud his appreciation of its success and suppress his qualifications. That she had the naturalist's habit of saturation in his materials he did hint—but hastened to add that she had "extracted" an essence instead of serving the reader an unpurified quantity, and this by a truly admirable concentration upon satiric value, "the hard intellectual touch" of which he chose to speak. As for the rest—well, he had quite given up the hope that she would ever really adapt herself to his conception of the art of fiction.

283

10

The Summing Up

IN HIS REVIEW of *The Custom of the Country* James had finally taken public notice of Edith Wharton's quality as a writer. A few weeks later she appeared in the *Times Literary Supplement* with an article that began with a reference—*her* first in print—to Henry James. "The Criticism of Fiction," though it makes no mention of James's recent comment upon her work, takes as its starting point his remarks on the current state of criticism. On this question she had long agreed with James. "It is true," she wrote, "that in Mr. James's sense of the word, the criticism of fiction is practically non-existent in England and America."

Creative writers themselves were, in general, more indifferent to criticism than they had been in any other period of literary history, and their attitude was both cause and result of the situation. It is difficult for us to realize today—in a period in which criticism is at least as vocal as the arts it operates upon—how halting was the voice of literary judgment in the early years of the century. As for the artists themselves—the presumptions of aestheticism on the one hand and of naturalism on the other still combined to discourage respect for any selective jurisdiction in the arts, while the low state of criticism seemed to justify the suspicion that no advice worth heeding would, at any rate, be likely to come from that quarter.

Such was not the attitude, however, of either James or Edith

Wharton. They were almost alone among American writers in their attempt to recall the critics to their proper task. It is to his failure to discover any real critical response to his work that we owe Henry James's prefaces to the New York Edition of his fiction. James wrote to William Dean Howells that the prefaces "are, in general, a plea for Criticism, for Discrimination, for Appreciation on other than infantile lines—as against the so almost universal Anglo-Saxon absence of these things; which tends so, in our general trade, it seems to me, to break the heart." Edith Wharton, in her article, "A Cycle of Reviewing," recalled her own bafflement and frustration in reading reviews of her books. Her critical attempts in *The Writing of Fiction* and elsewhere were prompted by a desire, similar to James's, to supply some light by which her own work as well as fiction in general might be evaluated.

Here was a problem that she had often discussed with W. C. Brownell, whose little book *Criticism* was also published in 1914, and made, in effect, the same declaration as the articles by James and Mrs. Wharton. Upon the dearth of mature, informed, responsible criticism based upon acknowledged standards and conscious of the disciplines and traditions of the art it professes to guide, both of Edith Wharton's friends and mentors agreed completely. Brownell's discovery of the difference between the state of affairs in the English-speaking countries and in France had been elaborated as early as *French Traits*, a book that James undoubtedly read in 1889 when it may have seemed a confirmation of some of his own discoveries in Paris during the previous decade. That *French Traits* was an important influence upon Edith Wharton herself has already been indicated. Both James and Edith Wharton joined Brownell in envying the French a "national turn of intellectual seriousness" which raised the level of journalism and maintained a criticism far more worthy of the name than the English or American reviewers' guide to book-buyers. In France, as they saw, the *compte-rendu* might be perfunctory, but the literary essay had long been what Mrs. Wharton was to call "an organized process of appraisal." In her 1914 article, taking a further cue from James, she wrote:

The contempt of critics is general among creative writers of all tongues and traditions. But though the French novelist may, and often does, speak as slightingly of his analyst as the Anglo-Saxon, yet French literature is conscious of criticism, and has been modified by it to a degree no thoughtful French writer could seriously deny. The French intelligence, moreover, perpetually exercises itself in conversation upon questions of literary interest, thus creating an atmosphere of critical sensibility into which the novelist is born . . . The generation of Sainte-Beuve is gone, that of MM. Anatole France, Jules Lemaître, and Émile Faguet is going; but two such generations leave in the minds succeeding them so rich a deposit and so high a standard that French literary criticism, at one of its least original moments, is still a valuable contribution to literature . . . In a society where every sort of artistic creation has always been accorded the seriousness of attention that sport, politics, and finance monopolize in other countries, some kind of critical criterion is in any case bound to form itself, whatever the indifference of authors or the relative inadequacy of critics. There is not a hack reviewer on a daily paper in France who does not, as it were, know by which handle to pick up his subject . . .

As James had already pointed out in his "The Art of Fiction," published in 1884, fiction itself takes form and character from the critical atmosphere into which it is born. In his struggle to achieve a conscious order, a system of principles governing his own novels, he understood the inestimable advantage already enjoyed by the French. "Only a short time ago it might have been supposed that the English novel was not what the French call *discutable*. It had no air of having a theory, a conviction, a consciousness of itself behind it—of being the expression of an artistic faith, the result of choice and comparison." The novel, declared James, "must take itself seriously for the public to take it so." Here was an opening announcement of the struggle for a new aesthetic of the novel in which James engaged himself for the rest of his life. The impulse that had come to him from his French experience, particularly from the example of Flaubert, now translated itself into artistic efforts in which he was to be joined by such writers as Conrad and Crane and Ford Madox Ford.

Edith Wharton found herself engaged on the side of James in the fight for form and principle and against the naturalistic doctrine that fiction might be a haphazardly-cut "slice of life." "The best art must be that in which design is most organic, most inherent in the soul of the subject," she wrote. "This has been the case with the greatest French fiction, and the sense that it was so, necessarily and inevitably, has been the foundation of the best French criticism."

She sympathetically summarized James's campaign for critical standards in the writing of fiction when, in 1920, she reviewed Lubbock's collection of his letters:

> The writing of fiction was still, when his career began, an unformulated art in English-speaking countries. Only in France, and among men but slightly his elders, had an attempt been made to define the story-teller's main purpose and guiding principles, to enlarge and define his field. Henry James applauded, in this French group, "the infernal intelligence of their art, form, manner," but at once perceived their scheme to be too narrow and superficial. Yet the floods of tepid soap and water which under the name of novels are being vomited forth in England" seemed to him infinitely less "an honor to our race."

James, as she noted in the same review, suffered from nothing more keenly than from the realization that some of his most brilliant and creative contemporaries had no idea what he was doing or why. He complained to Gosse of Meredith's lack of literary standards which "reduces 'liking' and non-liking to the sort of use that a spelling out schoolgirl might make of them." "There are few sadder letters in the book," she observed feelingly, than the one "which answers Stevenson's sick protest at the 'Portrait of a Lady'." Mrs. Wharton well understood James's distress: "He could not see how so vigorous a creative faculty, combined with so sensitive an artistic feeling, could be unsustained by any general theory of art; how it could be only a vague Planchette-like state of possession."

Edith Wharton urged respect for criticism upon the writers whose work might be molded into more perfectly expressive form by the self-consciousness the critics could give them. James had pointed out that the "slice of life" theory embodied an essential fallacy:

> The principle of selection having been involved at the worst or the least, one would suppose, in any approach whatever to the loaf of life with the arrière-pensée of a slice . . . there can be no such thing as an amorphous slice, and . . . any waving aside of inquiry as to the sense and value of a chunk of matter has to reckon with the simple truth of its having been born of naught else but measured excision . . . It has thus had connections at the very first stage of its detachment that are at no later stage logically to be repudiated; let it lie as lumpish as it will—for adoption, we mean, of the ideal of the lump—it has been tainted from too far back with the hard liability to form, and thus carries in its very breast the hapless contradiction of its sturdy claim to have none.

And in her own characteristic, less jocular language, Mrs. Wharton echoed:

> It may well be that some new theory of form as adequate to its new purpose as those preceding it, will be evolved from the present welter of experiment; but to imagine that form. The bondless gush of "life" to be tasted and savored, must be caught in some outstretched vessel of perception; and to perceive is to limit and to choose. The novelist may plead as much as he pleases for the formless novel, the unemphasized notation of a certain stretch of a certain runnel of the stream of things; but why has he chosen that particular stretch of that particular runnel? Obviously, because it reflected or carried on its current, more things he thought worth studying and recording . . . The novelist who proclaims himself beyond and above selection and composition, and considers it his business merely to reproduce with all possible veracity any casual "cross-section" of life, regardless of aesthetic significance, on the plea that "wo Ihr's packt, da ist es interessant," is very much like the man who goes into the garden to pick a peach, any peach. No matter how good he thinks all peaches, the chances are that he will take the trouble to choose the best in sight . . . The novelist

most averse to composition will instinctively exercise the same selection in choosing a subject, and once selection is exercised, why limit its uses, why not push it to the last point of its exquisite powers of pattern-making, and let it extract from raw life the last drop of figurative beauty?

James read Edith Wharton's "The Criticism of Fiction" with delight, happy to find her at his side in his campaign, pleased also that she had obviously appreciated the remarks on her which he had tucked into his own essay. She had just returned to Paris after a motor tour of Algeria and Tunisia, and he wrote her from London:

I took up the Lit. Supp. to find you in such force over the subject you there treated, on that so happy occasion, that the beautiful firmness and "clarity," even if not charity, of your nerves and tone clearly gave the lie to any fear I should entertain for the effect of your annoyance. I greatly admired by the same token the fine strain of that critical voice from out the path of shade projected upon the desert sand, as I suppose, by the silhouette of your camel. Beautifully said, thought, felt, inimitably *jeté*, the paper has excited great attention and admiration here—and is probably doing an amount of missionary work in savage breasts that we shall yet have some comparatively rude or ingenious betrayal of. I do notice that the flow of the little *impayables* reviews meanders on—but enfin ne désespérons pas.

The date of this letter is June 2, 1914. By the end of the month the Austrian Archduke's assassination made the battles of critics and novelists seem a minor matter, even to Henry James and Edith Wharton.

Her own contribution to the theory of fiction is slight. After 1914, she made occasional statements about literary theory, and in *The Writing of Fiction*, published in 1925, attempted a summary of her aesthetic creed. But beyond a few practical hints on the procedures of composition, she had little to add to doctrines already expressed in James's prefaces and essays. It would not be unjust to say that her critical views are, on the whole, James's

289

own, somewhat simplified and now and then modified by a com-
monsense practicality. We have already seen that she agreed with
him in considering the location of point of view a "central difficulty" of the novelist, and subscribed to James's preference for a
"reflecting consciousness" of maximum luminousness, most capable of comprehending the significance of the events witnessed. It
was on this basis, as she explained, that she chose the narrator of
Ethan Frome. She agreed with James, in principle, that this consciousness should be shifted as seldom as possible during the
course of the work, though she felt that some of his gymnastics
performed towards this end made for as much artificiality as the
older, looser method. On the whole, despite her suspicion of
instances where she thought his devotion to theory had led to
excesses of contrivance—she referred on a number of occasions to *The Sacred Fount, The Awkward Age,* and *The Golden
Bowl,* in particular—she considered James the great modern ren-
ovator of the art of fiction. She also adopted, if not entirely
correctly, his view of the moral significance of the fiction
writer's "subject."

Yet she herself often quoted Goethe's saying about the gray-
ness of theory, the greenness of life's golden tree. Her subscription to the Jamesian formal aesthetic was only on certain occasions matched by a resemblance of practice. What she owes to
James as a theoretician of fiction is something more general than
any particular rule or method. Concerning *The Writing of Fiction,* she wrote Brownell: "I really poured out my faith and my
reverence of my art." Although the doctrines she supports are
only partially exemplified in her own writing, the faith and the
reverence for the art of fiction, the seriousness of her feeling that
the utmost dedication of craft was due her profession itself may
be the most significant of James's effects upon her.

In May, 1913, Edith Wharton wrote her publisher that she was
contemplating a new book. Its subject was uncertain, but its
form—aggressively non-Jamesian—was clear. "As to subject,
I am wavering between two, which I have had in mind for a long
time. In both cases the scene would be laid chiefly, if not alto-

gether, in America, and the novels are both planned somewhat on the lines of "The House of Mirth" and "The Custom": that is, they would deal with a group or groups of people, and with a series of events rather than a central situation." It will be recalled that she had summarized the meaning of James's private (though not public) response to *The Custom of the Country* as, "James had long since lost all interest in the chronicle-novel, and cared only for the elaborate working out on all sides of a central situation." Obviously, she was determined to proceed with her next major work according to her own conception of the art of fiction.

It is difficult, from so sketchy a description, to tell what her contemplated subjects for this new novel were. One may have been the story that emerged as *The Age of Innocence*, not published till 1920. The other almost certainly grew into a novel called "Literature" which intermittently occupied her for several years before being abandoned finally after the war. "Literature," of which the unfinished manuscript survives in Yale University's collection of Edith Wharton's papers, was to be a novel about the adventures of a writer in the modern jungle of publishing, magazines, and literary cliquism. Its subject is the making of a literary reputation—such as Mrs. Wharton herself had gained. She planned it on a large scale, and it was, as already indicated, to be a "chronicle." "It is to be rather a full and leisurely chronicle of a young man's life from his childhood to his end," she wrote early in 1914.

The outbreak of war changed all her plans, and left her little time or inclination for such large projects. She shared with James the sense that the whole foundation of social life was changing beneath her feet and that all the presuppositions upon which her fiction was based were undergoing a major alteration. While "Literature" foundered, eventually to sink out of sight, she occupied herself with slighter efforts, *The Glimpses of the Moon* and *Summer*, among other projects, though she continued to hope the work might be revived. But it never emerged. Or perhaps one should say it did emerge, much later and much transformed, in a new novel about an American writer of different background and history. Certain general features and many minor marks connect the scrapped "Literature" with *Hudson River Bracketed* and its sequel, *The Gods Arrive*, published in 1929 and 1932. In this terminal work, she reached the very extreme of her method as a "chronicle-novelist" whose broad narrative, sweeping ever onward like an endless tide, was the very reverse of James's strictly ordered and confined art.

One can only speculate concerning the views James might have offered Edith Wharton as each of her later books—again as many as she had already published before his death—came off the presses after the war. Certainly his death did not end their literary relationship. There were to be touches of his influence more or less evident in much of what she continued to write. But her talent had already defined itself most characteristically in *The House of Mirth* and *The Custom of the Country* and the method and intention of these works was to dominate over other notes in what she would now produce.

She continued to publish short stories, but these were intermittent, and for the most part minor, accompaniments to her efforts in the novel. *Xingu and Other Stories*, the collection issued in 1916, brought together eight stories of diverse significance written over as many years. One of these, "Bunner Sisters," is a curious third example (along with *Ethan Frome* and *Summer*) of her effort to portray at length the life of the poor and humble. This novelette, actually drafted many years earlier, probably in 1891 or 1892, belongs in atmosphere with "Mrs. Manstey's View," a story of the New York slums which was her first published prose. At the time she began to write she undoubtedly felt the influence of such local colorists of that era as H. C. Bunner whose name her sisters so coincidentally bear. It is interesting to reflect upon the failure of her effort at that early date to persuade the editors of *Scribner's Magazine* to accept "Bunner Sisters." Like *Ethan Frome* much later, it was a somber story of meager lives, told with some strength and artistry, but *Scribner's* did not publish it until the success of the later story had vindicated her ability to work in this vein. Meanwhile, it seems probable, her editors had directed her toward the role of critic of polite manners, for

The Summing Up

which her background so obviously suited her. It was a role she did embrace and fulfill herself in, even though we may read self-doubt in an observation set down among her unpublished papers that "to the student of human nature, poverty is a powerful lens, revealing minute particles of character imperceptible to the prosperous eye. Wealth keeps us at arm's length from life, poverty thrusts us into stifling propinquity with it."

Such subject-matter always exercised a certain attraction for her. Her treatment in *The House of Mirth* of Lily Bart's sojourn among the city poor belongs to the same mood, which though an unfrequent one in her writing, is not unrelated to her repeated attempts to come to grips with social material outside her personal sphere—the factory scenes and unsophisticated lives that are part of *The Fruit of the Tree*, the "Main Street" origins of the Spraggs and Moffats in *The Custom of the Country*, and of Vance Weston, the hero of her last two novels.

In this mood she was, perhaps, least in contact with James. It is not merely that his interest in such subject-matter was small—James had also made a foray into the world of the poor in *The Princess Casamassima*. But the complex brew of ingredients he poured into that novel has a quite different taste altogether from Edith Wharton's treatment of the depressed lives of the stagnant New England village and the city slum. As "Bunner Sisters," *Ethan Frome*, and *Summer* showed, she thought it worth-while to depict these worlds for their own sake, and her characters in the stories are predictable products of their environment, naturalistically viewed. James, however, placed that exotic bloom, Hyacinth Robinson, at the center of his book and surrounded him with intellectual and social stimulants from the mixed world of revolutionary avant-gardism that offered multifarious promptings to his complex nature. Anything so "simple" as Mattie Silver, or Eliza Bunner, or Charity Royall of *Summer*, would have bored him.

Her little-known masterpiece, *Summer*, published in 1917, is an *Ethan Frome* made more coherent in tone, more moving emotionally, because it eliminates the awkward presence of a Jamesian fine intelligence to register a tale of primitive passion in the

New England hills. Charity Royall's story is not told in terms the character herself could have given utterance to; it is the author rather than an intruded narrator who reports upon her heroine's experience. The result is at once more old-fashioned and more comfortable. Here is the inarticulate subject rendered as Flaubert rather than James would have done; we see the thought and emotions of Charity in the objective translation of the mind which stands outside of the story, the writer's own. And indeed this is an essential difference in method which marked her off from James in almost all that she subsequently wrote. She did not again tackle "un coeur simple," but she was increasingly preoccupied with the satirical display of personalities incapable of self-understanding, like Undine Spragg. As a writer she enjoyed the sound of her own voice; her own presence is an essential element in the pattern of her fiction.

And yet *The Age of Innocence*, published in 1920, contains some of the most obvious resemblances to James's works to be found anywhere in her writing. Is it perhaps a final monument to his influence? To begin with, her central theme might fairly be called his own favorite one—the theme of innocence and experience, the contrast of the strength of each state with that of the other which it annihilates. Newland Archer of *The Age of Innocence* seems to belong to the company of James's tender American initiates; like Lambert Strether, like Isabel Archer, like Christopher Newman, he encounters the sweetness of the state of knowledge in a European or Europeanized American of the opposite sex. And Ellen Olenska, the already-initiated, is one of those whose eyes the Gorgon has not blinded but fastened open, as she says, "so that they're never again in the blessed darkness." Innocence seems to triumph in the dénouement, for May, sweet and ignorant, holds fast the man so allured by Ellen. And how does she do it? By a species of guile, a guile of innocence which is like that of Maggie Verver of *The Golden Bowl*. Like Maggie, similarly threatened with the loss of her husband, she does not hesitate even to lie in order to win and to preserve. When she tells Ellen that she is to have a child even before she is sure of it herself—and sends Ellen into exile across the seas—she is not unlike

Maggie telling Charlotte, *her* husband's lover, that she cherishes no ground of complaint against her, and sentencing her rival to return to America forever.

But the abstract moral comparison of character out of which this theme emerges is not Edith Wharton's only, not even her chief interest in the book. *The Age of Innocence* is another kind of triumph, a triumph of documentation in which the décor of material existence—the interiors of houses, the minutiae of costume, the paraphernalia of work and leisure—are supremely important because they symbolize the qualities of period and class. Her chief characters are only more distinctly marked members of a crowd of social types; her constant references to current gossip and news and local scene locate them in a particular moment of history. This was never so for James, not even in the early novel whose bare plot may actually have provided some sort of model for *The Age of Innocence*. Certainly there is something in the central situation, the return of the Countess Olenska to her American family, that reminds us of the arrival in New England of Eugenia Young in James's *The Europeans*. But Mrs. Wharton's elaborate reproduction of the manners and mores of New York society in the 1870's is a splendid achievement of satiric archaeology, whereas James made no attempt to survey the Boston of the forties, being content to delineate a handful of characters as representatives of the American and European.

But surely, one may speculate, Mrs. Wharton had James to thank for the novel's epilogue, the last chapter in which an older Archer sits on a bench outside Ellen Olenska's house in Paris and contemplates what he has made of his life. Long ago he had not accepted and he would not now accept the "flower of life" which Ellen Olenska offered. As he sits on his bench he is almost James's Marcher in the story "The Beast in the Jungle," whose destiny proved to be simply that nothing would ever happen to him. There is even an echo of names—Archer is almost Marcher, and both stories contain a May, though May Bartram is the Ellen of Edith Wharton's situation, not its May. In an earlier chapter Archer foresees his own fate in words that unquestionably echo James's: "His whole future seemed suddenly to be unrolled before him; and passing down its endless emptiness he saw the dwindling figure of a man to whom nothing was ever to happen." And yet, Newland Archer's renunciation of Ellen is decisively different from Marcher's of May Bartram because there is another May in his life, the wife to whom this sacrifice is tendered, and because also, in Edith Wharton's view, the sacrifice has been tendered to a social principle. "After all, there was good in the old ways."

Finally, *The Age of Innocence* seems Jamesian in technique in its close-knit continuity of story and a certain restrictedness of point of view. Yet, as Joseph Warren Beach, who stressed these resemblances some years ago, observed most acutely, "Everything is rendered through the consciousness of Newland Archer, but nothing is made of his consciousness. [Newland Archer] is hardly more than a device for projecting a situation and characters more real than himself. We do not dwell with him in the narrow prison of his predicament as we dwell with Fleda Vetch or Maggie Verver." And indeed, one may go further and observe that a high proportion of the novel is not even projected through Archer at all, but through the old-fashioned authorial eye, which is endowed with a greater objectivity and range. It is precisely these which her differing needs, her differing aims as a novelist, required of Mrs. Wharton. Despite its many Jamesian notes *The Age of Innocence* is not, after all, as close to his essential spirit as *The Reef*, the one major work in which she embraced both his method and intention. More replete with echoes of his themes than any other of her works, it is yet directed towards the object most native to her talent from first to last, the scrutiny of society, the outward rather than the inward gaze.

The Age of Innocence, which won a Pulitzer Prize, remains, with *Ethan Frome*, the most familiar of Edith Wharton's works and its Jamesian echoes may have helped to fix with finality the impression that she was his constant imitator. Yet the principal tone of the book is one absent in James. It is a retrospective novel of American manners, while James's American backgrounds are almost exclusively of the present, whether it be the present of his youth or age. His tradition, his "past," he discovered in older cultures still to be visited by the contemporary explorer. Edith Wharton's age of innocence was an America inaccessibly vanished, and she memorialized it in a spirit of satire tempered with nostalgia. How quaint, how preposterous and pathetic, and yet how endearing was this ancestral time, she seems to be saying. The American past became henceforth for her the favored term of a comparison with the contemporary. In the four novelettes of the series "Old New York"—*False Dawn, The Old Maid, The Spark*, and *New Year's Day*—she soon after evoked the remote forties and fifties, and the sixties and seventies of her own youth. Significantly, each of these slight pieces, as indeed *The Age of Innocence* also, is woven of treasured bits of authentic legend or the author's actual memories of this extinct world which she displays with tender irony. This treasuring of the authentic is quite different from James's well-known attitude toward his *données*—that they should be as slender as possible, just a germ, no more, to initiate his imaginative aftergrowth. She was, as he was not, interested in real history, and the comparison of a faithfully reconstructed past with the society bursting into form before her.

She had already begun as early as *The House of Mirth*, and in short stories even earlier, to portray this new society in fiction that borrowed little from James, concentrating upon the typical comedy of social interaction rather than upon the inner consciousnesses of her characters. *Glimpses of the Moon*, written during the war as a relief from larger tasks, reads like the potboiler it undoubtedly was meant to be, for the plot is banal and the characters thinly conceived. Susy Branch and Nick Lansing— unlike Lily Bart and Lawrence Selden of *The House of Mirth*, whom they resemble—decide to marry and live on "nothing a year" in the fashion of Thackeray's Becky and her Rawdon. Their enterprise is a romantic if not a practical failure; they part, each to plunge again into the life of social parasitism and seek alternate mates; they return to one another resolved to live more ideally. Yet this book is better than its plot and its leading characters wherever these give way to the study of manners, "the air purged at a stroke of all the old sentimental and romantic values," which James had found in *The Custom of the Country*. James, of course, would have been interested in Susy and Nick (as has been noted he was repeatedly intrigued by the way money supports refinement and lack of it produces genteel black-guardism—vide Madame Merle, Kate Croy, Charlotte Stant). But for him the characters would have been everything and the surrounding tissue of social typicalities unimportant. It was the other way around for Edith Wharton.

With *The Mother's Recompense, Twilight Sleep*, and *The Children*, published in 1925, 1927, and 1928, she reached the full maturity of her powers as a social satirist. These novels are too little appreciated today—perhaps because readers want more Jamesian notes from the author of *The Age of Innocence*. They were successfully serialized in popular magazines and they are often accused of being as formulaic and slipshod as most of the fiction provided for the same audience. As a matter of fact, they are unsentimental, even austere stories of personal passion, deftly placed in a medium of ironic social observation. They owe very little to James in the strength of either element.

In *The Mother's Recompense*, Kate Clephane returns from a divorcée's exile in Europe to find that the old censures have passed taking with them all the terror and significance of her own old rebellion. She finds also that her grown daughter is about to marry the man who was her own former lover. The second discovery involves a near-duplication, it will be noted, of the dilemma confronting Darrow in *The Reef* when he recognizes a former mistress in the fiancée of his step-son-to-be. James had remarked that the earlier novel reminded him of a tragedy by Racine—and Kate's fatality of passion is perhaps even more reminiscent of the compulsive, illicit emotion of, let us say, Phèdre. In her interest in such unacknowledged feelings Mrs. Wharton became bolder rather than more timid as time went on. She passed beyond James in a psychological realism that is certainly French, perhaps even originating in Racine, but more immediately present in the novels of her friend Paul Bourget, whose influence on her work has generally been overlooked.

With its ironic turn-about establishing as well contrasts of times and manners, *The Mother's Recompense* is as precisely localized in a satiric medium as *The Reef* was lifted out of the particulars of time and place. Here, certainly, she reversed the direction pointed by *The Reef*, going back from the example of the mature James to her native inclination for comedy of manners. More important than *The Reef* as an antecedent, therefore, is the story "Autres Temps," first published in 1911 and later included in the "Xingu" collection, which anticipates that part of the novel's plot which involves the opportunity for comic comparisons of manners—the divorcée's return to her daughter in a changed America—and nothing of the tragic complications of living and dead loves which stem from *The Reef*.

In *The Mother's Recompense*, Kate Clephane's return to America is an opportunity for Edith Wharton to portray the transformation of New York society from the days before World War I to the roaring twenties that succeeded it. Here was a world of a kind James had anticipated in *What Maisie Knew* and *The Awkward Age* in which the treasured term "tradition" was absolutely and finally dissevered from the authority of wealth and position. James did not live to see the jazz age, with its wasters, its flappers, and its bohemia, but it is doubtful that he would have returned to the kind of interest expressed by these works of his middle period. But Edith Wharton, now in her sixties, increasingly absorbed herself in the study of these evolving social phenomena; she admired the explorations into this same area of a young writer just then emerging, F. Scott Fitzgerald.

One exception in this transformed world is Kate's daughter, who is not only her mother's supplanter in the triangular central tragedy but, curiously, her mother's representative in its diagram of social values. Anne Clephane is atavistic, a conservative among her contemporaries, a strong young votary of old standards and scruples. In each of the two succeeding novels Edith Wharton wrote there is such a youthful figure near the center—Nona Manford in *Twilight Sleep* and Judith Wheater in *The Children*. Of these, Anne is the most "memorial," to use the word applied to her by her creator, most conscious of past forms as containers of value, Judith the most instinctive and primitive, her sense of virtue springing from some depth of heart rather than from a conscious tradition. But each of these girls is the still center about which Mrs. Wharton's briskly disintegrating scene pulses and eddies.

Years before, when writing *The House of Mirth*, Edith Wharton declared that a frivolous society could provide the subject of tragedy because of what it destroyed. And as her own society crushes the flower-like Lily Bart, so the later world of America in the booming twenties isolates and mortifies Nona Manford. *Twilight Sleep* again involves the same near-incest pattern of passion we have seen in two books already—Nona's father falls in love with his step-son's wife. But here, even more than in *The Mother's Recompense*, this theme has dwindled to subordinate importance. What this novel is about is the ethos of a new civilization which Edith Wharton saw in triumphant progress, a civilization based on the avoidance of pain (as though we could all live in a sort of perpetual "Twilight Sleep"), a denial of guilt and responsibility, a pursuit of personal content at all cost. If she were writing today Edith Wharton would probably call her novel "Miltown." Her suggestion would probably be that we cannot and must not try to escape from the anxieties which are our mortal portion and, more than that, our sources of moral decision.

Twilight Sleep and *The Children* are both brilliant exposés of social futility, scathing presentations of the empty agitation of the rich and idle. Pauline Manford, Nona's mother, is a pathetically energetic New York lady of fashion whose time and emotions are desperately crowded into a calendar of "activities" which include as of equal significance the latest eurythmic exercises for reducing the hips and the problems of her children. In *The Children*, Edith Wharton looks at this same kind of American family abroad, the constantly divorcing and re-marrying Wheaters and their friends who crowded the Riviera beaches not far from Mrs. Wharton's home at Hyères. They seemed to her a new race, despicable and appalling, a race of humans without purpose or dignity, neither knowing nor needing any traditional sanctions. To measure their heedlessness Mrs. Wharton used two significant figures in the novel—Martin Boyne, the weary traveller who has come back from a career in deserts and jungles to a Europe as changed as Mrs. Clephane's New York, and Judith, oldest of the Wheater children. Martin, for a brief moment, falls in love with the girl—and here is another instance of hopeless and unreasoned "Racinian" passion—but this is not as important as the cause in which they are leagued, the desire of the Wheater children to remain together as a family. Judith struggles to defend her brothers and sisters out of some untaught instinct of heart, while Martin's judgments are based on the nearly vanished traditions of responsibility only he remembers; together they represent a frail continuity of virtue in the midst of chaos.

The vision of these three novels is coherent and matured. They are held together by a strength of social appraisal which is Edith Wharton's final wisdom as a novelist. She had no further reach to explore. Significantly, her last completed work is a pair of novels or a two-part novel which is less a new fictional world than an exercise in self-appraisal. She ended her career, as so many writers begin theirs, with a novel about a novelist. *Hudson River Bracketed* and *The Gods Arrive* compose a parable of the modern artist's life which is valuable to the student of Mrs. Wharton's own career and personality. Yet despite much vigor of presentation they are weakened by the uncertain nature of the hero's psychology as well as of that of the only other seriously-regarded character, Halo Spear. Mrs. Wharton's satiric vivacity is evident here and there in scenes and characters that range from "Euphoria, Mo." to Bloomsbury, but the tone too often returns to the sentimental when she deals with her central story.

Even more truly than in the case of her other "chronicle novels" there is "no reason why they should ever end." Never had she so completely disregarded James's lesson of economic shaping than in *Hudson River Bracketed* and *The Gods Arrive*. The second work could have sustained a sequel no less than the first; nothing but the death of her artist-hero might have halted the onward-rolling episodes. In its sprawling inclusiveness the method nearly justifies itself in the same terms as had *The House*

of Mirth or *The Custom of the Country* for it again enables the
novelist to display society in scene after varied scene. But these
earlier examples had their own kind of control, a hard certainty
about the significance of the major characters and their relation
to the setting, which this story lacks. Yet in pronouncing these
final products of Mrs. Wharton's age to be failures we can still
note the choice of method they affirm. Could she have viewed
her Vance Weston with the same cool detachment with which
she had regarded Undine Spragg—even if not with the same
distaste—she would again have demonstrated the validity of the
method which was peculiarly hers.

At the very last she still exhibited preoccupations that might
seem Jamesian, for *The Buccaneers*, on which she was at work
when she died, was to relate the European adventures of naïve
American heiresses. As far as one can tell from the published
fragment, she intended once more, as in *The Age of Innocence*, a
historical study of manners. She may herself have thought she
was closing her *oeuvres* upon a Jamesian note, for in her autobiography, also written in her last years, she had come to conclude,
"Henry James was essentially a novelist of manners, and the
manners he was qualified by nature and situation to observe were
those of the little vanishing group of people among whom he had
grown up, or their more picturesque prototypes in older societies."

Obviously, this description does not fit the more abstract moral
drama of *The Golden Bowl* which she herself had even emulated
once in *The Reef*. And as a matter of fact it does not even fit the
James of, let us say, *The Portrait of a Lady*. Nan St. George of
The Buccaneers is really not at all like Isabel Archer, whose
exercise of freedom brought her into touch with moral complexities possible in all times and places. She seems simply to be a
charming and intelligent young daughter of wealthy New York
in the 1870s who bunglingly marries the wrong English milord
(and will re-marry the right one). What Mrs. Wharton's statement seems to define is what, after all, was ultimately most usable
to her in James. This she could partake of even after she had
become indifferent to his formal principles and deepest themes.

Not surprisingly, when Edith Wharton died in 1937, most summaries of her career fell back upon the easy if insufficient formula that had satisfied her earliest reviewers. Her craftsmanship was still "emphatically the craftsmanship of Henry James, less subtle, less original, less rhetorical," but unmistakably his—as Henry Seidel Canby concluded in the *Saturday Review of Literature*. But now there was a paradoxical addition to the early judgment. To most commentators those later works that were more and more free of James's particular lessons—the series that had come after *The Age of Innocence*—seemed evidence not so much of the final solidification of a personal style as of the leaching out from her work of any sense of style at all, original or borrowed. To these critics she seemed to have become less and less of a craftsman, more and more of a facile entertainer whose work for the serializing women's magazines was the "vice," as Canby put it, of her later years. Her evolution thus viewed could be considered the very opposite of James's. He had ended his career as an austere priest of art, so dedicated to formal principles that he had sacrificed popularity; Edith Wharton seemed to have gained a larger, if less discriminating audience as her artistic method grew more lax.

If our summary of her literary career is just, she thus suffered a double misestimate of her achievement. Condemned early for a discipleship that had never been as exact and constant as her critics declared, she ended by being condemned as well for her later work, which, though it was less and less easily comparable to the work of James, had an overlooked excellence at times which was quite unlike his—an excellence of a kind James himself had recognized when he praised *The Custom of the Country*.

Though she was still popular with a reading public that was indifferent to questions of form and originality in any case, Edith Wharton's standing with the critics and with sophisticated readers was generally low at the time of her death. Part of the explanation was certainly non-literary—the result of the fact that lingering economic depression had made "social significance" seem a necessary qualification for art. *Ethan Frome*, with its implicit criticism of the tragic possiblities of life on a marginal New

England farm, was more than ever respected as an exception to her general rule, but there was little satisfaction with her studies of the rich and suspicion altogether of her own ability, as a daughter of riches, to see life whole. When her autobiographical volume, *A Backward Glance*, came out three years earlier, at the darkest moment of national crisis, William Troy had felt it necessary to caution his *Nation* readers, "Nothing could be more foolish than to throw down this book with the objection that its background, its people, and its events seem lacking in vital significance to the harried and very much preoccupied reader of today." She herself was aware that her interests as a writer and her own social history had alienated her at the moment from many. "At present," she wrote in the autobiography, "the demand is that only the man with the dinner pail shall be deemed worthy of attention and fiction is classed according to its degree of conformity to this rule."

Well before the thirties, however, she had been criticized because of her subject matter—the rich, the foreign, the aesthetic. Her attention to the lives of the wealthy seemed undemocratic, her interest in the European scene disloyal, her preoccupation with culture pretentious. In short, she was a snob. Since the end of the Civil War there had been a regular demand by the critics for "the great American novel." No one was very certain what it would be like when it appeared, but there was general agreement that it would concern itself with life both native and common. In the light of such an expectation, one reviewer of *The Valley of Decision* complained, "Why must a beautiful talent like Mrs. Wharton's turn to foreign lands to find the inspiration for work such as this?" But *The House of Mirth* had equally offended some because it showed the uncommon and privileged in American society. With only a few exceptions each of her subsequent works had produced some dissatisfaction on the score of suitable subject.

In 1927, Edith Wharton took up these charges in an article titled "The Great American Novel," published in *The Yale Review:* "It would appear that in the opinion of recent American reviewers the American novelist must submit to much narrower social and geographical limitations before he can pretend to have produced *the* (or the *greatest*, or even simply *an*) American novel . . . The great American novel must always be about Main Street, geographically, socially, and intellectually." And she affirmed, "The novelist's—any novelist's proper field, created by his particular way of apprehending life, is limited only by the bounds of his natural, his instinctive interest."

The following year, in the London *Spectator*, she wrote of the same matter in a more personal fashion: "Of late . . . a serious charge has been brought against me. It is that I write only about the rich! I will not pause to controvert this by giving a list of my tales which deal with divers classes of people; my point is other. Supposing I *did* write only about the rich—what then? If I did the chances would be that it was because they happened to be the material most 'to my hand.' "

In critical obloquy because of her subjects, she was kept company, of course, by Henry James. James had long been charged with a damning artistic preoccupation with lives lived in a foreign milieu of riches and culture, and it was well known—and resented—that he lived abroad and associated with the privileged of wealth and "high breeding." That Edith Wharton had also transferred her home from America to Europe, there, moreover, to enjoy the benefits of James's friendship, seemed to make her case not only similar to his but the familiar result, again, of his bad example. Arm linked in arm they seemed to have turned their backs upon their native land and the proper responsibilities of the American novelist, preferring foreign materials for their fiction as they preferred a Mayfair or a Faubourg Saint-Germain environment for themselves.

James's loss of his audience during his final period, the alienation he suffered as the monumental efforts of his last years were appreciated by fewer and fewer readers, was certainly assisted by this general view of his disaffection as an American which culminated in the sense of outrage many felt when he renounced his citizenship. It remained for Van Wyck Brooks to argue in 1925 that his final works were difficult and insubstantial because their author had chosen to live abroad. Less sensitively and eloquently than Brooks's *Prilgrimage of Henry James*, Vernon L. Parrington's final judgment of James was argued on the same basis. James had failed because of a mistaken "nostalgia" for the culture of aristocratic societies in the place of the "homely realities" of his birthplace.

Parrington pointed out the analogy with Edith Wharton. Both, he declared, had "erected this suppositious culture into an abstract *tertium quid*, something embodied in the choicer spirits of a class that for generations presumably had cherished them." When Parrington reviewed *The Age of Innocence* in 1921, he perfectly anticipated the sociological argument of the next decade:

> But when one has said that the craftsmanship is a very great success, why not go further and add that it doesn't make the slightest difference whether one reads the book or not, unless one is a literary epicure who lives for the savor of things. What do the van der Luydens matter to us; or what did they or their kind matter a generation ago? Why waste such skill upon such insignificant material? . . . If she had lived less easily, if she had been forced to skimp and save and plan, she would have been a greater and richer artist, one significant because more native, more continental . . . But unfortunately her doors open only to the smart set; the windows from which she surveys life open only to the east, to London, Paris, Rome . . . Mrs. Wharton is our outstanding literary aristocrat. She has done notable things, but she has paid a great price in aloofness from her own America. There is more hope for our literature in the honest crudities of the younger naturalists, than in her classic irony; they at least are trying to understand America as it is."

Thus, a curious mixture of personal and literary hostility enveloped the reputations of both Henry James and Edith Wharton. Of course there was a certain confusion in an argument which explained both James's difficult and unpopular final phase and the meretriciously "readable" novels of the successful Mrs. Wharton by means of the same cause. But it was enough for the critics to decide that expatriation and the wrong choice of materials had somehow blighted the talents of each.

There has since been a revolution of taste, that has brought James to the front of American writers. Pioneers like Edmund Wilson and Pelham Edgar and William Troy had almost immediately protested the Brooks-Parrington diagnosis of James's "case," and stated the grounds for understanding the true meaning of his artistic evolution. For nearly twenty years now the recognition of James's greatness has been firmly established and the old charges against him have fallen into disrepute (though there is some indication that they can be revived, as Maxwell Geismar has illustrated in his recent attack, *Henry James and the Jacobites.*)

Henry James has come to seem not the least but the most American of writers whose themes are deeply rooted in our cultural consciousness. His discoveries and refinements of the craft of fiction have become the technical assumptions of a whole generation of writers, and of teachers and students of the art of fiction, for whom the novel has come into its own—as he would have wished—as the greatest of modern literary forms. With the growth of James's fame, Edith Wharton has emerged as a figure of renewed interest, no longer judged hostilely because of her preoccupation with the foreign scene and the wealthy. She awakens curiosity in the new generation of novel-readers because of her association with James and the assumed likeness of their artistic characters—and this association and assumption, which had once discredited her, now create a fresh appeal.

But no Edith Wharton revival is likely to base itself securely on such credit by association. If her materials, now more tolerable, were often the same, it is clear, as we have shown, that her use of them was different from that of Henry James. As James's work came to final maturity, he became less and less concerned with the definition of types and customs; she, on the other hand, went on from book to book to trace the growth of new social configurations. She made a particular study of the later history of Americans abroad, after the First World War, describing phenomena James could hardly have dreamed of as she took note of the ways of the Riviera drifters who people such a novel as *The Children.*

It is doubtful if James would have found any new stimulus in these developments—he had long before anticipated what interest they might offer him in *What Maisie Knew*. James's late representatives of the rich, his contemporary "princes" and "princesses," his heirs and heiressess "of all the ages," were only conveniently the modern moneyed class because only among this class could he find situations of freedom suitable to his moral dramas. Edith Wharton, on the other hand, moved, as we have seen, from the "Racinian" *The Reef* to the later novels of social analysis where she found among the wealthy no royal images of moral conflict, but the clownish and the mean, privilege without principle, leisure without grace.

James's themes, though ethical, were the essential and permanent issues of human personality; he was, as Pelham Edgar wrote in 1933, "the essential novelist," who had taught himself to neglect "those excrescent attachments of fiction"—the reformatory, the argumentative, the sociological—in order "to concentrate all the powers of his intellect on the artistic presentation of human behaviour under conditions designed to reveal character at the maximum of intensity." To Edith Wharton these very "excrescent attachments" became of the highest significance; her ethical impulse, which is either castigatory or memorial, always bears reference to a particular time or place.

In rediscovering the value of her achievement we will have to assume that it was of a different sort from his. It must be admitted that for her peculiar art of satiric observation, expatriation may have occasionally had a damaging effect. When her subject was an America she knew only at second hand like the "Euphoria, Illinois" which nurtures Vance Weston in *Hudson River Bracketed*, she produced a picture that was not so much satiric as grotesque. An art of satiric observation depends on the author's ability to observe. Wisely, she took her hero in that novel, further and further East—to New York and to Europe—where she could operate with greater authority.

Of course, James was the greater writer, the truer and more abundant genius. And there is, even in Edith Wharton's best work, a thin and wintry quality traceable, perhaps, to the inadequacy of her attachment to life, the weakness of her sense of what makes it valuable. Her most persistent intellectual resource was the rationalism that stripped her of a conventional religious faith in her youth but left behind no sense of the mystery of life and of the grandeur of human capacity for goodness and depravity. She regarded naturalism as the enemy of art, with its animus against selectivity and form, and yet her view of human events almost certainly owed something to the naturalist philosophy of social determinism which makes good and evil only relative conditions.

In James, on the contrary, one discerns an inexpugnable attachment to transcendent values, a veritable "New England heritage," for all that he was a cosmopolitan New Yorker whose language betrays no trace either of conventional religion or Emersonian exaltation. What James's "beliefs," if any, were remains something of a mystery, but he never, I think, could have reached the dead level of Edith Wharton's skepticism. Hers, at best, was a view of a universe bleakly governed by "unpetitionable powers," as she describes them in her poem, *Moonrise over Tyringham.* Consequently character, in her books, never exudes that radiance, as of some immortal and beautiful spirit imprisoned in time and circumstance, which can be felt to flow from James's greatest figures. Certainly not Mattie Silver—and not even Lily Bart, Justine Brent, Kate Clephane or Halo Tarrant, the most complex and interesting of Edith Wharton's heroines—is as illumined with a sense of human possibility as Isabel Archer.

Reviewers often accused Edith Wharton of hard-heartedness towards her characters—as when Francis Hackett in *The New Republic* complained of her treatment of Charity Royall in *Summer:* "What one dislikes . . . is the undoubted purpose of the author to dish the heroine for the sake of dishing her. One really suffers on account of the pace at which Mrs. Wharton hurries over the poignancy of a human record to arrive at a cruel predicament. The feeling is certainly established before the end that as a human being Charity Royall is nothing to her author, she is merely a creature to be substantiated in detail in order that a dramatic sensation can be properly pulled off." James, the true

309

solitary with few unguarded, intimate relationships, really adored life. He could never cease his passionate absorption in it, his wonder at new human revelations, as the breathless notations in his journals often show. Edith Wharton almost always had closed the case of her characters before her story was under way. An insatiable traveller and a searcher into books, a woman of restless curiosity, she nevertheless expected less and found less wonder in human personality than did James.

Perhaps her emotional limitations had, ultimately, biographic origins. Her own life, despite its outer glitter, was singularly dry and empty. A child of aging, primly respectable parents who, it seems, were truly "Victorian" in the trite sense of offering their daughter no preparation for life's most commonplace realities, she married a man she never loved, and when he became a neurotic invalid, ruthlessly freed herself from bondage to him. Her one passionate attachment was to Walter Berry, and this never became the union she apparently hoped for. She had no children and she did not marry again after her divorce. Yet was this severance from emotional satisfaction any greater than James's? James never married at all, never, as far as we can tell, fully loved any woman, it will be hastily pointed out. He did have, however, a richly emotional family life; he had enjoyed in his childhood the atmosphere of the strongly affectionate James family, with parents, brothers and a sister to whom he was devoted until their or his own death. But above all, his renunciations, whatever their cause, did not seem to have left him with any irremediable sense of having missed the best of life. His art seems truly to have had the function Hawthorne spoke of when he described his stories as serving "to open up an intercourse with the world." It was the window through which, not in bitterness and disappointment but in love and joy, he regarded the whole of experience, being, as he said of Milly Theale, "afraid of nothing he might come to by living with enough sincerity and enough wonder."

But in the last analysis, her personal qualities did not disable Edith Wharton in the discovery of her own kind of work. If she found human beings inadequate, if her emotional expectations were unfulfilled, she was all the more trenchant in her definition of human frustrations. Her books are repeatedly concerned with the effect upon the individual of denial enforced by family, society, the meanness of others. And enveloping these situations there is always her vision of the changing sand in the social hour-glass, the pathetic replacement of class by class. Irony and detachment, her way of meeting her own fate, was her artistic mood.

Appendix

Lady into Author:
Edith Wharton
and the House of Scribner

A NOVELIST, surely, is just someone who writes novels. In this competence he is unlike other men, but not necessarily in the rest of his character. In particular, he need not be more inept in the practical management of his life than a specialist in another line. This would be too obvious to state were it not for the fact that the ancient legend persists that creative artists of any kind must be either saints or fools, persons inadequate in everything except the practice of a unique gift. The fact seems to be that a successful novelist is more likely to be a person of well-developed practicality. He has had to learn along the way that books are not only expressions of the spirit, but also end-products in a complex manufacturing process, objects of cost and price in the book-trade.

Yet one cannot help some surprise in finding this true of Edith Wharton. Was she not, to begin with, a "lady" out of a time and world when the word meant absolute indifference to business? Even the men of her class were, as she describes them in many of her stories, too proud and too ignorant of the methods of money-making to apply their intelligence to augmenting an inherited wealth. If they had any artistic talent at all, they were content to remain genteel dabblers; art seemed to them to be one of those higher activities which by its very nature should fail to pay. Mrs. Wharton, on the other hand, deserved the name of a professional in every sense. She trained herself to work assiduously at her craft, to be tirelessly self-critical, to measure her work by an absolute standard. And at the same time she developed an effective grasp of the commercial values that govern a literary career. She was never sentimental about the meaning of success or fame; she believed they should and could be made to reward the artist materially.

Her emergence as artist and literary merchandiser is visible in a nearly-continuous series of letters which she exchanged with representatives of her publishers, Charles Scribner's Sons, for over thirty years. The existence of such a record is a piece of extraordinary fortune. Writers seldom remain with a single house for so long and more seldom still do letters survive to preserve the fugitive episodes that once meant so much to the actors. That the letters were written at all is largely due to Mrs. Wharton's long residence abroad—many of the discussions they illustrate would have taken place in the publisher's office otherwise. That they have survived at all is due to the almost unique stability of the Scribner firm in a period when dissolutions and mergers eliminated the files of other firms. As it is, this unpublished correspondence presents in full the progress of that relationship in which the author is at once the creator for all time and the seller of goods in today's market. The incidents selected here may help to remind us that our favorite writers are generally human beings prompted by many claims, not all of them elevated, dwellers in a material as well as a mental world.

First publication is, like first love, an occasion of ideality. "I did not know how authors communicated with editors, but I copied out the verses in my fairest hand, and enclosed each in an envelope with my visiting card," Edith Wharton recalled long afterwards. The young society woman of twenty-seven had suddenly reverted to a girlhood interest in poetry-writing; hardly aware of what change in her life she was initiating, she mailed a still-girlish poem, "The Last Giustiniani," to the unknown editor of *Scribner's Magazine*. Edward L. Burlingame replied with a check for twenty dollars. "As long as I live I shall never forget my sensations," she wrote of the moment when she stood in the vestibule of her Madison Avenue house and opened his letter. ". . . I was to appear in print." *Scribner's Magazine* would print her work—poems, stories, essays, serial novels—nearly eighty times again, and the publishing firm of which it was a part would put her writing into a round two dozen volumes. But that moment in July, 1889, was, of course, unlike any other. On a later day, when her novel *The House of Mirth* had sold its 100,000th copy, she wrote Burlingame, "well, it's all great fun, and you did it all by accepting 'The Last Giustiniani!' "

Burlingame's encouragement and guidance and also the friendly piloting of William Crary Brownell, the distinguished head of Scribners book-publishing department, were to be long and gratefully relied on. She called Burlingame "my first and kindest critic," and to Brownell she would write, "I live really with and *on* very few people, and you are one of my unfailing references." Both men became personal friends, and so did Charles Scribner, their chief. Towards these three men and towards the firm as a whole Edith Wharton undoubtedly felt a personal loyalty which has since grown old-fashioned in the publishing business. Nevertheless, she was not slow to understand her relationship with the *impersonal* interest of the publisher. Let us look at her a little later, in 1899 when her first collection of short stories had been out six weeks. Mrs. Wharton wrote Brownell:

> You will pardon my saying that I do not think I have been fairly treated as regards the advertising of "The Greater Inclination." The book has now been out about six weeks, and I do not think I exaggerate in saying that it has met with an unusually favorable reception for a first volume by a writer virtually unknown . . .
>
> So much for my part in the transaction: now as to Mr. Scribner's. I have naturally watched with interest the advertising of the book, and have compared it with the notices given by other prominent publishers of books appearing under the same

317

conditions. I find that Messrs. MacMillan, Dodd and Mead, McClure, Harper, etc. advertise almost continuously in the daily papers every new book they publish for the first few weeks after publication, giving large space to favorable press-notices; in addition to which, they of course advertise largely in the monthlies. So far, I have seen once, in a Sunday paper, I think, an advertisement of "The Great Inclination," with a line or two from the "Sun" review, which appeared in the same shape in "Scribner's" for May, without the addition of any of the many notices since come out.

In calling your attention to these facts I don't of course flatter myself that there is any hope of modifying the business-methods of the firm; but I think myself justified in protesting against them in my own case.

If a book is unnoticed or unfavorably received it is natural that the publisher should not take much trouble about advertising it; but to pursue the same course towards a volume that has been generally commended seems to me essentially unjust. Certainly in these days of energetic and emphatic advertising, Mr. Scribner's methods do not tempt one to offer him one's wares a second time.

It is difficult to judge how much justice there was in this complaint. The whole question of book-advertising is one that authors rarely view in the same way as do publishers, whose advertising budget on a book is usually in proportion to *expected* sales. While authors have always argued that a book can be sold in direct ratio to the advertising expended upon it beforehand, "the trade" replies that a book is not a tube of toothpaste; it must win its way with a much more limited public whose buying cannot be so easily compelled—a book by a completely unknown author is a very speculative venture, and the publisher cannot afford to concentrate expenditure upon it. The dispute is an old one, and probably it will continue as long as books are published. It is interesting to see Edith Wharton assume the classic author position at the very outset of her career, assume it so strenuously, in fact, that she nearly broke with Charles Scribner's when her association with the firm had barely begun.

The threatened transfer did not take place. Six months after publication Edith Wharton acknowledged, "I am very much pleased with the sale of 'The Greater Inclination,' though I knew from the number of letters I have received from publishers that it must be doing well . . ." But of course it was the solicitation of rival publishers that she wanted Scribners to note in considering her success. And her meaning became clear two days later in another letter to Brownell: "Since writing you the other day I have received a letter from a leading publisher who had already written me twice on the subject—offering me 15% on any volume I will give him. I am just finishing a short novel of 30 to 40 thousand words, and I do not wish to enter any agreement with another publisher without asking you if you care to consider the publication of a volume of that length and what terms you would make." Scribners met the bid of the unnamed rival firm in the contract for her novelette, *The Touchstone*, published the following year.

Already upon the publication of her first book of fiction Mrs. Wharton had shown a capacity for gauging her weight and bringing it to bear. She did not gain a position of effective bargaining power, however, until 1905 when *The House of Mirth* achieved its popular success. The conception of this work had itself represented a new stage of growth for the author. She was already forty-two years old; she had written one historical novel which had achieved a certain limited distinction; chiefly she was known for her unemphatic short stories in the manner of Henry James. The novel she now launched in the pages of *Scribner's* was to overturn completely the general view of her, for it was planned as a full-scale study of contemporary life, a realistic, even sensational, presentation of the hidden world of the very rich. Writing it, moreover, she learned for the first time the value of consistent application. Edward Burlingame, issuing one of those fortuitous challenges that often determine the careers of artists, had forced her to the achievement. She recalled afterwards how "amid the distractions of a busy and hospitable life, full of friends and travel, reading and gardening," she had dawdled over her first chapters until one day Burlingame asked her if she could furnish a serial to take the place of one that had unexpectedly been withdrawn from the magazine. It would have to be ready in four or five months. Meeting this exigent assignment bent her, she later declared, to the discipline of daily writing, turning her "from a drifting amateur into a professional."

Her professionalism meant also that she would be able to take herself seriously as a seller of goods. Although her confidence in her artistic powers was still uncertain (it had needed strong persuasion from Brownell to convince her that the book showed "a certain amount of architecture"), she understood the meaning of popular acceptance. "After the Enormous Sales of 'The House of Mirth' which I predict for next November you will see my prices leap up!" she wrote, not altogether in jest, when the serial was only three months old. And when serious negotiations were started for her next book, she elaborated: "As to the terms, it seems to me that the incipient popularity of 'The House of Mirth' might permit me to name [an advance of] $8,000 . . . and perhaps you would think it reasonable, if the sale of the volume exceeded 10,000 to raise the royalities to 20%." Her expectations were more than confirmed, and in her next contract her royalty, never greater previously than fifteen per cent, was increased to twenty per cent, as she had proposed.

The House of Mirth was a resounding success. After 30,000 copies had been sold in the first three weeks of publication, Brownell was moved to caution her against extravagant hopes: "It is not a love story, you know, after all; and if it sells as few books that are have done, shall we not have to revise our ideas of the dear public?" But the curve refused to flatten. By the end of the month 60,000 copies had been ordered from the publisher and ten days later 80,000 orders prompted Charles Scribner to declare to Mrs. Wharton: "I do not remember that we have ever published any book the sale of which has been so rapid." In another ten days sales reached the 100,000 mark. The success of The House of Mirth continued, and for the next four months it was listed as the nation's top best-seller. In the fall of 1905 she was already at work upon her next novel, The Fruit of the Tree, and when Scribner announced that the 100,000th copy of The House of Mirth had been sold, she outlined to him her plans for the new work—and reminded him about the royalty increase she expected. There is a bit of jocular menace in her description of her new hero: "... he is going to be a *very* strong man; so strong that I believe he will break all records. Perhaps in consideration of his strength you will think it not unreasonable to start with a 20% royalty? If you were to refuse, he is so violent that I don't know whether I can answer for the consequences!"

The Fruit of the Tree, though it did mark the advance in earning power Edith Wharton expected, turned out to be a difficult book to write—and it did not match its predecessor's success. Writing the successor to a "hit" is always a crucial task for an author, for in it he is expected to demonstrate that he has more than a one-book talent. And Edith Wharton, though she had already published ten earlier volumes, must have felt that the phenomenal triumph of *The House of Mirth* posed such a problem for her. She suffered intervals of self-doubt during the composition of *The Fruit of the Tree*, and Burlingame's encouragement and advice were never needed more. "You will never know what a slough that note of yours dragged me out of!" she wrote him in one letter, and in another, "Your answer puts a finger on the two points that were troubling me"; and in conclusion, "I appreciate so much the trouble you take in writing me at various stages of the work, and giving me your impressions so fully and so sympathetically." The search for a title gave infinite bother—it took her almost a year to decide upon after distressfully embracing and rejecting a half-dozen other possibilities.

It was not a lucky book. It started well enough, for on publication day orders had reached 50,000 copies, and a week later, over 60,000 orders had been received in the Scribner office. But sales did not continue to mount as they had for *The House of Mirth*. The business panic of 1907 undoubtedly depressed the sales of books in general—this, at any rate, was the comforting explanation offered by Charles Scribner when he wrote Edith Wharton in February, 1908, "I fear that you may be disappointed that the sale is not larger, and I did hope it would come closer to *The House of Mirth*, but independently of any question of the relative popularity of the two books the great and sudden change in business conditions is sufficient to account for most of the difference." But it is obvious that the novel had also failed to hold on to the public interest the earlier work had captured. For the first month it was among the better-selling fiction (third on the lists furnished by leading bookstores), and then it sank out of sight while other volumes claimed greater attention.

The Fruit of the Tree had been a determinedly different book from The House of Mirth. It was a "problem novel" concerned with the issue of reform in a modern industrial town, and several other unexpected themes were thrown in for good measure, the justification of a "mercy-killing" being the most conspicuous. Reviewers noted that the author seemed to be overly anxious to demonstrate that she could handle a task entirely unlike the one that had come so readily to her hand before. Whether or not it was actually an inferior novel is perhaps not so much the question —the public had shown again that it wanted repetition and not surprises from a writer who had once struck its fancy. It is interesting, at any rate, to see the relief with which Burlingame welcomed Edith Wharton's next novel, The Custom of the Country, in the late summer of 1908. He wrote Charles Scribner after reading the scenario she sent him that he thought it would do much to revive interest in Mrs. Wharton's work. "It is distinctly and aggressively in the earlier field . . ." This book, which Edith Wharton referred to as "my new étude de moeurs," was to depict the social encroachment of the "new rich" upon the authority of the old—a drama she could describe from the same depth of intimate knowledge brought to The House of Mirth. Charles Scribner liked her plan as well as Burlingame had. He wrote her, "A story from you with such a presentation of contemporary society and such a girl from the West climbing into it would be sure of its interest and readers. I could not let it go elsewhere—even for the magazine."

The problem solved itself on this occasion partly because Mrs. Wharton found it impossible to write the book in time to meet the original magazine schedule. Her husband's illness and the attendant disturbance of her personal life prevented her from

working with the consistency she needed; the task was temporarily laid aside and new, less ambitious projects taken up in the
interval. It was not until the fall of 1911 that she again was able to
discuss serial publication of the novel, which was run in the
magazine in 1913. Book publication followed immediately after
the last installment.

The years 1908 to 1913, a period of personal tribulation,
turned out to be the most brilliant span of Edith Wharton's
entire career. *The Custom of the Country* is an acknowledged
satiric masterpiece, and during the same period she also wrote
Ethan Frome and *The Reef*, each an achieved monument of separate character. In addition, she published other volumes of stories,
poetry, travel-reporting during these years. Her apprenticeship as
an artist was over. She herself felt that *Ethan Frome* marked a
climax of self-realization. *The House of Mirth* had turned her
from an amateur to a professional, as we have seen, but *Ethan
Frome* represented a still greater surety. "It was not until I wrote
Ethan Frome that I suddenly felt the artisan's full control of his
implements," she asserted in her old age. "From that day until
now I have always felt that I had my material fairly well in
hand." And this was the moment at which Edith Wharton's
relations with Charles Scribner's Sons began to go aground. Of
the books just mentioned, one, *The Reef*, was published by D.
Appleton. Here was a break of the utmost significance, a fore-
warning of her definite transfer to Appleton five years later.

Friction seems to have arisen over *Ethan Frome*. It is at present
impossible to say just how Burlingame, Brownell and Charles
Scribner responded to the manuscript of what has become the
best known of all Edith Wharton's books. The Scribner-Whar-
ton file of correspondence is silent at this point; a gap of nearly a
year interrupts the steady exchange of letters, and we can only
infer the discussions that took place sometime between August,
1910 and July, 1911. Perhaps Mrs. Wharton's publishers failed to
anticipate the enormous vogue of this stark tale, a work strikingly
unlike anything she had ever before submitted to them. Her previous foray out of the subject-area defined by *The House of
Mirth* had been *The Fruit of the Tree*, a failure from the pub-

lisher's viewpoint. It is just possible that the prospects of this new venture, put forward while the promising *Custom of the Country* still remained unfinished, seemed meager. That such fears might have been justified is seen in the fact that *Ethan Frome* was judged to be "painful" and poorly composed, and "at first had much less success than my previous books," Mrs. Wharton later recalled. Probably her publishers would have preferred to see "The Custom" completed first, and when, after *Ethan Frome* was published it was still not forthcoming, there may have been a certain irritation expressed at the delay of something so much more certain, seemingly, of immediate reception. In addition, *Ethan Frome* was a work of that awkward in-between length which book-publishers have always disliked, too short to be called a novel, too long to be part of a group of short stories.

What remains of the correspondence pertaining to *Ethan Frome* is dated after its publication on September 30, 1911, and reveals a dispute over sales and advertising which recalls the near falling-out over her first fiction volume, *The Greater Inclination*. At the end of November she had written Charles Scribner:

> I am somewhat puzzled by the figures you give regarding the number of copies sold [of *Ethan Frome*]. You say that at the date of writing 4200 copies have been sold. I must have had a dozen letters from friends in New York and Boston, dated about Nov. 1st, and saying that the first edition was then sold out and the book absolutely unobtainable, and as I supposed you must certainly have printed 5000, your figures are naturally a surprise . . . As far as it is possible to judge from reviews and from the personal letters constantly pouring in, "Ethan" is having a more immediate and general success than "The House of Mirth," and this impression was corroborated for me the other day, by a friend who sailed about November 1st, and who told me that when she tried to get it at Brentano's they told her it was out of print and that they had more demand for it than for any novel published this autumn.—So you can understand my being surprised at the figures you give . . .

Scribner replied:

Your letter of the 27th disturbs me and I must write some particulars about the sale of "Ethan Frome" at the risk of seeming to disparage it. We are paying every attention to the book and the sale has kept up without a break but the quantities ordered are small and the sale has not been on the same plane with that of "The House of Mirth." As you know, the book has been splendidly reviewed both here and in London and undoubtedly the more discriminating readers have bought it eagerly but we have not secured for it the interest of the large public which supports the best sellers. Nothing is more difficult to meet than statements of an author's friends who report that a book is selling tremendously or cannot be had at the best bookstores. Retail clerks are very apt to say whatever they think a customer wishes to hear.

This diplomatic reply did not put an end to Mrs. Wharton's feeling that *Ethan Frome* had somehow been unjustly treated. She wrote again to Scribner:

I am very much surprised that the sale of "Ethan Frome" should have been so small, considering the wide attention it has attracted. It seems to me to have been very little advertised by you, either at the time of its appearance in the Magazine, or when it was published in book form; and I should of course expect that, in the case of a novel of the importance of "The Custom of the Country" you would give it as much publicity as my former novels.

And Scribner answered:

I am sorry that you were of the opinion that "Ethan Frome" was not well treated respecting advertising. The fact is we spent much more upon it than we can afford on a book selling at that price and very much more than we spend upon most full sized novels. The money actually put out for advertising, not including posters and circulars, was not less than $1,000. If the book had seemed to respond we might have spent even more but continuous advertising must now depend more or less upon the returns.

Such an exchange was a far more serious matter now than when she had been the fledgling author of *The Greater Inclination*. With a promptness that must have taken the breath even of the experienced Scribner, Edith Wharton replied with the stroke she had once only threatened.

> Since I last wrote you I have received from Messrs. Appleton a very high offer for a novel. As I was just finishing the short novel I have been working on during the last year, and as the terms they offered are so advantageous, I have decided to give them the tale in question, which they are to publish in September or early October.
>
> I believe this will be to your advantage as well as mine, as it will perhaps be the means of reaching a somewhat different public, and—if the story is a success—will in some sort act as a preparation for "The Custom of the Country."

The blow must have fallen heavily at the House of Scribner after the harmony of twenty-three years. Scribners' chief stated almost tearfully,

> It has taken me a month to recover from the shock caused by your announcement that you had arranged with Appletons for the publication of your next book, though indirectly a report to that effect had reached me. Of course I am very sorry to lose the honor of exclusive publication for you and it will be a little difficult for me to explain to others why you made the change. But I try to be broad minded about it and to be contented with "The Custom of the Country" now assured for the Magazine.

The novel given to Appleton was *The Reef*, which she had planned as early as 1910. At that time the Scribner office had probably been unenthusiastic about the prospect of a further project interposed before the still-uncompleted *Custom of the Country*. Burlingame sent a memorandum to Charles Scribner which advised that it would be good strategy to take the new book, though they were not eager for it, rather than let it go to some rival. But now, in 1912, they had no choice in the matter.

By giving the book to Appleton, Edith Wharton did more than obtain higher payment for her work—and put herself in a position to bargain for similar terms in the future from her old publisher. She had also succeeded in rearranging the sequence of publication which had been fixed by her agreements with a single firm. *The Reef*, orginally scheduled by Scribner to *follow* "The Custom," would probably not have appeared in the magazine or in book form until 1914. Appleton was able to bring it out immediately, in 1912.

As regards money, of course, the precedent of this contract with Appleton was to be most significant. As soon as *The Custom of the Country* was issued in 1913, Edith Wharton opened the question of advance royalties on future books, mentioning that Appleton had paid $15,000 on the appearance of *The Reef* (only $5,000 had been put down by Scribner for "The Custom"), and concluding, "In the event of your taking my next novel I should expect a somewhat larger advance royalty." Scribner, with the melancholy that was beginning to sound in all his letters to her, answered:

> The advance paid by the Appletons seems to me very large and I question whether the book has yet yielded that much as royalty. Perhaps in their desire to secure a book from you they went a little further than was safe . . . I hope you think $10,000 sufficient [on your next novel]. I cannot remember that we have ever advanced as much as that on any novel.

Scribners did not publish another novel of hers until *A Son at the Front* in 1923, for which the terms were exactly what she had asked this time—a royalty of twenty per cent with a $15,000 advance.

The Reef had gone right to press without prior serialization in *Scribner's Magazine* or elsewhere, but Edith Wharton was becoming aware that she could command higher magazine prices than *Scribner's* had been paying her. While *The Custom of the Country* was running in the magazine and delighting readers ("I have never received such letters as I am getting about it!" she wrote after the first installment), she received invitations from editors who were willing to make higher bids for her future stories. "I have had an offer of $12,500 for my next serial from a New York magazine," she wrote Scribner. "Before considering it, I want to let you know, though I think it is doubtful if you will care to publish another of my works serially." Scribner matched this offer, "though the price named," he observed, "was a little more than we have ever paid".

The truth was, of course, that a magazine like *Scribner's* was unable to compete with the mass-circulation women's magazines and weeklies that now offered prices few writers were so fastidious as to scorn in exchange for an imponderable loss of "prestige." *Scribner's*, like *Harper's*, the *Century*, the *Atlantic*, constantly lost writers to the growing "slicks." Edith Wharton herself had published an occasional story in *Cosmopolitan* and *Collier's*, but she had preferred to appear in *Scribner's* or another of the older group whose readers possessed her own background and tastes. Now she too prepared to greet the more numerous public the popular magazines represented, a public already aware of her through her successful books.

The Custom of the Country did not, of course, achieve the mass sales enjoyed in 1913 by books like *Pollyanna*, *V.V.'s Eyes* and *Laddie*. With its satirical view of American life, Edith Wharton's novel headed straight against the native complacencies that these best-sellers promoted. She herself was well aware of this. Among the papers left at her death is a clipping of an advertisement of Gene Stratton Porter's current "true blue story." Mrs. Wharton underlined in red pencil the admonishing information that *Laddie* had reached the three million mark, being a book that, as the advertisement went on, "goes to the heart of a vast reading public because it is true to life, a picture of genuine American people—people who love their homes, who figure neither in newspaper nor divorce court; who are the source of the real vitality of the nation." In time, the public would accommodate itself to a less flattering account of "genuine American people." By 1921, Mrs. Wharton's own *Age of Innocence* would be on a list of the year's best-sellers which was headed by Sinclair

Lewis' *Main Street*. But even in 1913 there were already enough readers who appreciated her work to make it worth the capture. She must have received many offers like that "from a New York magazine." In October, 1914, Edgar Sisson, editor of *Cosmopolitan*, wrote her a letter in which he offered $15,000 for the serial rights of her "next available novel." The letter, which she sent on to Charles Scribner, is an interesting specimen of the energetic salesmanship which now met her at her doorstep. Editor Sisson listed the many distinguished writers already appearing in his pages and unctuously declared that he longed to add to his catalogue "the foremost woman novelist in America." Scribner, reading this letter, realized its power immediately, and made no effort to hold Mrs. Wharton to the $12,000 previously agreed on, insisting only that the book publication of the promised work be reserved for him. Mrs. Wharton then wrote that she had decided to refuse the *Cosmopolitan* offer, after all. "I don't think I could have tolerated the idea of appearing in a Hearst publication," she explained. But other bidders were soon given better reception. At the end of the war pieces began to appear from her pen in the *Ladies' Home Journal* and *Woman's Home Companion*, and in the twenties she regularly sent her fiction to these two and to the *Saturday Evening Post, McClure's, Redbook, Delineator* and the *Pictorial Review*, the last pair being the steady recipients of her novels until her death in 1937.

The new novel Scribner hopefully looked forward to was to flit before him like marsh fire for a number of years and finally blink out. Its unfinished manuscript survives for scholars to see in the Yale Library. "Literature," as Edith Wharton intended to call it, was to be a chronicle of a writer's career—it may very well have been undertaken by Edith Wharton at this time in an attempt to clarify her own choices in the world of publishing. She began work on it in the fall of 1913 and planned it on an ample scale of 170,000 words. It would be ready, she thought, by the end of 1915. But hardly had she settled on her new fiction than the outer world about her changed overnight. The invasion of Belgium had almost immediately swept her into the current of active war-work which engaged the energies of sympathetic

329

Americans in Paris, and at the end of 1914 she admitted to Scribner that she had been forced to set the new serial aside. Again and again, as new war activities engrossed her, she tried to return to it, but by the spring of 1916 she confessed, "I have every hope of finishing 'Literature' after the war, but it is on too large a scale to be taken up now. What I am doing is much slighter . . . It is to be called 'The Glimpses of the Moon,' and it has begun so well that I almost think I may promise it to you for next November or December."

Perhaps Scribner chose the wrong moment to remind his author that publishing schedules were not so easily revamped; perhaps he failed to realize that she had put "Literature" so firmly out of sight for the time being that *The Glimpses of the Moon* might as well have been accepted as a substitute. But he had just taken a long story of hers, "Bunner Sisters," for the magazine, and with "Literature" still in the offing he foresaw a jam-up: "I really can't see how it is possible to make room for this new story. We have two definite engagements for other serials. Of course we should welcome it as a book at any time and would pay an advance on a 20% royalty for the sale of $15,000." *Glimpses of the Moon* did not go to Scribners, however; it was held by Mrs. Wharton until 1922 when it was published by Appleton.

Meanwhile, the break with Scribners was about to achieve itself at last. In August, 1916, instead of coming dutifully back with the finished manuscript of "Literature," Edith Wharton wrote Robert Bridges, the new editor of *Scribner's Magazine*: "I am taking a few weeks rest at Fontainebleau and am making use of my leisure to write a 'long short' story, of the dimensions of 'Ethan Frome.' . . . I expect to finish it in a few weeks and I imagine it will reach a length of about 30,000 words. I should like to know if you would like this for the magazine, for, as you know, I always offer everything first to *Scribner's*." The new fiction was *Summer*, the tale of a country girl's passion which is a companion piece to the wintry *Ethan Frome*. It is, some will agree, equal to the more widely-appreciated story, a work with a curious and individual strength. But Scribner wrote that there would be no place for it in the magazine: "Mr. Bridges and I were both reluctant to let the new short serial get away from us but did not see how we could do otherwise, for there seemed no chance of printing it next year; and this would not only have disappointed your expectation of prompt publication but would have interfered with the longer serial, about which we are still hoping to hear something definite."

It is easy to say, now, that Scribner was waiting for a ghost-book while real-bodied opportunities walked by. He had every reason, however, to expect "Literature" to make its appearance, for Edith Wharton had always finished her projects heretofore; even *The Custom of the Country* had eventually rewarded his patience. He risked the loss of *Summer* as a serial, therefore, counting on it still as a book-publication. "I understand that your short serial has been arranged for by the McClure Company and that they are highly pleased with it," he noted at the end of 1916. "Can we not now agree for book publication? I would suggest 20% royalty with an advance of $1,000. But the long customary bond had finally worn through and the book was already Appleton's. Edith Wharton wrote:

> Your letter of December 27th has just come, enquiring about the book publication of "Summer," my short serial appearing in McClure's. I always prefer, as you know, to publish with you, and always offer you first whatever I write; but when I offered you "Summer," and the other tale I have been writing at the same time, you wrote me you would have no place in the magazine for either of them for a long time to come, and that you preferred to wait till I could finish "Literature" after the war.
>
> In consequence of this answer, I took up a long standing offer of Messrs. Appleton, which combined serial publication in one of several magazines with book publication by them, on terms so advantageous that, in view of your refusal, I should not have felt justified in rejecting the opportunity.
>
> I regret very much that "Summer" should not be appearing in Scribner's where I already feel more at home than anywhere else.

It was nearly two months later before Scribner replied, summing up the situation:

I received your letter about publication of "Summer" but I had already heard of your arrangement with Messrs. Appleton. Our Magazine is sometimes as much a source of trouble as a benefit to our book publications, for it seems impossible to explain satisfactorily why we cannot use serials. I find that during the last two years of twenty-four numbers contributions by you have appeared in eight and we were expecting that you might wish us to begin "Literature" at the beginning of 1918, for I do not think you ever wrote that the writing of it was postponed until after the war but only that you felt unable to go on with it under present conditions. We should have been very glad to have bought the serial rights of "Summer" for use elsewhere and thus secured the book but I received the impression that that would not be agreeable to you as you preferred to know just where the story would be published. However, evidently my letters were not satisfactory and there is no one here to blame but myself. I do cordially appreciate the support you have given the Magazine and the house even if we are a little disappointed by this transfer.

However much the ground would be gone over, no common view of the matter would emerge between them. One fact was obvious: she had been writing at a rate no single magazine could keep up with. Years before, when her output had principally been short stories and articles, Brownell had commented somewhat dryly upon her simultaneous appearance at all compass-points of the magazine world, and she had admitted, "I don't wonder that my recent magazine-ubiquity suggests to you feats of quail-eating and other betting exploits." Burlingame had warned her against becoming a "magazine bore" and she had agreed that it was better to "espacer a little." It was better, certainly, for the growing artist to school herself to a harder standard than publishability, but there were other dangers from her editors' standpoint. When, for example, the *Century* published her series of articles on Italian gardens in 1903 (while *Scribner's* pages were occupied by other pieces by her), it naturally followed that the book-publishing Century Company would put out the collected volume of sketches, making *Italian Villas and Their Gardens* the first intrusion of another publisher upon her booklist. There was not to be another until *The Reef*, probably because Edith Wharton began soon afterwards to concentrate upon longer fictions. As long as she wrote no more than one novel a year, *Scribner's Magazine* would use it in installments and the book house could issue the volume in the month of the last installment. But now, once more, she was planning more works than *Scribner's* would place in its own pages, and this time the works in question were novels. Appleton's had seen the possibilities in the situation when it offered her not only a higher bookprice, but placement in one or another of *several* magazines.

One is tempted to say simply that Edith Wharton had decided to dispense with the handicap of sentiment; Appleton in combination with the popular weeklies could top *Scribner's* prices for her work and give it prompter circulation, and that was that. She herself seems to have come to this conclusion with some regret. When *Summer* was out, she wrote Brownell, whose friendly counsel she expected as of old, "I believe I forgot to have a copy of "Summer" sent for [you]—or rather what I really forgot was, that it was not published by Scribner! I never can get used to any other origin, and always sit down and weep under the willow tree when I remember Jerusalem—I don't know why Mr. Scribner didn't want 'Summer,' but I'm glad he does want the article on 'The French' that I'm doing now, for I can't imagine where else, in the vast 'fatras' of American magazinery, it would find even one comprehending reader."

Scribner, of course, would have protested that he *had* wanted *Summer* as a book, if not as a serial. He persisted in hoping that her transfer was only temporary and belatedly offered an arrangement similar to Appleton's. ". . . If you write another novel I hope you will give us a chance at it, unless you have contracted with Appleton," he wrote in the spring of 1918. "We are as well able to secure for you serial publication as any other house and it does not seem fair to limit our publication to such as appear in our own Magazine". She again went over the old ground, making it clear that this was no longer possible:

> In your letter you ask why I have not offered you a novel for a long time. You do not, I suppose, mean for publication in *Scribner's*, as I have offered you *two*, since the war, to replace "Literature," the subject of which it was really impossible to treat, with the world crashing around one. I offered you "Summer," & you said you preferred to wait for "Literature," and then I suggested another, which I have never finished. I should always prefer to have my novels appear in *Scribner's* and I refused all other offers for these two until you had declined them. But as you had never made any previous proposal (as far as I can remember) to "place" one of my novels in another magazine, I naturally, when you declined these two, accepted the offer which had long before been made by Appleton.
>
> Whenever you want a novel for *Scribner's* I shall be glad to give it to you; and meanwhile I hope you may occasionally want a short story.

She submitted with this letter a short story which Scribner replied that he would be glad to take for the magazine, "but the difficulty is that we cannot afford now to pay the old price. For some time you have been receiving $1,000 for your stories. This is greatly in excess of what we are paying anyone else and $500 would seem enough at this time. The present story is longer than the average and we could pay $600 for it, with permission to divide it into two parts, if it seems desirable." One might suspect Scribner of expressing his annoyance by means of this show of retrenchment were it not a generally-known fact that *Scribner's Magazine* had failed to yield a profit to its owners for three or four years. The statement that the magazine now had to cut expenses was literally true. To the rest of her letter he replied with a wearied review of the past, the conviction becoming plainer to him that Mrs. Wharton did not want the house to have any of her books unless they had previously appeared in *Scribner's*.

I have not the heart to reread the old letters but you certainly interpreted them to mean something never intended by me. My understanding was that we had definitely engaged "Literature" as a serial and there was no question of "replacing" it with another, but pending its completion, which was delayed and for how long I did not realize, you suggested that we use another which you appeared to regard as a less important story. As we did not see how we could use two in rapid succession, we preferred to abide by our first agreement for "Literature." In the initial case of "The Reef" we did not decline it as a serial for we were not asked to consider it, nor was it serialized anywhere. Since then when we have had to decline a serial of yours ourselves, it does not seem to me that we should lose the book, particularly when the serial is accepted by a magazine with no book department. We might then have at least an even chance at the book.

You now write that you will be glad to give us a serial for the Magazine but make no mention of book publication, from which I might infer that unless we can use the serial, you will prefer another publisher. Is not this treating us with less consideration than our previous relations entitle us to expect? I think it would be generally regarded that we had managed your books fairly well and they certainly have had our best attention. But I do not make any personal appeal. You know that we will gladly welcome any opportunity to publish for you. Meanwhile I am glad to know that your interest in the magazine continues.

She returned:

I think you will find in referring to my letters that I said it might be difficult to write "Literature" after the war, for the simple reason that these four years have so much changed the whole aspect of life that it is not easy to say now what one's literary tendencies will be when the war is over.

As to the fact that I have not asked you to publish novels which you had refused to take as serials—such as "Summer," for instance—my answer is, simply, that I have received in the last few years such large offers that in my present financial situation I cannot refuse them. At the moment I have offers of $15,000 for the serial rights of a novel from three different

335

magazines, with offers of the same amount in advance royalties from Appleton & Co. for publication of each of these novels. I can sell short stories for $1,000 apiece to any number of magazines, and articles for $500 or $600 apiece and though my old affection for Scribner makes me always wish to see my name on your list the last few years have been such a strain on me financially owing to a great reduction of my income, to the heavy taxes we are all suffering from, and to the unprecedented demands for help on all sides, that I feel I must profit by such offers as those I have mentioned, the more so as I write so slowly.

I am very glad to give you "The Seed of the Faith" for $600 if you will do me the favor not to mention the price ...

Forced to it, she conceded that though she felt more at home in the pages of *Scribner's* than anywhere else in "American magazinery," she did not care to reserve book-publication for the firm when other publishers would top its prices. She probably did "need" as much money as she could earn. Though she still had considerable private income, however diminished, she lived on an imperial scale—constantly travelling, maintaining two princely homes in France, employing a staff of servants—and at the same time giving to the charities that still engaged her attention.

"Literature," the novel for which Scribner had foregone other books, still failed to materialize. Though she had produced *Summer* and *The Glimpses of the Moon*, and shorter pieces in the interim, just as she had turned out *Ethan Frome* and *The Reef* while *The Custom of the Country* lingered by the way, she was unable to get back to work on this comprehensively-planned study of an American writer. She began to realize that her difficulty was not merely lack of time and opportunity. The cataclysms of the war had done more than rob her of these—they had fractured the very world in which her novel was to have been situated. In the last year of the war she admitted to Brownell, "I am doing my best to function literarily, being indeed a-thirst and a-hunger for my own job. But it is a good deal like writing a novel while balanced on a tight-rope to attempt portraying this convulsed world. That is why I have given up 'Literature,' temporarily, though I like it best of all my 'données,' and hope to get back to it when the air clears. At present writing is next to impossible." But the war ended, and the subject still would not revive under her hands. In the fall of 1919 she wrote Scribner:

> In the first relief from war anxieties I thought it might be possible to shake off the question which is tormenting all novelists at present: "Did the adventures related in this book happen before the war or did they happen since?" With the resulting difficulty that, if they happened before the war, I seem to have forgotten how people felt, and what their point of view was. I should feel ashamed of these hesitations if I did not find that all novelists I know are much in the same predicament. Perhaps it will not last much longer and we shall be able to get back some sort of perspective; but at present, between the objection of the public to the so-called war-stories and the difficulty of the author to send his imagination backward, the situation is a bewildering one. As you know, I several times, during the war, offered to replace "Literature" by other novels, which did not involve the study of such complex social conditions and dealt with people less affected by the war. As you preferred to wait for "Literature" these two tales, "Summer" and "The Marne," were given to other magazines, and I continued to hope that I should see my way to going on with "Literature."

Charles Scribner protested once more,

> I know I cannot expect you ever to understand our point of view about the last two serials; I don't think you ever offered to replace "Literature" with one of them; it was rather that one of them might be used to precede "Literature," which you hoped to write very soon. We did not expect the war to last so long nor to bring such terrible changes.
> I do not want you to feel trammelled in any way by our old agreement, either as to story or price. When you are disposed to give us a chance let us know about the story and we will see whether we can pay the price, but give us enough time.

There was really no longer any hope of "Literature," though it died lingeringly. In the spring of 1921 Edith Wharton told

Brownell, "The war dealt that masterpiece a terrible blow. I still 'carry' it about with me, and long to make it the dizzy pinnacle of my work; but *when* did it all happen? And what repercussions did 1914-1920 have in my young man? I wrote Mr. Scrbiner early in the war, and offered him several 'Ersatzes,' among them 'Summer' and 'The Marne,' but he preferred to wait. I don't yet despair of situating the tale; but there isn't enough perspective yet." But "Literature" never emerged again. Or perhaps one should say it did emerge, much later and much transformed, in a new novel about an American writer of different background and history. Certain general features and many minor marks connect the scrapped torso of "Literature" with *Hudson River Bracketed* which was published by Appleton in 1929.

Meanwhile, Scribner was being forced to the realization that his house would henceforth play only an occasional role in Edith Wharton's career. A series of essays on French life had been placed in *Cosmopolitan* after *Scribner's* declined to accommodate more than a single article on the subject in 1917 (she had apparently overcome her repugnance to appearing in a Hearst publication). Under the arrangement now customary with Appleton, the articles were collected in a book—*French Ways and Their Meaning*, published in 1919. The following year Scribner's put into a volume the articles on Morocco which she had been contributing to *Scribner's Magazine*, but also in 1920 she gave Appleton the book that won her more fame than anything she ever wrote in her long career—*The Age of Innocence*. When this novel was awarded the Pulitzer Prize and became the fourth-best-selling book of the following year—outdistancing even Edith M. Hull's *The Sheik*—Charles Scribner must have sighed ruefully. In February, 1921, he wrote, "I should so much prize an opportunity to talk with you about your work, for I have not abandoned the hope of securing future novels. The loss of your books was the greatest blow ever given to my pride as a publisher."

They did meet in Europe that summer and she agreed to give another novel to Scribners. It was *A Son at the Front*, the rather belated "war story" which ran in the magazine in 1923. It was hardly another *Age of Innocence*. Tactfully enough Scribner observed, "I might wish that the story was not so exactly a war novel (as clearly indicated by its title) but I recognize its quality and power. The presentation of Paris during the war was certainly well worth doing; indeed how could you refuse to make a permanent record of these wonderful years, of which you had such intimate knowledge." As Scribner obviously feared, the success of the book was only moderate. Somewhat defensively, the writer herself declared that she was satisfied with its sales: "The result seems to me as satisfactory as can be expected. I do not write 'jazz-books' and never expected to be a best-seller. The success of 'The Age of Innocence' was, I believe, due to the accident of my having resuscitated old New York at a time when the contrast was great enough to amuse the curiosity of a new generation. I believe my books have a certain staying power which, at any rate, I would far rather think they possess than the qualities requisite at present for a sensational sale." But Scribner would far rather have had *The Age of Innocence.*

Scribner tried, after *A Son at the Front,* to arrange a contract for her next novel providing serial publication in one of the popular magazines instead of in *Scribner's,* but she wrote him, "I have not been well this winter, and do not like to make any more engagements at present, especially for a novel. I work more slowly, and have to be careful to avoid fatigue, so that my dates are uncertain, and I think it best to decline the offer. I may add that, although I was delighted to give you *A Son at the Front* for $15,000, I have been receiving much higher prices from other magazines than that offered by the *Designer.*" There was really no ground for further hope, but Scribner then offered to pay $20,000 for the serial rights of her next book. The following month—it was June, 1923—she visited America to receive an honorary doctorate from Yale, and she saw Scribner once again. "Your brief visit here," he wistfully wrote, "seems scarcely real as I could see so little of you, but that brief interview was better than nothing. I was depressed to hear that the next novel must go to Appleton, for I thought that contract was completed and the future at least open to us. We have been thinking of a complete set of your books in a fine limited edition. . . ."

But *A Son at the Front* was the last volume of her fiction to be published by Charles Scribner's Sons. *Scribner's Magazine* got just one more story from her—the long "Her Son" which was submitted to the magazine through D. Appleton in 1931 when *Scribner's* was able to offer the special inducement of its new policy of running such outsize "long-short" stories in a single issue. By this time, Scribner, Burlingame and Brownell were all dead, and Mrs. Wharton's relationship with the House of Scribner had become mostly the concern of the clerical employees who mailed out royalty payments on her old books.

Charles Scribner had vainly hoped for her return to his fiction list during his last years, and watched each new work go to Appleton with a pang. He was obviously surprised each time anew to read or hear of one of her stories going to another magazine or book-publisher without having been first offered to him. "I did not think of mentioning 'The Old Maid' to you when I last saw you as it was in Messrs. Appleton's hand many months before I had finished *The Age of Innocence*," she wrote in embarrassed explanation in 1922, after Scribner had discovered the novelette in the current *Redbook*. "It is a novelette dealing with the long-ago-New York, and together with another tale of the same kind is to form a volume called 'Old New York,' which I agreed to give the Appletons when 'The Age of Innocence' was still in its infancy. Thank you for the offer to publish these tales, but as you see, the arrangement was made with Messrs. Appleton long before you came to see me last summer." The following year he came upon 'False Dawn' in the same fashion in the *Ladies' Home Journal*, and again his melancholy regret is heard: "You know of my great interest in your work and my willingness to compete with anyone for its publication. I read your rather long short story in the *Ladies' Home Journal* but I don't suppose that is what you referred to when you were last in my office and said that your next book had been engaged under the old arrangement." And so even with her next novel, *The Mother's Recompense*, when the threnody was taken up by Charles Scribner's brother, Arthur: "I suppose that the book publication of your new novel appearing in Pictorial Review is already arranged and that there is no possibility of our securing it."

Edith Wharton did do one last book for Scribners. In the fall of 1920 she had proposed some articles for the magazine on the art of fiction. These were pondered carefully and written slowly, for in these pages, as she wrote Brownell after they were finished, "I really poured out my faith and reverence of my art." They appeared in the magazine in 1925 and with an additional essay on Proust made up *The Writing of Fiction* published that year. Her final contribution to the magazine was a memorial essay on her old Scribner editor, W. C. Brownell, done at Charles Scribner's request in 1928. This and *The Writing of Fiction*, her artistic credo, were a not ungraceful farewell to her association with the firm which had witnessed her artistic maturing from its beginnings.

Charles Scribner had called the loss of Edith Wharton's books "the greatest blow ever given to my pride as a publisher," and the force of this statement comes home to us when it is recalled that it was made after close to fifty years as head of the House of Scribner. In 1936, six years after his death, Scribner's Sons produced one book which was at least partly hers—the play *Ethan Frome* by Owen and Donald Davis, to which she wrote an introduction. Young Charlie Scribner became almost as excited as his father might have been, and planned an omnibus volume of her stories to follow this project. He wrote Mrs. Wharton in tones suitable to a reconciliation accomplished after sore division: "I cannot tell you how happy I am to be publishing this book for you and to have another volume in prospect. My father would have been delighted as he felt very keenly the unfortunate differences which led to your going to another publisher and often spoke to me about it." But the next year she too was dead.

References

EDITH WHARTON's account of her own life, *A Backward Glance* (1934), is the necessary starting point for any biographical discussion of her, though how much it must be supplemented and corrected is demonstrated by the documentary evidence which is the main reliance of this book. It has been, nevertheless, a constant source of her opinions and self-descriptions and a uniquely valuable ingredient throughout, since no other biographical outline of her career exists. James's autobiographical volumes do not go beyond his youthful years, and it is only at the present moment that the task of comprehensive biography, based on exhaustive study of original sources, has been undertaken by Leon Edel in his still-uncompleted *Henry James*. Mr. Edel's three volumes thus far issued—*The Untried Years* (1953), *The Conquest of London* (1962), and *The Middle Years* (1962)—incorporate much new material concerning James's career up to, but not yet including, the years of his friendship with Edith Wharton. General impressions of James and Mrs. Wharton have been set down by a number of their acquaintances but are perhaps most conveniently available in two books published in 1947: Simon Nowell-Smith's *The Legend of the Master*, which culls many printed sources for anecdotes of Henry James, and Percy Lubbock's *Portrait of Edith Wharton*, which gracefully stitches together recollections contributed by a number of her friends.

It will be seen that the principal basis for the larger portion of this book has been unpublished letters, and those directly referred to are recorded in the following chapter notes in the order of their use, though several hundreds of others provided context and interpretation of a more general sort, and go unitemized. Where letters exist in print this is indicated, but it should be remembered

345

that the printed edition of James's letters edited by Mr. Lubbock contains few that are not reduced by deletions, and many of the passages pertinent to my inquiry had to be located in the fuller manuscript versions. References to printed sources have been reduced to a minimum. *A Backward Glance* and *Portrait of Edith Wharton* have made so constant a contribution that specific citations seemed unnecessary, but the occasional help of other printed works is acknowledged.

Unless otherwise indicated the letters cited were found in the Houghton Library at Harvard University. My citations indicate date and the names of senders and recipients, for the most recurrent of whom I use the following abbreviations:

WB	Walter Berry	GL	Gaillard Lapsley
PB	Paul Bourget	PL	Percy Lubbock
WCB	William Crary Brownell	CEN	Charles Eliot Norton
ELB	Edward L. Burlingame	EGN	Elizabeth Gaskell Norton
WDH	William Dean Howells	SN	Sara Norton
JHS	A. John Hugh-Smith	CS	Charles Scribner
HJ	Henry James	HS	Howard Sturgis
WJ	William James	EW	Edith Wharton
MCJ	Mary Cadwalader Jones		

Letters indicates that the letter in question appears in whole or partial form in Percy Lubbock's *The Letters of Henry James* (New York, 1920), 2 vols.

Bold-face numerals refer to the pages of the present work.

When letters are undated by the sender, brackets [ ] indicate probable date, if known.

Chapter I: Foreshadowings and Beginnings

25: HJ to Henry James, Sr., 10 May 1869; HJ to MCJ, 22 Jan. 1912.

346

26: HJ to Lucy Clifford, 18 May 1912 (*Letters*, II, 234–36); HJ to MCJ, 20 Aug. 1902; Henry James's friendship with Constance Fenimore Woolson is lengthily discussed by Leon Edel in *The Middle Years*, and her letter is quoted *op. cit.*, p. 92.

27: *Vernon Lee's Letters*, with a preface by her Executor, Irene Cooper Willis (1937, privately printed), provided texts of her letter to her mother, 11 July 1884 and 25 July 1885 (for the use of this rare volume I am indebted to the Colby College Library).

28: "Lady Tal" is included in Vernon Lee's *Vanitas: Polite Stories* (London, 1892); HJ to WJ, 20 Jan. 1893.

29: Notebook entry, 18 Nov. 1894, *Notebooks of Henry James*, ed. by F. O. Matthiessen and Kenneth B. Murdock (New York, 1947), p. 177; *The Middle Years*, p. 93; HJ to Margaret Brook, Ranee of Sarawak, 28 Jan. 1894.

32: HJ to Grace Norton, 28 Dec. 1880; IIJ to Elizabeth Boott, 11 Dec. 1883.

34: *47 Unpublished Letters from Marcel Proust to Walter Berry*, Black Sun Press (Paris, 1930), contains the texts of letters written between 1916 and 1922.

38: The most complete biographical study of Paul Bourget is Albert Feuillerat, *Paul Bourget: Histoire d'un esprit sous la Troisième République* (Paris, 1937); Edith Wharton's "Souvenirs du Bourget d'outremer" was published in *La Revue Hebdomadaire* (June 1936).

44: Three copies of Edith Wharton's fugitive *Verses*, C. E. Hammett (Newport, 1878), are in the Yale University Library, one is in the Harris Collection of Brown University. As Edmund Wilson has noted: "There is a legend . . . that her first book of poems, which she had secretly printed, was discovered and destroyed by her family," *Classics and Commercials* (New York, 1950), p. 413, but an unpublished manuscript note in the Yale University Library records Edith Wharton's remembering that her mother had been in the habit of keeping a notebook of the young poet's exercises, and finally "perpetrated the folly of having a 'selection' printed"; her early contribution to the *World* was identified and described by me in " 'Eadgyth' Wharton in the New York *World*, 1879," *Yale University Library Gazette*, XXX (Oct. 1955), 64–69; Allen Thorndike Rice to Henry Wadsworth Longfellow, 12 Aug. 1879.

46: Henry James's *A Small Boy and Others* (1913) gives his recollection of the Old New York of his youth.

47: "The Sense of Newport" in *The American Scene* (1907) gives his later vision of Newport.

51: Mary Cadwalader Jones in *Lantern Slides* (Boston, 1937, privately printed), gives details of her recollections of Edith Wharton; EW's letter to MCJ concerning their first meeting is quoted by Wayne Andrews, *The Best Short Stories of Edith Wharton* (New York, 1958).

52: HJ to MCJ, 23 Oct. 1902 (*Letters*, I, 401–3); HJ to MCJ, 8 Nov. 1906, 30 Sept. 1911, and 10 Oct. 1911 give recollections by James of their early friendship.

Chapter II: Outre-mer

53: Edith Wharton's professional development between 1889 and 1899 as well as in later years can be minutely followed in the letters she exchanged with her Scribner's editors, Edward L. Burlingame and W. C. Brownell, and with Charles Scribner. Not only have a long series of her own letters been preserved in the Scribner archives, but many of the letters to her as well. A large number of her letters to W. C. Brownell were deposited at his death in the Amherst College Library. I am indebted to these two sources for my study of this correspondence (for a description of her relations with the house of Scribner see Appendix). EW to ELB, 14 Dec. 1895; EW to ELB, 21 Oct. 1893.

References

55: EW to ELB, 10 July 1898.

58: Henry James recorded his earliest impressions of European travel in *A Small Boy and Others.*

59: WJ to Robertson James, 2 Jan. 1870 (from a letter in the possession of Mary James Vaux, quoted by Edel, *The Conquest of London,* pp. 335–36).

61: EW to WCB, 25 June 1902; EW to Vernon Lee, 5 Oct. 1907; "Letters from Edith Wharton to Vernon Lee," by Hilda M. Fife, *Colby Library Quarterly,* series III, no. 9 (Feb. 1953), pp. 143–44.

64: EW to ELB, 30 July 1894.

64ff.: The friendship of Henry James and Paul Bourget is described in Albert Feuillerat's biography and in "A Literary Friendship—Henry James and Paul Bourget," by I. D. McFarlane, *The Cambridge Journal,* IV (1950–51), 144–61; the following James letters provide a view of James's attitudes toward Bourget: HJ to Robert Louis Stevenson, 19 Mar. 1892 (*Letters,* I, 188–90); HJ to Henry Adams, 15 June 1892; HJ to CEN, 4 July 1892 (*Letters,* I, 193–97); HJ to Robert Louis Stevenson, 17 Feb. 1893 (*Letters,* I, 199–201); HJ to Robert Louis Stevenson, 5 Aug. 1893 (*Letters,* I, 204–7); HJ to WJ, 29 Dec. 1893; HJ to Edmund Gosse, 23 Aug. 1894 (*Letters,* I, 217–20); HJ to George du Maurier, 12 Sept. 1894; HJ to WJ, 30 Sept. 1895; HJ to WJ and Alice James, 4 Sept. 1896; HJ to WJ, 7 Aug. 1897; HJ to WJ, 22 Apr. 1899 (*Letters,* I, 315–17); HJ to PB, 18 Aug. 1898 (*Letters,* I, 286–90); HJ to Mrs. W. K. Clifford, 8 Sept. 1902; HJ to EW, 11 Aug. 1907 (*Letters,* II, 78–81).

65: James records exchanging themes with Bourget in *Notebooks* (20 June 1887), pp. 76–81.

66: HJ to WJ, 29 Dec. 1893; HJ to PB, 26 Sept. 1893; HJ to PB, 5 Feb. 1894; HJ to PB, 20 Apr. 1894.

67: HJ to Edmund Gosse, 23 Aug. 1894 (*Letters,* I, 217–20).

69: PB to HJ, 14 Mar. 1896; PB to HJ, 26 May 1896.

70: HJ to WJ, 22 Apr. 1899; PB to HJ, 30 Aug. 1899.

72: HJ to Henrietta Reubell, 12 June 1892.

Chapter III: The Mount

74: HJ to MCJ, 20 Aug. 1902 (*Letters,* I, 395–97).

75: HJ to WJ, 22 Apr. 1899 (*Letters,* I, 315–17).

76: *Notebooks,* p. 23; Henry James, "An American Art Scholar: Charles Eliot Norton," in *Notes on Novelists, with Some Other Notes* (New York, 1914).

77: EW to WCB, 25 July 1902.

78: HJ to MCJ, 23 Oct. 1902 (*Letters,* I, 401–3).

80: Edward Wharton to CEN, 19 Aug. 1906.

82: CEN to George W. Curtis, 14 July 1864, in *Letters of Charles Eliot Norton,* ed. by Sara Norton and M. A. DeWolfe Howe (London, 1913), Vol. I, p. 274.

83ff.: Biography of Norton is provided in Kermit Vanderbilt, *Charles Eliot Norton: Apostle of Culture in a Democracy* (Cambridge, 1959), and a sketch by John Jay Chapman, *Memories and Milestones* (New York, 1915).

84: CEN to John Ruskin (quoted in Vanderbilt, p. 120); CEN to WDH, 4 Oct. 1903 (quoted in Vanderbilt, p. 153); CEN to WDH, 29 Aug. 1903 (quoted in Vanderbilt, p. 153); EW to WCB, 20 Mar. 1902.

85: CEN to Henry B. Fuller, 30 May 1895, in *Letters of Charles Eliot Norton,* vol. II, p. 225; Edith Wharton's notes and drafts for *The Valley of Decision* are in the Yale University Library; EW to CEN, 19 Nov. 1901; EW to CEN, 26 Nov. 1901; EW to CEN, 3 May 1902; EW to EGN, 4 Mar. 1928.

86: CEN to Samuel Grey Ward, 10 Mar. 1902, in *Letters of*

Charles Eliot Norton, vol. II, p. 319; EW to EGN, 2 Nov. 1928.

87: EW to SN, 7 July 1909; HJ to MCJ, 9 June 1903; EW to WCB, 11 Aug. 1903.

88: HJ to MCJ, 31 Dec. 1903.

89: EW to WCB, 7 Jan. 1904; HJ to WJ, 10 Apr. 1903; HJ to WJ, 24 May 1903 (*Letters*, I, 415–23).

92: HJ to MCJ, 23 Oct. 1904.

93: HJ to WJ, 7 July 1905 (*Letters*, II, 34–35); HJ to Lee Childe, 4 Jan. 1906; EW to CEN, 1 July 1905; HJ to Edmund Gosse, 27 Oct. 1904 (*Letters*, II, 19–22).

Chapter IV: English Hours

96: HJ to MCJ, 16 July 1905.

98ff.: Descriptions of Howard Sturgis are provided by Gerard Hopkins, intro. to *Belchamber* by Howard Sturgis (World's Classics Edition, London, 1935), George Santayana, *Persons and Places: The Background of My Life* (New York, 1944), *The Diary of Arthur C. Benson*, ed. by Percy Lubbock (London, 1926), as well as by Edith Wharton in *A Backward Glance* and by Percy Lubbock in *Portrait of Edith Wharton* and *Mary Cholmondeley: A Sketch from Memory* (London, 1928).

102: EW to WCB, 7 Jan. 1904; EW to WCB, 2 Feb. 1904; EW to WCB, 28 Feb. 1904; HJ to HS, 8 Nov. 1903 (*Letters*, I, 428–30).

104: Edith Wharton reviewed *Belchamber* in *The Bookman*, XXI (May 1905); E. M. Forster's comment on *Belchamber* appeared in his review of *A Backward Glance* in *New Statesman and Nation*, VII (23 June 1934).

107: An introductory essay on Percy Lubbock appears in Marjory Grace Harkness' *A Percy Lubbock Reader* (Freeport, Me., 1957).

108: Percy Lubbock's *Shades of Eton* (London, 1929) contains the recollection of his first meeting with James.

109: E. M. Forster's *Aspects of the Novel* (New York, 1927) analyzes *Roman Pictures*.

110: Edith Wharton's letters to A. John Hugh-Smith are in the collection of the Yale University Library, where I have been privileged to study them; EW to JHS, 18 Oct. 1925.

111: HJ to EW, 22 Mar. 1906.

112: HJ to EW, 29 Mar. 1906; HJ to EW, 2 Apr. 1906; HJ to EW, 4 Apr. 1906.

114: HJ to WJ, 4 May 1906 (*Letters*, II, 50–51).

115: HJ to GL, 6 May 1906.

116: HJ to MCJ, 18 June 1906.

Chapter V: The Dance upon the Aubusson Carpet

121: HJ to EW, 21 July 1906.

123: HJ to EW, 13 Mar. 1912 (*Letters*, II, 227–29).

124: HJ to EW, 11 Nov. 1906 (*Letters*, II, 56–58); HJ to WJ, 29 July 1876 (*Letters*, I, 50–52); *Notebooks*, 25 Nov. 1881, p. 25.

125: HJ to EW, 4 Dec. 1912 (*Letters*, II, 281–86).

128: HJ to EW, 11 Aug. 1907 (*Letters*, II, 78–81).

132: EW to WCB, 30 July 1908; EW to WCB, 16 Aug. 1908.

133: HJ to MCJ, 18 Nov. 1906.

134: HJ to Thomas S. Perry, 16 Feb. 1907; HJ to Lee Childe, 19 Feb. 1907; HJ to HS, 20 Mar. 1907; HJ to HS, 13 Apr. 1907

(*Letters*, II, 72–74); HJ to G. W. Prothero, 13 Apr. 1907.

135: HJ to Henry James, Jr., 17 Apr. 1907; HJ to William James, Jr., 26 Mar. 1907 (*Letters*, II, 71–72).

136: EW to SN [n.d.]; EW to JHS, 16 May [1909]; EW to CEN, 5 May 1907; *A Motor Flight Through France* (New York, 1908).

137: EW to ELB, 30 Mar. 1907; HJ to EW, 11 Aug. 1907 (*Letters*, II, 78–81); HJ to HS, 14 May 1907.

138: HJ to WJ, 30 Apr. 1907; HJ to Henry James, Jr., 17 Apr. 1907; HJ to W. E. Norris, 23 Dec. 1907 (*Letters*, II, 84–87).

139: HJ to EW, 4 Oct. 1907; HJ to WB, 5 Oct. 1907; *Letters of Henry James to Walter Berry*, Black Sun Press (Paris, 1928) contains the texts (with deletions) of some of James's letters to this friend; HJ to EW, 24 Nov. 1907.

140: HJ to MCJ, 8 Dec. 1907; HJ to EW, 2 Jan. 1908 (*Letters*, II, 90–92).

141: HJ to EW, 7 Jan. 1908; HJ to EW, 11 Mar. 1908; HJ to EW, 29 Mar. 1908; HJ to HS, 23 Apr. 1908.

142: Jacques-Émile Blanche, *Mes Modèles* (Paris, 1929).

143: HJ to Ellen Emmet, 26 Nov. 1908 (*Letters*, II, 107–10).

145: HJ to Mrs. Henry White, 29 Dec. 1908 (*Letters*, II, 117–118); HJ to WB, 10 Feb. 1909; HJ to SN, 13 Feb. 1909; HJ to EGN, 13 Sept. 1909; HJ to EW, 19 Nov. 1911 (*Letters*, II, 208–10); HJ to EW, 29 June 1912.

Chapter VI: The Eagle and the Worm

146: Edith Wharton, "Henry James in His Letters," *Quarterly Review*, CCXXXIV (1920).

148: EW to JHS, 6 Feb. 1909.

149ff.: Excerpts from Edith Whartons' diary have been published by Wayne Andrews in the introduction to *The Best Short Stories of Edith Wharton* (New York, 1958).

151: EW to ELB, 27 Mar. 1908.

152: HJ to GL, 14 Apr. 1908; EW to WCB, 7 June 1908.

153: HJ to GL, 13 Oct. 1908.

154: HJ to EW, 13 Oct. 1908 (*Letters*, II, 104–5); EW to CS, 20 Oct. 1908; André Gide, "Henry James (an unsent letter to Charles du Bos)" reprinted in *The Question of Henry James*, ed. by F. W. Dupee (New York, 1945).

155: HJ to HS, 2 Nov. 1908; HJ to MCJ, 2 Nov. 1908.

156: HJ to HS, 21 Nov. 1908; HJ to EW, 21 Nov. 1908; HJ to Henrietta Reubell, 21 Dec. 1908.

157: HJ to WB, 12 Dec. 1908; HJ to GL, 4 May 1909.

158: JHS to PL, 17 Feb. 1938; EW to JHS, 26 Dec. [1908]; HJ to EW, 16 Dec. 1908; EW to SN, 10 Feb. 1909.

159: EW to JHS, 6 Feb. [1909]; EW to JHS, 14 Mar. [1909]; HJ to WB, 10 Feb. 1909.

160: HJ to EW, 19 Apr. 1909 (*Letters*, II, 123–25); HJ to GL, 4 May 1909.

161: EW to SN, 5 May 1909; EW to JHS, 8 June [1909]; HJ to GL, 16 Aug. 1909; HJ to WB, 18 Aug. 1909; HJ to EW, 13 Dec. 1909 (*Letters*, II, 142–44).

162: EW to SN, 5 May [1909]; HJ to GL, 1 Jan. 1910.

163: See Appendix for description of Edith Wharton's break with Charles Scribner's Sons in 1912 and events leading up to it; Anna Bahlmann to WCB, 21 Jan. 1910; EW to JHS, 2 Mar. [1910].

164: HJ to EW, 8 Feb. 1910 (*Letters*, II, 156–57); HJ to SN, 15

Mar. 1910; HJ to EW, 10 June 1910 (*Letters*, II, 163–64).

165: HJ to EW, 9 Sept. 1910 (*Letters*, II, 168–69); EW to SN, 14 Oct. 1910; EW to JHS, 9 Dec. 1910; EW to JHS, 21 Jan. [1911].

166: HJ to EW, 9 Feb. 1911 (*Letters*, II, 175–78).

167: HJ to EW, 20 Dec. 1911; EW to JHS, 21 Jan. [1911]; EW to CS, 27 Mar. 1908.

168: EW to WDH, 18 Feb. 1911; MCJ to WDH, 28 Feb. 1911; WDH to EW, 3 Mar. 1911; Edmund Gosse to EW, 14 Feb. 1911.

169: HJ to EW, 9 Feb. 1911 (*Letters*, II, 175–78); EW to SN, 21 May 1911; HJ to SN, 26 June 1911.

170: EW to SN, 3 July [1911]; HJ to GL, 17 July 1911.

171: HJ to SN, 17 Aug. 1911.

172: EW to JHS, 6 Aug. 1911; EW to SN, 26 Aug. 1911.

173: HJ to GL, 5 Sept. 1911; HJ to MCJ, 10 Aug. 1911; HJ to MCJ, 17 Aug. 1911; HJ to HS, 10 Oct. 1911.

175: HJ to EW, 27 Sept. 1911 (*Letters*, II, 197–98).

176: HJ to WB, 27 Sept. 1911; HJ to MCJ, 17 Oct. 1911; HJ to EW, 25 Oct. 1911.

177: HJ to EW, 2 Dec. 1911; HJ to MCJ, 4 Jan. 1912; HJ to EW, 22 Dec. 1911.

178: HJ to GL, 12 Jan. 1912; HJ to EW, 5 Feb. 1912; HJ to EW, 24 Feb. 1912.

179: HJ to GL, 13 Feb. [1912]; HJ to HS, 20 Feb. 1912.

180: HJ to HS, 22 Feb. 1912; HJ to EW, 29 Mar. 1912; HJ to EW, 12 May 1912.

181: HJ to HS, 1 July 1912.

182: HJ to HS, 20 July 1912; HJ to Mrs. William James, 23 July 1912.

183: HJ to Mrs. William James, 31 July 1912; HJ to EW, 3 Aug. 1912; HJ to EW, 6 Aug. 1912.

185: HJ to HS, 9 Aug. 1912; HJ to Mrs. Humphrey Ward, 24 Oct. 1912 (*Letters*, II, 265–67); HJ to EW, 6 Sept. 1912.

186: HJ to HS, 11 Sept. 1912; HJ to WB, 28 Oct. 1912; HJ to Mrs. Humphrey Ward, 24 Oct. 1912; HJ to EW, 18 Nov. 1912.

187: HJ to HS, 10 Dec. 1912; HJ to MCJ, 31 Jan. 1913.

188: HJ to EW, 3 Feb. 1913; HJ to HS, 13 May 1913; HJ to PL, 3 May 1913; HJ to EW, 2 May 1913.

Chapter VII: The Real, Right Thing

190: JHS to PL, 17 Feb. 1938; HJ to EW, 9 June 1913.

191: HJ to MCJ, 31 Oct. 1913; HJ to GL, 30 June 1914.

192: Charles Scribner's copy of the "birthday letter" sent to American friends of James is in the Scribner file along with Edith Wharton's form-letter returning contributions, 14 Apr. 1913; EW to CS, 17 Apr. 1913.

193: HJ to WB, 8 Feb. 1912 (*Letters*, II, 217–20); HJ to EW, 29 Mar. 1912; HJ to EW, 2 May 1913.

194: EW to JHS, 4 Sept. [1913].

195: HJ to HS, 4 Aug. 1914.

195ff.: *Fighting France: From Dunkerque to Belfort* (New York, 1915) contains Edith Wharton's war reports, most of which were sent in letters to James.

196: HJ to EW, 6 Aug. 1914.

197: HJ to EW, 19 Aug. 1914 (*Letters*, II, 391–92); HJ to EW, 6 Aug. 1914.

References

198: HJ to EW, 30 Aug. 1914; HJ to EW, 3 Sept. 1914.

199: HJ to EW, 21 Sept. 1914 (*Letters*, II, 405–6); HJ to EW, 13 Oct. 1914; HJ to EW, 17 Oct. 1914 (*Letters*, II, 414–16).

200: HJ to HS, 4–5 Aug. 1914 (*Letters*, II 382–85); HJ to Mrs. Alfred Sutro, 8 Aug. 1914 (*Letters*, II, 388); HJ to EW, 1 Dec. 1914 (*Letters*, II, 425–26).

201: HJ to EW, 20 Oct. 1914; HJ to EW, 9 Nov. 1914. 201ff.: On the history of *Literature* see Appendix; the manuscript of *Literature* is in the Yale University Library. 201: EW to CS, 23 Feb. 1914; EW to CS, 29 Dec. 1914; EW to CS, 30 Jan. 1915.

202: EW to CS, 30 Mar. 1916; EW to CS, 13 Apr. 1918; EW to WCB, 21 Apr. 1921.

203: Henry James, *Notes of a Son and Brother* (New York, 1914); HJ to Viscount Wolseley, 7 Dec. 1903; HJ to Rhoda Broughton, 1 Oct. 1914 (*Letters*, II, 408–9).

205: EGN to PL, [n.d.].

206: HJ to EW, 5 Mar. 1915.

207: HJ to EW, 23 Mar. 1915; HJ to EW, 3 Apr. 1915 (*Letters*, II, 465–68).

208: HJ to EW, 23 May 1915; HJ to Henry James, Jr., 24 June 1915 (*Letters*, II, 477–79).

209: HJ to EW, 2 Oct. 1914; HJ to EW, 23 May 1916.

211: HJ to Grace Norton, 28 July [1883] (*Letters*, I, 100–2).

Chapter VIII: The Continued Cry

217ff.: Reviews of *The Greater Inclination* in: *Springfield Republican* (2 Apr. 1899), *New York Outlook* (8 Apr. 1899), *Hartford Gazette* (5 Apr. 1899), *Philadelphia Telegraph* (1 Apr. 1899), *New York Commercial Advertiser* (20 May

1899), *The Bookman* (June 1899), *New York Musical Courier* (May 1899); John D. Barry's review and following article appeared in the *Boston Literary World* (1 Apr. 1899 and 13 May 1899).

220: *The Touchstone* was reviewed in the *Atlantic Monthly* (Sept. 1900); *The Descent of Man and Other Stories* was reviewed in *The Independent* (Dec. 1903).

221: EW to WCB, 25 June 1904; EW to WCB, 7 Jan. 1904.

222: EW to WCB, 25 July 1902; WCB to EW, 6 July 1904; "Henry James" by W. C. Brownell, appeared in the *Atlantic Monthly* (Apr. 1905), was reprinted in *American Prose Masters* (New York, 1923); EW to WCB [n.d., 1905]; EW to WCB, 14 Dec. 1924.

223: WCB to CS on James's *The Sacred Fount,* quoted in Roger Burlingame, *Of Making Many Books* (New York, 1946), pp. 36–37.

224: "William C. Brownell" by Edith Wharton appeared in *Scribner's Magazine,* LXXXIV (1928).

226: "Henry James in His Letters" by Edith Wharton appeared in the *Quarterly Review* (July 1920); *The Writing of Fiction* by Edith Wharton (New York, 1925).

228: Edward Clark March's comment on *The House of Mirth* appeared in *The Bookman,* XXVI (Nov. 1907) in the course of his review of her later work, *The Fruit of the Tree.*

Chapter IX: Correspondences and Differences

245: HJ to WDH, 25 Jan. 1902.

246: CS to Arthur Scribner, 12 July 1899; EW to WCB, 25 July 1902.

247: HJ to MCJ, 20 Aug. 1902 (*Letters,* I, 395–97).

248: HJ to Mrs. Humphrey Ward, 26 July 1899, and previous letter [n.d.] (*Letters*, I, 320–27).

249: HJ to Mrs. Humphrey Ward [n.d.], quoted by Mrs. Ward in *A Writer's Recollections* (New York and London, 1918), Vol. II, p. 223.

250: HJ to EW, 17 Nov. 1906 (*Letters*, II, 56–58); H. C. Dwight, *Putnam's Monthly*, III (1907–8), 593.

254: EW to CS, 22 Nov. 1905; CS to EW, 20 Nov. 1905.

257: HJ to EW, 30 Aug. 1907; HJ to EW, 4 Oct. 1907.

258: EW to CS, 12 Oct. 1907.

259: HJ to EW, 24 Nov. 1907; HJ to MCJ, 8 Dec. 1907.

261: Concerning Edith Wharton's use of James's suggestion in "The Pretext," see Millicent Bell's "A James 'Gift' to Edith Wharton," *Modern Language Notes*, LXXII (1957), 182–85.

262: HJ to EW, 7 Jan. 1908.

264: Edith Wharton, "The Writing of Ethan Frome," *The Colophon*, XI (Sept. 1932); Edith Wharton, intro. to *Ethan Frome*, Modern Student's Library Edition (New York, 1922).

265: John Crowe Ransom, "Character and Characters," *American Review*, VI (1935–36).

266: Lionel Trilling, "The Morality of Inertia," *Great Moral Dilemmas*, ed. by Robert MacIver (New York, 1956).

267: HJ to EW, 25 Oct. 1911.

271: EW to ELB, 27 Jan. 1908; EW to ELB, 12 Feb. 1908.

272: CS to EW, 17 Mar. 1908; EW to ELB, 27 Mar. 1908; Morton W. Fullerton, "The Art of Henry James," *Quarterly Review*, CXX (1910).

275: HJ to EW, 4 and 9 Dec. 1912 (*Letters*, II, 281–86); HJ to HS, 10 Dec. 1912.

280: HJ to EW, 31 Jan. 1913; HJ to EW, 3 Feb. 1913; HJ to EW, 9 June 1913.

282: "The New Novel," *Notes on Novelists* by Henry James (London, 1914).

Chapter X: *The Summing Up*

284: Edith Wharton, "The Criticism of Fiction," *Times* [London] *Literary Supplement* (14 May 1914).

285: HJ to WDH, 17 Aug. 1908 (*Letters*, II, 98–104); Edith Wharton, "A Cycle of Reviewing," *Spectator*, CXLI (Nov. 1928), Supplement, 44–45.

286: Henry James, "The Art of Fiction," *Longman's Magazine*, Sept. 1884.

289: HJ to EW, 2 June 1914 (*Letters*, II, 369–71).

290: EW to WCB, 13 Mar. 1926.

291: EW to CS, 19 May 1913; EW to CS, 23 Feb. 1914.

293: "Poverty is a powerful lens . . . propinquity with it" occurs among other remarks in unpublished critical fragments of Edith Wharton's in the Yale University Library.

296: Joseph Warren Beach, *The Twentieth Century Novel* (New York, 1932).

303: Henry Seidel Canby, "Edith Wharton," *Saturday Review of Literature* (21 Aug. 1937).

304: William Troy, "Flower of Manhattan," *The Nation* (May 1934); review of *The Valley of Decision* by Richard Henry Stoddard, *Saturday Evening Mail and Express* (22 Feb. 1902).

305: Edith Wharton, "The Great American Novel," *The Yale Review*, new series, XVI (1927); Edith Wharton, "A Cycle of Reviewing," *Spectator*, CXLI (Nov. 1928); Van Wyck Brooks, *The Pilgrimage of Henry James* (New York, 1925).

References

306: Vernon L. Parrington, "Henry James and the Nostalgia of Culture," *Main Currents in American Thought*, vol. III (New York, 1930); Vernon L. Parrington, "Our Literary Aristocrat," *The Pacific Review*, June 1921.

307: Edmund Wilson, "The Pilgrimage of Henry James," *The Shores of Light* (New York, 1952); Pelham Edgar, "The Essential Novelist? Henry James, *The Art of the Novel*" (New York, 1933); William Troy, "Henry James and the Young Writers," *The Bookman* (June 1931); Maxwell Geismar, *Henry James and the Jacobites* (New York, 1964).

Appendix—Lady into Author: Edith Wharton and the House of Scribner

As already noted, the bulk of Edith Wharton's correspondence with members of the firm of Charles Scribner's Sons is preserved in the company's archives, where I have been privileged to examine it. In addition to Edith Wharton's own letters, the Scribner file contains copies of letters written to her, and in notes taken from "Letter Books" now missing there are synopses of some letters which no longer exist in entirety. In addition, certain of Edith Wharton's letters to Scribner editor W. C. Brownell have been deposited in the Amherst College Library, where they were placed at my disposal. I am, again, deeply grateful to the custodians of both these collections.

317: EW to ELB, 23 Nov. 1905; EW to WCB, 2 Nov. 1913

318: EW to WCB, 25 Apr. 1899.

319: EW to WCB, 26 Sept. 1899; EW to WCB, 28 Sept. 1899.

320: EW to WCB, 5 Aug. 1905; EW to WCB, 26 Mar. 1905; EW to WCB, 19 May 1905; WCB to EW, 26 Oct. 1905; CS to EW, 30 Oct. 1905; CS to EW, 10 Nov. 1905; CS to EW, 20 Nov. 1905.

321: EW to CS, 22 Nov. 1905; EW to ELB, 30 Aug. 1906; EW to

ELB, 1 Dec. 1906; EW to ELB, 30 Mar. 1907; CS to John Kendrick Bangs, 14 Oct. 1907.

322: CS to EW, [n.d.] Feb. 1908; ELB to CS, 4 Aug. 1908; EW to ELB, 7 June 1908; CS to EW, 9 Aug. 1907.

323: CS to EW, 16 Nov. 1911.

324: EW to CS, 27 Nov. 1911.

325: CS to EW, 13 Dec. 1911; EW to CS, 28 Mar. 1912; CS to EW, 10 Apr. 1912.

326: EW to CS, 3 May 1912; CS to EW, 12 June 1912; ELB to CS, 26 July 1910.

327: EW to CS, 2 Nov. 1913; CS to EW, 14 Nov. 1913; EW to CS, 26 Jan. 1913.

328: EW to CS, 17 Apr. 1913; CS to EW, 16 May 1913.

329: Edgar G. Sisson to EW, 16 Oct. 1914; EW to CS, 14 Nov. 1914; EW to CS, 21 Dec. 1914; EW to CS, 23 Feb. 1914; EW to ELB, 28 Mar. 1914.

330: EW to CS, 30 Mar. 1916; CS to EW, 19 May 1916; EW to Robert Bridges, 2 Aug. 1916.

331: CS to EW, 21 Sept. 1916; CS to EW, 27 Dec. 1916; EW to CS, [n.d.] Dec. 1916.

332: CS to EW, 16 Feb. 1917; EW to WCB, 31 Oct. 1902; EW to ELB, 22 Feb. 1904.

333: EW to WCB, 20 Aug. 1917.

334: CS to EW, 13 Mar. 1918; EW to CS, 13 Apr. 1918.

335: CS to EW, 6 May 1918.

336: EW to CS, 23 May 1918.

337: EW to WCB, 27 July 1918; EW to CS, 12 Sept. 1919; CS to EW, 29 Sept. 1919.

338: EW to WCB, 21 Apr. 1921; CS to EW, 9 Feb. 1921.

339: CS to EW, 19 Dec. 1921; EW to CS, 10 Dec. 1923; EW to CS, 1 May 1923; CS to EW, 16 May 1923; CS to EW, 17 July 1923.

340: EW to CS, 15 Feb. 1922; CS to EW, 19 Nov. 1923.

341: Arthur Scribner to EW, 6 Mar. 1925; EW to CS, 19 Sept. 1920; EW to WCB, 13 Mar. 1926; Charles Scribner, Jr., to EW, 25 Feb. 1936.

Index

Index

INDEX

Book of the Homeless, The, 202, 209
Bookman, The, 104, 228
Bosanquet, Theodora, 176, 211
Bostonians, The, 41, 43, 231, 237, 269
Bourget, Paul, 11, 30, 37–40, 45–46, 55–56, 59–73, 75–77, 83, 88–89, 108, 128–30, 132, 140–41, 149, 215, 261, 298
Bourget, Mme. Paul (Minnie), 66–67, 70, 72–73, 128
Breuil, Jean de, 180, 206–7
Bridges, Robert, 330–31
Bronson, Mrs. Arthur, 41, 65
Brontë, Emily, 90
Brooks, Van Wyck, 305–7
Brownell, William Crary, 11, 53–54, 61, 77, 84, 88–89, 101, 111, 132, 148, 163, 202, 221–27, 246, 252, 272, 285, 290, 317, 319–20, 323, 332, 333, 336, 338, 340–41
Browning, Robert, 41, 50–51
Buccaneers, The, 106, 252, 302
Bunner, H. C., 292
"Bunner Sisters," 292–93, 330
Burlingame, Edward L., 30, 53–55, 64, 137, 151, 271, 317, 319, 321–23, 326, 332, 340

Cambon, Jules, 129
Canby, Henry Seidel, 303
Calderon, George, 110
Carlyle, Thomas, 83
Century Company, The, 333
Century Magazine, 64, 82, 328, 332

Chapman, John Jay, 83
Chevalier of Pensieri-Vani, The, 84
Childe, Lee, 134
Children, The, 298–300, 307
Cholmondeley, Mary, 111
Clairmont, Jane, 233
Claudel, Paul, 131
Clifford, W. K., 25
Clifford, Mrs. W. K. (Lucy), 25
Cocteau, Jean, 131
Codman, Ogden, 50, 82
Collier's Magazine, 328
"Confessional, The," 132, 247
Conrad, Joseph, 268, 286
Cooper, James Fenimore, 224
"Copy," 232
Cosmopolis, 65
Cosmopolitan Magazine, 328–329, 338
Craft of Fiction, The, 106, 108
Crane, Stephen, 286
Crawford, Marion, 52
Criticism, 285
"Criticism of Fiction, The," 284, 289
Crucial Instances, 74, 220, 230, 232, 235, 246–47
Cruelle Énigme, 64
Curtis, Daniel S., 41–42, 65
Curtis, Mrs. Daniel S., 41–42, 65
Curtis, George William, 82
Curtis Publishing Company, 254
Cust, Henry, 97
Custom of the Country, The,

368

Index

371

Index

INDEX

377

Index

379

C.2